Prayers in
the Precincts:

The Christian Right in
the 1998 Elections

Prayers in the Precincts:

The Christian Right in the 1998 Elections

Edited by

John C. Green

Mark J. Rozell

Clyde Wilcox

Georgetown University Press
Washington, D.C.

To our Brothers and Keepers

Luther A. Green
Kenneth N. Rozell
Kevin D. Wilcox

Georgetown University Press, Washington, D. C.
© 2000 by Georgetown University Press. All rights reserved.
Printed in the United States of America

10 9 8 7 6 5 4 3 2 1   2000

This volume is printed on acid-free offset book paper.

Library of Congress Cataloging-in-Publication Data

Prayers in the precincts : the Christian right in the 1998 elections/
    edited by John C. Green, Mark J. Rozell, Clyde Wilcox.
        p.   cm.
    Includes index.
    ISBN 0-87840-774-X (cloth : alk. paper).—ISBN 0-87840-775-8
(pbk. : alk. Paper)
        1. Conservatism—United States.   2. Conservatism—Religious
aspects—Christianity.   3. United States. Congress—Elections,
1998.   4. Christianity and politics—United States.
5. Evangelicalism—United States.   6. Fundamentalism—United States.
7. United States—Politics and government—1993– I. Green, John
Clifford. II. Rozell, Mark J. III. Wilcox, Clyde.
JC573.2.U6P73   2000
320.52′0973—dc21   99-36840
                                                        CIP

CONTENTS

ACKNOWLEDGMENTS

We are grateful for the assistance of Kim Haverkamp of the Bliss Institute of Applied Politics at the University of Akron for preparing the manuscript for publication and to Rachel Goldberg for assistance in proofreading the manuscript. We thank John Samples of the Georgetown University Press for his interest and assistance throughout the development and completion of the project. Finally, we appreciate the scholarly support of our colleagues at the University of Akron Department of Political Science, The Catholic University Department of Politics, and the Georgetown University Department of Government.

J.C.G.
M.J.R.
C.W.

CONTRIBUTORS

Andrew Appleton is assistant professor of political science and associate director of the division of government studies at Washington State University. He is coeditor of *State of the Party Profiles* and author of *Party Politics* (2000).

Michael Buckley is assistant professor of political science at Eastern Washington University.

Charles S. Bullock III is Richard B. Russell Professor of Political Science at the University of Georgia. He is a widely published author on the politics of the South and the coauthor of *Runoff Elections in the United States* and coeditor of *The New Politics of the Old South.*

Allan J. Cigler is Chancellor's Club Teaching Professor of Political Science at the University of Kansas. His research and teaching interests include political parties, participation, and interest group politics.

Joel Fetzer is a visiting scholar with the Center for International Studies/Pacific Council on International Policy at the University of Southern California. His research focuses on immigration and on religion and political behavior.

Christopher P. Gilbert is associate professor and chair of the department of political science at Gustavus Adolphus College, St. Peter, Minnesota. He is the author of *The Impact of Churches on Political Behavior.*

John C. Green is director of the Ray Bliss Institute of Applied Politics at the University of Akron and the author of numerous studies on the Christian Right in American politics. He is coeditor of *The State of the Parties* (2d ed.).

Christian Grose is a Ph.D. candidate in political science at the University of Rochester, New York.

James L. Guth is professor of political science at Furman University, Greenville, South Carolina. His work on religion and politics has appeared in many journals and collections. He is coauthor of *Religion and the Culture Wars: Dispatches from the Front.*

Ted G. Jelen is a professor of political science at the University of Nevada, Las Vegas. His most recent book is *A Wall of Separation? Debating the Public Role of Religion.*

James Lamare is professor of political science and Dean of the Dorothy F. Schmidt College of Arts and Letters at Florida Atlantic University. He is the author of *Texas Politics: Economics, Power, and Policy* (6th ed.).

Burdett A. Loomis is professor of political science and interim director of the Robert J. Dole Institute for Public Service and Public Policy at the University of Kansas. He has written extensively on legislatures, interest groups, and public policy.

Matthew C. Moen is professor and chair of the department of political science at the University of Maine. His latest book on the Christian Right is *The Transformation of the Christian Right.*

Kenneth T. Palmer is professor of political science at the University of Maine. He is the coauthor of *Maine Politics and Government.*

James M. Penning is professor of political science at Calvin College, Grand Rapids, Michigan. He is coeditor with Corwin Smidt of *Sojourners in the Wilderness: The Christian Right in Comparative Perspective.*

David A. M. Peterson is a Ph.D. candidate in political science at the University of Minnesota. His research interests are religion and politics, political behavior, and mass media influences on public opinion.

J. L. Polinard is professor and chair of the department of political science at the University of Texas-Pan American. He is the coauthor of *Electoral Structure and Urban Politics* and *State of the Local Politics.*

Mark J. Rozell is associate professor of politics at The Catholic University of America. He is coauthor of *Second Coming: The New Christian Right in Virginia Politics* and the coeditor of two books on Christian Right politics in the United States.

Richard K. Scher is professor of political science at the University of Florida and the author of *Politics in the New South* (2d ed.).

Corwin E. Smidt is professor of political science at Calvin College, Grand Rapids, Michigan. His research focuses on religion and politics. He is coauthor of *Religion and the Culture Wars: Dispatches from the Front.*

Mark C. Smith is a Ph.D. candidate in political science at the University of Georgia. His research focuses on religion and politics and he holds an M.A. in the history of Christianity from Trinity Evangelical Divinity School.

J. Christopher Soper is associate professor of political science at Pepperdine University. His latest book is *The Challenge of Pluralism: Church and State in Five Democracies.*

Robert J. Spitzer is professor of political science at State University of New York, Cortland. His books include *The Right to Life Movement and Third Party Politics, President and Congress,* and *The Politics of Gun Control.*

Harold W. Stanley is associate professor and chairman of the department of political science at the University of Rochester, New York. He is the author of numerous articles on voting, political parties, and elections, and of the books *Voter Mobilization and the Politics of Race; Senate vs. Governor, Alabama 1971;* and *Vital Statistics in American Politics.*

Kenneth D. Wald is professor of political science at the University of Florida. He is the author of *Religion and Politics in the United States* (3d ed.).

Maureen Tartaglione is a Ph.D. candidate in political science at the University of Florida.

Clyde Wilcox is professor of government at Georgetown University. His latest book on the Christian Right is *Onward Christian Soldiers? The Religious Right in American Politics.*

Robert D. Wrinkle is professor of political science and director of the Survey Research Center at the University of Texas-Pan American. He is the coauthor of *Electoral Structure and Urban Politics* and *State and Local Politics.*

1

The Christian Right and the 1998 Elections: An Overview

John C. Green

The 1998 election can only be described as a defeat for the Christian Right. Several of its most prominent supporters were retired by the voters, many allies lost close contests, and the movement was a liability in some high-profile races. These losses were especially galling to movement activists because major gains were widely anticipated: the Clinton-Lewinsky scandal was expected to mobilize conservative religious voters and the mid-term election was supposed to be a good one for the Republicans. However, the 1998 election was not a debacle for the Christian Right. Many of its key supporters were reelected, some new allies gained office, and the movement was an asset in some important races (Green et al. 1998).

Of course, 1998 was an unusual election by any reckoning. The congressional results were historic, with the Democratic net gain of five seats representing the first mid-term advance by the party in the White House since 1934. However, the Republicans actually won the congressional election, posting the highest popular vote margin since 1946. In fact, incumbency dominated the election, with a near-record number of office-holders facing little or no opposition. The campaign was waged against the backdrop of prosperity at home, (mostly) peace abroad, and an acrimonious debate over the impeachment of the president, all of which contributed to the unusual results (Jacobson 1999).

A seismic metaphor is helpful in putting this odd election in perspective. If the 1994 election is thought of as an "earthquake" that transformed the political landscape, then 1998 was an "aftershock" that settled the disturbed landforms. In 1994, the Republicans won a historic victory, taking control of Congress for the first time in forty years; the Christian Right made a small but important contribution to this victory (see Rozell and Wilcox 1995). One cost of the Republican victory was an enlarged and unwieldy coalition, where the Christian Right was a contentious element. Republicans then experienced consolidation in 1996, in which the movement participated (see Rozell and Wilcox 1997). The consolidation continued in 1998. On balance, however, the Republicans maintained their 1994 gains, and the Christian Right has retained a prominent niche in national politics.

The essays in this volume are state-level case studies of Christian Right activity in the 1998 elections, and they describe the movement's niche in some detail, in both defeat and victory. Our task here is to set these case studies in context by describing the salient characteristics of the Christian Right and giving an overview of the 1998 campaign.

The Christian Right in American Politics

The Christian Right is a social movement dedicated to restoring "traditional values" in public policy by mobilizing evangelical Protestants and other conservative religious people to political action (Green et al. 1996). And like other movements, it is fundamentally about challenging political institutions in order to redress its grievances. Since its inception in the late 1970s, the Christian Right has focused this challenge at the ballot box, with special attention to the Republican Party (Oldfield 1996). These efforts can be usefully described by different strata of activity, with leaders and organizations at the top, activists in the middle, and potential voters at the bottom. From this perspective, the Christian Right, properly so called, is all three strata set in movement politically. The movement has many strengths, and numerous weaknesses, and can play several roles in electoral politics. These are worth reviewing before we turn to 1998.

Strengths

The Christian Right's strengths derive primarily from the vitality of evangelical Protestantism (Jorstad 1993). Of particular importance is the internal structure of this distinctive religious tradition. Evangelicalism combines orthodox Christian beliefs with intense individualism. This combination has created a highly decentralized set of religious organizations, including thousands of small denominations, parachurch groups, and independent churches. Even the largest bodies, such as the Southern Baptist Convention (the largest Protestant denomination in the country), are actually voluntary alliances of the component institutions. This environment puts a premium on aggressive, entrepreneurial leaders who are adept at recognizing discontent among religious people, identifying opportunities to respond to such discontents, and organizing the resources to bring the two together.

These leadership skills can be effectively applied to politics if the opportunity presents itself. Over the last generation, social and economic forces have increasingly brought evangelicals into contact with lifestyles and worldviews they find abhorrent (Wilcox 1992). Government policies directed at protecting, extending, and enforcing these rival values have been a particular irritant, especially when they dealt with matters easily linked to traditional morality: sexual conduct, abortion, women's roles, family arrangements, education, crime, and the legal status of religion itself.

These discontents have allowed leaders to recruit a corps of zealous activists, which can, on the one hand, provide the resources for movement organizations and, on the other, engage in political activity (Leege 1992). Like other politically involved Americans, these activists are largely middle class, with the personal skills and resources necessary to be effective in politics (Guth et al. 1994). Although churches themselves are rarely a formal part of the movement's organization, they are key to its success: the close-knit religious communities and related communication networks are a fertile source of activists and a potent forum for their activities (Gilbert 1993; Green 1999).

A final movement strength is the relative size and cohesiveness of evangelicalism in the mass public (Green et al. 1996, chap. 10). Nationally, white evangelicals make up about one-quarter of the adult American population and are even more numerous in southern and midwestern states. The high degree of religious commitment among them allows for effective mobilization on the basis of moral appeals, church communities, and religious networks. By way of reference, evangelicals are about as numerous as Roman Catholics, and somewhat larger than Mainline Protestants or the secular population. Although they are hardly a political monolith, mobilizing just one-half of this large tradition would produce a voting bloc more numerous than African Americans and roughly ten times larger than Jews or Episcopalians. When combined, these strengths can be formidable.

Weaknesses

The nature of evangelical Protestantism also poses weaknesses for the Christian Right. For one thing, evangelicals have been very difficult to organize for politics, even at the elite level (Jelen 1991). One special problem has been the otherworldly orientation of these deeply religious people, many of whom have little interest in politics, and others who are outright hostile to it. Another equally serious problem is religious particularism, where long-standing theological differences among evangelicals have seriously inhibited political cooperation. It has been even harder to reach out beyond evangelicalism to members of other traditions who might share their political concerns, particularly Catholics and African Americans. The entrepreneurial tendencies among evangelical leaders have been a further drag on cooperation, as each leader has incentives to pursue his or her own interests.

Another weakness is the intense and sometimes extreme views of movement activists. The very opinions that motivate these people to engage in politics often make them difficult to work with. This problem has seriously interfered with political alliances with secular conservatives. Central to these difficulties is the movement's social issue agenda, which is quite controversial in many quarters. Attempts to set priorities, broaden the movement's goals, or compromise on such issues can become a source of conflict. The division between "pragmatists" and "purists" is common in movement politics, of course, but may be especially problematic in the Christian Right because of the movement's religious dimension (Green, Guth, and Hill 1993).

Finally, the Christian Right's organizing activity and controversial agenda can produce equally intense countermobilization by opponents, particularly liberal social movements, many of which draw on the natural opponents of evangelicals, such as religious progressives and the secular population (Wilcox 1994). Also, many important social institutions are often critical of the Christian Right's agenda, including the news media, the entertainment industry, public and higher education, and the professions. In addition, key elements of the movement's agenda are not especially popular with the general public, making it possible to mobilize large blocs of voters in opposition. When combined, all these weaknesses can present serious obstacles to the movement.

Political Roles

The basic role the Christian Right can play is to be in *contention* politically: exploiting its strengths and overcoming its weaknesses to the point where it can effectively challenge political institutions. In this context, the term "contention" has two meanings, each quite appropriate to the Christian Right: being competitive politically and being a source of controversy. Over the last twenty years, the Christian Right has become competitive in many parts of the country, partly because of and partly in spite of the controversy it generates (Rozell and Wilcox 1996). However, the movement is not yet in contention everywhere and may never be (Green, Guth, and Wilcox 1998).

Once in contention, the movement must then achieve influence, and here one can imagine two opposite approaches. On the one hand, the Christian Right can seek *consolidation* with other interests on behalf of a common agenda. On the other hand, it can engage in *confrontation*, warring with other interests and demanding attention to its own agenda. Consolidation and confrontation are not mutually exclusive categories, of course, and elements of both can occur in a given election. Both options have potential benefits and costs. Consolidation often increases the chance of victory but at the risk of not achieving the movement's substantive goals in government. Confrontation often increases the risk of electoral defeat but holds out the prospect of achieving substantive goals in government. The American two-party system generates strong incentives for the consolidation in elections, but movements exist precisely because the two-party system produces incentives for confrontation over policy.

Movement contention, consolidation, and confrontation take place in the context of candidate-centered politics. In contemporary American elections, candidates themselves are the most dynamic element of campaigns, with their quality and efforts usually decisive (Salmore and Salmore 1989). Thus, the impact of the Christian Right comes chiefly from its association with candidates: strong candidacies usually help the movement "succeed" at the polls and poor ones produce high rates of "failure." The movement has thus become deeply involved in the recruitment of candidates as well as nomination and general elections battles.

However, neither contention, consolidation, nor confrontation guarantees success at the polls or in government. Elections involve many factors besides the behavior of the Christian Right, and most are far beyond the control of the movement, including the conduct of campaigns, the activities of other interests, and real world events. The movement can become part of a consolidated coalition and still lose at the ballot box; similarly, bitter confrontations can sometimes produce stunning victories. Indeed, the former occurred in the aftershock of 1998 and the latter in the 1994 earthquake.

Table 1.1 offers an overview of the case studies in this book, using the foregoing categories as guidelines. The first division is horizontal, between twelve states where the Christian Right was in contention in 1998 and two states were the movement was not in contention. We focus on the former because they best illustrate movement activities, but we could have included numerous other states where the movement was not in contention in 1998. The second division is vertical, ranging from states where the movement largely practiced consolidation within the Republican Party to places where confrontation occurred. We have arrayed our state studies across this dimension in a rough-and-ready fashion. Within these categories, we offer a further division based on the relative degree

Table 1.1 The Christian Right in 1998: Summary of Case Studies

Roles	Movement In Contention		Movement Not In Contention	
	States Where Movement Had Relative		States Where Movement Had Relative	
	Failure	Success	Failure	Success
Consolidation				
	South Carolina	Texas		
	Georgia	Virginia		
	California	Florida		
Mixed				
	Alabama	Michigan		
	Washington	Minnesota		
	Kansas	Illinois		
Confrontation				
			New York	Maine

of success the movement enjoyed in 1998. So, for instance, South Carolina and Texas were examples of consolidation in 1998, but the movement suffered major losses in the Palmetto state and experienced considerable success in the Lone Star state. With this rough categorization in mind, we can turn to an overview of the 1998 campaign.

Movement Strengths and Weaknesses in 1998

How did the Christian Right cope with its strengths and weaknesses in 1998? Overall, the movement had some success in exploiting its strengths but suffered from its weaknesses. These trends can be seen in a brief review of three strata of the Christian Right.

Leadership and Organizations

In 1998, the Christian Coalition was challenged as the flagship movement organization. To some extent this situation came from changes within the Coalition itself. The departure of Ralph Reed after the 1996 election unsettled the organization, and his replacements, former Reagan cabinet official Donald Hodel and former congressman Randy Tate, were not as effective. The Coalition's membership growth leveled off, its finances and programs declined, and the enthusiasm of some its activist corps waned (Gerson 1998). This organizational instability continued after the 1998 election and continues at this writing (Balz 1999; Szabo 1999). In addition, the Coalition lost its longstanding appeal for tax-exempt status in a ruling by the Internal Revenue Service. Disillusionment with the 1996 election results, including the Dole campaign and the lack of attention to social issues by the Republican Congress, contributed to a broader reassessment of the pragmatic style championed by Reed and the Coalition. Some other Christian Right organizations also experienced retrenchment as well.[1]

However, other elements of the movement experienced growth and expansion, and chief among these was a loose network of groups allied with Focus on the Family (Focus), including the Family Research Councils (FRC) and the Campaign for Working Families (CWF). This expansion gave Focus founder James Dobson, FRC and CWF head Gary Bauer, and their associates greater prominence, rivaling that of Pat Robertson and the Christian Coalition. A third problem for movement organizations was the siphoning off of movement resources into the GOP: Ralph Reed became a campaign consultant, some activists joined the Federation of Republican Assemblies (a conservative faction within the Republican camp at the state level), and Gary Bauer prepared to run for the 2000 Republican presidential nomination. In addition, some hard-core movement activists defected to minor parties, such as Howard Phillips's U.S. Taxpayers Party.

These trends represent a new variation on the old theme of organizational diversity. The Christian Coalition was prominent in nearly all the states covered here, but stronger in some places (South Carolina and Texas) and weaker in others (Michigan and Maine). The Focus on the Family affiliates were nearly as strong, though less involved in grassroots politics. Numerous state and local Christian Right organizations were still active and influential, and the movement was often allied with other conservative groups, especially the Right to Life committees. The Michigan and California case studies offer a fuller look at the diversity and vitality of Christian Right organizations; the Maine case study chronicles organizational problems and decline.

Despite this instability, the Christian Right retained formidable resources in 1998. The Christian Coalition claimed some 2 million members, 2,000 local chapters, an informal liaison network associated with perhaps 100,000 churches, and a budget of $17 million. The Focus network was roughly of equal size, claiming more than 2 million members, 34 state affiliates, and connections to thousands of churches; in 1997–1998, the CWF political action committee grossed some $7 million. In the 1998 campaign, the Christian Coalition claimed to have distributed some 45 million voter guides, made over 1 million telephone calls, and expended some $3 million on campaign activities. The Campaign for Working Families spent $3 million in support of primary and general election candidates, and its leaders were involved in numerous campaigns.

These resources allowed the movement to continue its high level of political activity in many states, often under trying circumstances. Partly for this reason, two longstanding weaknesses have abated. First, religious particularism among the various kinds of evangelical Protestants appears to have declined (Rozell, Wilcox, and Green 1998). The tensions between fundamentalists and pentecostals are much less likely to disrupt political activity than in the past. Second, the evangelical community has become more accepting of political activity by religious people. For example, a 1998 survey found that 75 percent of evangelical Protestants in the mass public agreed that "it is important for organized religious groups to stand up for their beliefs in politics," and only 25 percent agreed that "organized religious groups of all kinds should stay out of politics." In contrast, comparable figures for the nation as a whole were 52 percent and 45 percent, respectively.[2]

Other weaknesses remain in force, however. For instance, the competitive tendencies among evangelical leaders were problematic, and the multiple movement organizations often failed to cooperate and sometimes fought one another. The South Carolina and Georgia case studies illustrate these tensions. The movement organizations have also continued to have difficulties with recruiting support from nonevangelicals, despite high-profile efforts with regard to blacks, Hispanics, and Catholics. The retrenchment of the Christian Coalition led to the abandonment of projects designed to bridge these gaps, such as the Catholic Alliance and the Samaritan Project (aimed at Catholics and African Americans, respectively.) And as the California study reveals, the movement may have alienated many ethnic minorities, especially Hispanic evangelicals, because of its opposition to immigration.

Activists

As in the past, the Christian Right deployed an extensive activist corps in the 1998 campaign. Though the exact numbers are not known, a careful review of group claims, conservative mailing lists, and comments by reliable observers suggests that overall the activist corps probably numbered about 150,000, down from 1996. Some of these activists were part of well-coordinated local chapters and others were less sophisticated solo operators (Berkowitz and Green 1997). These activists participated in a variety of settings, from Christian Right operations to party committees to candidate organizations. The activist corps was also involved in a wide variety of activities, from raising money to running campaigns. However, its most common tactic remained distributing voter guides in churches.

The dedication and intensity of the Christian Right activist corps has become legendary, and it is a staple of all the case studies. The movement activist corps appears to have been most numerous in states with large populations of evangelicals that have become politically competitive in recent times, especially southern states such as Virginia. Highly competitive states with smaller evangelical populations, such as those in the upper Midwest and West Coast, appear to have had fewer activists. And in some states the level of activism has been very modest. For example, in Maine, a small number of evangelicals combined with a tradition of political independence limits the movement.

The movement activists are also known for their zealous and sometimes extreme views. Not surprisingly, conflict with other activists, particularly with moderate Republicans, is much discussed in the case studies. Such conflicts were common even in places where the Christian Right was relatively strong, such as Texas, and were especially sharp in states where the movement was weaker, such as Illinois and Washington. During much of the 1990s, such conflicts were tempered by pragmatism among movement activists, leading to consolidation rather than confrontation (see the Texas and Florida case studies).

However, in 1998 there was a strong resurgence of "purism" among Christian Right activists, especially those linked to the Focus networks. Rallying to the call of "principle over politics," these activists provoked some intense confrontations, examples of which are found in the Kansas and Washington case studies. Yet another weakness reappeared among activists in 1998: a skepticism about the efficacy of political action, leading to renewed interest in nonpolitical activities. Although these sentiments were common during the campaign, they came to public notice after the election—and the impeachment and trial of President Clinton. Paul Weyrich, a longtime leader of the movement, spoke for many when he publicly questioned the ability of the Christian Right to "change the culture" via political action (Van Drehle 1999). A book by former leaders of the Moral Majority sounded similar themes (Thomas and Dobson 1999). Whatever these sentiments may mean for the future of the Christian Right, they represented a decline in movement activist enthusiasm in at least some places.

The Christian Right also faced much stiffer opposition in 1998 than in 1996. Groups dedicated to opposing the movement were especially active. Perhaps the greatest expansion came from secular groups, such as People for the American Way (PFAW) and Americans United for the Separation of Church and State (AU). Operating through its political action committee, PFAW Voters Alliance, PFAW spent $2 million on a television ad campaign aimed at increasing voter turnout, in addition to extensive get-out-the-vote efforts in key states. This effort included the deployment of field staff and alliances with other progressive groups. AU ran a focused campaign against political activity in churches, titled "Project Fair Play." AU activists distributed some 80,000 letters to ministers, informing them of the legal implications of distributing voter guides and promising to file complaints with the IRS when churches distributed Christian Right voter guides.

Perhaps the most interesting aspect of this expanded opposition was the continued growth of religious progressives at the grass roots. The Interfaith Alliance (TIA), an ecumenical group with substantial support among mainline Protestants, was particularly important. Unlike in 1996, when it attempted its own voter guide program, in 1998 TIA launched a program to educate religious people about political action. Titled "Call to a Faithful Decision," the program encouraged voter education, a candidate civility code, and candidate and issue forums; provided guidelines for political action by clergy and religious organizations; and opposed voter guides in houses of worship. These efforts added to the repertoire of activities by religious progressives. More traditional political activities also expanded in 1998, especially the voter programs of African American churches. Indeed, in some states such efforts by these churches were extraordinary.

There is considerable anecdotal evidence that these efforts bore fruit. Some churches refused to allow voter guides to be distributed on their premises, an occurrence common enough to provoke a public counterattack by Christian Right leaders. These efforts may have been especially effective in Catholic congregations. However, in at least some cases, these efforts backfired, prompting some skeptical churches to actually distribute voter guides. Interviews with local activists suggest that the education efforts of TIA were the most effective in interfering with voter guide distribution, particularly in mainline Protestant and moderate evangelical churches. Couched in the language of faith, these messages offered both good reasons for avoiding voter guides and alternative strategies for encouraging good citizenship by church members. In addition, higher levels of turnout among liberal voters and especially African Americans in key races suggest the get-out-the vote programs enjoyed some success. Several of the case studies make reference to these efforts.

Mass Support

What about support for the movement in the mass public in 1998? A survey taken before the fall election suggested that the movement faced both challenges and opportunities in this regard. Overall, the movement appears to have gained some measure of public support in 1998. A preelection survey found that 60 percent of the public believed the Christian Right represented "most" or "some" of their values, and 40 percent felt the movement represented "few" or "none" of their values.

Predictably, evangelicals were the most likely to report shared values (78 percent, most or some) and secular people the least (44 percent, most or some).[3] All told, the core constituency of the movement remained somewhere between one-sixth and one-fifth of the electorate, depending on how movement support is measured. The public was still largely opposed to many of the core issues of the Christian Right's agenda. For example, only 13 percent of the public agreed that abortions should be banned and another 30 percent agreed they should be limited to cases of rape or incest or when the woman's life was in danger.[4]

Political Roles in 1998

When taken together, the foregoing evidence suggests that the Christian Right was in contention in many states in 1998 as in 1996. However, the movement did not fare as well as in 1996 or 1994. This change can be seen in candidate recruitment, nomination battles, and general election campaigns. As in the past, the movement's weaknesses were most evident at the level of candidate recruitment, which produced some intense confrontations in 1998 (Green, Guth, and Hill 1993). In contrast, the movement's strengths were most evident in general election campaigns, which often involved consolidation.

Candidate Recruitment

Like other movements, the Christian Right can have the widest influence in candidate-centered politics when it participates in the actual recruitment of candidates, but candidate recruitment creates a classic political dilemma for the movement: whether to back candidates that best articulate the movement's values or to support candidates that have the best chance of being elected. Movement purists tend to advocate the former, while pragmatists are at least equally concerned with the latter. This dilemma becomes especially intense when candidates arise from within the movement itself.

More often than not, self-starting movement candidates bring to the fore the Christian Right's weaknesses, including its internal divisions and unpopular issue positions. Even when pragmatic leaders advise against it, the activist corps is often impressed by such candidates' commitment to the movement's agenda. Besides having unpopular issues positions, self-starters frequently lack other credentials, such as previous political experience and a well-developed agenda on other issues of concern to voters. Not surprisingly, such candidates rarely win. Few obtain major party nominations, and those who do tend to lose by large margins. However, the combination of unpopular issue positions and lack of electability can generate ferocious confrontations between Christian Rightists and other kinds of activists.

There appear to have been more self-starting movement candidates in 1998 than in 1996. A good example was David Miller in Kansas and the candidates described in the New York case study. There Randall Terry, the founder of the antiabortion group Operation Rescue, unsuccessfully sought the Republican congressional nomination in a competitive upstate district. However, both Terry and an ally in a nearby district, James Pierce, failed to win the GOP nomination, gaining minor party nominations instead, a result reflecting New York's unique multiparty system. Although their weak showing at the polls had no effect on the outcome, such minor party forays sometimes do, as reported in the Washington case study, where a movement candidate running under a minor party label contributed to the defeat of a moderate Republican incumbent. The Minnesota case describes the mixed impact of the candidacy of Jesse "The Body" Ventura on the fortunes of the movement in the state.

As in the past, the Christian Right helped recruit a number of candidates associated with the movement but also with more mainstream credentials. Examples include a return appearance of Bob Dornan, one of the movement's original supporters in Congress (see California case study), and first-time candidates Gex Williams in Kentucky, Gary Hofmeister in Indiana, and Mike Fair in South Carolina (the last three were campaign clients of former Christian Coalition head Ralph Reed). The South Carolina case study tells of the primary defeat of Fair—at the hands of another candidate with movement support. All these candidates lost in the general election, at least in part because of their association with the movement. A similar situation occurred for a handful of movement supporters in the House who ran for the Senate, including John Ensign in Nevada, Mark Neuman in Wisconsin, Bob Inglis in South Carolina, and Linda Smith in Washington.

However, the movement did help recruit winners in 1998, including Robin Hayes in North Carolina and Tom Tancredo in Colorado, and a movement supporter, Congressman Jim Bunning, won a close Senate race in Kentucky. Sometimes candidates arise with good movement credentials and wider political appeal; an example is Mark Earley in Virginia (see the Virginia case study). Just as movement-backed candidates may be too conservative for their districts, sometimes GOP candidates may be too moderate, such as Nancy Hollister in Ohio and Delbert Hosemann in Mississippi, both widely touted candidates who lost in 1998. And weak conservative candidates can hurt the mobilization of evangelical voters, as the Georgia case study shows. The Michigan case study shows yet another side of this situation: candidates hostile to religious sensibilities, like the Democratic gubernatorial nominee, can fare as poorly as candidates too closely tied to the Christian Right.

In 1998, the Christian Right was once again active in ballot issues. A political referendum on a single issue in the movement's agenda resembles the situation of a self-starting candidates. And as with self-starters, such efforts frequently fail, largely because they present an unpopular issue in isolation. A good example of this pattern can be seen in the Washington case study regarding an antiabortion ballot measure. The Michigan case study shows the opposite pattern, where the Christian Right joined with a broad array of religious groups to defeat an assisted suicide measure. The Maine case study covers the repeal of a gay rights measure, where the movement succeeded in a low voter turnout. Across the nation, the Christian Right backed losing abortion and school voucher referenda in 1998 but prevailed in same-sex marriage referenda in Hawaii and Alaska.

Nomination Politics

More pragmatic Christian Rightists have sought to minimize the problems of movement self-starters by becoming involved in the rough-and-tumble of nomination politics. In some cases, movement activists have helped recruit credible candidates who shared their goals, but mostly they have supported or opposed candidates recruited by other means. This process is quite informal and mostly local, involving three-way contacts among candidates, activists, and leaders. Under the best circumstances, this kind of involvement reduces the risks to the movement since the disagreements between purists and pragmatists can be negotiated around a particular candidate. This seems to have happened with Dan Lundgren in California and in several races in Virginia in 1997 (see the California and Virginia case studies).

There is no guarantee, of course, that such a process will succeed. In 1998, several bitter confrontations occurred, including Governor Fob James's renomination struggle in Alabama, the fight for the U.S. Senate nomination in Illinois, and the battle over the GOP gubernatorial nomination in Kansas. These three examples are discussed in detail in the respective case studies and cover the range of typical outcomes. In Alabama, the poster child for the Christian Right, Governor Fob James, won a narrow primary victory and then went down to defeat in the general election. But in Illinois, Peter Fitzgerald, a candidate viewed as too extreme, won the nomination and then prevailed in the fall. Meanwhile in Kansas, a popular sitting governor crushed a movement candidate and in the process damaged the Christian Right's influence in the Kansas Republican party. Movement pragmatists and party regulars alike steadfastly warned against the first and third outcomes, and movement purists yearn for the second category.

The 1998 primary campaign witnessed a more concerted effort than in the past to contest nominations by the Christian Right. Here Gary Bauer's CWF had a high profile. A good example is the $230,000 spent by CWF on behalf of Tom Bordonaro in California. CWF also spent on behalf of Linda Smith's and Peter Fitzgerald's primary contests, in Washington and Illinois, respectively. This extensive use of a political action committee (PAC) to raise and spend campaign funds for the movement was an unusual tactic by the Christian Right. Indeed, one has to hark back to the mid-1980s to find a similar, albeit smaller, effort. Interestingly, such spending was a prelude to Pat Robertson's 1988 presidential campaign, much as the 1998 effort may have been a first step in Gary Bauer's presidential plans (Hertzke 1993).

Pragmatism was not entirely absent from the Christian Right in 1998, however. Movement operatives either did not oppose or got behind the nomination of many centrist candidates as well. Good examples include the Bush brothers—Jeb in Florida and George W. in Texas—John Engler in Michigan, and James Gilmore in Virginia in 1997. As several of the case studies point out, the Christian Right does best when it participates as part of a broader conservative coalition led by a mainstream candidate. The Minnesota case study of the Republican victory in the lower state legislative chamber illustrates this point. Nomination rules are important to outcomes, and control of the GOP party apparatus matters as well, although it does not guarantee success (see the Washington, Minnesota, and Texas case studies).

Campaign Support

Once candidates are nominated, the Christian Right can campaign on their behalf. If candidate recruitment and nomination struggles tend to bring out the movement's weaknesses, then general election activities tend to reveal its strengths. Most of the case studies point to the positive effects of the movement's grassroots activities. In most cases, the distribution of voter guides was the centerpiece of these efforts, but movement activists performed a wide variety of roles, including the raising of funds for favored candidates. These efforts can be critical to Republican candidates of all stripes. A good example of this impact can be seen in the Illinois case study, where strong support from the right-to-life constituency was critical to Peter Fitzgerald's victory. And the major wins of the brothers Bush in Florida and Texas involved strong support from the Christian Right constituencies combined with backing from a wide range of other groups.

However, the general election efforts of the Christian Right did not appear to be as successful in 1998 as in 1996 or 1994. From the point of view of the movement, the most startling election results were in the

South, especially the defeat of Governors David Beasley of South Carolina and Fob James of Alabama, and the narrow loss of Senator Lauch Faircloth in North Carolina. These incumbents were strong movement backers presumably running in the heart of the movement's strength. The most common explanation for their defeat was that the Christian Right's organizational weaknesses undermined its ability to turn out its prime constituency of evangelical Protestants. A prime piece of evidence for this hypothesis came from television network exit polls, which showed self-identified members of the religious right to have made up 13 percent of the electorate, down from 15 percent in 1996 and 17 percent in 1994 (Neal and Morin 1998). Other analysts speculated that a larger slice of the movement's constituency may have voted Democratic once they got to the polls, a point supported by the Christian Coalition's own postelection poll.[5]

There is some truth to these explanations. The movement's weaknesses did appear to limit turnout among evangelical Protestants in some places, and some Democratic candidates did receive higher than usual support from evangelical voters. The Georgia case study shows this result quite convincingly. However, nationwide measures of voter behavior show a more complicated pattern. Although turnout among evangelicals was down roughly five percentage points from that of 1994, they remained a strong Republican constituency, with 70 percent voting for House Republican candidates in 1998, up from 68 percent in 1994.[6] Self-reported religious contacts by voters show a similar pattern. In 1998, 16 percent of evangelicals claimed to have been contacted by a religious interest group, almost the same as the 15 percent in 1994. There was modest decline in the percentage claiming political information was made available in their church, from 24 percent in 1994 to 20 percent in 1998.[7] Overall, then, the Christian Right appears to have matched its performance in recent elections with its prime constituency in 1998.

The election results may have turned less on the weaker effort of the Christian Right than on other factors. First, 1998 involved a broader electorate than in 1994. Although turnout was typical of a midterm election, participation by Democratic constituencies, such as African Americans and blue-collar workers, was up, in some cases nearing all-time highs. Liberal voters, from feminists to environmentalists, also turned out in large numbers. The much anticipated voter malaise did occur—but among conservatives, especially secular ones (Neal and Morin 1998). Thus, the electorate was more diverse in 1998, quite apart from the efforts of the Christian Right.

The 1998 election was also characterized by a broader opposition. We have already noted the expanded opposition to the Christian Right from religious progressive and secular activists. The Republican Party also faced more sophisticated foes. For one thing, the Democrats recruited a number of very strong candidates, especially in the South, who were adept at dealing with cultural issues. The Democratic Party was well funded and effective as well. Interest groups allied with the Democrats were also very active in 1998. Drawing on the tactics of 1996, labor unions, environmentalists, and feminists undertook extensive issue advocacy campaigns and get-out-the-vote drives. New interests, like the gambling industry in South Carolina and Alabama, were quite potent in some states. In key races, these Democrat strengths dovetailed with Republican weaknesses. The GOP fielded some poor candidates, as the Georgia case study reveals, and the Republican campaign efforts suffered from poor strategy and coordination. Republican interest group allies were also quite active but were simply outclassed in some instances (Magleby 1999).

Finally, the 1998 campaign was characterized by a broader issue agenda than in 1994. The Republicans and many of their allies banked on the country's disgust with the Clinton-Lewinsky scandal to carry the day. However, most of the public was tired of the scandal and very critical of the Republican approach to the topic. Thus, the Republicans offered little in the way of an affirmative agenda, and this hurt their candidates in close races (Neal and Morin 1998). Christian Right leaders complained with some merit about the lack of emphasis on social issues and the fixation on scandal by the GOP. But in all fairness, many of these same movement leaders strongly supported the Republican strategy on the scandal.

In sum, the electoral environment in 1998 was quite different from that of 1994—to the surprise of most pundits and politicians. The broader electorate, opposition, and issue agenda worked against the interests of the Christian Right quite apart from the movement's own weaknesses and mistakes. From this perspective, the remarkable thing is that more Christian Right candidates were not defeated. Indeed, if more races had been competitive, the Democrats might well have won the election in fact rather than just symbolically. As it was, most movement allies already in office were reelected.

Was the 1998 aftershock just a bad year for the Christian Right or was it a prelude to a final collapse in 2000? Will the Republican coalition continue to consolidate, crushing the movement's niche in national politics? Will a nasty confrontation help give the Democrats a big victory in 2000? The following case studies offer a wealth of detailed information with which to answer this question, and the concluding chapter offers some informed speculation on the subject. One thing is certain: the Christian Right will be very active in the 2000 campaign.

NOTES

1. Unless otherwise noted, the conclusions in this chapter are based on the author's interviews with several dozen movement activists during and af-

ter the 1998 campaign and on an extensive review of the documents and Web sites of political organizations.

2. These data come from the 1998 National Survey of Americans on Values conducted by the *Washington Post,* Kaiser Family Foundation, and Harvard University. This survey was graciously made available by the *Washington Post.*

3. These data also come from the 1998 National Survey of Americans on Values.

4. These data come from the 1998 National Election Studies. The 1998 National Election Studies were conducted at the University of Michigan and made available by the Interuniversity Consortium for Political and Social Research.

5. The Christian Coalition postelection poll showed 54 percent of religious conservatives voted Republican, compared with 67 percent in 1994.

6. These data come from the 1998 and 1994 National Election Studies.

7. These data come from the 1998 and 1994 National Election Studies.

REFERENCES

Balz, Dan. 1999. "The Christian Coalition: A Staff to Match Its Goals?" *Washington Post,* 12 March, A15.

Berkowitz, Laura, and John C. Green. 1997. "Charting the Coalition: The Local Chapters of the Ohio Christian Coalition." In *Sojourners in the Wilderness: The Christian Right in Comparative Perspective,* edited by Corwin E. Smidt and James M. Penning, 57–74. Lanham, Md.: Rowman & Littlefield.

Gerson, Michael J. 1998. "Christian Coalition in Unprecedented Crisis." *U.S. News and World Report,* 16 February, 33, 36.

Gilbert, Christopher P. 1993. *The Impact of Churches on Political Behavior.* Westport, Conn.: Greenwood Press.

Green, John C. 1999. "The Spirit Willing: Collective Identity and the Development of the Christian Right." In *Waves of Protest: Social Movements Since the Sixties,* edited by Jo Freeman and Victoria Johnson, 153–68. Lanham, Md.: Rowman & Littlefield.

Green, John C., James L. Guth, and Kevin Hill. 1993. "Faith and Election: The Christian Right in Congressional Campaigns 1978–1988." *Journal of Politics* 55:80–91.

Green, John C., James L. Guth, Lyman A. Kellstedt, and Corwin E. Smidt. 1998. "The Religious Right and the 1998 Election: A Defeat, Not a Debacle." *Christian Century,* 23–30 December, 1238–45.

Green, John C., James L. Guth, Corwin E. Smidt, and Lyman A. Kellstedt. 1996. *Religion and the Culture Wars: Dispatches from the Front.* Lanham, Md.: Rowman & Littlefield.

Green, John C., James L. Guth, and Clyde Wilcox. 1998. "Less than Conquerors: The Christian Right in State Republican Parties." In *Social Movements and American Political Institutions,* edited by Anne N. Costain and Andrew S. McFarland. Lanham, Md.: Rowman & Littlefield.

Guth, James L., John C. Green, Lyman A. Kellstedt, and Corwin E. Smidt. 1994. "Onward Christian Soldiers: Religious Interest Group Activists." In *Interest Group Politics,* 4th ed., edited by Allan Cigler and Burdett Loomis, 55–76. Washington, D.C.: CQ Press.

Hertzke, Allen D. 1993. *Echoes of Discontent.* Washington D.C.: CQ Press.

Jacobson, Gary C. 1999. "Impeachment Politics in the 1998 Congressional Election." *Political Science Quarterly* 114(1):31–52.

Jelen, Ted G. 1991. *The Political Mobilization of Religious Belief.* Westport, Conn.: Praeger.

Jorstad, Erling. 1993. *Popular Religion in America.* Westport, Conn.: Greenwood Press.

Leege, David C. 1992. "Coalitions, Cues, Strategic Politics, and the Staying Power of the Religious Right." *Political Science and Politics* 25:198–204.

Magleby, David B. 1999. "Outside Money: Soft Money and Issue Ads in Competitive 1998 Congressional Elections." Unpublished report, Brigham Young University.

Neal, Terry M., and Richard Morin. 1998. "For Voters, It's Back Toward the Middle." *Washington Post,* 5 November, A3.

Oldfield, Duane M. 1996. *The Right and the Righteous: The Christian Right Confronts the Republican Party.* Lanham, Md.: Rowman & Littlefield.

Rozell, Mark J., and Clyde Wilcox. 1995. *God at the Grass Roots: The Christian Right in the 1994 Elections.* Lanham, Md.: Rowman & Littlefield.

———. 1996. "Second Coming: The Strategies of the New Christian Right." *Political Science Quarterly* 111:271–94.

———. 1997. *God at the Grass Roots, 1996: The Christian Right in the American Elections.* Lanham, Md.: Rowman & Littlefield.

Rozell, Mark J., Clyde Wilcox, and John C. Green. 1998. "Religious Constituencies and Support for the Christian Right in the 1990s." *Social Science Quarterly* 79(4):815–21.

Salmore, Barbara G., and Stephen A. Salmore. 1989. *Candidates, Parties and Campaigns.* 2d ed. Washington D.C.: CQ Press.

Szabo, Liz. 1999. "Christian Coalition Official Reassigned; Robertson's Own Leadership Increases." *Virginian Pilot,* 2 June, A1.

Thomas, Cal, and Ed Dobson. 1999. *Blinded by Might.* Grand Rapids, Mich.: Zondervan.

Van Drehle, David. 1999. "Social Conservatives' Ties to GOP Fraying." *Washington Post,* 28 February, A1.

Wilcox, Clyde. 1992. *God's Warriors.* Baltimore: Johns Hopkins University Press.

———. 1994. "Premillenialists at the Millenium: Some Reflections on the Christian Right in the Twenty-first Century." *Sociology of Religion* 55:243–62.

2

South Carolina: Even in Zion the Heathen Rage

James L. Guth

For the past three decades, South Carolina has provided a marvelous case study of the Christian Right's development as a force within the Republican Party. The movement appeared as a partisan actor earlier than in most states, manifested a wider variety of forms, and sustained greater influence over a longer period than almost anywhere else. As a result, the Christian Right has established a stronger beachhead in the South Carolina GOP and perhaps had greater electoral impact than in other locations (see Smith 1997, ch. 5).

Nevertheless, the Christian Right faces formidable challenges in South Carolina, as elsewhere. As long-term demographic changes gradually challenge the religious dominance of conservative Protestantism, movement activists clash frequently with other elements of the Republican Party, especially the business wing, and Christian Right forces fight among themselves at critical junctures. As the election of 1998 demonstrates, the proper convergence of political forces can still push the Republican Party, the movement's adopted home, from its dominant position in South Carolina politics, reminding us that all social movements, whatever their resources, are often constrained by external events and that their activities can be countered by more effective mobilization by other political actors.

Prologue: The Religious Context

South Carolina has long laid claim—with several other states—to being the "buckle" of the southern Bible Belt. Although rapid economic development and massive in-migration from other parts of the United States and the world have diversified the urban population, religion is still dominated by conservative Protestants, especially Southern Baptists, the state's (and nation's) largest Protestant denomination. Indeed, Southern Baptists still constituted over 40 percent of the church members in 1990, although that proportion has probably declined at the brink of the new millennium. South Carolina also has a large number of mainline Protestants from the United Methodist Church (14 percent), the Presbyterian Church in the U.S.A. (4 percent), and the Evangelical Lutheran and Episcopal denominations (3 and 2 percent, respectively). There are also numerous (and mostly uncounted) independent fundamentalist congregations, usually Baptist, and many new nondenominational charismatic churches, often quite large, located in the state's burgeoning suburban areas. Other evangelical denominations, such as the Presbyterian Church in America (PCA), have also benefited from urban growth and play a noticeable political role. The African American community is served by several black Baptist denominations (16 percent of the state's church members) and many other historically black churches such as the African Methodist Episcopal Church, Zion (Bradley et al. 1992, 31). These churches and their clergy continue to have an important place in South Carolina politics.

For most of the twentieth century, the centrality of race in South Carolina politics precluded any large role for religion (see Guth 1995). This situation gradually changed in the 1960s and 1970s, as Republicans challenged the historic Democratic monopoly of state politics. The rising GOP of the 1950s and early 1960s reflected the religious coloration of its new urban, often "immigrant," leadership: upper-status mainline Protestants such as Episcopalians, Presbyterians, Methodists, and some "First Church" Southern Baptists. But other religious forces soon crashed the party. Beginning with the infusion of separatist fundamentalists from Bob Jones University in two waves after 1964, a succession of religious groups and organizations have "migrated into," "infiltrated," or "invaded" the GOP (the appropriate metaphor depending on the observer's attitude). By 1990 the charismatic and Pentecostal allies of 1988 presidential aspirant Marion G. "Pat" Robertson had became major actors in the party leadership, while the much larger body of conservative Southern Baptists moved more slowly, but with greater electoral impact, toward the GOP (Smith 1997).

By 1994 the Christian Right had become a major, if not yet the controlling, force in the South Carolina Republican Party. In that year the Right's favored gubernatorial candidate, David Beasley, a born-again Southern Baptist (and Democratic convert), won the Republican primary against two more mainstream candidates. With the united support of both the "new" GOP religious establishment and its "old" business elites, Beasley defeated incumbent Democratic Lieutenant Governor Nick Theodore in the general election. The 1994 election also gave the GOP a solid majority in the state House of Representatives (after several conservative Democrats moved across the aisle) and even left the party in a workable position in the state Senate, still in Democratic hands.

The 1996 Republican presidential primary revealed that the Christian Right was a crucial political force but was by no means monolithic. At least some conservative Protestant activists were in the camps of almost every declared Republican aspirant, even Lamar Alexander and Steve Forbes. Still, Senator Bob Dole and his nemesis, Pat Buchanan, divided most of the Christian Right forces, with the Kansas senator attracting the "pragmatists" and Buchanan the "purists." State Christian Coalition chair Roberta Combs assisted Dole, while many local coalition officials worked for Buchanan. Alumni and faculty of fundamentalist Bob Jones University, always a factor in the state GOP, revealed similar divisions. In the fall campaign, Christian Right activists of all descriptions coalesced behind the Republican ticket, allowing Dole (and incumbent Senator Strom Thurmond) to carry the state comfortably and returning the state's four Republican House members to Washington. Exit polls showed that 75 percent of white evangelical Protestants voted Republican for statewide offices and in U.S. House races. As a result, the Christian Right appeared to have solidified its institutional position within the state's dominant party (Guth and Smith 1997).

Well ensconced in a powerful state party that appeared on the verge of recreating a "one-party" South Carolina, the Christian Right seemed poised to enjoy some success on its "pro-family" agenda. Few observers anticipated that within two years the GOP would suffer a surprising defeat in the governor's race, fail to unseat a vulnerable Democratic U.S. senator, and be on the defensive on policy questions. In the remainder of this chapter, we focus on three 1998 elections critical to the movement: the defeat of incumbent Governor David Beasley, the reelection of U.S. Senator Fritz Hollings, and the Republican victory in the race for the Fourth District congressional seat. In combination, these stories reveal both the weaknesses—and the continuing strength—of the Christian Right in South Carolina.

The Beasley Administration and the Politics of Morality

At the beginning of 1997, Governor David Beasley seemed in a strong position to win reelection. Beasley had antagonized some Republican leaders by his patronage policies and garnered some bad publicity for questionable uses of state-owned aircraft and implausible claims to past athletic prowess (Fox 1995), but these seemed minor problems. South Carolina's economy was booming, the budget was in surplus, and the governor had struck a public tone of conciliation and cooperation during his first two years. Beasley sought to maintain the uneasy coalition between business Republicans and social conservatives in both personnel and policy. As Oran Smith has observed, he appointed enough Christian conservatives "to make the Republican establishment nervous, but not enough to satisfy the [Christian] Coalition" (Smith 1997, 129). He also tried to focus on both economic development and moral issues. The former task was easiest: Beasley succeeded in attracting new business to the state, ably following in the footsteps of his predecessors, Republican Carroll Campbell and Democrat Dick Riley (Hoover 1998a). In addition, he focused on other "consensual issues" for Republicans, including property tax reduction, welfare reform legislation, and tougher sentences for criminals (Associated Press 1997).

Moral issues proved more recalcitrant. During his first two years in office, Beasley established a high profile as a Christian Right spokesman, addressing abstinence education, homosexuality, and welfare reform from both state and national venues (Pope 1995). By the summer of 1996, these issues had become more visible in South Carolina and Beasley's responses increasingly identified him with religious conservatives. A variety of gay rights controversies were capped by a bitter struggle in Greenville, where the conservative Greenville County Council condemned gay lifestyles as "incompatible with community values." This action elicited a storm of protest from liberals, including many mainline Protestant clergy, and eventually drew a boycott of the area by the Atlanta Olympics torch committee. At Beasley's request, the state legislature passed the antigay Defense of Marriage Act, a major legislative priority of the Christian Right groups, especially the American Family Association and Palmetto Family Council (Karr 1996).

Other social issues received considerable attention from the governor. His administration propounded new restrictive regulations on abortion clinics, ended free condom distribution to poor families by the state department of health (Breckenridge 1997), and supported local government regulation of adult entertainment. And in late February 1997, the legislature overwhelmingly approved Beasley's partial-birth abortion prohibition, setting up a potential confrontation with the federal courts. These and other social issues became front-page news, energizing Christian Right forces and mobilizing their opponents as well. Although many of the governor's policies were not strong enough to satisfy the most militant elements of the Christian Right, they did serve to antagonize more liberal political forces, including some moderate members of the governor's own party.

Whether Christian Right activists would ultimately have coalesced enthusiastically behind Beasley is uncertain, because he soon splintered that constituency by a dramatic turnabout on a highly symbolic issue: the presence of the Confederate battle flag over the state capitol. He had promised during his 1994 campaign to keep the banner flying, but after receiving the report of his race relations commission, considering the pandemic of racial incidents (including church burnings), and engaging in "much prayer," Beasley decided that the controversial symbol should be removed to another place on the statehouse grounds. (Cynical observers attributed his new stance to pressure from the business community to "modernize" South Carolina's image.) During the first two years of his term, he sought a quiet negotiated settlement among state legislators, but when this failed, he decided to go public in 1997. Endorsed by five previous governors, including both Senator Strom Thurmond and U.S. Secretary of Education Dick Riley, Beasley's plan created a firestorm within the Republican Party. Many of the governor's own legislative partisans (and other Republican state officials) refused to follow his lead.

Beasley's action divided the religious community as well, but not entirely along the expected lines. For several weeks, hundreds of clergy from all over the state lined up on opposite sides, expressing themselves through marches, full-page newspaper advertisements, lengthy position papers, and well-scripted news conferences (South Carolina Christian Action Council 1997). Predictably, most mainline Protestant, Catholic, and Jewish religious leaders joined African American clergy in supporting Beasley's plan. Perhaps more surprisingly, a great many conservative Southern Baptists, Pentecostals, and charismatics also stood behind Beasley, organized by Dick Lincoln, the governor's own pastor and a leader of the conservative wing of the state Baptist Convention (Kirkland 1996).

Other conservative clergy, however, vocally opposed the governor's proposal, warning that he was threatening religious support for his re-election campaign in 1998 and wasting precious political capital that could be used on vital moral issues (Hammond 1996). Indeed, the South Carolina Baptist Convention was so divided that it failed to take a position, merely publishing opposing views in the *Baptist Courier*. The contributors there drew heavily on religious imagery—on both sides—and spoke with a vehemence uncharacteristic of church publications. Although polls showed a slight plurality of citizens favoring his plan, the governor's campaign was doomed to failure. After protracted maneuvering in the legislature, Beasley despaired of finding an acceptable solution and gave up, promising not to raise the flag issue again (Tanner 1997). In the end, he both angered former supporters among the flag's defenders and failed to assuage any of its critics, who were angered by his capitulation. Ironically, then, Beasley's effort to resolve an historic grievance of the African American community in "Christian" fashion served only to erode his "religious" coalition. Once again, the issue of race bedeviled Southern politics (Key 1949), this time within the ranks of the Republican Party and its allies on the Christian Right.

Beasley might have survived the flag fiasco had he not taken on the gambling industry, in what some saw as an effort to reunite his original religious constituency. From the time of his election through the legislative session of 1996, Beasley never concealed his distaste for the rapid proliferation of 30,000 video poker machines in gas stations, convenience stores, and video arcades all over the state. Although there was considerable question about the legal status of the industry because of a state constitutional prohibition of lotteries, voters in most counties had refused to ban the machines in a 1994 referendum. This referendum was overturned in the courts, ironically opening the entire state to video poker, as the South Carolina Supreme Court avoided a definitive ruling on the issue, obviously loath to jump into a political maelstrom. Beasley moved in where the court feared to tread. In his 1998 state of the state address, he warned that "a cancer"—gambling—had spread its tentacles into every part of South Carolina. In the absence of definitive court action, the governor proposed to ban the game through legislation, creating an uproar among gambling entrepreneurs and among the growing thousands of predominately blue-collar South Carolinians devoted to the pastime. Indeed, Beasley had attacked what was now a major South Carolina industry, with revenues well over $2.4 billion in 1998 (Hammond 1998).

The governor's campaign for a ban got off to a good start with favorable preliminary action in both the state house and senate. Legislators reported strong support from antigambling activists all over the state, drawn from both mainline and evangelical Protestant communities, as well as from some social service groups alarmed by the growing numbers of problem gamblers and the social ills deriving from addiction. A well-publicized incident in which an infant died in a overheated car as its mother played video poker for several hours gave added impetus to the antigambling forces. A number of Christian Right organizations supplemented legislative lobbying by litigation, harassing local proprietors with suits alleging violations of various state laws or local ordinances (Munro and Foley 1998).

The industry's counterattack was somewhat delayed, but eventually massive, mobilizing thousands of the small business people whose stores benefited from the traffic and revenues generated by the ubiquitous machines. Gambling forces argued that the governor should allow individuals the right to play games of chance, accept the inevitable, and raise state funds by increasing license fees and boosting taxes (but not too much) on the industry. After much maneuvering, the governor's ban passed the

Republican house but was stymied by a last-ditch filibuster in the Democratic senate, precipitated in part by a clumsy GOP effort to link Democratic senators' support for video poker to organized crime (Holland 1998).

The battles over the Confederate flag and gambling converged with personal grievances to foster Republican opposition to Beasley's renomination. One prominent Republican, Lexington county sheriff Jim Metts, first announced that he would run against Beasley in the primary but then decided to run as an independent in the fall campaign. Although Metts eventually withdrew, for several months he not only served as a rallying point for Republicans disappointed with Beasley but also spread some damaging allegations about the governor's personal lifestyle and marital fidelity. These statements were widely reported by the state and national press and were later circulated by Democratic Party officials as well. Although vehemently rebutted by Beasley (and later retracted by Metts), by all accounts these rumors reduced Christian Right enthusiasm for the governor, already eroded by the flag battle. Metts also reminded Christian Right activists that Beasley's father-in-law continued to operate an abortion clinic in Alabama, presumably demonstrating the governor's insufficient zeal on the issue (Hoover 1998e; Hoover and Hammond 1998).

Nevertheless, as late as the spring of 1998 most observers still expected Beasley to win reelection without undue strain. Indeed, his position was strong enough to deter much competition for the Democratic gubernatorial nomination. Beasley's 1994 opponent, Nick Theodore, decided to run for his old job as lieutenant governor, and other major Democratic figures, such as Mayor Joe Riley of Charleston and college president Alex Sanders, opted against the race. In the end, only Democratic minority leader Jim Hodges of Lancaster was willing to serve as the party's sacrificial lamb (Hoover 1997c). Discouraged by the frustrations of leading a legislative minority (another job nobody wanted), Hodges resigned from the legislature to devote full time to what seemed to be a hopeless campaign.

The Old and the New: The U.S. Senate Race

A long-time target of the GOP and its Christian Right allies was veteran U.S. Senator Ernest "Fritz" Hollings, who sought reelection in 1998. A former governor and seemingly permanent junior senator, Hollings had long appeared vulnerable to electoral attack, barely defeating a weak Republican challenger in 1992. By turns charming, irascible, and sometimes arrogant, Hollings maintained his own unpredictable course in Washington, voting at times with his liberal Democratic colleagues, at other times with conservatives, but always bringing home the bacon on pork-barrel legislation. Christian Right leaders regarded him as a foe of most of their treasured causes and targeted him for defeat in 1998, especially after he voted to sustain President Clinton's first veto of the national partial-birth abortion bill.

Despite Hollings's apparent vulnerability, no strong GOP opponent materialized immediately. After former governor Carroll Campbell and other party heavyweights decided not to run, Fourth District Congressman Bob Inglis found himself in the somewhat surprising role as the front-runner for the nomination. First elected to Congress in 1992, Inglis had unseated a seemingly popular Democratic incumbent with a massive grassroots mobilization that drew support from all wings of the large conservative Christian community in his home base of Greenville. His forces had included numerous campaign strategists and workers from his own Presbyterian Church in America (PCA).

Although much of the press had mistakenly attributed his original success to the Christian Coalition, Inglis had never enjoyed warm relations with the Coalition. He held its activists at arm's length, although he always did well on the group's legislative scorecards. The congressman's iconoclastic antipolitician rhetoric had endeared him to some constituents and antagonized others. Pledging to serve only six years in the House, he ignored the usual rules of pork-barrel politics by refusing to seek his district's "fair share" of federal road funds and other benefits. More important, he not only applauded Beasley's stance on the Confederate flag but went even further, publicly lecturing state Republicans for their failure to attract black voters. He explicitly repudiated the time-honored "Southern strategy" of the GOP, calling it "immoral." None of these actions endeared Inglis to party officials, nor did they win over many African Americans to his staunchly conservative campaign (Hoover 1997d). The congressman also injected himself into the state controversy over gambling by urging federal officials to take action against legal violations by the industry, thereby attracting the enmity of gaming interests. And Inglis's customary refusal to accept PAC donations had worked to his political and rhetorical advantage in the narrow confines of a congressional district but put him at a competitive disadvantage in a Senate race against Hollings, a noted cultivator of PAC managers.

The GOP Primaries

By the time of the GOP primaries in the summer of 1998, both Governor Beasley and Representative Inglis had attracted Republican opposition. Opponents sought to capitalize on the discontent they had aroused by putting together a coalition representing the Southern heritage crowd, Christian Right dissidents, and—especially in the governor's case—gambling interests. Beasley won renomination in the primary, but lawyer and political unknown William Able drew a significant protest vote (28 percent) with his support for video poker and for a referendum on a state lottery. In the Senate race, Inglis had more formidable opposition. Stephen Brown, former head of the Greenville County Republican Party, as well as a Southern Baptist deacon, Sunday School teacher, and conservative stalwart, entered the contest. He embarrassed Inglis across South Carolina by winning county convention endorsements, bolstered by the support of Southern traditionalists, some religious fundamentalists, and hard-line secular conservatives, all of whom had grievances with the congressman (Hoover 1997b). Nevertheless, Inglis eventually won the primary with over 74 percent of the vote against Brown and a minor candidate.

Although Beasley and Inglis emerged as victors, the contests fit the classic model of the "divisive primary" and were a harbinger of diminished enthusiasm for both candidates among movement conservatives, especially on the Christian Right. Dissatisfaction with the Republican administration's policies on abortion, law enforcement, and education (where the governor had not pushed vouchers and school prayer with enough enthusiasm) had increased the sniping at Beasley by Christian Right activists. The movement was still split between hard-line and more moderate elements, as evidenced by a division that flared into open conflict in the Republican primary for superintendent of education, where factions of the Christian Coalition backed different candidates. More moderate elements, led by state coalition chair Roberta Combs, supported Governor Beasley's chosen candidate, David Eckstrom, the brother of the Republican state treasurer, while the purist wing supported Jim White, a Hanahan businessman. Eckstrom defeated White handily in the primary, 53 to 21 percent, with another conservative candidate drawing 14 percent. Despite the solid victory, the campaign left yet more divisions within the GOP—and the Christian Right (Bandy 1998a, 1998c).

Strife in God's Home District, the Fourth

As always, the GOP and Christian Right factional alignments were in full display in the race for the fourth congressional district seat being vacated by Representative Inglis. The media-chosen front runner, State Senator Mike Fair, was well known in the district (and state) not only for his former heroics as a quarterback for the University of South Carolina but for his adamant social conservatism, a hallmark of his many campaigns and long legislative career. Bolstering his candidacy was Ralph Reed, former executive director of the national Christian Coalition, who had quickly signed Fair on as one of the first clients for his new consulting service (Hoover 1997a). Fair immediately drew the support of the Greenville County Republican convention, many Christian Coalition activists, Bob Jones graduates (he was a member of a BJU-affiliated independent Baptist church), and many conservative Southern Baptists. Fair's much-publicized connection with Reed, his endorsement by well-known upstate conservative politicians, and subsequent plugs from national Christian Right figures such as Phyllis Schlafly and Gary Bauer did little to widen his appeal to more moderate voters (Bandy 1998b). Nor did a stamp of approval from presidential hopeful Steve Forbes, pursuing his own reconciliation with Christian conservatives, prove to be of much electoral value.

Several other Republican candidates challenged Fair, each with his own constituency. While antiabortion activist and BJU alumnus Frank Raddish threatened to pull a few votes away from Fair on the right, other candidates aligned themselves at varying (but small) distances to his left on the political and religious spectrum. Jim DeMint, a public relations entrepreneur, inherited much of Inglis's campaign organization and his implicit endorsement. DeMint stressed economic issues attractive to the small business community but was quite acceptable to most social conservatives. Like Inglis, he was an adherent of the conservative Presbyterian Church in America (PCA) and drew on PCA churches for activists, but like his mentor, he was not particularly close to the Christian Coalition and Bob Jones community. Nevertheless, for many Christian Right activists DeMint was an acceptable second or third choice, and his campaign worked hard to establish that position through back channels.

Candidate Howell Clyborne, Jr., a public hospital executive, was often seen as the candidate of the "old" GOP establishment. He had served as a Republican leader in the state legislature, as an aide to former Governor Campbell, and as a close ally of the state's business community, which funded his campaign quite generously. Clyborne was "establishment" in religious terms as well, belonging to an old-line Southern Baptist congregation and avoiding harsh rhetoric, but not conservative stances, on social issues. The primary field was completed with Spartanburg state Senator James Ritchie, a Methodist who counted on division among the dominant Greenville (and Christian conservative) forces to eke his way into a runoff, thereby becoming the candidate of the anti-Fair forces.

The campaign revealed few detectable policy differences among the candidates: most took socially conservative stands and wanted lower taxes, although they differed on how to reform the national tax system. As expected, Fair led the field in the first primary but won only 32 percent of the vote, with DeMint capturing 23 percent and Clyborne coming in a close third with 22 percent. In the runoff, DeMint surprised some observers by defeating Fair, supposedly the candidate with the most zealous followers, carrying over 53 percent of the vote (Hoover 1998c). Many attributed Fair's defeat to a lackluster campaign and inarticulate debate style, but the reason lay more in the structure of GOP politics in South Carolina. Even in Republican primaries, candidates with too strong an identification with the Christian Right movement seldom command a majority; Fair was simply unable to expand his constituency to include a substantial contingent of "business" Republicans (Bandy 1998b). (It is important to note that establishment Republicans like Clyborne, who appeal only to the business community, typically fare no better. Winning candidates need both traditional Republican constituencies and the new social issue conservatives.)

The Campaign and General Election

The general election campaign turned into one of the hardest-fought and most expensive battles in South Carolina electoral history. Indeed, the phrase "total mobilization" comes to mind as an apt description. Not only the usual suspects but a variety of outside actors became involved in the campaign on both sides. On balance, however, the changes in the cast of characters and the expansion of the South Carolina political universe worked to the advantage of the recently hard-pressed Democrats.

This shift in fortunes was evident in both the gubernatorial and senate races but appeared first in the governor's contest. Far behind in all the polls, Democratic gubernatorial candidate Jim Hodges took a tremendous gamble in early 1998: he linked the growing public concern over the quality of education in South Carolina with calculated revisions in state gaming policy. An active Methodist layman, Hodges had long shared the characteristic opposition of his church to the influx of gambling, fighting the rise of video poker as a legislator and opposing a state lottery. His new position was that voters should have the final word on both: video poker revenues (if voters approved the existence of the industry) and proceeds from a new state lottery (if the voters endorsed the requisite constitutional amendment) should be allocated to education funding (Hoover 1998b).

In one stroke, then, Hodges adroitly created both the issue basis and the organizational network for an upset victory. His new platform had a cross-class appeal: better education for the middle-class, abundant video poker for blue-collar voters. At the same time, he laid the groundwork for a new Democratic organizational network, attracting generous campaign funding from entertainment interests, virtually neutralizing the usual Republican advantage in money (Hammond and Smith 1998). As the video poker interests had already exhibited considerable skill at mobilizing both beneficiaries and participants in the gaming industry, Hodges could also hope for industry muscle at the precinct level, filling the long-vacant holes in Democratic operations, especially in Republican-leaning suburban areas.

By August, Beasley was clearly on the defensive, as Hodges's new appeal drew him upward in the polls. Indeed, by late summer the competing campaigns addressed few other issues. Lavish financing by entertainment interests allowed Hodges to commission and run truly masterful political spots featuring "Bubba," a Georgia convenience store operator who "just luuuuved" David Beasley for depriving South Carolinians of a lottery, permitting both Bubba and the state of Georgia to make a killing on ticket-hungry neighbors. Although the Republicans countered in the same spirit, focusing on the economic and social costs of gambling, their spot had little impact. Finally, Beasley yielded to the swelling tide of pro-lottery sentiment by saying that he would no longer stand in the way of a referendum vote on a constitutional amendment (Associated Press 1998). This concession, like Beasley's earlier retreat on the flag issue, did little to mollify his critics but disappointed an already distrustful conservative Christian constituency. Beasley's belated attempt to revive his campaign with a proposed automobile tax cut failed to divert attention from gambling issues (Strope 1998).

Where Hodges overcame significant obstacles to overtake the incumbent Republican governor, Senator Hollings deployed the resources of incumbency enthusiastically, stressing to voters the advantages of seniority for securing pork-barrel benefits and drawing invidious comparisons with Inglis's ideological refusal to support even home-state boodle. At various points, Hollings resorted to personal attacks, once referring to Inglis as a "goddam skunk," in addition to milder imprecations. The senator also assailed Inglis's proposal for Social Security reform, suggesting to senior citizens that they might be out in the cold if the congressman moved to the other side of Capitol Hill (Hollings and Inglis 1998). The Hollings campaign was reinforced by substantial spending by the Democratic Senatorial Campaign Committee and friendly interest groups. Press reports also credited Hollings with using his resources to re-create an effective Democratic campaign organization on the ground. Trapped in Washington as his House Judiciary Committee considered the impeachment of President Clinton (which he vocally supported), Inglis never really got his campaign rolling. The congressman's self-denying ordinance against PAC money left him with less than half the cash available to Hollings. Even the uncoordinated soft-money spending by the Republican Senatorial Campaign Committee hurt rather than helped, since the spots run by the committee were in bad taste, mean-spirited, and immediately repudiated by Inglis himself (Hoover 1999c). And despite nominal support from the U.S. Chamber of Commerce, the Christian Coalition, and other conservative groups, the Inglis campaign could not match the extensive Hollings organization (Edsall 1998; Moore and Vinson 1999).

On election day, the Democrats won both major statewide contests, with Hodges capturing 53 percent of the vote and Hollings 52 percent. Their combined organizational efforts and coattails carried some other statewide Democrats to victory. Although Republican Lieutenant Governor Bob Peeler prevented Democrat Nick Theodore from reclaiming his old office and both Attorney General Charlie Condon (a Christian Right favorite) and GOP Secretary of State Jim Miles held on as well, other Democrats did better. The party took the state treasurer's job and the comptroller general's office by extremely narrow margins, giving Democrats a majority on the powerful state budget and control board, a legislative-executive committee responsible for the budget. The Democratic candidate for superintendent of education, Inez Tenanbaum, rode the Democratic wave to an impressive victory over David Eckstrom, once again frustrating Christian conservatives disturbed with state educational policy. The Democrats also reduced the Republican margin in the state house of representatives and added slightly to their own narrow edge in the state senate.

Still, the Democratic waters failed to perturb the 4–2 Republican majority in the state delegation to the U.S. House. All the incumbent Republicans and Democrats running for reelection triumphed. Republican Jim DeMint easily captured the fourth congressional district, defeating Democratic State Senator Glenn Reese, in a race that was notable only for civility and courtesy. The two candidates toured the district together for debates and often seemed to agree more than disagree. DeMint won the support of both economic and social conservatives while carefully distancing himself from the Christian Coalition. For his part, Reese, an active Southern Baptist layman, insisted that he was a member of "the coalition of Christians," though not the "Christian Coalition," and actually outflanked DeMint on the right on issues such as television censorship. Still, the low-key contest was never in doubt, and Reese himself saw his candidacy primarily as a means to maximize Democratic turnout by "filling the ticket."

Interpretation

The outcome of the 1998 South Carolina elections certainly represented a setback to the growing state power of the GOP and provided at least a reprieve for the Democratic Party. The victory not only restored party morale but also disoriented the Republican rank and file and was widely interpreted as a defeat for the Christian Right. What were the most critical elements accounting for the victory? What lessons should be drawn about the future of the Christian Right?

Strategic decisions by candidates obviously played a critical role in the outcome. Governor Beasley consistently weakened himself by actions of his administration, antagonizing past supporters and failing to build new constituencies (Hoover 1998d). Representative Inglis had also created a legislative and political record that presented some difficulties during the campaign. Senator Hollings used the powers of incumbency skillfully, taking advantage of both his own resources and his opponent's miscues. Perhaps most important, Democratic candidate Jim Hodges combined popular positions on two emerging statewide issues by his masterful link between education and gambling, as exit polls showed that 60 percent of the voters approved a lottery for education. Until Hodges made that link, his campaign was clearly a long shot, even given Beasley's problems.

To some indeterminate extent the national environment also worked to the Democrats' advantage, even in South Carolina. Although all the polls showed that Bill Clinton was notoriously unpopular among white South Carolinians, the impeachment episode mobilized key Democratic constituencies such as blacks in support of the president and, more vitally, behind the party's statewide candidates. At the same time, Christian Right activists seem to have been dispirited, hardly responding to their leadership's effort to make Clinton's immoral behavior the focus of the campaign (Hoover 1998f). For many, the leadership strategy drowned out much more vital items on the Christian Right agenda. The strong divisions within Christian Right ranks from the series of disputes over the previous four years did not help either.

By contrast with previous elections, in 1998 the Democrats had the unique advantage of superior organization. This was produced by the combination of Senator Hollings's massive effort to mount strong campaigns in every county and the lavish funding of the Hodges campaign by the video poker operators, who provided a very substantial part of the total campaign spending. The poker campaign focused on strong Democratic constituencies, such as the African American community, and, along with Hollings's effort, probably increased turnout. These organizational efforts were supplemented by similar mobilization drives by Democratic candidates in some local areas, helping statewide candidates.

Although the Democrats' new organizational life had several sources, the most striking development in South Carolina electoral politics was the sudden arrival and prowess of the new gaming industry. The industry not only provided a very substantial (and as yet undetermined) amount of campaign money for both Democratic coffers and independent expenditures but also built a major political machine. One Greenville Democratic activist reported his disappointment with the minuscule turnout of volunteers in his precinct a few days before the election—but all that changed on election day:

> What happened between that sparsely attended training session and the crowded moment at the same Hollings headquarters on election day? The video poker industry came through. For the effort at East North Street, video poker money supplied 12 vans and 12 employees to drive the vans. More video poker employees were given the day off so they could volunteer. As it turned out, all-day volunteers were paid $50. In addition, dozens, perhaps hundreds, of middle school and high school students were recruited to go door-to-door in predominately black neighborhoods. This helps explain the high turnout in those neighborhoods with most votes going to the Democrats. (Ezell 1998)

Whether such organization can be replicated in the future probably depends upon whether gambling interests perceive a stake in a particular election. Indeed, Democratic leaders were quick to warn the faithful against assuming the permanence of the new alliance. For the foreseeable future, however, the Christian Right and the GOP face a new and formidable opponent.

The video poker forces were not the only ones targeting the African American community. Most observers also saw the election of 1998 witnessing the revival of an old religious force in South Carolina politics: the African American clergy. Despite the tense relations in recent years between the Democratic state leadership and black voters, both the Hodges and Hollings campaigns did everything possible to activate black religious leaders and their followings, with frequent campaign stops in black churches and assiduous attention to clergy. Even those African American pastors strongly opposed to gambling—a significant number—regarded issues such as education, civil rights, and welfare programs as more important to their people. Seldom in recent campaigns have these churches been as visible as in 1998.

More surprising than the mobilization of gambling interests in 1998—or even the revival of church-based activity among black Christians—was the clear ineffectiveness of Christian conservatives. Although there are no firm public poll data on the electoral behavior of conservative Christians in 1998, experienced observers agree on two conclusions. First, conservative Christians were not as energized as in previous years, perhaps reducing their turnout. Second, those who did vote were slightly less prone to choose the GOP. A Christian Coalition survey discovered that among the 40 percent of the voters who called themselves "Christian conservatives," the governor had received 71 percent, probably down a few crucial percentage points from 1994 (Hoover 1998f).

As we have seen, several factors worked against Christian Right unity in 1998, but why did the gambling issue not activate conservative Christians, given the historic opposition of their churches to this social evil? Initial religious reactions to the Beasley proposal to ban video poker were very positive. Certainly a great many South Carolina church leaders had actively lobbied the legislature for the governor's proposed ban on video poker in early 1998 (Phifer and Kirkland 1998). Even later, the State Baptist Convention Executive Committee declared October 25 a day of prayer, when clergy and churches were to "preach, pray and talk" about the issue (Kirkland and Deaton 1998).

As it turned out, this opposition was difficult to convert into electoral effectiveness. First, the gambling issue became so enmeshed in the partisan campaign that some pastors felt very uncomfortable attacking gambling—because that was tantamount to endorsing the GOP. Even the strongest Republican clergy tried the impossible: to separate their opposition to gambling from partisan choices. For example, one widely publicized election-eve statement issued by two hundred South Carolina Baptist clergy cautioned that they "did not intend to lift up or put down any political candidates" (Kirkland and Deaton 1998). Second, even in the strongest Christian Right churches many pastors refrained from action because some of their working-class members were also video poker aficionados. (In fact, one large purveyor of video poker machines was also a born-again member of a large, politically active Spartanburg charismatic church and took out statewide, full-page newspaper ads denying that gambling was "un-Christian.") In more affluent churches, middle-class parishioners often supported a state lottery to finance better education, confident that they would pay little of the cost. So, despite ubiquitous church signs deprecating gambling, the customary Christian Coalition voter guide distribution, and some use of phone banks, the modest religious counterorganization failed to bolster the GOP side. Ironically, *after* the election both church bodies and individual pastors became much more outspoken about gambling, preparing for the legislative and referenda contests soon to follow (Hinkle 1998). Nevertheless, the Christian Right's organizational and legislative strengths were not transformed into electoral resources during the 1998 campaign.

Epilogue

The Republican defeat did not signal the end of religious politics in South Carolina, of course. The governor-elect's office soon announced that Hodges would precede his inauguration with a pilgrimage to important churches across the state—mostly African American and mainline Protestant congregations (Hoover 1999a). At Greenville's Springfield

Baptist Church, a historic black congregation, Hodges exhorted the faithful to join "his crusade" for educational funding. Speakers repeatedly attributed Hodges's victory to divine intervention. State Senator Ralph Anderson told the worshippers that "it was your prayers on November 3rd that made the difference," while Rev. John Corbett, pastor of the church, saw Hodges's victory as "a beacon of light in a sea of despair." Rev. S. C. Cureton, vice president of the National Baptist Convention USA, observed that "for 12 years we had nothing to rejoice about. Praise God tonight that Jim Hodges has brought us back." Even one of the few whites present, Greenville County Democratic chair Johnnie Fulton, an Episcopalian, struck a biblical theme, saying that in Hodges Democrats had "found their Moses." This Moses, noted another speaker, was "as strong as Samson and as wise as Solomon" (Hoover 1999b).

Like the triumphal tour, Hodges's inaugural featured the new religious coalition behind the Democratic victory. The ceremonies began with morning prayer at the Washington Street United Methodist Church, the capital city home of many prominent Democratic politicos, past and present. The Reverend William Kennett, a Methodist minister and old friend of Hodges, conducted the service. The theme was the Democratic one of "inclusion" of "men and women, black and white, Jew and Christian, Protestant and Catholic," illustrated by the identity of the prominent religious and political figures attending (Hammond 1999). The audience, however, included few conservative Protestants, a forewarning of the difficulty the new governor would face in building winning coalitions for his legislative agenda. Indeed, within a few weeks Hodges was confronting stiff resistance from the Republican House over his education, gambling, and taxation policies, a resistance buttressed by Christian Right activists. The new chief executive would indeed require the prescience of Moses, the strength of Samson, and the wisdom of Solomon to make the 1998 Democratic revival a truly "Great [Political] Awakening."

And what about Christian conservatives? Although they were now deprived of access to the state's top executive office, there was no indication that the Christian Right was about to disappear. Whatever the fortunes of particular organizations, Christian conservatives constitute a substantial portion of South Carolina's population, as much as half the electorate in Republican primaries, and some of the most engaged activists in the state, although they are seldom monolithic in that activism. The persistence of the moral issues triggered by economic modernization and population change will continue to provide incentives for political organization. And although many obituaries for the Christian Right were recycled in 1998, a wiser voice was that of Neal Thigpen, a political scientist, sometime state official, and moderate Republican activist, who had observed the Christian Right from close quarters. Thigpen warned that the movement might appear dead, but appearances are misleading: "you drive a stake through their heart, and they still keep coming." Or, as Christian Coalition leader Al Padgett predicted with just as much confidence: "We'll be back" (Hoover 1998f).

NOTE

Although the accounts in this chapter derive to some extent from "participant observation" of politicians and preachers, the author wishes to express his gratitude to many individuals who provided information and insight. The almost daily press reports of Dan Hoover and James Hammond of the *Greenville News* and the weekly columns of Lee Bandy of the Columbia *State* are absolutely essential reading for any student of South Carolina politics. Oran Smith has written several works on South Carolina politics and has always been generous with his insights. A number of politicians and political activists from both parties have shared their views with me over the past few years, although they are certainly not responsible for my interpretations: Representatives Bob Inglis and Jim DeMint, Lieutenant Governor Nick Theodore, State Representative Sara Manly, and Secretary of Education Dick Riley. And when one has taught political science long enough, former students can be sources of information as well as inspiration; I thank Greenville County Democratic chair Johnnie Fulton, Beasley cabinet member Lewis Gossett, and former South Carolina Democratic Party chair Frank Holloman. The chapter also benefited from discussions with my colleagues Danielle Vinson, who shared with me the results of her own research, and Brent Nelsen, who participated in some of these events as a Republican activist.

REFERENCES

Associated Press. 1997. "Beasley Gets Mixed Reviews." *Greenville News,* 14 July, 1D.

———. 1998. "Beasley Says He'll Allow Lottery." *Greenville News,* 10 August, 1B.

Bandy, Lee. 1998a. "Doing Unto Others." *The State,* 19 July, A1.

———. 1998b. "Fair Set Up Own Defeat." *The State,* 28 June, A1.

———. 1998c. "With Only a Right Wing, GOP Can't Fly." *The State,* 2 August, 1A.

Bradley, Martin, Norman M. Green, Jr., Dale E. Jones, Mac Lynn, and Lou McNeil. 1992. *Churches and Church Membership in the United States, 1990.* Atlanta: Glenmary Research Center.

Breckenridge, Mona. 1997. "Beasley Gets State to Abstain from Condom Handouts." *Greenville News,* 10 January, 10.

Edsall, Thomas. 1998. "In South Carolina, the Democrats' Last Stand." *Washington Post National Weekly Edition,* 12 October, 12.

Ezell, Walter. 1998. "South Carolina Democrats Must Remain Vigilant to Keep Party." *Greenville News,* 6 November, 9A.

Fox, William. 1995. "Beasley Used State Jet for Religious Outings." *Greenville News,* 26 October, 1A.

Guth, James L. 1995. "South Carolina: The Christian Right Wins One." In *God at the Grass Roots: The Christian Right in the 1994 Elections,* edited by Mark J. Rozell and Clyde Wilcox. Lanham Md.: Rowman & Littlefield.

Guth, James L., and Oran P. Smith. 1997. "South Carolina Christian Right: Just Part of the Family Now?" In *God at the Grass Roots, 1996: The Christian Right in the American Elections,* edited by Mark J. Rozell and Clyde Wilcox. Lanham Md.: Rowman & Littlefield.

Hammond, James T. 1996. "Ministers Say Beasley Twisting Flag's Meaning." *Greenville News,* 12 December, 1A.

———. 1998. "Session Opens with Video Poker on Front Burner." *Greenville News,* 14 January, 1A.

———. 1999. "Patriotic Tunes Steal Show." *Greenville News,* 14 January, 1B.

Hammond, James T., and Tim Smith. 1998. "$8.1 Million Fuels Governor's Race." *Greenville News,* 20 October, 1A.

Hinkle, Don. 1998. "Gambling Proponents Prevail Against Governors." *Baptist Courier,* 12 November, 6.

Holland, Jesse. 1998. "Filibuster to Stall Video Poker Ban on Hold." *Greenville News,* 22 March, 3B.

Hollings, Ernest P., and Bob Inglis. 1998. "Hollings, Inglis Offer Vision of Social Security's Future." *Greenville News,* 22 October, 13A.

Hoover, Dan. 1997a. "Fair Shows Off New Ralph Reed-Led Campaign Team." *Greenville News,* 23 July, 1D.

———. 1997b. "Greenville Chairman Seeks GOP Senate Nod." *Greenville News,* 2 October, 1D.

———. 1997c. "Hodges May Make Run for Governor as Democrat." *Greenville News,* 27 April, 1F.

———. 1997d. "Inglis Says He's Still Reaching Out to Blacks." *Greenville News,* 17 August, 2B.

———. 1998a. "Beasley: 1997 Was Rosy Year Economically." *Greenville News,* 16 January, 1C.

———. 1998b. "Has Poker Money Had an Effect?" *Greenville News,* 10 May, 1F.

———. 1998c. "DeMint Upsets Fair in GOP Runoff." *Greenville News,* 24 June, 1A.

———. 1998d. "Errors Sealed Beasley's Doom, Say Top Republicans." *Greenville News,* 5 November, 1A.

———. 1998e. "Metts Quits Governor's Race, With Apologies." *Greenville News,* 17 May, A1.

———. 1998f. "Religious Right Stung GOP at Polls." *Greenville News,* 23 November, 1D.

————. 1999a. "Gov.-elect Hodges to Speak to Churches Around the State." *Greenville News,* 5 January, 1B.

————. 1999b. "Hodges Pre-Inaugural Tour Visits Greenville." *Greenville News,* 7 January, 1B.

————. 1999c. "Inglis Calls GOP Attack Ads Key Factor in Election Loss." *Greenville News,* 3 February, 1B.

Hoover, Dan, and James T. Hammond. 1998. "Beasley Again Denies He Had Affair." *Greenville News,* 29 September, 1B.

Karr, Gary. 1996. "Beasley Signs Measure Banning Same-Sex Marriages." *Greenville News,* 21 May, 2D.

Key, V. O., Jr. 1949. *Southern Politics in State and Nation.* New York: Alfred A. Knopf.

Kirkland, Don. 1996. "Pastors Back Governor's 'Desire' For Reconciliation." *Baptist Courier,* 19 December, 2.

Kirkland, Don, and Todd Deaton. 1998. "S.C. Pastors Say Lottery Won't Improve Education." *Baptist Press Release,* 23 October.

Moore, William, and Danielle Vinson. 1999. "South Carolina Senate." In *Outside Money: Soft Money and Issue Ads in Competitive 1998 Congressional Elections,* edited by David B. Magleby and Marianne Holt, 63–71. Provo, Utah: Brigham Young University.

Munro, Jenny, and Mike Foley. 1998. "Anti-Gambling Group Videotapes Local Stores." *Greenville News,* 8 August, 1B.

Phifer, Amy, and Don Kirkland. 1998. "Baptists Join S.C. Effort to Rid State of Video Poker." *Baptist Press Release,* 21 January.

Pope, Charles. 1995. "Beasley Becoming Voice for Religious Conservatives." *The State,* 13 July, B1.

Smith, Oran P. 1997. *The Rise of Baptist Republicanism.* New York and London: New York University Press.

South Carolina Christian Action Council. 1997. "A Statement from South Carolina Religious Leaders Concerning the Confederate Battle Flag." *Greenville News,* 19 January, 5F.

Strope, Leigh. 1998. "Republicans Focus on Cutting State's Car Tax." *Greenville News,* 17 October, 2B.

Tanner, Robert. 1997. "Warring Camps Reject Confederate Flag Proposal." *Greenville News,* 22 March, 1D.

3

The Christian Right in God's Country: Texas Politics

James Lamare, J. L. Polinard, and
Robert D. Wrinkle

If pressed, many native-born Texans would argue that God almost certainly is from Texas, probably from Lubbock (maybe Abilene). And, increasingly, religious belief in Texas is not separated from political belief. As one observer put it, "Almost nowhere else has the religious right grown as rapidly as in Texas" (Beinart 1998).

If you wanted some advice about how to vote in the 1998 Texas elections, various organizations associated with the Christian Right developed voters guides from answers submitted by candidates to questions tendered by these groups. The following questions were among those used to develop one such guide.

"Do you believe that Jesus Christ was the son of God, died for the sins of man, rose the third day and presently sits at the right hand of God?"

"Do you believe that prayer, other religious activities and/or posting the Ten Commandments in public schools and other public places would violate the [U.S. Constitution]?"

"Do you believe our Founding Fathers based the Constitution on biblical values and intended our leaders to have those values?"

In addition, this particular guide included six questions concerning the candidate's beliefs relating to abortion, questions about the legitimacy of homosexuality, and general questions concerning the relationship between moral and ethical conduct, both public and private, and religious beliefs (Ivins 1988).

It is an understatement to say that religion holds a paramount position in Texas society; there is no devil in the following details. Ninety-six percent of all Texans express a religious commitment. Less than 1 percent profess no belief in a deity, regardless of the fact that, until her mysterious disappearance in 1995, the state was home for Madalyn Murray O'Hair—one of the country's most prominent atheists.[1] Most, around 60 percent, are Protestants, with about one-third of the state's population affiliated with the Baptist Church. A quarter of Texans are Roman Catholics, a figure that largely reflects the religious preference of Hispanics—the state's largest minority group. Only 1 percent of the population is Jewish.

Regardless of denominational preference, fully 92 percent of Texans believe that religion is "important" in their lives. Most, some 70 percent, routinely attend religious services. Eighty-six percent pray at home at least once a week. A majority proclaim a traditional commitment to their religion, while one-fifth characterize their religious fervor as fundamental, evangelistic, or charismatic. A mere 4 percent think of themselves as "New Age." More than seven of every ten adult Texans believe that the Bible is God's word and that all its prophecies will transpire. A majority "say that (they) have been born again or have had a born-again experience." Nearly two-thirds respond affirmatively when asked if they had "ever tried to encourage someone to believe in Jesus Christ or accept Him as . . . Savior," a response registered by around 45 percent of a national sample of Americans (Tinsley 1999). Only a small minority (around 8 percent) hold that a public school is no place for "reading the Lord's Prayer or Bible verses" (Lamare 1998, 16).[2]

Thus, overall, Texans are conservative in their religious beliefs and practices. In the past religiosity has played a distinct but rather diffuse role in shaping Texas politics. Candidate selection, issue advocacy, and policy options have been affected by the salience of religion in the state. Laws regulating the distribution and sale of alcohol, the permissibility of various forms of gambling, and retail sales on Sunday have reflected a sensitivity to religion for most of this century. The advent of a more direct and specific impact of religion on politics can be traced to the rise of abortion as a policy issue and to the upheaval in lifestyle choices that rocked the country and the state during the 1960s and 1970s.

For example, after *Roe* v. *Wade,* the abortion case that originated in Texas, opened the door to a woman's right to choose to have an abortion, Texans quickly developed strong stands on this issue. Entering the 1990s, the public was slightly more pro-choice (46 percent) than pro-life (39 percent). A clear majority, regardless of their position on abortion, claimed that before voting, they made "a point to find out the candidate's position on abortion." This search was more pronounced among pro-life supporters. Moreover, by a margin of 58 to 36 percent, pro-life partisans were more inclined than pro-choice Texans to cast their ballot solely on the basis of a candidate's stand on abortion (*Texas Poll* 1990).

The often intense public reaction in Texas to abortion and other controversial social issues has been fertile ground for the growth of organizations opposed to what is perceived to be the moral and cultural decay of the United States. Many of the groups associated with the Christian Right have been active in mobilizing conservative public opinion for direct political action. Often, the ideological wellspring feeding these organizational activities is found in the teaching and tenets of Christianity. The most prominent social conservative or Christian Right organizations to emerge in the Lone Star State are the Texas Eagle Forum (an affiliate of Phyllis Schlafly's Eagle Forum), two major antiabortion entities (American Family Association of Texas and Texans United for Life), and the Texas Christian Coalition (TCC), the largest of these groups.

The Texas Christian Coalition is an offshoot of Pat Robertson's Christian Coalition. Dick Weinhold, the chief fund raiser for Robertson during his unsuccessful 1988 bid for president, established the TCC in 1991. It has grown from an initial 10,000 members and 38 county chapters to a current membership and support base estimated at 200,000 located in 100 county chapters. With its political ideology firmly embedded in Christianity and biblical teachings, the TCC is committed to five fundamental goals: to represent Christians and traditional values before government, to take public stands on issues, to train Christians to be effective leaders in social and political arenas, to keep Christians throughout the state fully informed about policy matters and proposed legislation, and to protest any bias against Christians and defend the legal rights of Christians.

The TCC's policy platform comprises a comprehensive social conservative political agenda, touching on an extensive array of economic, educational, moral, and lifestyle issues, including a flat tax, an end to the marriage tax penalty, no state income tax, and balanced government budgets. While remaining steadfast in its opposition to abortion (except in cases involving the possible death of the mother), it favors parental consent before any minor can obtain an abortion and it opposes partial-birth abortion and the use of tax money for funding abortions. Public schools are encouraged to teach a basic curriculum emphasizing, reading, writing, mathematics, science, and history rather than teaching about "sinful" alternative lifestyles or "anti-American politics." Parents should be kept fully informed by the public education system regarding what is being taught in the classroom. They are encouraged to become deeply involved in the education of their children and they should have a choice over the schools, including private schools, to which they send their children and should have the option of providing home schooling.

Federal government intrusion in local school business is out; prayers in school are in. Protecting and guaranteeing victim rights and utilization and enforcement of the death penalty are supported by the TCC. Convicted criminals should serve their full sentences. The TCC opposes judicial activism and gun control but fervently advocates the sanctity of marriage, unless the partners are of the same sex. It views homosexuality as sin and consequently condemns the extension of workplace benefits to the partners of homosexuals (Texas Christian Coalition).

Funding for social conservative organizations comes from a variety of sources, including membership contributions, outside donors, and financial assistance from parent national associations. It is difficult to uncover the funding base of these groups, given that there is no required reporting of their revenues. One major financial supporter of social conservative organizations in Texas is Dr. James Leininger of San Antonio, who, according to the *Texas Observer,* has contributed some $2.1 million to several of the state's social conservative organizations (Nathan 1999). Dr. Leininger, who is worth an estimated $340 million, is listed among the richest one hundred Texans and the four hundred wealthiest Americans. He initially earned his fortune from the manufacture of high-tech hospital beds designed for the comfort of patients who must endure long stays in hospitals. Leininger's Kinetic Concepts International (KCI) grew rapidly during the 1980s owing to its dominant position in the sales of these beds. Dr. Leininger sold KCI in 1998 for $875 million but still holds a one-third ownership share in the company. He also has various other business interests, including a 10 percent share in the San Antonio Spurs. Several of his business interests directly produce and promote Christian material and messages.

Strategies and Outcomes

Social conservative groups have utilized a variety of effective strategies aimed at gaining political leverage in Texas. More specifically, they have been successful in obtaining a foothold in the state's political party system, in scoring some electoral wins, and in the direct lobbying of political decision makers.

Political Parties

Parties mobilize and inform voters, design political agendas, recruit and choose political leaders, and provide an organizational fulcrum for officeholders, once in government. In the recent past, social movements in Texas, such as those composed of Chicano activists, supporters of former Alabama governor George Wallace, and the followers of Texas billionaire Ross Perot, largely rejected participating in the established two-party system, opting instead to contest Texas elections through a third party.

Although these efforts have enjoyed some successes, in the main they have had a short shelf life. The reasons for the inevitable flame-out of third parties are manifold. They include the enduring psychological attachment of many eligible voters to one of the two established parties, the difficulty experienced by third parties in gaining access to the Texas ballot, and the disincentive facing third-party candidates running in elections where the victor is determined on a "winner take all" basis—most Texas elections require a majority vote to win (Lamare 1998).

Wisely, the Christian Right in Texas has eschewed the third-party route to gaining electoral and political influence in the state. Rather, social conservatives have concentrated on becoming a part of, and securing control over, the established parties, especially the Republican Party. The GOP has made a fast and dramatic rise in Texas in recent years. Entering the 1978 elections, only one Republican (Senator John Tower) had won a statewide election since Reconstruction. Twenty years later, following the 1998 elections, no Democrat had won a statewide race in two election cycles, and the GOP tide was beginning to reach the down-ballot races as well. In effect, Texas enters the new millennium as a one-party GOP state in statewide election, and the Christian Right is hitched firmly to the Republican wagon.

The influx of Republican migrants into the state and the defection of conservative Democrats to the GOP account for most of the party's success. As part of being a party on the move, the GOP has been open and accessible to individuals and groups seeking political standing and clout. Moreover, it has drifted more and more toward issue stands and ideological positions that embrace the social and cultural agenda of the Christian Right (see Layman 1999). The organizational foundation of Texas's major political parties rests squarely upon partisans who cast ballots in closed primaries. A vote in the primary serves as a ticket to attend the party's precinct meeting, which occurs immediately after the polls close on primary night. Historically, these precinct conventions are lightly attended (fewer than ten people is not uncommon), offering a prime opportunity to any group with sound organization skills and a dedicated if numerically small following.

Christian Right groups have taken to these precinct conventions, especially those of the Republican Party, like ducks to water. Their members undergo training on how to participate fully in the precinct meetings, with an eye to being elected chair of the precinct. As a result, social conservatives have been successful in capturing precinct chair posts and subsequently in choosing the delegates to the Republican Party's district convention. The principal function of the district convention, which is held within three weeks of the primary, is the selection of delegates to the party's state convention.

By 1994, more than 60 percent of the six thousand delegates and six thousand alternates attending the GOP's state party convention were affiliated with the social conservative movement (Bruce 1997, 35). Since voting at the party convention is based on district units, social conservatives only had to comprise a majority of delegates within sixteen or more of the party's thirty-one districts to exercise power. And, indeed, by 1994, they had effectively gained control over the GOP's state convention and, in so doing, a strong foothold in the Texas Republican Party.

The result: social conservatives now have a major voice in selecting key party personnel and in writing the party's platform. In 1994, for example, they elected a sympathetic candidate, Tom Pauken, to the position of chair of the Texas Republican Party, despite the fact that Pauken was not the favorite of the party's gubernatorial candidate, George W. Bush. Two years later, the campaign committee of GOP presidential candidate Robert Dole recommended a slate of 123 Texans to be delegates to the national party convention in San Diego. All, of course, were strong supporters of Mr. Dole. However, the Christian Right-dominated state Republican Party rejected many of these recommendations and instead selected social conservatives to take their place.

Even United States Senator Kay Bailey Hutchison originally was rebuffed by the state party because of her soft abortion stance. After Governor Bush intervened on her behalf, she was added to the delegation on an at-large basis. In another testimony to the strength of the religious conservatives, Bush himself was denied the position of chair of the 1996 national delegation in favor of state party chief, and social conservative, Pauken. The vice chair of the delegation was Dick Weinhold, then director of the Texas Conservative Coalition. It is estimated that 70 percent of the delegates who journeyed to the 1996 Republican National Convention in California were social conservatives (Bruce 1997, 39).

Since 1994, the Christian Right has continued to be well represented on the committee charged with writing the platform of the state Republican Party. In 1998, for example, one of the thirty-one members of the platform committee was Cathie Adams, president of the Texas Eagle Forum. Not surprisingly, the platform became a showcase for social conservative policy stands. The 1998 platform, for instance, was replete with language staunchly opposed to the federal government in general, governmental intrusion into people's lives, homosexuality, pornography, abortion, the cloning of humans, and sex education in schools (other than the teaching of abstinence) and was equally strongly in favor of parental choice in selecting schools for their children (including sending their kids to private school at the expense of the state and the right to home-school), preserving and extending the sanctity of property rights, and celebrating the preeminent importance of the individual and the family. The religious tone of the platform clearly resonated in the preamble's incantation: "We believe in you. We believe you are a sacred being created in the image of God" and, "We welcome all Americans into our ranks to work for those values we hold dear—God, family, and country!"

Today, the top echelons of the Texas Republican Party are staffed mostly by individuals identified with the Christian Right. The state chair first came to statewide attention when, responding to former Governor Ann Richards's support for gay rights, she placed a black wreath at Richards's campaign headquarters with the inscription, "Death to the Family." The vice chair is president of an organization that contends the separation between church and state is a myth. The state party's male representative to the Republican National Committee presides over the Texas Home School Coalition, and the female representative is a former official in the Eagle Forum. The chair of the most recent state party platform committee is the former director of projects of Texas Right to Life (Beinart 1998).

Elections

Social conservatives are deeply involved in trying to affect who wins electoral office in Texas. During the 1998 campaigns, the Texas Christian Coalition distributed 2 million voter guides, and its members made 50,000 get-out-the-vote phone calls. Not content with simply influencing electoral results through mobilizing and persuading, the Christian Right has also taken direct aim at winning political office, particularly a majority of seats on the state's fifteen-person state board of education (SBOE).

Texas is divided into fifteen distinct geographical districts from which each member of the SBOE is elected. Since voter turnout in these elections is usually less than 15 percent of eligible voters, running a competitive race is not overly difficult or expensive, especially if a candidate has the support of organized political activists. The SBOE is charged with the responsibility of establishing policy for Texas's primary, secondary, and vocational schools. Among other things, it assists in budget preparation for public schools, approves textbooks for classroom usage (always a controversial process), evaluates whether schools are achieving policy goals, reports to the legislature on the progress being made by schools toward meeting policy objectives, administers the Texas Permanent School Fund, and oversees the financial performance of school districts. Several controversial issues have appeared on the board's agenda, including reviewing textbooks to spot whether they contain any "liberal" or "politically correct" messages, rebuffing federal control over local schools, and deciding on the proper place for sex education in the curriculum.

The Christian Right has been successful in winning seats on the state board of education. By 1994, one-third of the board's membership was composed of social conservatives. In 1996, the Christian Right made an all-out but ultimately unsuccessful effort to capture three more SBOE seats, which would have given social conservatives a majority. It renewed its efforts to gain the elusive majority in the 1998 SBOE races. Social conservative candidates contested five of the seven positions that were up for grabs. They were victorious in three of these contests, leaving social conservatives with six seats on the state board, still two shy of a majority. Republicans now hold a nine-to-six edge over the Democrats in membership on the state board of education.

However, the Christian Right members are not always on the same page with their fellow Republican board members. Indeed, some of the most heated controversies on the SBOE have pitted the social conservatives against moderate Republicans. The fighting has been so intense that the board has recently been described as "the most divided, most embattled, most uproarious political body in Texas" (Burka 1998).

Overall, the 1998 elections were a GOP walkover. The GOP repeated its 1996 performance of winning every statewide election. Republicans now hold all statewide executive positions, including the positions of governor, lieutenant governor (who, although less visible than the governor, generally is recognized as the most powerful officer in the state), attorney general, comptroller of public accounts, and commissioners of both agriculture and the general land office, as well as the three elected seats on the Texas Railroad Commission (which regulates the state's oil and natural gas industry). Eight of the nine members of both the Texas Supreme Court and the Texas Court of Criminal Appeals, the state's two highest courts, are Republicans. The GOP has a slim majority in the thirty-one-person Texas Senate. Only the one hundred fifty-member state house of representatives is under the control of the Democrats, but here, too, the Democratic prospects appear grim. The Republicans gained four seats in the 1998 election and now, with seventy-two seats, are only four short of being the majority in this chamber. In short, the 1998 elections left the Republicans with their most political clout in Texas government since Reconstruction days.

The marquee campaign of 1998 was, of course, that of Governor Bush. The outcome was never in doubt. Democrat Gary Mauro threw himself on the sword for the party as a sacrificial candidate but never got within sight of Bush either in the polls or on the campaign trail. Bush offered an ideal model for bridging the ideological divisions within the GOP. He emphasized the positive virtues of conservatism, which, with the possible exception of the issue of abortion, may be enough to keep the Christian

Right supporters in the fold, while at the same time he avoided the divisive politics that had splintered and isolated the Republicans in so many other states.

Governor Bush's victory, however, may have been a mixed blessing for the Christian Right. Put simply, his win owed little to and did little for the social conservatives in his party. In truth, the Christian Right had nowhere else to go in this election, and had every evangelical conservative stayed home on election day, it would not have altered the outcome. Indeed, the talk following the election focused on the different constituencies that Bush had been able to attract, particularly the traditionally Democratic Hispanic vote, and on the potential to use the statewide election as a springboard to the presidential nomination in 2000. And the Bush mantra of "compassionate conservatism" seemed to be a deliberate attempt to separate his ideology from the more dogmatic social agenda. Nonetheless, the 1999 Texas legislative session has been marked, at least in part, by conspicuous attempts by Governor Bush to avoid alienating the social conservatives. He has supported vouchers for private schools, opposed increased state gun control in the wake of the Littleton, Colorado, school tragedy, supported parental-notification legislation applying to minors who seek abortions, and remained mum on whether he will sign an enhanced anti-hate crimes bill if the bill passes the legislature and includes gays as a protected group. Still, as we discuss more fully below, the divisions within the Texas GOP run deep, and the Christian Right remains suspicious of the governor's conservative credentials; for many of them, the apple does not fall far from the tree.

Individuals, groups, and organizations associated with social conservative causes were financially active in supporting many of the candidates who competed in the 1998 electoral contests. Leading the parade of contributors was Dr. James Leininger. Throughout the 1990s, it is estimated that Dr. Leininger has spent some $3 million on elections in Texas and another $3.2 million on attempting to sway public opinion (Nathan 1999; Castillo 1998) In 1996, he contributed nearly $60,000 to social conservative candidates for state board of education elections. Two years later he donated $51,000 to Christian Right candidates for the SBOE, including $40,000 to Shirley Piggot, a physician who heads the Victoria chapter of the American Family Association, and some money to Donna Ballard of Midland (Nathan 1999; Castillo 1998; Stutz 1998a). Ballard was a member of the state school board between 1995 and 1997, when she lived in the Woodlands, a planned community located north of Houston. While on the board, she was called "the most controversial member of the board—perhaps in the entire history of that body" (Ivins 1998). Although her 1998 campaign attempted to portray her incumbent opponent, El Pasoan Rene Nunez, as promoting the teaching of homosexuality in the curriculum, she lost (as did Dr.

Piggot). Nunez raised $35,000 for his campaign, most of which came from Texas-born rock star Don Henley (Stutz 1998a).

Dr. Leininger's campaign largesse supported the campaigns of others seeking state office in the 1998 Texas election. It is estimated that Leininger donated a total of more than $1.8 million of his own money that year to candidates and political action committees.[3] Following the May primaries, for example, he gave $175,000 to the Texas Republican Party, the largest single contribution received by the state GOP. Much of this money was used by the party to fund the campaign of Rick Perry, who became the first successful GOP candidate for lieutenant governor (Nathan 1999, 13). Leininger personally gave Perry nearly $57,000. Moreover, he underwrote, along with two other Texas businessmen (petrochemical executive William McMinn and telecommunications executive James Mansour), a $1.1 million loan that was credited to the Perry campaign. This loan represented almost 10 percent of all of the funds raised by Perry (Tolley 1999), and it was secured during the last week of the campaign, just in time for Perry to mount a last-minute media blitz that is credited with helping him edge his Democratic rival, John Sharp (Bryce 1999).

Perry's election ensures Leininger direct access to the lieutenant governor, who, as mentioned previously, is the most powerful person in the Texas senate and, some say, the state. Hence, Leininger was, after the 1998 election, well positioned to lobby the legislature for special projects, particularly state-funded vouchers to be used by parents who choose to send their children to private schools. Two pro-voucher groups associated with Dr. Leininger—Putting Children First and the Children's Educational Opportunity—made campaign contributions worth an estimated $1.37 million in 1998 (Castillo 1998). In total, Lieutenant Governor Perry received at least $500,000 in campaign contributions from pro-voucher groups (Stutz 1998b).

Lobbying

Social conservatives have been very active in the direct lobbying of policymakers in Texas. The most publicized victory achieved as a result of these lobbying efforts was the decision reached in July 1998 by the state board of education to unload stock in the Walt Disney Company. Over a twelve-month period prior to this decision, the American Family Association (AFA) of Texas led a campaign urging this divestiture. AFA/Texas was appalled because, in its judgment: "The world's largest family entertainment company has extended company insurance benefits to the live-in partners of homosexual employees, but not unmarried partners of hetorosexual employees; allowed homosexual celebrations in its objectionable films; allowed a convicted child molester to direct a Disney movie; published a book aimed at homosexuals; and promoted numerous other anti-family policies and activities" (American Family Association of Texas).

AFA/Texas collected five thousand signatures on a petition urging state agencies that had a financial investment in Disney to drop the company from their portfolios. It also produced a video entitled "Dumping Disney: How Texas Is Bankrolling the Disney Empire" and supplied it free of charge for showing to audiences across Texas. Officials of AFA/Texas addressed several legislative committees and administrative agencies, expressing profound outrage over Disney's activities. When Wyatt Roberts, chair of AFA/Texas, testified before the state board of education, he recited lyrics from musical groups that recorded for the Disney label (Hollywood Records) that he claimed advocated suicide and extolled violence (American Family Association of Texas). The state board of education voted eight to four to discontinue investing the Permanent School Fund in the Disney corporation. It is estimated that this action resulted in a $45 million withdrawal of Disney stock. Attempts by social conservatives to have other state agencies, such as the Texas Teachers Retirement System and the Texas Employment Retirement System, which hold shares in Disney, follow suit have not been successful.

The Christian Right in Texas generally supports a state-funded voucher program that would provide taxpayer money to parents who wish to send their children to private schools. This proposal was high on the legislative agenda of state leaders, including Governor George W. Bush and Lieutenant Governor Rick Perry. Moreover, well-funded organizations, including the Texas Public Policy Foundation, Putting Children First, and the Coalition for School Choice, unleashed impressive lobbying efforts to ensure that state-funded vouchers would become law in Texas when the Seventy-sixth Texas Legislature convened in January 1999.

The bill that was debated in the legislature involved a five-year experimental plan that would permit some parents of economically disadvantaged children residing in Texas's six largest counties to transfer their children to private schools if the students failed any part of the state's mandated standardized skills test. As public schools in Texas are funded in part on a formula that includes attendance, school districts from which these children departed would lose taxpayer money to the private schools in which these students enrolled. Texans, by a slim 46–43 percent margin, favored the general idea of school vouchers. Even more, 54 percent, supported legislation creating a pilot program that allowed students from low-performing schools to enroll in state-funded private schools. Interestingly, a majority of African Americans and Hispanics, as well as Anglos, favored this plan (Ray 1998).

One of the major proponents of school vouchers, as mentioned above, is Dr. James Leininger, who has financially backed the major lobbying organizations pushing for voucher legislation (Nathan 1999; Mandel 1999). Indeed, Leininger is a major contributor to a program initiated in the poverty-stricken Edgewood School district, which is located in San Antonio. This program provides tuition grants ranging between $2,000 and $4,000 to parents who wish to move their children from Edgewood into a private school of their choice. The parents of more than 800 children took this offer when the school year began in 1998 (Cisneros-Lunsford 1998a, 1998b). Religious schools stand to gain the most from voucher plans.[4] For instance, only 6 of the 837 students who initially left the Edgewood school district under the voucher program enrolled in a nonreligious school, with about half transferring to Catholic schools (Mandel, 11).

The Christian Right also lobbied the Seventy-sixth Texas Legislature for the passage of various bills restricting access to abortions. Of the five bills addressing this controversial area, the parental consent bill, requiring parental consent before an abortion could be performed on a minor teenager, was given the best chance of passing in the 1999 legislative session.

Constraints on the Christian Right in Texas

The Christian Right certainly has made substantial and significant inroads into Texas politics. Throughout the 1990s, it has expanded its support base and its political influence in the state. Nonetheless, there are several constraints that affect, and may very well limit, the future political impact of social conservatives.

Internal Conflict

There are signs that the Christian Right in Texas is not as unified in its issue positions as it might seem on first blush. For example, a clear division has emerged over the state-funded school voucher proposal. At the heart of this conflict is the question of government control over private schools. Private schools that would receive money from the state probably would be required to administer the Texas Assessment of Academic Skills (TAAS), a standardized test designed to measure student performance in mathematics, reading, and writing. As a rule, social conservatives oppose TAAS, essentially arguing that schools spend far too much time teaching students how to pass the test rather than concentrating on teaching the normal curriculum. Prominent Republican (and president of the Texas Eagle Forum) Cathie Adams envisions the voucher program and its attendant state-mandated requirements, "as a back door approach to control every private school in Texas. Vouchers are coupons for control. Whoever holds the purse strings is the one who will call the shots" (Stutz 1998b).

Opposition Groups

The Christian Right's rise to importance has spawned some groups intent on countering its political influence. In 1996, for instance, a loose-knit, diverse group of clergy organized as the Texas Faith Network with the purpose of offsetting the Christian Right. Its first major action was to disrupt the social conservatives' campaign tactic of distributing voter guides at churches (Bruce 1997, 38). The Texas Faith Network was successful in stopping this practice in some congregations. Many of its members lobbied against state-funded school voucher proposals presented to the Seventy-sixth Texas Legislature.

The most prominent opposition group is the Texas Freedom Network (TFN), founded in 1996 by Cecile Richards, the daughter of former Texas Governor Ann Richards. TFN claims a membership of three thousand. It was formed solely to challenge the Christian Right. In addition to monitoring the activities of social conservatives, TFN keeps tabs on the campaign contributions of the Christian Right, including the amounts raised, the sources of funds, and the candidates who benefit from these donations. Since their inception, however, the Texas Freedom Network and the Texas Faith Network have been unable to develop either the resource base or the ideological wherewithal among their members to compete with the Christian Right on a level playing field. However, the split among social conservatives over a state-funded school voucher scheme provided an opportunity for these groups to ally with the Texas Eagle Forum to impede the passage of legislation in 1999 that would implement this plan.

Limited Support Base

There is little doubt that the ranks of supporters of Christian-based political organizations have grown over the last two decades. At its peak in the early 1980s, approximately one in ten adult Americans supported the Moral Majority; in 1996 nearly 16 percent of the U.S. public endorsed the Christian Right. The current social conservative movement is filled mainly with partisans who identify with the Republican Party and have strong feelings against gay rights and abortion. As impressive as these gains in supporters have been, however, doubts have been raised over whether the religious right "can expand its support much beyond its current base" (Wilcox, DeBell, and Sigelman 1999, 191).

A 1994 Texas Poll found that 25 percent of Texans had never heard of the Christian Right and that 36 percent were unaware of conservative Christians. Equal minorities—some 23–25 percent—had either a favorable or an unfavorable view of these groups; the rest, at around 35 percent, were neutral. Though nearly two-thirds of Texans considered themselves "conservative Christians," only 27 percent identified with the term "Christian Right." In making their voting decision, 20–23 percent said that they were less likely to choose a candidate tied to the Christian Right or the conservative Christians. Only 14 percent said that a candidate connection with the Christian Right would sway their vote. A majority of Texans indicated that candidate proximity to social conservatives would not influence their vote one way or the other (Stahl 1994). Moreover, efforts to extend recruiting in Texas have not been overwhelmingly successful.

The Bush Factor

As indicated above, perhaps the most important obstacle to the growing influence of the Christian Right within the Texas GOP is, ironically, the popularity of Governor Bush. Recall that social conservatives have been at loggerheads with the governor along many fronts, including the selection of key party personnel at the Republican state convention, opposing some of his policy proposals, and questioning his overall commitment to the Christian Right agenda. Bush is by no means a liberal, or even a moderate by most standards, but within the Texas GOP, his brand of "compassionate conservatism" is greeted with suspicion by the Christian Right.

The following anecdote captures the essence of the conflict. On the night of Robert Dole's acceptance speech at the GOP National Convention in San Diego in 1996, some journalists and Texas GOP delegates were having a late snack at the hotel where the Texas delegation was housed. A political analyst for one of the Texas television stations observed that if Dole lost, it was clear that Governor Bush would be a major player in the 2000 race. The two GOP delegates, both of whom were social conservatives, immediately responded, "We hope not. He's not one of us."[5]

The most glaring problem that Bush has with the religious wing of his party is his perceived softness on the abortion issue. In addition, Bush takes what in the GOP is a strong pro-immigration stance (a position that contributed to his record-setting support from Mexican Americans in the 1998 election). The GOP state platform calls not only for eliminating welfare benefits for undocumented immigrants but also for ending automatic citizenship at birth for babies of Mexican nationals who cross into the United States to give birth. The governor's positions on education and taxes also have put him at odds with some Christian Right groups.

Thus, in many ways the most serious opposition facing the governor has come from the social conservative wing of his own party and not from the Democrats. As his campaign for the presidency expands and intensifies, the governor will have to negotiate a treacherous path between not alienating social conservatives, who are both politically very active and very willing to work against him, and not, in placating the religious right, diminishing his appeal to both moderate Republicans and mainstream voters in general.

There is room for compromise here; certainly, there have been stranger bedfellows in politics than Governor Bush and the evangelicals. Without a GOP president, the Christian Right has little influence over executive policy. Thus, being a potential winner in 2000's presidential sweepstakes may trump ideological reservations, at least in the short run. If Bush's staying power is confirmed by early primary victories, and the more ideological of the GOP presidential wannabes fall by the wayside, the Christian Right may swallow hard and jump on the bandwagon. And, on Bush's side of the bed, the disproportionate influence of the Christian Right on the GOP nominating process may encourage the governor to tread carefully with respect to issues that might cause problems for presidential candidate Bush.

Conclusion

The Christian Right is an integral part of Texas politics. The messages that social conservative groups preach have attracted a reasonably large following, including some people willing to contribute the financial wherewithal that keeps the Christian Right organized and poised to act politically. Indeed, social conservatives have achieved such notable political successes as their dominance of the state's Republican Party, their strong foothold on the state board of education, and their successful efforts in lobbying policymakers on behalf of their social and political agenda. Moreover, their sheer presence helps shape the ongoing political debate in the state and serves as a nettlesome thorn in the sides of groups and officeholders who do not abide by their mandates, principles, and programs.

The future of the movement, however, is far from clear. There are several factors that may hamper its ability to expand its prominence or even maintain its current status. In recent years, social conservatives have experienced discord within their ranks, and the recent call by national leaders to reconsider the direct involvement of the Christian Right in the electoral process may serve to further exacerbate these divisions. Redirecting the energies of the faithful away from national and statewide electoral politics and more toward community activities may reduce their visibility in the national arena while enhancing their impact on local political development. The very success of the Christian Right has spawned groups opposed to its agenda and tactics. Moreover, the Christian Right may be reaching a point where its membership base will not expand as rapidly as in the past.

More immediately, the state stewardship and presidential aspirations of Governor George W. Bush may blunt the most extreme ideas of the Christian Right. The allure of power at the top level may soften the ideological rigidity of the movement, a process that could further erode the strong foundation of the Christian Right if Governor Bush were successful in his quest to become president.

Still, actors in the Texas political process, particularly Republicans, ignore the influence of the Christian Right at their peril. Barring a conscious decision to withdraw from direct political action, the various groups that make up Texas's Christian Right will continue to be major players in the process in the near future.

After all, God may be from Fort Worth or Houston or . . . .

NOTES

1. The disappearance of O'Hair eventually led the FBI to become involved. In April, 1999, after securing a search warrant, the FBI conducted a two-day search for O'Hair's remains in a pasture on a 5,000-acre ranch in the Texas Hill Country. The search has yielded no remains as of this writing.
2. For further information see Martin 1975. 1990.
3. This estimate is provided by the Texas Freedom Network. See Castillo 1998.
4. Recent research suggests that Texas parents choose to send children to private schools for religious or racial reasons rather than for reasons relating to quality education. See Stewart, Wrinkle, and Polinard (in press).
5. One of the authors of this chapter was the political analyst involved in the conversation.

REFERENCES

American Family Association of Texas. http://www.afatexas.org/document/boycotts
———. http://www.afatexas.org/document/news/other/dumped.htm
Beinert, Peter. 1998. "The Big Debate: George Bush Battles the Republican Right." *New Republic,* 16 March, 21.
Bruce, John M. 1997. "Texas: A Success Story, At Least for Now." In *God at the Grass Roots 1996: The Christian Right in the American Elections,* ed-

ited by Mark J. Rozell and Clyde Wilcox. Lanham, Md.: Rowman & Littlefield.

Bryce, Robert. 1999. "The Polls He Bought." *Texas Observer,* 5 February, 11–12.

Burka, Paul. 1998. "Disloyal Opposition." *Texas Monthly,* December, 140.

Castillo, Jaime. 1998. "Anti-voucher Group Blasts Contributions." *San Antonio Express-News,* 26 March, 20A.

Cisneros-Lunsford, Anastasia. 1998a. "CEO Says 871 Students Have Received Vouchers." *San Antonio Express-News,* 15 August, 13A.

———. 1998b. "Poor School District Loses 600 to Vouchers." *San Antonio Express-News,* 14 August, 1A, 11A.

Ivins, Molly. 1988. "Want Character? Check Public Records." *Monitor,* 12 October.

———. 1998. "Right-wing Win Would Be Schools' Loss" *San Antonio Express-News,* 2 October 1998, 3A.

Lamare, James W. 1998. *Texas Politics: Economics, Power, and Policy.* 6th ed. (Belmont, Calif.: Wadsworth).

Layman, Geoffrey C. 1999. "Culture Wars in the American Party System: Religious and Cultural Change among Party Activists since 1972." *American Politics Quarterly* 27 (1): 89–121.

Mandel, Jeff. 1999. "Edgewood under Siege." *Texas Observer,* 5 March, 8–11.

Martin, William C. 1975. "Texas and God." *Atlantic Monthly,* March.

Nathan, Debbie. 1999. "Saint Sickbed." *Texas Observer,* 22 January, 8–14.

Ray, Steve. 1998. "Poll: Texans Willing to Try Vouchers." *Corpus Christi Caller-Times,* 9 March.

Stahl, Lori. 1994. "Labels Draw Similar Support, Texas Poll Says." *Dallas Morning News,* 4 September, 10A.

Stewart, Joseph, Robert Wrinkle, and J. L. Polinard. 2000. "Public School Quality, Private Schools, and Race. *American Journal of Political Science,* in press.

Stutz, Terrence. 1998a. "Religious Conservatives Aim to Win Majority on Board." *Dallas Morning News,* 26 October, 18A.

———. 1998b. "School Voucher Issues Divide Conservatives." *Dallas Morning News,* 20 December, 1A, 8A.

Texas Christian Coalition. http://www.texascc.org

Texas Poll. 1985. April. The *Texas Poll* is published by Harte-Hanks Communications and the *Texas Poll* staff at the Office of Survey Research in the School of Communication at the University of Texas, Austin. Persons interested in obtaining *Texas Poll* data should contact the Office of Survey Research, School of Communication, University of Texas, Austin, Texas 78712.

———. 1987. Fall.

———. 1990a. Spring.

———. 1990b. Winter.

Tinsley, Anna M. 1999. "Poll: More Texans Are Going to Church." *Monitor,* 9 May, B1, 8.

Tolley, Laura. 1999. "Perry Report Lists Loan Backers." *San Antonio Express-News,* 16 January, 1A, 6A.

Wilcox, Clyde, Matthew DeBell, and Lee Sigelman 1999. "The Second Coming of the New Christian Right: Patterns of Popular Support in 1984 and 1996." *Social Science Quarterly* 80 (1): 191.

4

Georgia: The Christian Right Meets Its Match

Charles S. Bullock III and Mark C. Smith

Georgia's 1998 elections hinged on the mobilization of the core constituencies of the two parties. Although it involves a bit of hyperbole, the election can be cast as a face-off between the Christian Right and black ministers. African Americans became mobilized while Christian conservatives saw less at stake in 1998 than in other recent elections. In the end, Georgia's political landscape emerged almost identical to what existed at the beginning of the last election year of the century.

Christian conservatives have become the GOP's most consistent supporters in Georgia. Exit polls reveal that in 1994, white voters who identified with the Christian Right supported Republican Guy Millner over Democratic Governor Zell Miller by more than three to one, whereas among other white voters, the Democrat won three to two. In 1996, Christian Right whites chose Millner over Democrat Max Cleland for the Senate, again by more than three to one, while Millner lost among other whites 39 to 56 percent. In that year's presidential election, the margin was even more pronounced as Bob Dole outpolled Bill Clinton among the Christian Right by more than seven to one even as the president took a majority among other whites.

Whereas Christian conservatives were Republican stalwarts, black voters were even more cohesive in backing Democrats. Exit polls for 1994 and 1996 show black support for Republicans as low as 6 percent for Dole and no higher than 12 percent for Millner in his Senate bid.

These patterns persisted in 1998. African Americans continued to reject the candidacies of Republicans, giving only 8 percent of their votes to the nominee for governor (Millner again) and Senator Paul Coverdell.

With virtually no support among African Americans, GOP nominees in 1998 once again relied heavily on the Christian Right, whose identifiers backed Coverdell and Millner by 83 and 70 percent, respectively. Most whites who did not identify with the Christian Right rejected the Republicans, giving Coverdell 45 percent of their votes and holding Millner to 38 percent.

Setting the Scene

By any objective measure, 1998 was the epitome of a no-change election in Georgia. The partisan composition of the executive branch and the congressional delegation was unchanged while Democrats registered a net gain of one seat in each chamber of the general assembly. No Democratic incumbent above the county level lost, and Republican officeholders fared almost as well, with two house members being turned out. So why do disinterested observers as well as partisans generally agree that Republicans suffered in 1998?

To answer this question requires an understanding of the expectations going into the election. The 1990s had been the Decade of Democratic Decline in Georgia. At the beginning of the decade, Democrats held all but one congressional seat, 80 percent of the state legislative seats, and every statewide office. Except for a gradual growth in GOP strength in the legislature, Democrats remained as dominant as they had been for the last century. Beginning in 1992, Republicans embarked on a series of unprecedented successes. GOP congressional seats reached a record four in 1992, became a majority of seven in 1994, and grew to eight when Nathan Deal changed parties in April of 1995. In 1992, Coverdell upset Democratic incumbent Wyche Fowler to become only the second popularly elected senator of his party from Georgia, and Bobby Baker became the first Republican in more than a century to win a statewide state office when he secured a seat on the public service commission. Republicans unseated Democratic incumbents in 1994 to win the offices of state school superintendent and insurance commissioner and retained the office of attorney general, which came to them when the incumbent switched parties. The GOP also came within 33,000 votes of denying reelection to Governor Zell Miller.

Going into the 1998 election, Republicans dominated the congressional delegation, had more than 40 percent of the seats in the state legislature, and controlled the public service commission, filling all but one of its five seats. Moreover, although Democrats held three of every five seats in the legislature, Republican candidates for each chamber had polled more votes statewide than had Democrats in 1996, suggesting that Democrats owed at least some of their success to an apportionment system rendered antiquated by the state's phenomenal growth.[1] Given the upward slope of any line that one chose for plotting GOP electoral success, they entered 1998 expecting to capture the governor's office and other executive posts, and optimists even saw an outside chance of becoming the majority in one chamber of the legislature.

Republicans went into the election cycle buoyant, convinced by experiences thus far in the decade that they were the party of the future. As they saw their positions eroding, many Democrats also came to accept the GOP view of the future. One got the sense among some older Democratic legislators that they hoped to remain in the majority until they retired. *Après moi, le déluge.*

To achieve their 1998 objectives, Republicans needed to be united and they needed quality candidates. GOP operatives hoped to avoid fractious primaries at the top of their ticket by having a single serious candidate emerge. This scenario described the U.S. Senate contest, since no one challenged Coverdell, who had consolidated his primary electoral constituency by moving to the right (on the expansionist mode of a legislator's career, see Fenno 1978). Coverdell had not been the favorite of Christian conservatives in 1992 when he plodded through a five-person primary with 37 percent of the vote while the political novice most closely aligned with the Christian Right polled almost a quarter of the vote and missed the runoff by fewer than a thousand votes. In the runoff, despite nine terms in the state senate and two years as chair of the state GOP, Coverdell won a mere 1,600-vote victory over Bob Barr, who attacked the front-runner from the right. In office, Coverdell raised money for six years and avoided the deficiencies that Fenno (1996) identifies in Fowler's reelection campaign that enabled Coverdell to get to the Senate.

Greater uncertainty and thus greater concern surrounded the office that could do the greatest good for GOP expansion—the governorship. Early on, Mike Bowers, long-serving attorney general who switched parties just before the 1994 election, had the inside track. Party leaders drew criticism when at the 1997 state convention they anointed Bowers as the putative nominee (Heffernan 1997). Bowers was widely acknowledged as the individual who would end more than 125 years of Democratic control of the governorship. He had an unblemished record as attorney general and a military bearing developed while at West Point and later as a general in the reserves, and he could articulate the issues. A longstanding GOP theme had been that Georgia needed a two-party system in order to eliminate corruption. Bowers epitomized that by his outspoken criticism of state agencies and public officials for malfeasance. He had so angered the speaker of the state house that when pay raises were distributed to other elected department heads, his name was frequently omitted. This same independent streak made some Republicans queasy since

Bowers had quickly gotten behind Governor Zell Miller's aborted effort to remove the Confederate cross of St. Andrew from the state flag. On the other hand, he scored points with Christian fundamentalists for having gone to the Supreme Court to uphold Georgia's sodomy statute and for having been sued by a lesbian after retracting the offer of a staff position while he was attorney general.

No sooner had Bowers been hailed as the Moses who would lead the GOP to the Promised Land than human frailties emerged in dramatic fashion. In what was rumored to be a preemptive strike to get out information in the hands of a rival campaign manager, Bowers revealed a decade-long adulterous affair with his former secretary. Unlike President Clinton's denials of sexual dalliances, Bowers spent a day meeting one-on-one with reporters admitting that he had broken his marriage vows. Like Clinton, however, once the information was out, he continued his campaign and urged the press and the public to get over the affair and move on with him to a confrontation of the issues. Bowers's wife of some thirty years stood by him and the campaign continued.

The revelation caused some of those who had recently hailed him as the ideal "family values" candidate to rethink their commitment. Most damagingly, however, Guy Millner, the founder of the Norrell temporary help agency and reported to be worth well over $100 million, got into the race. Millner had come within 33,000 votes of victory in 1994 as gubernatorial nominee and he also ran competitively as the senatorial aspirant two years later. His wealth and name recognition, coupled with Bowers's problems, made Millner the instant front-runner. Despite his near misses, some in the party worried that no matter how much of his fortune he invested in the effort, Millner was unelectable. He no longer made gaffes like his question to a group of farmers, "Do you farm or do you work?" Nonetheless, even his supporters admitted that he was not someone you warmed up to quickly.

Millner had not been the initial candidate of choice of the Christian Right in 1994, although his campaign manager, David Shafer, did work to get him a share of support from that camp (Bullock and Grant 1995). He positioned himself as fervently pro-life, and his wife helped the cause by hosting prayer groups. Some pro-family groups worried because she was his third wife, but unlike Bowers, he did not have a mistress.

Two other offices attracted spirited fields in the Republican primary. Five candidates ran for lieutenant governor, which, like the governorship, would be open in 1998. The two aspirants most closely identified with fundamentalists were Clint Day, a former state senator who finished third behind Millner in the 1996 senatorial primary, and Pam Glanton, a three-term state senator from Atlanta's southern suburbs. Day's responses had pictured him as the most conservative senatorial candidate in 1996. Glanton's agenda in the Senate included focusing sex education in public schools on abstinence and promoting covenant marriage, which would make divorce more difficult for those who selected that option. She was strongly pro-life and sought to amend a stalking bill so that it could not be used against Operation Rescue or other antiabortion groups. One year the Christian Coalition used six of her proposals in constructing its legislative scorecard (Hendricks 1998).

A third candidate, Mitch Skandalakis, tried to establish credentials with the Christian Right by hiring as campaign manager former Christian Coalition political guru Ralph Reed. Skandalakis had potential problems, especially in the runoff, where Day was his single opponent. Skandalakis had once had good relations with Atlanta's politically active gay and lesbian community, which alienated some religious conservatives and may explain why Rev. Jerry Falwell gave his blessing to Day ("Day Gets Fake Endorsement" 1998). Offsetting the Virginia minister's assist to Day were letters sent to GOP primary voters by Reed and a former lobbyist for religious conservative issues who also worked for Reed's consulting firm, Century Strategies.

The GOP primary for attorney general also attracted a host of candidates, with one closely identified with Christian conservatives. Four aspirants came forward in hopes of wresting the state's chief law enforcement office away from the Democrat who had been appointed to complete Bowers's term when he resigned to campaign full-time for governor. All had conservative credentials, but Kip Klein, a former state house member, was the favorite with the greatest number of conservatives. Though Klein may have been more closely aligned with family issues in the minds of Republicans, his chief opponent, state senator David Ralston, was acceptable and was the favorite of the legal profession.

Primary Results

Despite a strong kick at the finish that saw him attract almost twice as large a share of the vote as had been predicted by the polls, Bowers came up short, failing by fewer than 3,150 votes to push Millner into a runoff. Between the time of the final polls and the actual vote, Millner slipped, and Bowers managed 40 percent of the vote.

Nomination of the lieutenant governor and attorney general required a runoff. Day and Skandalakis went through to the next round in the contest for the second highest post in the executive branch. Klein made it to the runoff but trailed Ralston. If one accepts that Day and Klein were the favorites with religious conservatives, then Christian activists suffered two losses in the runoff. If one gives Skandalakis the nod because of his Reed connection, then one candidate with ties to the evangelical community survived.

Indeed, the primaries were good to Ralph Reed's new consulting venture. Going into the general election, his stable included three statewide candidates. In addition to Skandalakis, Reed managed secretary of state nominee John McCallum—a young (twenty-eight) former staffer of Newt Gingrich who was married to former Miss America Heather Whitestone—and labor commissioner nominee John Frank Collins, a World War II veteran who had become a perennial candidate.

Reed also managed a number of state legislative candidates, including at least four who won contested primaries (Shipp 1998). A businessman and political novice knocked off a three-term senator in south Georgia, while in metropolitan Atlanta Reed's firm helped eliminate a ten-year veteran after criticizing the incumbent for supporting a pregnancy and family planning program directed at teenagers and for being out of touch with the constituency (Baxter 1998). Other Reed candidates challenged conservative Democratic incumbents. In the past, the GOP had steered clear of rural Democrats who agreed with Republicans on many issues, but 1996 had shown that even rural south Georgia Democrats were not out of reach.

Neither Reed nor the Christian Right more generally proved invincible in the GOP primaries. A Reed candidate came close but failed to unseat a candidate regularly thought by Christian conservatives to be unreliable. And on the south side of Atlanta an incumbent who aspired to GOP leadership in the House lost a runoff despite having NRA and right-to-life support. All four Republican House incumbents who stumbled in the primary had scores of at least 89 percent on the Christian Coalition scorecard after adjusting for absences, and two had perfect records. Support for the Christian Coalition agenda did not ensure renomination.

General Election Outcomes

Multiple explanations exist for the failure of the GOP to continue its upward trajectory in 1998. A simple one offered by a GOP campaign manager is that the Democrats "outclassed us at the top of the ticket." With anti-incumbency feelings at low ebb, Roy Barnes used his two decades in the state legislature to advantage by stumping Millner at debates with questions such as "How is the Georgia budget put together?" Moreover, Millner could not establish the rapport with voters that Barnes achieved. Even Republican campaign staffers said of the head of their ticket, "There's not much to like about Guy Millner," while another described him as "untrustworthy."

Millner was not the whole problem by any means. None of Reed's statewide candidates succeeded, in part because his stable lacked thoroughbreds able to keep up with the more experienced Democrats. The elderly Collins ducked reporters and was a no-show at the debate on statewide public television. Mike Thurmond, an African American and former state legislator, praised for moving people off the welfare rolls and into jobs during his tenure as head of the department of human resources, was the tortoise to Collins's hare. His active campaigning and strong black support enabled him to pull ahead in the closing days after trailing in the polls.

Youthful John McCallum had an appeal for young voters, but their low turnout rates made them a weak reed on which to build a campaign. His Democratic opponent had the benefit of two successful campaigns for the state legislature, the first of which involved unseating an incumbent. Cathy Cox, the number two at the secretary of state's office, exuded confidence and appealed to women who had a chance to elect the first Democratic woman to a statewide nonjudicial post.

Mitch Skandalakis proved to be Reed's biggest embarrassment as he was trounced in his bid to become lieutenant governor. Atlanta columnist Jeff Dickerson (1998, A18) labeled Skandalakis "this year's race- baiting GOP standard-bearer," a disastrous image that we will develop further later.

High hopes for picking up legislative seats also crashed. Not only did Reed-managed Republicans fail to unseat rural Democratic solons, but one of the Christian Right's most outspoken members lost his bid for a fourth term. Evangelical Presbyterian Church pastor Ron Crews, who had spearheaded efforts to ban partial-birth abortions and outcome-based education while creating the Legislative Prayer Caucus, fell to a Democratic woman in a district undergoing ethnic transformation.

All was not gloom and doom for Christian conservatives, however, as a lobbyist for some of their causes won an open senate seat. Susan Cable, whom Reed managed, commanded a larger share of the vote in her initial election than her Republican predecessor had obtained in three terms before being sidelined by ill health.

Although Republicans made no gains, the Christian Coalition continued to be active in Georgia. As it had since 1994, it prepared a report card analyzing the voting record of state legislators on roll calls of interest to the organization. It also distributed hundreds of thousands of voter guides in churches across the state. These tools had dulled by 1998. In 1994 they caught many outraged Democratic officeholders by surprise (Bullock and Grant 1995). But even a campaign manager with close ties to the movement speculated that the guides converted few opponents and were useful only when they mobilized the faithful. On this dimension he judged them deficient, observing that "something needs to be done to upgrade the message and update the techniques."

A stale approach—which we warned of after the 1996 election (Bullock and Smith 1997)—that failed to motivate could explain why the

Christian Right's share of the Georgia electorate has declined. A legislator with strong ties to the Christian Right criticized it for a lack of leadership at a time that the movement was fragmenting. In the two most recent exit polls conducted by news networks, the proportion of the white electorate that identifies with the Christian Right has shrunk. In 1998, only 19 percent of the white voters said they belonged to the Christian Right. As table 4.1 shows, four years earlier 26 percent of the whites who went to the polls identified with this cause.

Several reasons could account for the drop in Christian conservative identifiers. The activist quoted above suggests that they have been turned off and become less politically active than they were in 1994, when Republicans scored a major breakthrough as they became a majority of Georgia's congressional delegation for the first time in generations. A former Reed employee explained to us that 1994 gave conservatives their first opportunity to vote against Bill Clinton's agenda, and since he was not on the ballot, they took their frustrations out on his fellow partisans. Certainly 1998 did not evoke comparable enthusiasm among social conservatives. Indeed, after four years of GOP congressional control, some conservatives had become jaded. Some close to the religious movement in Georgia have observed that their followers were apathetic because the GOP had ceased to have a clear, conservative message (Austin 1999). According to a GOP party staffer, "Our people didn't go to the polls. We weren't doing anything that appealed to them."

Table 4.1 Mobilization of Democratic and Republican Base Groups, 1994–1998 (in percentages)

| Year | African Americans[a] | | Christian Right[b] |
	Exit Poll	Count	Exit Poll
1994	16	NA[c]	26
1996	24	21	22
1998	29	23	19

Sources: Exit poll results available on CNN.com/ELECTION/ and audits performed by the Georgia secretary of state.

[a]Figures are the percentage of the electorate that was black. The exit poll column reports figures from the exit polls conducted by the combined forces of the television networks and CNN. The "count" column reports the actual share of those who went to the polls who were listed on their registration forms as African American. The first such analysis was conducted by Georgia's secretary of state in 1996.

[b]Figures are the proportion of the white electorate that identified with the Christian Right.

[c]NA: Not available.

Republican Representative Len Walker (1999), who is a minister, noted "an overall general sense of disinterest" in the GOP ticket. Others active with religious conservatives complained that Millner had become too shopworn, Skandalakis too divisive, and Coverdell too moderate to mobilize the faithful to do the grassroots work necessary to get supporters to the polls. The Republican candidate for lieutenant governor had the unfortunate ability to mobilize the Democratic base while leaving the GOP base uninspired.

An alternative perspective contends that Christian Right identifiers have declined because it has become less acceptable to be seen as part of a conservative Christian movement. This explanation emphasizes that the mix of the white electorate has not changed in significant ways; rather, the liberal social climate has made some conservatives reluctant to acknowledge their support for a socially conservative agenda. According to a Republican legislator, the Christian Right has lost respect and credibility and is increasingly seen as "harsh and divisive and politically nonastute."

A third explanation is that the composition of the electorate is changing. New voters coming from out of state or registering pursuant to motor-voter legislation may be less likely to be religious conservatives. Though we cannot be sure of that proposition, it is clear that the Georgia electorate did change in at least one way.

Whether or not the Christian Right was mobilized, the Democratic base turned out in record numbers. Approximately a quarter of Georgia's voting age population and its registered voters are black, and thus African Americans are no longer underrepresented among potential voters. For several elections prior to 1996, because black turnout relative to white turnout had dropped, African Americans constituted a declining share of the electorate. As table 4.1 shows, this pattern has reversed in the two most recent elections. Exit polls show blacks voting at about the same proportion as their share of the electorate in 1996, meaning that black turnout equaled white turnout; in 1998, with black turnout up 13 percentage points in four years, it appears that blacks actually went to the polls at higher rates than whites.

In 1996, for the first time, Georgia's secretary of state—the office responsible for election administration—analyzed sign-in sheets to determine the race of those who voted (Mishou 1999). This audit shows that African Americans constituted 21 percent of the voters in the presidential election, and although that is below the exit poll estimate, it confirms that black participation has risen. The official tally for 1998 also places black participation below the exit poll figure but agrees that black participation continued to rise so that blacks went to the polls at about the same rate as whites.[2]

Several forces combined to encourage blacks to go to the polls. Toward the end of the campaign, Millner and his running mate, Skandalakis, ran ads widely perceived to be racist. Skandalakis, who was trailing in the polls and struggling to raise money, turned to the whipping boy used by conservatives at least since Governor Gene Talmadge in the 1930s and attacked Atlanta and its politics. In one television ad he characterized the city's black mayor as an incompetent boob and threatened that if elected he would "kick Atlanta's [bleeped out]." Skandalakis's history places this ad in a broader context. He became a significant player by defeating Martin Luther King III, for chair of the Fulton County Commission (Bullock and Dunn 1996). He paid an $18,000 fine a few years later for darkening the picture of a Democrat and adding an Afro hairdo in an effort to elect a Republican to the decisive seat on the Fulton Commission (Helton 1998).

Concerning his 1998 ads, Cynthia Tucker (1998), an African American editorial writer for the *Atlanta Constitution,* concluded that "Skandalakis' constant bashing of the mostly black administration of the city of Atlanta was so insulting that it created a backlash among black voters, who turned out in much higher numbers than expected to vote for Democrats" (G5). Criticism was not confined to the black community. Republican Representative Ralph Hudgens (1999), who represents part of the Athens community where the University of Georgia is located, asked rhetorically, "How can you be a Christian and actively support [Skandalakis's] campaign?"

Millner also injected race as he saw the election slipping away despite spending as much as $11 million of his own money. In the last week he began running ads critical of affirmative action in hopes of attracting white Democrats in south Georgia, a portion of the state where whites have remained more loyal to the party of their ancestors.

Black ministers were among the important players as they reacted to the Skandalakis and Millner ads. Our interviews with black activists indicate that ministers began preaching earlier and perhaps harder on the importance of voting. We were told of a minister in Albany who broke his rule of keeping campaigning away from his pulpit. A political scientist with extensive ties to black legislators and the Concerned Black Clergy noted that the amount of pulpit time devoted to the election was extraordinarily high and began five weeks before the vote (Cornish 1999).

The Democratic Party augmented the ministers' efforts. Historically elections in Georgia had stimulated little party coordination, with each candidate running independently of others on the same ticket. Outgoing Governor Zell Miller had begun changing this approach, and in 1998 Democrats running statewide undertook a highly publicized bus tour that wound around the state. In addition, realizing that contacted voters are more likely to turn out (Wielhouwer and Lockerbie 1994), the state party stockpiled funds for a last-minute blitz directed at the households of black voters. Since a voter's race is maintained on official registration materials, it is feasible to build a data file for black registrants. The Democratic Party claimed it contacted the households of African American voters five times during the last week of the campaign. Three of the contacts came via telephone, with one of these being a recording of President Clinton who urged the recipient to go to the polls. A statewide mailing used the Skandalakis television ad to suggest that he and Millner had threatened black voters that "We're going to kick your ass!" Pictures of the two candidates bracketed this inflammatory statement printed in bold letters. On the reverse side, recipients read that "The Millner/ Skandalakis Team Believes You're 'Killing' Georgia and They've Threatened to 'Kick Your Ass.'" Below six actions by the two candidates that could be interpreted as racist came the admonition, "You Get the Message. Get to the Polls Before Millner and Skandalakis Get to *You*."

In addition to a desire to keep Millner and Skandalakis away from executive power, African Americans had a positive incentive for voting. For the first time, three black candidates appeared on the Democratic statewide ballot. Thurbert Baker had been appointed to fill the post of attorney general when Bowers resigned to pursue the governorship. Mike Thurmond was running an underfunded effort to become labor commissioner, another job that had opened up when its incumbent saw himself as the next governor. Finally, Henrietta Canty walked away from a safe seat in the legislature to run for Insurance Commissioner. Election of any of these would mark the first African American to win a nonjudicial statewide position.

These factors combined to mobilize African Americans who constitute the Democratic base vote. When the herculean Democratic effort is juxtaposed against the Republican inability to inspire its base among Christian Right voters, it is easy to see why the GOP failed to make headway in Georgia. The contribution of the Christian Right was shrinking on two fronts—whites constituted a smaller share of the turnout and fewer religious conservatives showed up among whites who went to the polls. In the 1994 electorate, Christian Right whites outnumbered blacks by about five percentage points. By 1998, more black than self-identified Christian conservative voters went to the polls.

Although Republicans—and thus Christian conservatives—failed to make gains in 1998, one of their workers challenges any suggestion that Republicans suffered from their ties to the Christian Right or that the movement's message was potentially ineffective. Clint Austin (1999), a Century Strategies employee during the campaign who has worked for a number of Republican legislators, asserts that the agenda associated with the Christian Right dominated debate in a number of contests in which Republicans challenged conservative Democrats. He accuses Democrats of highjacking GOP initiatives much as President Clinton embraced some of Dole's more popular issues in 1996. For example, after a senior

House Democrat was criticized for voting for a teen sex-education program, he began running a radio commercial that featured "I Pledge Allegiance to the Lamb," a song familiar to Christian conservatives. In a Senate contest, as the Republican candidate's attacks intensified, his opponent trotted out an endorsement from a right-to-life group from an earlier campaign. In summing up Democratic strategy, Austin complains, "They stole our issues. They scare their base by saying 'I'm not one of them.' But they sound like a religious Right conservative. The Democrats are talking like us to steal our votes and our thunder."

Multivariate Models

To explore the relative impact of the Christian Right on elections, we include a measure for concentrations of Christian conservatives in multivariate models along with other potential predictors. If the hypothesis that religious conservatives did not respond to the GOP ticket in 1998 is accurate, then a negative relationship between our measure of evangelicals and share of the vote going to Republican candidates should emerge. While acknowledging problems in getting a perfect reading on the strength of religious conservatives by county, we retain the measure used previously (Bullock and Grant 1995; Bullock and Smith 1997), which calculates the proportion of fundamentalist and evangelical members as a share of all church members.[3] In 1994, a positive relationship often emerged between the incidence of religious conservatives and support for GOP candidates, whereas in 1996 no relationship typically emerged between these two variables.

We expect Republican support to be negatively related to the percentage of blacks among registered voters who turned out in record numbers, in part because of the admonitions of black clergy. Positive relationships are expected for three control variables—suburbs, region, and past GOP strength. The suburban variable assigns a 1 to counties that are part of metropolitan areas but do not contain a central city, since central cities in Georgia tend to be Democratic while Republicans have excelled in bedroom communities. To differentiate regions, a 1 is assigned to counties north of the fall line since the GOP has done much better in the northern half of the state. The measure of party strength is one developed by the Republican Party in Georgia and some other southern states (Aistrup 1996; Bullock and Shafer 1997) and is a weighted average vote share for statewide Republican candidates for an assortment of offices in recent elections. The figure used in this study is the one prepared in anticipation of the 1998 elections. We expect that Republicans will do better in suburban counties, in north Georgia, and in places where their party has shown strength in the past.

With one exception, table 4.2 shows that in 1998 Republicans performed *worse* in counties with concentrations of evangelicals than in counties where they were less numerous.[4] Only Coverdell did better in counties with higher proportions of evangelicals, but the coefficient for his election is one of three that is not statistically significant. The other two candidates for whom the percentage of evangelicals failed to achieve statistical significance were Ralston, whom many thought to be the best candidate on the GOP ticket, and Linda Schrenko, incumbent school superintendent. Ralston's standing with the legal community and some of Schrenko's policy stands may have been factors. She may have been seen as something of a martyr for the conservative Christian agenda with her attacks on the PTA and as a result of the battering she suffered at the hands of the Democratic-dominated state school board early in her term.

At the other end of the scale, Skandalakis, whose campaign embarrassed many Republicans, turned in one of the weakest performances in heavily evangelical counties. Only the nominee for agriculture commissioner, the least competitive Republican on the ticket, did worse in heavily evangelical counties than did Skandalakis. Collins, who had the third largest slope for the evangelical variable ($b = -.092$), along with Skandalakis, was managed by Ralph Reed. Having the former chief operative of the Christian Coalition seems not to have promoted Republicans in counties with concentrations of religious conservatives.

The sizable negative slopes for the evangelical measure common in 1998 mark a major break with the past. In 1994, Republican performance improved with the percentage of evangelicals, especially in counties in which Christian Coalition voter guides featured the contest. The slope for percentage of evangelicals was particularly large in top-of-the-ticket contests such as governor ($b = .127$), lieutenant governor ($b = .072$), and attorney general ($b = .072$). Two years later, the slopes were not statistically significant except in the presidential election and were slightly negative for two of four statewide contests (Bullock and Smith 1997). Millner's experience tracks with the change in the evangelical variable. When he ran for governor the first time, he did substantially better in counties with a high percentage of evangelicals ($b = .127$). When he ran for the Senate in 1996, the slope was positive ($b = .032$) but not significant. In 1998 when he made his second bid for governor, his performance suffered as the percentage of evangelicals increased ($b - -.073$). John Oxendine's evangelical slope changed from $b = .072$ in 1994 to $-.070$ when he ran for reelection in 1998.

Except for Schrenko, Republicans invariably ran significantly worse in counties having concentrations of African Americans. The relationship between percentage of blacks and support for the school superintendent may have been muted by the massive publicity that she received during her term coupled with the largely invisible campaign of her opponent. If

Table 4.2 Bases of Support for Republican Statewide Candidates, 1998

	a	Evangelicals	Suburb	Region	Party	Percentage Black	Adj.R2	F
Coverdell, U.S. senator	.389	.034 (.058)	.036* (.018)	-.014 (.013)	.349** (.125)	-.138* (.075)	.353	18.21***
Millner, governor	.134	-.073** (.029)	.026** (.009)	.036*** (.007)	.736*** (.061)	-.160*** (.037)	.855	187.57***
Skandalakis, lieutenant governor	.000	-.096** (.037)	.013 (.011)	.078*** (.008)	.836*** (.079)	-.131** (.047)	.819	143.98***
McCallum, secretary of state	.039	-.069* (.035)	.013 (.011)	.053*** (.008)	.850*** (.075)	-.194*** (.045)	.844	172.58***
Ralston, attorney general	.195	-.059 (.034)	.015 (.011)	.034*** (.008)	.686*** (.073)	-.266*** (.044)	.837	162.90***
Greer, agriculture commissioner	.105	-.110** (.031)	.038*** (.010)	.011 (.007)	.617*** (.067)	-.166*** (.040)	.781	113.95***
Oxendine, insurance commissioner	.434	-.070* (.034)	.013 (.011)	-.008 (.008)	.585*** (.073)	-.302*** (.004)	.797	124.99***
Collins, labor commissioner	.225	-.092** (.031)	.030** (.010)	.017* (.007)	.713*** (.067)	-.276*** (.040)	.859	192.75***
Schrenko, school superintendent	.131	-.048 (.035)	.014 (.011)	.008 (.008)	.855*** (.075)	-.064 (.045)	.750	95.55***
Baker, Public Service Commission	.367	-.068* (.032)	.013 (.010)	-.010 (.007)	.638*** (.069)	-.260*** (.041)	.804	130.25***

Standard errors in parentheses. *p ≤ .05 **p ≤ .01 ***p ≤ .001

this is the explanation for party strength being the only significant correlate of Schrenko's vote share, it provides support for the political chestnut that "I don't care what you say about me as long as you spell my name correctly"—at least when the opposition lacks the resources to develop anything approaching comparable name recognition—since much of the publicity surrounding Schrenko was negative.

Though all other Republicans ran significantly worse in counties with concentrations of blacks, the slope for Skandalakis was among the smallest (b = −.131), only half the magnitude of that for four of his fellow partisans. Millner, the other candidate widely accused of running racist ads, also suffered less than most of the GOP ticket (b = −.160). The three largest slopes occurred for the Republicans who faced black opponents, and the coefficients may be the result of concerted efforts by black voters to mark ballots for the Democratic nominees.

Of the control variables, past party voting is always a strong correlate of the 1998 results. The smallest slope, albeit still statistically significant, came for Coverdell, who ran an effective campaign against an opponent who never seemed to get on track. Republicans generally fared better in north Georgia, although this variable was not statistically significant for any of the incumbents (Coverdell, Oxendine, Schrenko, and Baker). The only other Republican who did not do significantly better in the north was the hapless agriculture nominee. Region made the most difference for Skandalakis and McCallum, the only Republicans who faced Democrats from south Georgia. The Democratic nominee for lieutenant governor, Mark Taylor, rolled up insurmountable leads in south Georgia by appealing to regional pride. All Republicans ran stronger in suburbia, although for only four were the slopes statistically significant. Here we have a curious combination of the two who ran the most expensive campaigns (Coverdell and Millner) and two who ran among the least expensive efforts (Greer and Collins).

The frequency of negative relationships between the proportion of evangelicals in a county and support for Republicans prompts a further check. Is it possible that evangelicals have become so much a part of the GOP that including a measure of party strength obscures a positive relationship between the presence of conservative Christians and Republican support? Reestimating the models without the party variable had no effect on the signs of the coefficients for evangelicals. The slope for Coverdell continues to be positive, although not statistically significant, while the remaining ones are negative.

Conclusions

The relationship between Christian conservatives and the GOP in 1998 differed sharply from what had existed only four years before. The

Christian Coalition continued to distribute roll call analyses of state legislators and voter guides in which Democrats scored poorly while Republicans performed well on the items selected for comparison. Voters who identified with the Christian Right still gave overwhelming support to GOP candidates. Ralph Reed had left Pat Robertson and established a consulting firm in Atlanta that worked with a number of Republicans. The GOP, which had registered impressive gains during the 1990s, thought itself poised to capitalize on vacancies in the offices of governor, lieutenant governor, secretary of state, and labor commissioner. The more optimistic Republicans even spoke of winning control of one house in the state legislature. Earlier in the election year it had seemed possible that religious conservatives could help propel the GOP to dominant party status.

These pipe dreams changed to nightmares on election night. None of the vacant offices fell into Republican hands. The string of gains in the legislature ceased. At least a part of the explanation for the change in GOP fortunes is that religious conservatives were not excited about the ticket. Our interviews indicate that some in the Christian Right thought the GOP no longer concentrated on relevant issues while others were turned off by the racial overtones in the messages of the most vocal candidates. The statistical analysis indicates that up and down the ticket, Republicans paid a penalty in counties where evangelicals were concentrated—just the opposite of the pattern four years earlier when the GOP tallied some of its biggest gains in Georgia and excelled in counties with Christian Right concentrations.

In striking contrast with evangelicals who failed to get their flocks inspired, black clergy approached the election with messianic zeal. The message came early and was frequently repeated that 1998 was a critical year for the future of black Georgians and that to protect that future, voting was essential. With these exhortations, African Americans cast more votes than did adherents of the Christian Right. If black pollster Harry Ross (1998) is accurate and many black voters feared that should Republicans win control of Georgia government the status of blacks would be set back a generation, then the record turnout is no surprise.

NOTES

We appreciate the research assistance provided by William Gillespie.

1. From 1990 through 1998, only Arizona and Nevada grew at faster rates than Georgia.
2. We cannot be sure of the cause for the disparity between the exit poll estimate and the official count of black participation. One possible explanation is that the exit poll misses those who vote absentee and this

component may have been disproportionately white. The GOP made an especially strong effort to get individuals who had participated in the GOP primary—almost all of whom were white—to request absentee ballots by sending out 650,000 application forms. In southwest Georgia, Republican congressional nominee Joe McCormick ran twenty-two percentage points stronger among absentees than among voters who went to the polls on election day (Bullock 1998). There is no way to know the racial makeup of the absentee vote, but McCormick's performance suggests that it was much whiter than on election day.

3. Denominations included among evangelicals are Assembly of God; Christian Missionary Alliance; Church of God of Anderson, Indiana; Church of God of Cleveland, Tennessee; Church of the Nazarene; Lutheran, Missouri Synod; Four Square Gospel; Independent Church (both charismatic and noncharismatic); Pentecostal Church of God; Presbyterian Church of America; Reformed Presbyterian; Southern Baptist; and Wesleyan. Data on membership in these denominations by county come from Bradley et al. (1990). The percentage of evangelicals is computed by summing the membership in these denominations and then dividing by the total church membership.

4. Variance inflation factors were inspected and multicollinearity was not a problem.

REFERENCES

Aistrup, Joseph A. 1996. *The Southern Strategy Revisited.* Lexington: University of Kentucky Press.

Austin, Clint. 1999. Telephone interview with Bullock, Austin, Texas, January 2, 1999.

Baxter, Tom. 1998. "Infighting Shows GOP Has Arrived." *Atlanta Journal,* 4 August, B4.

Bradley, Martin B., Norman Green, Jr., Dale E. Jones, Mac Lynn, and Lou McNeil. 1990. *Churches and Church Membership in the United States.* Atlanta: Glenmary Research Center.

Bullock, Charles S., III. 1998. "High Turnout in a Low Turnout Year: Georgia's Second Congressional District." Paper presented at the "Money, Media and Madness: Inside the 1998 Elections" Conference, Center for Congressional and Presidential Studies, American University, Washington, D.C., December 4.

Bullock, Charles S., III, and Richard E. Dunn. 1996. "Election Roll-Off: A Test of Three Explanations." *Urban Affairs Review* 32 (September): 71–86.

Bullock, Charles S., III, and John Christopher Grant. 1995. "Georgia: The Christian Right and Grass Roots Power." Chap. 3 in *God at the Grass*

Roots: The Christian Right in the 1994 Elections, edited by Mark J. Rozell and Clyde Wilcox. Lanham, Md.: Rowman & Littlefield.

Bullock, Charles S., III, and David J. Shafer. 1997. "Party Targeting and Electoral Success." *Legislative Studies Quarterly* 22 (November): 573–84.

Bullock, Charles S., III, and Mark C. Smith. 1997. "Georgia: Purists, Pragmatists, and Electoral Outcomes." Chap. 4 in *God at the Grass Roots, 1996: The Christian Right in the American Elections,* edited by Mark J. Rozell and Clyde Wilcox. Lanham, Md.: Rowman & Littlefield.

Cornish, Grady. 1999. Personal interview with Smith, Athens, Georgia, January 19, 1999.

"Day Gets Fake Endorsement from Paper." *Atlanta Journal-Constitution,* 8 August, B5.

Dickerson, Jeff. 1998. "Skandalakis Should Give Race Baiting a Rest." *Atlanta Journal,* 20 October, A18.

Fenno, Richard F., Jr. 1978. *Home Style.* Boston: Little, Brown.

———. 1996. *Senators on the Campaign Trail.* Norman: University of Oklahoma.

Heffernan, Tony. 1997. "A Message for Millner: 'Stay Out!'" *Bill Shipp's Georgia* 10 (May 26): 2.

Helton, Charmagne. 1998. "Mitch Skandalakis: Tax Issue Is Again a Main Focus." *Atlanta Journal-Constitution,* 10 July, C6.

Hendricks, Gary. 1998. "Pam Glanton: A Proud Advocate for Conservatism." *Atlanta Journal,* 8 July, C4.

Hudgens, Ralph. 1999. Telephone interview with Smith, January 14, 1999.

Mishou, Tom. 1999. Telephone interview with Bullock, January 15, 1999.

Ross, Harry. 1998. Personal interview with Bullock, Atlanta, Georgia, November 3, 1998.

Shipp, Bill. 1998. "GOP May Revive Massey Runoff Bid." *Bill Shipp's Georgia* 11 (27 July): 6.

Tucker, Cynthia. 1998. "Voters Offer Reed a Sermon on Race-baiting." *Atlanta Journal-Constitution,* 8 November, G5.

Walker, Len. 1999. Telephone interview with Smith, January 15, 1999.

Wielhouwer, Peter W., and Brad Lockerbie. 1994. "Party Contacting and Political Participation, 1952–90." *American Journal of Political Science* 38 (February): 211–29.

5

Virginia: Prophet in Waiting?

Mark J. Rozell and Clyde Wilcox

Virginia did not hold statewide elections in 1998. Other than referenda throughout the state, the only electoral contests were for the state's eleven congressional seats. As expected, every incumbent won reelection.

The only campaign to attract even marginal interest was in the eighth congressional district in northern Virginia, perhaps the most liberal seat in the Virginia delegation and held reliably by Democratic Representative James Moran. Demaris Miller, wife of former Reagan administration Office of Management and Budget Director Jim Miller, ran as the GOP nominee. An archconservative, Miller emphasized in her campaign Moran's support for the policies of President Bill Clinton, who was then tarred by a sex scandal. The fiercely independent Moran made national headlines in the campaign when he frequently blasted Clinton over the scandal and his Democratic colleagues could not reign in his criticisms of their president. At Clinton's urging, the First Lady called Moran to try to calm him down—to which Moran replied to Mrs. Clinton that if he were her big brother he would take the president outside and break his nose. Republicans lost their issue of the Clinton scandal in this race, and Moran incurred the wrath of many Democratic constituents who both let him know they didn't like his criticizing their president and voted for him in the general election. Moran won by more than a 2–1 margin.

Virginia's off-year state elections system meant that the major contests relevant to the study of the Christian Right were in 1997. That election year was a big success for the Christian Right. Possibly the movement's biggest achievement ever in Virginia electoral politics was in the race for attorney general. Republican State Senator Mark Earley—a Christian social conservative not only with ties to the movement but also with social issues positions compatible with the views of candidates strongly rejected by Virginians in recent years—won his race with the most votes of any of the three Republican statewide victors. In fact, his 58 percent vote was the largest this century for any GOP candidate for attorney general in Virginia.

As they had done so successfully in the past on many occasions, Democrats characterized the socially conservative candidate as an extremist and a threat to women's rights. Yet Earley won. And given the size of his victory and the fact that he outpolled even the victorious gubernatorial and lieutenant governor candidates, no one could credibly argue that his victory was an aberration due to electoral coattails.

What became clear in the 1997 campaign was that Mark Earley was a unique kind of Christian Right candidate. In the past Virginia voters had soundly defeated such Christian Right statewide candidates as former Moral Majority leader Michael Farris and Iran-Contra figure Oliver North, among others. But Farris and North could easily be attacked as extreme because of their controversial issue stands and the manner in which each of them presented his views. Neither one had experience in elected office. They were successful at mobilizing a movement but huge failures at establishing their credibility before a broader public.

What made Earley different were the following factors: First, he had served in the state senate for ten years and established a widely admired record for legislative effectiveness. Movement leaders have the luxury to take strong, noncompromising issue stands, but responsible legislators have to work with diverse constituencies and be willing to compromise goals in order to be effective. State newspapers consistently rated Earley one of the most effective in the state senate. Second, Earley had a long record of reaching out to diverse constituencies, and his voting record was widely reported as favorable to the interests of labor unionists and minority voters. It was simply not credible for opponents to characterize as a far-right extremist a man with a long record of support for civil rights and labor. Despite his conservative social issue views, he received endorsements from the *Washington Post* editorial page and a former state director of the NAACP—an organization he joined back in 1982, making him quite a rarity among white southern conservative Republicans.

Unlike Christian Right candidates in the state in the past, Earley was not identified only by his stands on social issues, and he ran a smart campaign in which he made little effort to draw attention to his social issues positions. Earley is a model of what scholar Allen Hertzke likes to call the "bilingual Republican"—one who is as comfortable speaking the secular language of politics as he is talking the language of the Christian Right.

This chapter examines the modern history of the Christian Right in Virginia politics. Special attention is given to the 1990s elections, particularly the latest statewide campaigns in 1997.

The Context

In his seminal *Southern Politics in State and Nation,* V. O. Key, Jr. (1949) described Virginia as a "political museum piece." He wrote: "Of all the American states, Virginia can lay claim to the most thorough control by an oligarchy" (19). At the time, the Democratic political machine of Harry F. Byrd dominated Virginia politics. Byrd served as governor from 1926 to 1930 and as U.S. Senator from 1933 until he retired in 1965. He assembled his machine from the county courthouse organizations of the landed gentry, who preferred stability to economic growth and were fiercely committed to racial segregation (Barone and Ujifusa 1993).

The Byrd machine succeeded by restricting participation. Long after the demise of his organization, the state still holds its gubernatorial and other statewide elections in odd-numbered years. This has long meant that organized interests can exert disproportionate influence in the general election because of the potential for lower turnouts in non-federal election years.

Another remnant of the Byrd machine is the system of no formal party registration. This restriction suited the Byrd machine's objectives during the era of single-party dominance of state politics. Today it means that in those rare cases in which a party nominates a candidate for statewide election by primary, all registered voters may participate.

In recent years Republicans nominated their candidates in large, statewide conventions that allowed almost any citizen to participate who was willing to pledge to support the party nominees and pay a registration fee. These conventions selected the candidates and passed the planks of the party platform. As the Republican Party grew, so did attendance at these conventions. For example, in 1994 more than 14,000 Virginians participated as delegates to the convention that nominated Oliver North for the U.S. Senate.

In the second half of the twentieth century, the GOP has held an open primary nomination for statewide election only three times: for governor in 1989, for senator in 1996, and for attorney general in 1997. The difference in nominating process has a profound impact on party nominations.

The party nominating conventions have favored candidates backed by organized interests, and most recently this has meant the Christian Right and the pro-life movement. Ralph Reed said that "the caucus-convention nominating process in the [Virginia] Republican Party is unusual in that it does tend to give [our] grassroots activists a greater voice than they have in primaries" (Reed 1994).

The evidence for Christian Right strength in GOP primaries is less clear only because of the limited number of cases. In 1989, the GOP gubernatorial primary favored the most conservative candidate, who won with less than 37 percent of the low-turnout vote in a three-way race. In 1996 the primary heavily favored the more moderate candidate in a two-way contest. In 1997, the attorney general primary favored a Christian social conservative who prevailed in a very low-turnout, multicandidate race.

The evidence is nonetheless clear that Christian Right influence on Republican nomination politics has hurt the party in general elections. The urban corridor that includes the D.C. suburbs has a majority of the state's population, and the northern Virginia suburbs are distinctive in their affluence, their relatively low levels of religious involvement, their social liberalism, and their many Republican voters. Many of these Republican voters are unwilling to support candidates strongly identified with the Christian Right and have defected in large numbers to moderate Democrats and even an independent candidate in some recent elections.

Virginia is a heavily Protestant state, full of Baptist and Methodist churches. Surveys show that nearly half of the state's residents profess an affiliation with an evangelical denomination and that more than 10 percent identify as fundamentalists. More than 40 percent of likely voters indicate that they believe that the Bible is literally true. The northern Virginia area has a sizable number of Catholics and even non-Judeo-Christian immigrants. John Green reports that "Virginia is one of the most cosmopolitan and diverse of the southern states, which are the most religious overall" (Green 1995; see Green et al. 1998).

During the 1970s and early 1980s, Virginia was home to the Moral Majority, a Christian Right organization based in the Bible Baptist Fellowship that was centered mainly in the fundamentalist Right. Reverend Jerry Falwell, former head of the Moral Majority, lives in Lynchburg, and his huge congregation is a major institution in that region of the state. In the 1990s, Virginia has been home to the Christian Coalition, an organization that grew out of Marion G. (Pat) Robertson's failed 1988 presidential campaign. Although that campaign appealed mainly to charismatics and Pentecostals, the Christian Coalition has sought to build bridges to other religious groups.

Not surprisingly, then, the Christian Right has long exerted influence on Virginia politics. In 1978, conservative Christians attended the state Democratic convention to support G. Conoly Phillips, a Virginia Beach car dealer who said that God had called him to run for the U.S. Senate. Phillips expressed surprise that the call had even specified the Democratic Party, for he would have preferred to run as an independent.

Campaign mentor Pat Robertson, the son of a former Democratic U.S. Senator, also urged that choice. Phillips lost the nomination, although his strong support surprised many observers. A smaller number of Christian conservatives participated in the GOP nominating convention, backing the eventual nominee, former state party chair Richard Obenshain. The nominee died in a plane crash, and the party committee eventually selected John Warner as the nominee. Warner went on to win a historically close race for the Senate.

The Republican realignment took on metaphysical overtones in the 1980s, as the Christian Right moved into the GOP. In 1981 the Moral Majority helped to mobilize some seven hundred delegates to the state GOP nominating convention, primarily to support lieutenant governor candidate Guy Farley, a former Byrd Democrat turned born-again Republican. Farley lost a bitter nomination fight in which opponents characterized him as a Christian Right extremist. Nonetheless, the GOP fielded a conservative ticket led by Attorney General J. Marshall Coleman, and Falwell embraced the Republican nominees. Falwell's open endorsement and activities on behalf of the GOP ticket became a focal point of contention in the campaign. Despite his large following among social conservatives, polls showed that Falwell was the most unpopular figure in state politics, and Democrats, led by moderate gubernatorial candidate Charles S. Robb, succeeded in linking Republican nominees to Falwell and the Christian Right. Republicans lost all three statewide offices, and this campaign inaugurated the Democrats' use of Christian Right support for the GOP as a wedge issue.

In 1985, Christian conservatives mobilized behind the gubernatorial candidacy of Wyatt B. Durette, a pro-life advocate who opposed abortion even in the cases of rape and incest. Durette advocated a constitutional amendment to ban all abortions. He also advocated organized nondenominational prayer recited aloud in schools and a constitutional amendment to permit those prayers (Cox 1985). Partially in response to pressure from his own backers, late in the campaign Durette said that he favored the mandatory teaching of creationism in the public schools. Once again, Falwell endorsed the GOP ticket, and again a moderate Democrat, Gerald Baliles, succeeded in portraying Durette as a pawn of the Christian Right. Once again, all three GOP candidates for state office handily lost.

In 1988, Pat Robertson's presidential campaign did poorly in the state primary but well in the local and congressional caucuses that selected delegates to the national convention. Because the state party central committee is selected out of those caucuses and the resultant state convention, Christian conservatives gained a strong foothold in the party apparatus.

In 1989, the GOP experimented with a party primary, its first since 1949. Coleman ran as the most conservative candidate on abortion and won the gubernatorial nomination in a close three-way contest. After the primary, the Supreme Court handed down the *Webster* decision that allowed states to enact certain abortion restrictions, and Coleman scrambled toward the middle on abortion in a general election race that centered on that issue (Cook, Jelen, and Wilcox 1994). Large numbers of moderate Republicans defected to support Democratic nominee L. Douglas Wilder, who became the nation's first elected black governor.

By 1993 Christian conservatives had a strong foothold in the party. The state GOP chair, Patrick McSweeney, had won office by appealing to the Christian Right, and our survey of the state central committee showed that about one-third of its members were strong supporters of Christian Right organizations and issues (Rozell and Wilcox, 1996). A number of organizations, including the Christian Coalition, Concerned Women for America, and the Family Foundation (associated with Focus on the Family) were active in Virginia politics, and their members were primarily Republicans. But in 1993 it was the Christian home-schoolers that dominated Republican politics.

The 1993 convention nominated Michael Farris for lieutenant governor. Farris was a former Washington state Moral Majority executive director and a former attorney for Concerned Women for America, and he currently heads a legal defense organization for home-schooling families. Farris's supporters were new to GOP politics, but they flooded the nominating convention. Farris won the nomination easily against a pro-choice moderate woman and longtime GOP activist, Bobbie Kilberg.

At the top of the ticket was former U.S. Representative George Allen, who appealed to Christian activists with promises to push hard for parental notification on abortion, support for charter schools, and rollbacks in the state's Family Life Education program. Yet unlike Republican nominees in earlier contests, Allen did not stress his socially conservative views. In fact, he portrayed himself as a moderate on abortion, favoring only limited restrictions on the procedure. He emphasized instead his promises to cut taxes and abolish parole. By contrast with the 1980s campaigns, when Christian Right leaders made uncompromising demands on GOP candidates as a condition for support, in 1993 these leaders decided to back a gubernatorial candidate who was not a purist on the social issues but was clearly a better choice from their perspective than the pro-choice Democratic nominee, Mary Sue Terry. Allen won in a landslide, as did the GOP attorney general candidate James Gilmore, who also was supported by, but not a part of, the Christian Right.

Farris, however, lost, running an extraordinary twelve percentage points behind the top of his ticket. Don Beyer, his Democratic opponent, characterized Farris as a Christian Right extremist who would ban books from public schools and whose ideas were dangerously out of the mainstream. Farris was a prolific writer and public speaker, and a number of passages from his writings and published statements gave Beyer ample and credible ammunition.

Robertson and the Christian Coalition were actually more supportive of Allen and Gilmore than of Farris. According to a good many accounts, Robertson considered Farris potentially damaging to the Christian Coalition's goal of becoming an organization with a reputation for taking reasonable stands on issues and party politics (Rozell and Wilcox 1996).

Allen benefited from the comparison with Farris. Voters could compare Allen and Farris and conclude that Allen was far more moderate. Farris mobilized a large number of social conservatives who then also voted for the rest of the GOP ticket. Terry failed in her attempts to get the public to accept that Allen, too, was a Christian Right extremist, although, according to Allen's own tracking polls, once in the campaign his momentum temporarily slowed when Terry ran ads linking Allen to Robertson and Falwell. Warner refused to back Farris, although he campaigned on behalf of the rest of the GOP ticket. In 1994 Warner again broke with the party and refused to support the Senate nomination of Oliver North. But there was one important difference: Warner merely refused to endorse Farris, whereas he openly opposed North and recruited a moderate Republican to run as an independent.

In 1994 Virginia attracted worldwide attention because of the GOP nomination of North. The Iran-Contra figure campaigned openly espousing his religious faith and socially conservative views. Although he ran against an incumbent senator tainted by scandal, voters strongly rejected North in a historic Republican election year. Once again, the Christian Right suffered a major setback and took much of the blame for the party defeat (Rozell and Wilcox 1995).

Warner's actions in 1993 and 1994 set the stage for his renomination battle in 1996. Social conservatives pledged to challenge Warner and to replace him with a more reliable conservative. Party centrists hailed Warner's actions as rare displays of political courage and pledged to work for his renomination. And there were signs of vulnerability for Warner. In both January and October of 1995, polls of likely primary voters showed that Warner and challenger Jim Miller were statistically tied (Lee 1995; Peter Baker 1996). Until mid-April 1996, it remained unclear whether Warner would be able to run for reelection in a primary, and it remained undoubtedly clear that, given his alienation from party leaders and activists, in a convention nomination he would lose.

A provision of a Virginia law allows the incumbent candidate running for renomination to request an open primary. Warner knew that an open primary was his only hope of winning. The Virginia GOP challenged the constitutionality of the state law that gave Warner the right to choose his own method of renomination. The state GOP charged that the law was an infringement on the party's constitutional right to select its own nominating process and its own candidate. The co-plaintiff in the suit was Delegate Robert G. Marshall, a social conservative and director of the American Life League. The federal judge threw out the lawsuit on April 16, 1996, guaranteeing Warner an open primary. It was the senator's most important victory. A poll released the same week as the court decision showed Warner for the first time with a substantial lead over Miller (Peter Baker 1996).

Despite all this good news for the senator, he could not take lightly the intraparty challenge. Miller had run for the GOP U.S. Senate nomination in 1994 and had come close to defeating Oliver North in the convention, despite having been heavily outspent by the Iran-Contra figure. The Virginia GOP lacked a tradition of statewide primaries, having held just one since 1949. For Warner, with strong Christian Right opposition to his candidacy and the potential for a low turnout, it was conceivable that he could lose renomination.

Indeed, the widespread conventional wisdom during the primary suggested that support from the Christian Right could deliver an upset victory to Miller. He had the support not only of the state party chair and national committee member, but also of former governor Mills Godwin, and he selected Farris as a campaign chairman. Farris maintained that he could easily deliver tens of thousands of Christian Right votes to Miller in a primary. Senator Warner had the support of established party figures (e.g., George Bush, Colin Powell, Dan Quayle, and Bob Dole) and a large fund-raising advantage that he used to great effect by running frequent television advertisements.

Ten days prior to the primary, the state GOP held its convention in Salem. In a straw poll of the three thousand delegates, Miller beat Warner by a 3–1 margin. Christian conservatives were a dominating force at the event that featured a battle between the party factions for state party chair and RNC member. The social conservatives won both votes easily.

The most dramatic moment of the convention came when Oliver North addressed the delegates and urged them to get behind Miller's candidacy. He asked each delegate to pledge $20 to Miller's campaign and actively work to identify and urge similar help from every 1994 North supporter. North mailed a plea to 16,500 supporters asking for their assistance for Miller's campaign.

Warner soundly defeated Miller, taking 66 percent of the popular vote. Although there were no exit polls and it is impossible to determine exactly how many non-Republicans participated, there is some telling evidence of Warner's broad-based appeal. For example, turnout was very strong for Warner in traditionally Democratic-leaning urban areas. Although turnout statewide was 15.9 percent, the turnout was significantly stronger in the Democratic strongholds of northern Virginia, including Fairfax City (21.5 percent), Falls Church (26.1 percent),

Arlington County (18.9 percent), and Alexandria (17.3 percent). In those four jurisdictions, Warner took 68 percent, 77 percent, 75 percent, and 78 percent of the vote, respectively.[1] Warner had benefited from non-Republican support that most likely could be attributed to his opposition to North and to his estrangement from the Christian Right.

In the eyes of most observers of the state political scene, with such a resounding renomination win, he was virtually assured reelection. For the Christian Right, Miller's loss continued their series of statewide electoral disappointments, for they had also failed to elect Farris or North. Once again it appeared that voters even in this conservative state were uncomfortable with candidates who were either from the Christian Right or very closely aligned with the movement. Perhaps the most apt comment after the primary came from former state GOP spokesman Mike Salster, who said that the Christian Right had been "spoiling for this fight for three years. . . . Now they have found their base, and it is 34 percent, not 50.1 percent" (Donald Baker 1996).

Despite some campaign pratfalls and heavy opposition spending, Senator Warner secured the endorsements of all of the eighteen newspapers that had made endorsements, including such reliably liberal editorial sources as the *Washington Post,* the *Norfolk Virginia Pilot,* and the *Fredericksburg Free-Lance Star.* He won reelection with 53 percent of the vote—a much closer contest than anyone had predicted—against a Democratic nominee who had spent over $10 million of his personal fortune in the campaign.

The exit polling data revealed that Christian conservatives did not sit out this election, as some had predicted, and that they overwhelmingly supported the senator's reelection. Fully 21 percent of the electorate were white self-described religious Right voters and they supported the senator by more than a three-to-one margin. The Christian Right comprised nearly 30 percent of the senator's overall vote total (CNN/*Time* Exit Poll).

The Christian Right did all it could to try to defeat the senator in the GOP primary and then ultimately supported him in the general election. The most telling example was the activity of the Christian Coalition. Although a January 1996 Christian Coalition scorecard gave the senator a 100 percent voting record for 1995, in June 1996 during the GOP primary the group's voter guide gave him a 20 percent rating (Miller received 100 percent). But then after the primary a new coalition guide gave the senator an 83 percent rating! The organization cleverly substituted issues on which to base its ratings according to the campaign and the group's preferred outcome. But for some of the congressional races, the coalition kept the issues the same for both the primary and the general election (Rozell and Wilcox 1997).

An Associated Press survey of the Virginia delegates to the Republican National Convention in 1996 showed the continued strength of the

Christian Right in the state party. Of the fifty-two delegates, forty eight responded to the survey. Among those, twenty-one responded that they considered themselves a part of the Christian social conservative movement, nineteen said "no," and eight chose "no answer." Among those who chose "no answer" were delegates Pat Robertson and Ralph Reed (O'Dell 1996). The delegation also included Farris, former National Right to Life spokesperson Kay Coles James, antiabortion leader Anne Kincaid, and Family Foundation (of the Focus on the Family) head Walter Barbee.

The Christian Right achieved most of its success through the continued support of the Allen administration. Until 1997, Virginia was the only state to refuse to accept federal education dollars through the Goals 2000 program. Christian Right groups lobbied hard for the governor to turn down the federal funds because of their belief that the money would force localities to accept nationally mandated values and standards and would therefore undermine educational choice. The governor launched a $300,000 "traditional values"-based series of advertisements to extol the importance of fatherhood. Called the "Virginia Fatherhood Campaign," the initiative was an outgrowth of the gubernatorial Commission on Citizen Empowerment. The governor supported initiatives in the state legislature to mandate parental notification on abortion for underage girls and to establish a new criminal category of "feticide" to declare the act of killing a fetus a murder. The former eventually gained approval. The latter failed.

The 1997 Elections

George Allen left the governorship very popular and with his political party in better shape than when he had been elected. The stage was set for continued GOP success with the uncontested nomination of Attorney General James Gilmore for governor. Gilmore's opponent was the incumbent two-term Democratic Lieutenant Governor Don Beyer. Although most analysts expected a close contest, Gilmore won a landslide victory with 56 percent of the vote.

Social issues were very visible in the campaign, although Gilmore could not easily be tagged a far-right extremist. Like Allen before him, Gilmore ran as a secular conservative but with strong backing from the Christian Right.

A media exit poll sponsored by the *Washington Post* and other sources attributed Gilmore's victory to the "family values" agenda. Interestingly, this conclusion was at odds with every other analysis that attributed Gilmore's victory solely to his appeal to eliminate Virginia's personal property tax, commonly called the "car tax." Virginians annually pay a tax of 4.5 percent of the assessed value of such items as automobiles and boats. Gilmore promised to rid the state of this hated tax, and numerous polls showed that voters flocked to his candidacy on the basis of that single-issue appeal.

Yet the *Post* reported the interesting finding that one-third of the electorate said that taxes was their leading issue, and one-third said that education was their leading issue. On the former, Gilmore picked up eight out of ten voters. On the latter, Beyer picked up an almost identical percentage of voters. About one in seven voters said they were most concerned about family values and moral decline. Those voters overwhelmingly went to Gilmore and provided him with the bulk of his margin of victory (Morin 1997).

The race for lieutenant governor in 1997 was much more typical than the high-profile 1993 campaign that had featured a strong social conservative. The GOP nominated a candidate who was controversial for other reasons. Former tobacco company executive John Hager had never held elective office, and he was an unrepentant promoter of tobacco interests as well as openly defensive of the industry's past efforts to alter the nicotine content in cigarettes. He also had a propensity to make off-the-cuff statements that were nothing short of embarrassing (Hsu 1997).[2] No one expected Hager to win in his race, but the more usual pattern in Virginia elections is for the lower-tier races to track closely with the gubernatorial results. Hager won strictly on coattails.

It is telling that whereas in 1993 state voters made the extraordinary step of substantially splitting their verdicts on the top two offices because of the controversial lieutenant governor nominee, they did not do the same in 1997. Both candidates lacked public office experience. Both had a history of making controversial and, to many, offensive statements. But only the Christian Right candidate was unacceptable to the electorate.

The most important story for the Christian Right in 1997 was the election of State Senator Mark Earley as attorney general. Before the general elections, Earley had to overcome three GOP opponents in a party primary, including Gil Davis, who was then the high-profile attorney for Paula Jones, the woman who sued President Clinton for sexual harassment.

While three GOP candidates ran mass media campaigns spending large sums on television advertising, Earley focused on lower-cost Christian radio and mass mailings. His campaign manager, Anne Kincaid, correctly told one of us several weeks before the primary that with strong Christian Right support in a predictably low-turnout primary, Earley would win easily. Kincaid's strategy was to keep a relatively low profile and to count on the social conservative base enthusiastically showing up at the precincts for Earley. The other three candidates focused on one another in their mass media advertising, opening the door for Earley. Less than 6 percent of eligible voters participated in the party primary, making the social conservative base the key to victory.

Although Earley ran as the social conservative candidate in the party primary, he did a masterly job at presenting himself to the general electorate as a mainstream conservative. In truth, his views on the social issues are not easily distinguishable from the views of Michael Farris and Oliver North. For example, Earley opposes abortion, even in the cases of rape and incest.

Yet the electorate did not consider him extreme, and many liberal-leaning editorial pages endorsed him. A key difference is that Earley lacked a controversial history like North's and he was not prone to sounding extreme, as did both North and Farris. Furthermore, Earley's involvement in social conservative activities was not with organizations such as the Moral Majority. Rather, he spent two years as a missionary in Manila.[3]

Like many social conservative candidates in the late 1990s, Earley did not emphasize social issues in his campaign. And when confronted with questions about his social issues views, he used moderate-sounding language. On abortion, not surprisingly, he emphasized the subissues of parental notification, parental consent, no late-term abortions, and no public funding for the procedure. He could credibly defend his views as moderate because of his ten-year record in the state senate: he sponsored and led the effort for the eventually successful parental notification requirement, a very popular position in the state, but he never introduced legislation to outlaw the procedure of abortion itself. When asked his views on the procedure generally, he merely responded that he respected current constitutional interpretation and had no plan as attorney general to challenge federal law in that area.

By focusing on certain popular restrictions on abortion and stating his intention not to attack abortion rights more generally, he made it difficult for opponents to characterize him as a threat. Democratic opponent Bill Dolan tried in vain to credibly link Earley to the extremist wing of the GOP. Dolan thought that he had the smoking gun to prove Earley's extremism when he learned of the GOP candidate's speech at a controversial pro-life rally called the "Field of Blood." A pro-life group placed hundreds of crosses on a Shenandoah Valley hillside to represent large numbers of abortions.

Dolan's campaign ran televised ads about Earley's participation at the event, and Earley responded with his own ad placing the onus on Dolan for negative campaigning and issue position distortion. Oddly, Dolan's campaign never rebutted Earley's characterizations, leaving the impression that Dolan perhaps had indeed embellished the story for political gain. According to Earley's media consultant, Dolan's support declined every day he ran that advertisement, and Earley ultimately carried 40 percent of self-described pro-choice voters (Johnson 1998). Dolan tried blasting Earley for accepting a $35,000 contribution from religious broadcaster Pat Robertson, but that tack failed as it had many times in the past when Democrats tried to link a GOP candidate to the extreme Right merely because of the source of a campaign contribution.

By the end of the campaign editorial pages were lambasting Dolan's campaign as excessively negative. The influential *Washington Post* four years earlier had enthusiastically endorsed Dolan in his first unsuccessful campaign for attorney general against Jim Gilmore. In 1997 the *Post* switched and supported GOP candidate Earley. The editorial ran on the Sunday before election day and strongly rebuked the tone and content of Dolan's campaign as undignified and inappropriate.

As of this writing in 1999, state political analysts portray Earley as the obvious front-runner for the GOP gubernatorial nomination in 2001. During his first year as attorney general Earley has identified himself with a number of mainstream issues, and he has not done anything to lend credibility to Dolan's campaign charge that he was "a stealth right-winger masquerading as a moderate" (Nakashima 1997).

Our earlier studies of the Christian Right in Virginia elections suggested that the movement fares best when it supports mainstream GOP candidates who back some, but not all, of the conservative social issues agenda. We noted as well that voters apparently are willing to make a distinction between GOP candidates who are from the Christian Right and those who merely are supported by the movement. In recent years voters in the state have consistently rejected Christian Right candidates and even candidates who aligned themselves closely with the movement by staking extreme social issues positions.

Gilmore and Hager clearly fit the model of GOP candidates backed by the Christian Right but not perceived as a part of the movement. Earley is a different kind of Christian Right candidate. He may, in a technical sense, be considered "from" the movement. But his reputation is very different from those of such socially conservative candidates as Oliver North and Michael Farris. Earley's record-breaking electoral victory suggests that a Christian Right candidate can be credible with secular voters in Virginia as long as he or she can claim a public record of distinction, rather than a record of social movement or even conservative movement activism. Earley's credible record of ten years' service in the state senate gave him the kind of mainstream credentials that neither Farris nor North could ever claim.

But perhaps most important is the lesson that a Christian Right nominee is electable statewide if he or she can credibly campaign as a broad-based coalition candidate with appeal beyond more typical ideological boundaries. Earley is unique among the Christian Right candidates we have encountered in our studies of the movement in Virginia Republican politics. He joined the NAACP in 1982, supported a state bill to mandate multicultural education in the public schools, and supported a bill to require nonunion employees to pay union dues or be fired. He attracted the endorsements of the state firefighters' union and immediate past president of the NAACP.

Earley continues to have critics who claim that he is hiding his truly extreme social issues views for now so that he can act on those views some day in the future as governor. The evidence to date suggests that Earley will run for governor as a mainstream conservative and that critics will once again have a most difficult time trying to characterize him as dangerously extreme.

Like the southern states generally, Virginia in recent years has become both more Republican and racially progressive. To those who see these dual trends as incompatible, Mark Earley's electoral success might give them some pause.

In 1999 the state became the first in the south since Reconstruction to achieve complete GOP control of the legislative and executive branches at the same time. Since the 1970s moderate Republicans in the state have decried the role of the Christian Right in the party and suggested that the movement is a hindrance to the GOP quest for majority status. Yet as the party achieved its longstanding goal of being the uncontested majority, the Christian Right also had its most substantial electoral achievement in the state and a credible chance at the governorship in the 2001 elections.

NOTES

1. Virginia State Board of Elections official results. Obtained by authors.
2. Hager mocked suburbanites in northern Virginia for, as he put it, getting "puckered up" over smoking and for their antipathy toward guns. In the 1970s he wrote company memoranda about experiments with enhancing nicotine levels in cigarettes. When the embarrassing internal memoranda were made public, he said he felt he knew what it was like to be raped. During the campaign he claimed that nicotine is not addictive.
3. To this day Earley maintains ties with the Filipino community in the United States. One of his campaign stops in 1997 was at a Filipino-American fund-raiser dinner at which Earley sang a traditional Filipino song in perfect dialect to the three hundred guests and handed out "Filipinos for Earley" bumper stickers (Nakashima 1997).

REFERENCES

Baker, Donald P. 1996. "With Warner's Victory, GOP's Right Wing Clipped for 3rd Time." *Washington Post,* 12 June, A8.

Baker, Peter. 1996. "Sen. Warner's Rising Lead Falls Short of Majority, Poll Finds." *Washington Post,* 18 April, B5.

Barone, Michael, and Grant Ujifusa. 1993. "Virginia." In *The Almanac of American Politics 1994,* 130–6. Washington, D.C.: The National Journal.

CNN/*Time* Exit Poll. 1996. Virginia U.S. Senate Race. Allpolitics.com

Cook, Elizabeth Adell, Ted G. Jelen, and Clyde Wilcox. 1994. "Issue Voting in Gubernatorial Elections: Abortion in Post-*Webster* Politics." *Journal of Politics* 56: 187–99.

Cox, Charles. 1985. "Baliles, Durette Dramatize Differences." *Richmond Times-Dispatch,* 3 November, C2, 6.

Green, John, C. 1995. Author interview by telephone. 17 January.

Green, John, Lyman Kellstedt, Corwin Smidt, and James Guth. 1998. "The Soul of the South: Religion and the New Electoral Order." In *The New Politics of the Old South,* edited by Charles S. Bullock, III and Mark J. Rozell, 261–76. Lanham, Md.: Rowman & Littlefield.

Hsu, Spencer, 1997. "In this Race, Issues Are Not at Issue." *Washington Post,* 22 October, B1, 8.

Johnson, Wayne. 1998. "Vote Earley—and Often." *Campaigns & Elections* (February): 42–45.

Key, V. O., Jr. 1949. *Southern Politics in State and Nation.* New York: Knopf.

Lee, Elizabeth. 1995. "Warner Tops Va. Poll." *Fairfax Journal,* 24 January, A1, 8.

Morin, Richard. 1997. "Family Values a Key to Result," *Washington Post,* 5 November, A1.

Nakashima, Ellen. 1997. "Republican Earley Breaks Tradition in Race Against Dolan." *Washington Post,* 21 October, B1, 4.

O'Dell, Larry. 1996. Author interview by telephone. 26 July.

Reed, Ralph. 1994. Author interview. Washington, D.C., 29 September.

Rozell, Mark J., and Clyde Wilcox. 1995. "Virginia: God, Guns and Oliver North." In *God at the Grass Roots: The Christian Right in the 1994 Elections,* edited by Mark J. Rozell and Clyde Wilcox, 109–31. Lanham, Md.: Rowman & Littlefield.

———. 1996. *Second Coming: The New Christian Right in Virginia Politics.* Baltimore: Johns Hopkins University Press.

———. 1997. "Virginia: When the Music Stops, Choose Your Faction." In *God at the Grass Roots, 1996: The Christian Right in American Elections,* edited by Mark J. Rozell and Clyde Wilcox, 99–114. Lanham, Md.: Rowman & Littlefield.

6

The Christian Right and the Republican Party in California: Necessarily Yoked

J. Christopher Soper and Joel Fetzer

After the midterm elections of 1994, the Christian Right in California was riding high. It had taken over the state Republican Party and helped to elect dozens of GOP candidates, and white evangelical voters, the core constituency of the Christian Right, represented nearly a quarter of all Republican votes in that election. Four years later, the Christian Right is being blamed for the GOP's worst electoral defeat in California in over forty years. Candidates closely affiliated with the Christian Right lost several races. Republicans were defeated in contests for governor, lieutenant governor, and the United States Senate, and the GOP lost seats in both the state senate and state assembly, both of which the Democrats control. How can a movement that had apparently achieved such prominence in 1994 have fallen so far in only four years?

The answer is that it hasn't. The Christian Right remains an important electoral faction within the state, but it is not and never has been a controlling one. When the movement has had a significantly pro-GOP impact, as it did in 1994, it has been because party candidates made overtures to Christian conservatives and thereby secured their support, but candidates also disguised the movement's prominence within the GOP. That election, in short, was the ideal example of the party's mobilizing its base by drawing sharp ideological divisions without alienating voters in the center. This politics of pragmatism worked because conservative Christians turned out in large numbers and voted for candidates who were in fact social-issue moderates within the party (Soper 1995). In 1998, by contrast, Democratic candidates effectively exposed the ties between the GOP and the Christian Right and exploited them successfully for their purposes. Fearful of too close an association with the Christian Right, Republican candidates tried to distance themselves from the movement, a tactic that in turn gave conservative Christians fewer reasons to participate in the election.

The difference in outcome between the elections masks a more significant similarity: the Christian Right and the Republican Party in California need each other. Absent a voice within the GOP, the Christian Right movement would have very little impact on the policy process. Without the active support of the Christian Right, the GOP cannot be the majority party in the state. Even in a bad election, such as 1998, conservative Christians are the most loyal constituency within the GOP, representing close to 20 percent of votes cast for Republican candidates. At the same time, however, an explicitly Christian Right Republican Party has no chance of winning statewide elections. California is not the most hospitable place for the Christian Right. The marriage between the GOP and the Christian Right is, therefore, not a perfect fit, but the party and the movement remain yoked together out of a mutual recognition of their need for each other.

The stakes for the Republican Party are very high in California. The state, already the most populous in the union, is certain to see its House delegation of fifty-two grow even larger after the census in the year 2000. Democratic control of the governor's mansion and both houses of the state legislature could have a dramatic impact on post-census legislative reapportionment that could shift the partisan balance of power in the U.S. House of Representatives. It is essential, therefore, that the Christian Right and the Republican Party find a way to live comfortably together in California, but the outcome of the 1998 midterm elections does not bode well for such an arrangement.

The Political Context

There are few states that have been as affected by Progressive political reforms as has California. Beginning at the turn of the century and continuing to the present, Californians have supported various political reforms that have weakened political parties and increased the opportunities for direct democracy. The most important Progressive legacies are the political primary election; the initiative, referendum, and recall votes; nonpartisan city elections; and the outlawing of preprimary endorsements by the parties. In a 1996 referendum, California voters further complicated the nomination process by adopting a blanket primary system, which was used for the first time in the 1998 party primary elections. From the standpoint of the Progressives, these reforms had the desired impact of sapping power from the political parties that were largely controlled by the railroads, Over time, however, these reforms have had the unintended consequence of strengthening the power of interest groups, which dominate the costly initiative campaigns, and fostering a politics of personality where candidates must raise substantial resources for elective office with little or no help from the parties (Gerston and Christenson 1995; Hyink and Provost 1998).

Democrats have had a substantial, though diminished, advantage in party registration over the Republicans for the past fifty years. The Democratic advantage over the Republicans among registered voters fell from 58 to 37 percent in 1950, 55 to 40 percent in 1970, and 46 to 35 percent in 1998. Democratic support is concentrated among racial minorities, urban voters, members of labor unions, and residents of Los Angeles and northern California. The Republican Party does best with white, older, more affluent voters, suburbanites, evangelical Christians, and residents of southern California, except Los Angeles. Republican voters are more dependable, which is one reason that GOP candidates win elections in California, but what is more important is that the link between parties and voters is weak in the state. The Progressive reforms have nurtured an electorate with a well-deserved reputation for political independence; crossover voting is common as the electorate rarely thinks or acts in party terms.

The Christian Right

As in other states, the impetus for Christian Right activism in California was a growing dissatisfaction among conservative Christians with the state's liberal social policies on abortion, gay rights, and religion in public schools. The religious convictions of conservative Christians provided them with clear priorities and policy stances and a well-integrated network of churches, television programs, and associations that made these voters relatively easy to mobilize. From a resource perspective, conservative Christians proved to be ideal for political activism as group leaders recruited members through sympathetic evangelical and fundamentalist churches (Gilbert 1993). Two significant groups emerged to challenge the state's liberal social policy: the Traditional Values Coalition (TVC) and the Christian Coalition. The TVC is the brainchild of the Reverend Lou Sheldon. Founded in 1981, the TVC claims a nationwide membership of one million, but its support is concentrated in California, where it has its national headquarters and where Sheldon has had a high profile on abortion and gay-rights issues for the past twenty years. Sheldon led the unsuccessful efforts to retain the state's antisodomy law in 1981 and to pass an initiative that would have prevented gay and lesbian people from teaching in public schools (Dunlop 1994). In 1998, the TVC aggressively opposed President Clinton's choice for ambassador to Luxembourg, James Hormel, who is gay, on the grounds that his confirmation would "advance a homosexual agenda." Prior to his hearings in the Senate, the TVC provided senators with copies of sexually explicit material from a gay-research center named for Mr. Hormel at the San Francisco Public Library (Shenon 1999).

The TVC is uncompromising in its social-issue conservatism; the voter guides it provided for the primary and general elections in 1998 focused exclusively on abortion, gay rights, and religion in public schools (Traditional Values Coalition 1998). Sheldon has said that the TVC will ask candidates if they have been faithful to their spouses and possibly put that information on the group's 2000 voter guides (Baum 1999). Though the group is small, it is a significant player in state politics, particularly within the Republican Party. This prominence was apparent in 1998 when Matt Fong, the GOP Senate candidate, donated $50,000 to the group prior to the party's primary election. Fong's donation gave the impression that he was trying to win Sheldon's endorsement for the political primary, but, as we will show later, the contribution caused considerable difficulty for Fong in the general election when he tried to portray himself as a social moderate.

The Christian Coalition has been active in California since shortly after Pat Robertson founded the group in 1989. The group has proved adept at establishing a network of grassroots support and mobilizing members for political activism at the state and local levels. The Coalition is the most significant Christian Right organization within the state, with a membership of several hundred thousand and forty local chapters. In the early 1990s, the Christian Coalition ran candidates closely affiliated with the movement in Republican primary elections. These candidates fared poorly, however, and the Coalition adopted a more pragmatic political approach to gain access to the party and policy process. In 1994, for example, the group supported dozens of "stealth" candidates who minimized their formal ties to the Coalition. The group also stressed a wider variety of conservative issues than the Traditional Values Coalition; the Coalition voter guides for 1998 included such issues as support for a balanced budget amendment and a flat-rate federal income tax. In addition, the Coalition all but endorsed socially moderate Republican candidates like Pete Wilson in his successful gubernatorial reelection bid in 1994, and Matt Fong in his unsuccessful campaign for the United States Senate in 1998. The Coalition is a powerful, though not dominant, movement in the state. In 1998 it distributed 4 million voter guides at sympathetic churches throughout the state.

Leaders of the Christian Coalition and the Traditional Values Coalition claim to be nonpartisan, but both organizations were instrumental in forging stronger links between the Christian Right and the Republican

Party in the early 1990s. California provided a paradoxical place for the Christian Right as it organized through the Republican Party, offering both opportunities and limitations to the movement's effectiveness. Weak political parties and a strong tradition of citizen movements allowed the Christian Right to have a dramatic impact on state party politics. Christian conservatives committed time and resources, and they turned out for party leadership elections to county and state committees to which few party members pay attention. By 1993 conservative Christians controlled thirty-eight of the fifty-eight county GOP central committees and were effectively in charge of a state Republican party that was, until the past decade, socially moderate (Nollinger 1993). When he was governor, for example, Ronald Reagan signed a landmark permissive abortion bill that was pushed through the assembly by Republicans in 1967 (Cannon 1998b).

The Christian Right's greatest impact has come in moving the party's caucus in the state assembly and senate in a more socially conservative direction. They accomplished this by mobilizing conservative Christians for Republican Party primary elections and by providing candidates with financial resources for an effective campaign. The Allied Business PAC, a political action committee formed in 1991 by four wealthy businessmen with close ties to the Christian Right, spent $9 million dollars from 1992 to 1997 for Republican Party candidates in state and local races (Bailey and Warren 1998). Allied sought candidates who supported the group's fiscally and socially conservative ideals. Candidates responded by adopting a more conservative platform on abortion, gay rights, and related "family values" issues. One of the group's founders, Rob Hurtt, won a seat in the state senate and became the minority leader in 1994 (Morain and Ingram 1995).

The Christian Right was the dominant force in the state party by 1993, but they could do little with it. Because it was weak, the state party had few of the resources that candidates needed and none of the sanctions that they feared. "Control" of the party, therefore, yielded very little policy influence for the Christian Right. GOP elected officials distanced themselves from the party apparatus when they wished; annual party conventions in the mid-1990s became a public feud between Christian Right activists and the socially moderate Pete Wilson. Wilson, recognizing the difficulty of pro-life candidates' winning statewide elections, urged the party to adopt a modified pro-choice position on abortion. Though he did appeal to evangelical voters in 1994 with more conservative positions on gay rights, Wilson accomplished few of the policy objectives of the Christian Right movement during his eight years in office.

The Christian Right also had little power to shape the issues debated within a given election. There is no state in the union where elections are more candidate centered than California; more often than not the Christian Right found itself responding to a set of issues defined for it by candidates or the media. Pete Wilson, for example, consistently used divisive wedge issues for his political purposes. The most notorious examples came in 1994 when he linked his reelection bid to support for Proposition 187, a referendum that called for cutting off undocumented immigrants' access to most public services, and in 1996 when he and the GOP supported an anti-affirmative action measure, Proposition 209. Wilson easily won reelection in 1994, and both propositions passed with the endorsement of Christian Right organizations. In the long term, however, the initiatives have proved disastrous for the GOP and the Christian Right. Proposition 187 mobilized the growing Latino population into the Democratic Party, while Proposition 209 further alienated African Americans from the Republican Party. Christian Right support for both initiatives has limited the movement's capacity to expand its base outside the white community (Fetzer and Soper 1997).

California's political culture has also provided a significant obstacle to the influence of the Christian Right. Though there are pockets of religious conservatism in California, in general the state is secular and moderate on the social issues of abortion and gay rights. A 1998 preelection survey found that 59 percent of Californians favored the Supreme Court's decision in *Roe v. Wade* strongly or somewhat strongly, while only 28 percent opposed the court's decision (*Los Angeles Times* 1998a).[1] The same poll showed, however, that a majority supported a ban on late-term abortions and a parental consent requirement for minors seeking an abortion. According to a 1993 poll, 21 percent of Californians could be categorized as part of the Christian Right—people who are both religiously and politically conservative. A much larger 54 percent, however, are secularists—people who are not religious or are not religiously active (California Opinion Index 1993). Even at the height of the Christian Right's ascendancy, the 1994 midterm elections, conservatives were a minority of the state's electorate. According to exit polls for that election, 29 percent of voters described themselves as conservative or very conservative, 17 percent as liberal, and 46 percent as moderate. The percentage of self-described conservatives and liberals increased in the 1998 midterm election, to 34 percent and 23 percent, respectively, but moderates were still the largest group at 43 percent (*Los Angeles Times* 1998b). The state may not be as liberal as is often assumed in the media, but it is not as conservative as it would need to be for the Christian Right to be a dominant electoral force. The winning formula for elections in California was and is to be found in the ideological center, which was not where the Christian Right and the Republican Party had positioned themselves for the 1998 elections.

The 1998 Elections

The Gubernatorial Election

The challengers for the 1998 gubernatorial race, Democratic Lieutenant Governor Gray Davis and Republican Attorney General Dan Lungren, were political veterans who had contemplated this run for years. Almost no one, however, predicted that Davis would win his party's nomination. His primary opponents, Al Checci and Jane Harman, spent $40 and $14 million, respectively, in the race, while Davis had trouble raising $9 million. In a state where candidates rely almost exclusively on paid television advertisements to reach the voters, it seemed impossible that Davis would be able to win the race. This was a year, however, when California voters preferred experienced candidates, a sentiment that Davis tapped into with his slogan "experience money can't buy." Davis also benefited from local television coverage of the campaign that focused more attention on the amount of money Checci and Harman spent than on specific issues they proposed. Davis easily won the Democratic primary. Lungren, in contrast to Davis, ran unopposed in the Republican Party primary. In a sign of his potential weakness, however, he failed to receive as many votes as Davis in the state's first-ever blanket primary.

Lungren was, in many respects, an ideal candidate for the Christian Right. As a member of Congress in the early 1980s, he coauthored the abortion-banning Human Life Amendment, and as the state's attorney general, he supported a 1993 ballot initiative that would have allowed parents to use taxpayer-financed vouchers to pay private school tuition, including for religious schools. More than 70 percent of California's voters rejected the initiative. During the gubernatorial campaign, Lungren made no secret of his support for vouchers and his opposition to abortion. He asserted that vouchers would "save the public school system," and he defended his pro-life position on religious grounds, stating in one of the debates that he was taking a "mainstream traditional Catholic approach to the issue" (Weintraub and Katches 1998). Though his views on these issues were consistent with those of the Christian Right, they were not in sync with those of the state's electorate. In the campaign, Davis marginalized Lungren as too conservative for most California voters on such issues as abortion, education, gun control, and the environment while portraying himself as the ideological centrist (Brownstein 1998a).

Not surprisingly, Lungren did very well among Christian conservative voters, besting Davis by a margin of 87 to 13 percent. Conservative Christians, however, constituted only 7.6 percent of all voters in this election.[2] In addition, Lungren's cues to Christian conservatives likely had the effect of moving the sizable secular vote toward Gray Davis. Voters with no religion represented 16 percent of the electorate, and they supported Davis by a 77 to 23 percent margin. Even more significant is the support Davis garnered among self-described moderates. While 69 percent of "middle of the road" voters chose Davis, only 28 percent supported Lungren. These voters constituted 43 percent of the total electorate. Davis ended up defeating Lungren by a margin of 58 to 38 percent to become the first Democratic governor in the state of California in sixteen years.

A final feature of this race worth considering is the Latino vote. Latinos represent 30 percent of California's population, and they are the fastest-growing ethnic group in the state. They had not, however, been very politically active in the past or so predictably Democratic in party affiliation or voting. Wilson's support for Proposition 187 in 1994, however, changed all that. This classic wedge issue proved effective for Wilson in the short run as it mobilized his base and divided Democrats, but the longer-term impact has been to reinforce an anti-immigrant, racist image of the Republican party among Latinos. Proposition 187 also mobilized this growing part of the electorate like no other issue before it; the Latino percentage of the electorate increased from 8 percent in 1994 to 13 percent in 1998 (Block 1998). To cement the relationship between Lungren and Wilson, Spanish stations broadcast Democratic commercials showing the two joining hands in a victory celebration. A mailing from the Democratic Party urged voters to "send Wilson and Lungren a message: We haven't forgotten what you did" (Tobar 1998). In what might be proof of the biblical adage that the sins of the father are visited upon the sons, Latinos supported Davis by a margin of 71 to 29 percent.

The United States Senate Election

That Barbara Boxer won reelection by a 53 to 43 percent margin in the 1998 Senate election was surprising; that she did so by convincing the voters that she was the ideological moderate and her opponent, Matt Fong, the extremist is astounding. Her victory says much about the problems facing the Christian Right in California.

Boxer ran virtually unopposed in the Democratic Party primary, and she made a strategic decision to spend very little money during the primary or the early part of the general election. Fong, by contrast, had a competitive primary campaign against car-alarm magnate Darrell Issa that left Fong penniless at the start of the general election. Though outspent by his primary opponent, Fong benefited from an electorate that favored experienced candidates over political outsiders and from the state's first-ever blanket primary, which allowed Democrats, independents, and third-party affiliates to vote for Republicans. According to exit polls, Fong did particularly well among Democrats and independents, a fact that should have helped him during the general election.

By all accounts, this ought to have been a highly competitive race. Fong led Boxer in the polls taken directly after the primary election. The *National Journal* had pegged Boxer as the most liberal member of the U.S. Senate, which was probably true. A one-term Senator, Boxer was a very controversial figure in California because her views on abortion, gay rights, health care, and other social issues were more liberal than those of the state's electorate. According to a poll taken in September, a third of likely voters had an unfavorable impression of Boxer, compared with just 14 percent who viewed Fong unfavorably. Although she had urged the Senate to have a public hearing on the sexual harassment charges against then-Senator Bob Packwood, Boxer said almost nothing about President Clinton's moral problems. The rhetorical high point for Fong's campaign came during one of the televised debates when he described Boxer's silence on the issue as "deafening."

Fong, by contrast, seemed the ideal Republican candidate. He was a member of a well-known and respected Democratic political family, an Asian American who could blunt Democratic charges that the Republican Party was unsympathetic to racial minorities, and a social-issue moderate who could presumably appeal to the state's political independents and moderates who control election outcomes. Fong favored keeping first-trimester abortions legal but opposed funding and late-term abortions. He opposed a law allowing benefits for domestic partners but supported a ban on discrimination against gays and lesbians in housing and employment. He also said he would vote to confirm the nomination of James Hormel for the ambassadorship to Luxembourg. His views on social issues were closer than his Democratic opponent's to those of the electorate as a whole, and Fong, it seemed, simply needed to remind the voters what they disliked about Boxer in order to win the race (Perry 1998).

To shore up his support with conservative Christians in the party, however, Fong contributed $50,000 to the Traditional Values Coalition before the GOP primary. This helped to secure Sheldon's endorsement for the socially moderate Fong when he was locked in a close primary battle, but it become an albatross that Boxer hung around his neck during the general election. When news of the contribution leaked in October, gay Republicans threatened to rescind their endorsement of Fong. The angry response from GOP gays and lesbians prompted Fong to sign a written pledge to support the California Log Cabin Republicans on a wide range of issues (Marinucci and Wildermuth 1998). This in turn angered conservative Christians within the party. As one member of the California Christian Coalition indicated in a letter on the group's Web page, "I'm getting a lot of mail on Fong, most asking why you would ever vote for him" (Christian Coalition of California 1998).

Despite this debate within the Christian Right, the Christian Coalition tailored its voters guides to present Fong and Boxer as further apart on abortion and gay rights than they actually were (Christian Coalition 1998). The group's 1998 guides gave the candidates' views on partial-birth abortion and homosexual adoption of children. This indicated a real difference between Fong and Boxer on these moral issues. The candidates would have appeared identical on these issues, however, had the coalition offered their positions supporting first-trimester abortions and the confirmation of James Hormel as ambassador to Luxembourg. As in 1994 and 1996, the coalition supported socially moderate candidates under the pragmatic assumption that the Christian Right would benefit in the long run with the Republican Party in power. Christian conservatives appeared to have shared that view, voting for Fong over Boxer by a margin of 88 to 12 percent.

The controversy over Fong's contribution to the TVC provided Boxer with a convenient way to portray Fong as a social-issue conservative, which she needed to do to secure support among moderate voters. Because she had a significant financial edge over Fong, Boxer dominated the only medium that matters in California politics, television, and she skillfully portrayed her opponent as an extremist on abortion, gun control, gay rights, and the environment (Warren 1998). Fong never effectively countered her charges. Boxer converted what ought to have been a political liability—her own very liberal record on social issues—into a political windfall. According to a *Los Angeles Times* exit poll, the strategy worked as Boxer carried the moderate vote on election day by a margin of 64 to 33 percent. A majority of voters who focused on social and moral issues also supported Boxer. According to the exit polls, 17 percent of the voters indicated that abortion was one of the most important issues in deciding their vote. Boxer took 60 percent of those votes. Thirty percent of those polled said that a major influence in their vote was that the candidate "shared their moral and ethical values." Boxer won 54 percent of those votes.

These results are significant because in past elections moral issues have been clear winners for Republican candidates. On abortion, for example, the electorate was pro-choice in 1994 and 1996, but pro-life voters were far more likely to base their decision on that issue. This meant that Republican candidates could secure Christian-conservative support with a modified pro-life position without having to fear a mobilization of pro-choice voters against them. In 1998, by contrast, moral issues benefited Boxer as she defined herself as the ideological moderate and her Republican opponent as the extremist. Fong suffered from a decline in conservative voting and from his inability to sell his social-issue moderation to moderate voters. The race demonstrates that social-issue conservatism, even if it is more real than imagined—as in the case of Matt Fong—is an electoral liability in statewide races in California.

The United States House Races

If the U.S. Senate election illustrated what happens when conservative Christians back a social moderate, two closely watched U.S. House races demonstrated the ineffectiveness of Christian Right support for social conservatives. In particular, these races showed how the Christian Right can get its favorite candidate nominated in the primary but thereby torpedo the GOP's chances in the general election.

In District 22 (Santa Barbara/San Luis Obispo), state and national Christian Right forces managed to deliver the GOP nomination to conservative Tom Bordonaro in the first round of the special election after having overwhelmed Brooks Firestone, the socially moderate favorite of establishment Republicans. Following Democrat incumbent Walter Capps's death in the middle of his first term, officials called a special election for January of 1998 to fill his vacated seat. Democrats in the district quickly rallied around his widow, Lois Capps, as their nominee, but Republicans endured a bloody contest between Firestone and Bordonaro in the first round of a special election. Endorsed by such GOP leaders as Gerald Ford and Newt Gingrich (Purdham 1998), the pro-choice Firestone hoped to beat Capps by appealing to the ideological center in this historically Republican district. Instead, Firestone fell victim to a devastating series of television ads targeting his alleged position on partial-birth abortions. Funded and directed by the "Campaign for Working Families" (Bathen 1998), a political action committee affiliated with Gary Bauer's Family Research Council, the ads appear to have influenced socially conservative GOP voters to shift their support to Bordonaro (Dionne 1998).

Come the runoff election in March, however, Bordonaro proved incapable of beating Capps despite favorable advertising by Bauer's group and the Christian Coalition. In the end, Capps appears to have received not only the votes of Democrats but also as many as two in five of Firestone's first-round voters. Such socially moderate Republicans seem to have deserted their party's "extremist" candidate in favor of the more "mainstream" Democrat (Cannon 1998a). Bordonaro repeated his poor performance against Capps in June's blanket primary and November's regular election, garnering 41 and 44 percent of the vote, respectively ("'98 Election: Congress" 1998a; "'98 Election: Congress" 1998b).

Despite Bauer's characterization of his PAC's role in the special election as a "net plus" for conservativism, a conservative Christian should take little comfort in the results. Rather, this contest suggests that the type of pro-life, socially conservative candidate favored by the Christian Right is simply unelectable in many parts of the state. Or as Democratic Representative Martin Frost of Texas argued about this and similar races, "Republicans are following a path that will lead to their own destruction" (Cannon 1998a).

The story in Garden Grove (District 46) was much the same, only more so. Site of the vicious 1996 battle between Latina neophyte Loretta Sanchez and conservative firebrand Bob Dornan, this district witnessed a second clash between these combatants in 1998. Like Lois Capps, Sanchez was assured of the Democratic nomination. Establishment Republicans, on the other hand, probably would have preferred anyone but Dornan as their nominee. They feared—rightly—that he would further alienate Latinos from the Republican Party, lose to Sanchez in the general election, and end up bringing down other GOP candidates running in overlapping districts. Republican leaders from the Lincoln Club of Orange County therefore asked Dornan not to run and instead backed Lisa Hughes, a moderately pro-choice attorney who chaired the State Lottery Commission. Ardent pro-lifer "B-1 Bob" was not to be dissuaded, however, launching a roughly $1.5 million primary campaign against Hughes and his two other Republican rivals ("'98 Election: Congress" 1998a, 46; Mecoy 1998). Such Christian Right PACs as the Campaign for Working Families, Eagle Forum, California Right to Life, Republican Coalition for Life, and the Pro-Life PAC of Orange County also bypassed the three other GOP contenders and donated at least $14,800 to Dornan just before the primary (Federal Election Commission 1998a, 1998b, 1998c, and 1998d). In the end, Dornan's name recognition and conservative PAC money paid off, netting him 49 percent of Republican primary votes versus Hughes's 27 percent ("'98 Election: Congress" 1998a, 46).

Yet as in the Capps-Bordonaro race, the Republican nominee could not beat the Democratic incumbent in the general election. Had nothing changed since their 1996 matchup, Sanchez might still have outpolled Dornan in 1998. In the intervening two years, however, Dornan had been busy committing political suicide in this majority immigrant district by antagonizing Latinos. First, he persuaded his former GOP colleagues in the House to investigate his charge that voter fraud by noncitizens had cost him his seat in 1996. Though some about-to-be-officially-naturalized immigrants did vote in that election, even the Republican-controlled House eventually concluded that Dornan would have lost anyway (Mecoy 1998). Second, he proposed that "election observers" be posted outside polling places, presumably to ensure that only U.S. citizens were allowed to vote. Third, Dornan carried out an outrageously insensitive campaign to win back Latinos from Sanchez. Latino business and community leaders were not amused when he showed up uninvited at a private Cinco de Mayo celebration. Dornan also took to spicing up his talks with bits of mangled Spanish, sporting a wristwatch with a picture of the Virgen de Guadalupe (a Mexican saint), and claiming his "pro-family" views made him the "only true Latino" in the race. But what most outraged Latino voters was a Dornan campaign flyer that juxtaposed an image of the revered *Virgen* with illustrations of partial-birth abortions. "I threw it in the trash immediately," said one Chilean American from Santa Ana (Associated Press 1998; "'98 Election: Congress" 1998a, 46; Roll Call 1998; Schrader 1998a). On election day the Forty-Sixth District voiced its disapproval of such tactics, giving Sanchez 56 percent of the vote to Dornan's 39 percent ("'98 Election: Congress" 1998b, 23–24). Even the previously loyal Vietnamese American population seems to have deserted Dornan in 1998, perhaps viewing his attacks on Latinos as implicating Asian immigrants as well (Schrader 1998b).

The political dynamics of this race do not lack irony. In 1994 the Christian Right adopted the pragmatic strategy of backing Pete Wilson, a moderate on abortion and gay rights, and thus at least tolerated his attacks on immigrants (Soper 1995). It remains a very open question just how upset conservative Christians were at his anti-immigrant campaign; white evangelicals in the United States and California have certainly had their nativist streak.[3] But at any rate, the state's Christian Coalition had never made immigration a key issue. After Wilson's impressive reelection victory, however, conservative Christians could be forgiven for believing that immigrant bashing pays at the polls. Yet in 1998, the Christian Right's support of Dornan—despite or even partly because of his reputation as a nativist—led to electoral catastrophe.

State Assembly and State Senate Races

Republican defeats in the gubernatorial, House, and Senate races overshadowed what was an even more disastrous outcome for the party in the state assembly and senate. The Democrats increased their majority over the Republicans by five seats in the assembly to a comfortable 48–32 margin, and by two seats in the senate for an equally imposing 25–15 advantage. The most noteworthy defeats for the GOP came at the expense of two incumbents closely affiliated with the Christian Right: Rob Hurtt and Jim Morrisey. A well-known evangelical Christian, Hurtt was a cofounder of the powerful Allied Business PAC, a big-money backer of conservative candidates, and a former GOP minority leader. Morrisey had a solidly conservative voting record on social and moral issues. Unfortunately for Hurtt and Morrisey, their districts overlapped with the 46th Congressional District. Dornan's decision to run against Sanchez in that contest made it difficult for the Republican incumbents as it galvanized the Latino population against Dornan, who has a well-deserved anti-Latino reputation. Hurtt and Morrisey got caught in the crossfire.

Their efforts to distance themselves from Dornan did not succeed, and the newly mobilized Latino voters supported Democratic candidates up and down the ticket (Bailey 1998).

The biggest impact of the Republican defeats in the state assembly and senate will come after the 2000 census. With a Democratic governor and comfortable margins in both of the state houses, the Democratic Party will dominate the politically significant redistricting battle in California. California is almost certain to gain seats after the census is taken, increasing from fifty-two to perhaps as many as fifty-four or fifty-five congressional seats. The influence that the Democratic Party will have in redistricting the state could affect the national balance of congressional power.

Exit Poll Analysis

As in previous years, belonging to the Christian Right dramatically increased one's chances of voting for a Republican candidate. And as in 1996, this pro-GOP influence remains robust after statistically correcting for the effects of education, income, gender, ethnicity, and age (see table 6.1).[4] The logistic regression coefficients in the first column of table 6.1 indicate, for instance, that a forty-year-old, white, non-Christian Right Protestant woman who holds a bachelor's degree and receives a household income of $35,000 per year would have a 34 percent chance of voting for Dan Lungren. If this hypothetical voter were the same on all characteristics except that she belonged to the Christian Right, however, her likelihood of casting a ballot for Lungren[5] would more than double to 83 percent. Even if a member of the Christian Right had the most pro-Democratic demographic characteristics possible (i.e., was twenty-five-years-old, white,[6] and female with a graduate degree and household income less than $20,000 per year), her probability of voting for Lungren would fall only to 73 percent. Or in other words, simply knowing that a person belongs to the Christian Right allows us to predict with at least 73 percent accuracy that she or he will vote for the GOP gubernatorial candidate. No other variable in table 6.1 can boast such impressive predictive power.

Prospects for the Future of the Christian Right in California

Conventional wisdom has it that one of two things will happen in the relationship between the Republican Party and the Christian Right in California. One scenario is that the GOP, to become more competitive in a state that is liberal on traditional social values, will abandon its ties to the

Table 6.1 Determinants of Gubernatorial, U.S. Senate, and
U.S. House Vote

	GOP Gubernatorial Vote	GOP Senate Vote	GOP House Vote
Independent Variables			
Christian Right	2.213**	2.062**	1.982**
Catholic	−.092	−.218**	−.264**
Jewish	−1.600**	−1.481**	−1.604**
Other religion	−.915**	−1.095**	−.783**
Secularist	−.961**	−1.076**	−1.045**
Education	−.082	−.026	−.063*
Income	.182**	.165**	.184**
Female	−.273**	−.408**	−.358**
African American	−1.585**	−1.368**	−1.882**
Latino	−.984**	−1.032**	−1.154**
Asian	−.133	.292	−.375*
Other race	−.096	−.082	−.129
Under age 30	−.214	−.106	−.148
Over age 64	.215*	.261**	.233*
Constant	−.414*	−.271	−.210
Model Statistics			
Sample size (N)	2810	2815	2631
Percentage correctly predicted	69.6	67.6	68.4
χ^2	526.0***	529.6***	524.4***
Degrees of freedom	14	14	14
Pseudo R^2	.158	.158	.166

NOTE: Data from *Los Angeles Times* 1998 exit poll. Estimates obtained by dichotomous logistic regression. Pseudo R^2 calculated according to Aldrich and Nelson (1984, 56–57). Education and income both range from 1 to 6. See note 2 for operationalization of the Christian Right variable. Cases with missing data deleted listwise.
*p <.10, two-tailed test
**p <.05, two-tailed test
***p <.05, one-tailed test

Christian Right (Jeffe 1998). As we have noted in our review of the 1998 election, there is some logic to this argument. The Republican Party got clobbered among moderate voters, who are the largest percentage of the state's electorate, and it is reasonable to assume that the GOP will move to the ideological center on abortion and gay rights. A clean break between the GOP and the Christian Right, however, is simply not going to happen. It is unthinkable that the state party, which conservative Christians ostensibly control, would support a dramatic change in the party's plank on abortion and gay rights. What is more important, conservative Christian voters provide considerable resources for the party and its candidates, and they represented close to 20 percent of the voters cast for party candidates in the 1998 election. A clean break with the Christian Right would further solidify the Republican Party's minority status in the state.

At the other extreme, a second possibility is that evangelicals will quit the GOP. The leading interpretation among Christian Right leaders for the party's dismal showing in 1998 is that the GOP failed to mobilize its religious base because it did not stress conservative social issues in the campaign (Brownstein 1998b). Indeed, while in 1996 self-identified born-again Christians in the United States were five percentage points *more* likely to vote than the average voting-age citizen, two years later they were two percentage points *less* likely to participate than the typical voting-eligible American.[7] It is a stretch to say that conservative Christians have received much from the GOP for their electoral loyalty over the past decade, and it is possible that the Christian Right movement could in the future run its own candidates in Republican Party primaries or even bolt entirely from the party. The implicit threat behind Gary Bauer's decision to run for the GOP presidential nomination is that he intends to leave the Republican Party if it does not remain faithful to its conservative platform on traditional social issues. This is, however, an empty threat. Minnesota's election of Jesse "The Body" Ventura notwithstanding, third-party movements stand almost no chance of gaining a foothold in the American two-party system, and this strategy assumes that the core of the Christian Right movement—white evangelical Christians—would leave the GOP because it was not conservative enough on social issues. This political divorce is hard to imagine, however, given the extent to which conservative Christians are mobilized into the Republican Party.

The 1998 electoral outcome in California points instead to a less dramatic future for the Republican Party and the Christian Right: a tenuous balance between them. The movement and the party are necessarily yoked, and though it is not always a marriage made in heaven—for either partner—it beats the alternatives. What is most likely is that the Republican Party, taking a page from the Democrats, will emphasize those social-issue positions that are popular both with their conservative Christian base and among moderates. California, for example, is pro-choice, but a majority of Californians favor a ban on partial-birth abortions. The party is not likely to nominate an unabashedly pro-life candidate for statewide office, but candidates will certainly support a ban on late-term abortions and will oppose government funding for them.

The state is generally liberal on gay rights, but Californians oppose the legalization of gay marriages and homosexual adoption of children. That California will have a referendum against gay marriages on its ballot in 2000 will likely help GOP candidates show their fidelity to conservative moral principles without alienating moderates. It could well become an ideal wedge issue for the GOP in 2000. There is, in short, room for a balance on moral issues if the right kinds of issues predominate in a given election.

Efforts by the GOP to nominate more moderate candidates should get a boost from the state's adoption of a blanket primary, which favors candidates who can make appeals to a broad electorate (Cannon 1998b). Finally, leaders of the Christian Right have demonstrated that they are essentially pragmatic. Both the Christian Coalition and the Traditional Values Coalition have supported socially moderate Republican candidates in the past, and there is no reason to think that they will not in the future. Whether or not this is a sell-out of the movement's original purposes is debatable, but the fact remains that when faced with the choice between what is, from their perspective, a less-than-ideal Republican and a perfectly awful Democrat, conservative Christians select the former. A person writing on the Web page for the Christian Coalition of California indicated just this attitude: "Christians should band together and vote for the candidate that makes the most sense, and not divide our votes while the worst possible candidate gains the advantage" (Christian Coalition of California 1998). What is harder to predict is whether or not socially moderate party candidates will excite conservative Christians sufficiently that they will turn out in large numbers.

Finally, one of the most fascinating future developments in religion and politics in the state will be the political evolution of Latino evangelicals. Typically conservative on social issues such as homosexuality but liberal on economics and the rights of ethnic minorities, today's *evangélicos* appear to vote as disproportionately Democratic as their Catholic cousins. One first-generation Salvadoran American[8] interviewed at a Pentecostal-oriented, Spanish-speaking church in Los Angeles explained that he had voted for Gray Davis so as not to reward the Republicans for their dirty methods of electioneering. The U.S. resident of twenty years also preferred many of Davis's policies, such as his stand on bilingual education. Though this Latino Pentecostal was not dead-set against voting for a Republican candidate in the future (and actually was fond of Ronald Reagan), he did not see himself supporting the GOP unless it adopted "more just" positions on immigration and welfare reform. Given the extent to which the state's Republicans have shown themselves hostile to immigrants and welfare recipients, however, such a kinder, gentler GOP is not likely to appear anytime soon. Nor do the Golden State's Republicans enjoy a reputation for being more successful than Democrats in solving the problems that mattered most to our informant: violence, unemployment, and dysfunctional schools. For at least the medium term, then, California's Latinos—whether Protestant or Catholic—are likely to remain solidly in the Democratic fold. Since Latinos are a growing part of California's electorate, this alliance does not bode well for the GOP or the Christian Right.

NOTES

1. The data analyzed in this chapter were collected by the *Los Angles Times* and distributed by the Roper Center of Storrs, Connecticut. Responsibility for the analysis and interpretations in this work nonetheless rests solely with the authors.
2. We defined "Christian Right" respondents as Protestant or "other Christian" (often a euphemism for evangelical) whites who viewed "morality and family issues" as one of the two most important factors in deciding whom to choose as governor. Though strictly religious criteria (e.g., being a Protestant Christian who claimed to have been "born again") would have been preferable, the *Los Angeles Times* did not ask a "born-again" or equivalent question in its 1998 exit poll. The base category for the series of religious dummy variables in table 6.1, then, consists of Protestant or other Christians who are not white and/or who did not view morality and family issues as one of the two most important factors in the gubernatorial race. In other words, the base category consists by and large of ethnic and mainline Protestants.
3. Though recently the National Association of Evangelicals has tended to favor immigrant rights (1993, 1995), in the 1950s and 1960s it endorsed the racist national-origin quota system (1957, 1965). In California, the late immigration activist Harold Ezell "made a personal commitment to the Lord as a young boy" yet coauthored Proposition 187 and argued that undocumented immigrants should be "caught, skinned and fried" (Ezell 1986; Pignatora 1998). And though the Christian Coalition took no official position on the initiative (a nonaction that angered many Latino evangelicals), the group's president reported that "most of our members were definitely in support of it (Zipperer 1995).
4. Although students of voting behavior often control for partisan identification as well, we chose not to in table 6.1 because we view partisanship as primarily an intervening variable between the vote and more arguably exogenous regressors such as religion, gender, and income.
5. The pro-GOP effect of belonging to the Christian Right was only slightly less powerful in determining the vote for U.S. Senate and House candidates. In the Senate race, our hypothetical non-Christian Right Protestant would have a 39 percent chance of voting for Fong (the GOP standard-bearer), while her otherwise identical Christian Right col-

league would have an 83 percent probability of doing so. Corresponding figures for the House election differ only trivially from the Senate results (39 percent and 82 percent, respectively).
6. In principle, ethnic minorities may belong to the Christian Right. Given our data-induced definition of its members (see note 2 above), however, the models in table 6.1 do not allow Christian Right voters to be non-white.
7. Calculations are based on analysis of the full 1998 American National Election Study (postelection sample) and of the cross-sectional segment of the 1996 American National Election Study (pre- and postelection sample). These data were collected by the Center for Political Studies at the University of Michigan and distributed by the Interuniversity Consortium for Political and Social Research of Ann Arbor, Michigan. Neither the collectors nor the distributors of these surveys bear any responsibility for the analysis and interpretation in this chapter.
8. Though probably most Latino evangelicals in California are ethnic Central Americans (e.g., Guatemalan, Salvadoran, or Honduran Americans), a few are Chicanos or even Peruvian Americans.

REFERENCES

Aldrich, John H., and Forrest D. Nelson. 1984. *Linear Probability, Logit, and Probit Models.* Newbury Park, Calif.: Sage Publications.
Associated Press. 1998. "Candidates Want Voters to Know They Are Best Catholic for Job." State and Local Wire, 28 October.
Bailey, Eric. 1998. "Hurtt, Morrisey Seek Distance from Dornan." *Los Angeles Times,* 16 August, B1.
Bailey, Eric, and Peter M. Warren. 1998. "Power PAC Steps out of Spotlight." *Los Angeles Times,* 15 June, A3.
Bathen, Sigrid. 1998. "The Politics of Abortion." *California Journal,* April, 22–23.
Baum, Geraldine. 1999. "Appetite for Political Scandal Altering Political Menu." *Los Angeles Times,* 10 January, A1.
Block, A. G. 1998. "The Wilson Legacy." *California Journal,* November, 6–10.
Brownstein, Ronald. 1998a. "Davis Appears to be Making Right Move by Shifting Issues to the Center." *Los Angeles Times,* 19 October, A5.
———. 1998b. "Republicans to Face Struggle for Party's Soul." *Los Angeles Times,* 8 November, A1.
"'98 Election: Congress." 1998a. *California Journal,* July, 31–37; 46.
"'98 Election: Congress." 1998b. *California Journal,* December, 18–24.
California Opinion Index. 1993. "Religion and Politics," September.
Cannon, Lou. 1998a. "Democrats Boosted by Capps' Win in California." *Washington Post,* 12 March, A4.

————. 1998b. "The California GOP: A House Divided." *California Journal*, November, 18–21.

Christian Coalition. 1998. *1998 Christian Coalition Voter Guide.*

Christian Coalition of California. 1998. "CC Member Forum—Matt Fong," 29 October, < http//www.ccca.org>

Dionne, E. J. 1998. "Internal Strife Hurts GOP Chances." *Denver Post*, 24 March, B1.

Dunlop, David W. 1994. "Minister Stresses Anti-Gay Message." *New York Times*, 19 December, A8.

Ezell, Harold. 1986. "A Call From the Wall: Interview with Harold Ezell, Western Regional Commissioner of the U.S. Immigration and Naturalization Service." *Full Gospel Business Men's Voice*, 9 September, 3–13.

Federal Election Commission. 1998a. "Cornelius M. Coronado, Jr.: Committees Who Gave to This Candidate." http://herdonl.sdrdc.com/cgi-bin/can_give/H8CA46047

————. 1998b. "James Gray: Committees Who Gave to This Candidate." http://herdonl.sdrdc.com/cgi-bin/can_give/H8CA46039

————. 1998c. "Robert Kenneth Dornan: Committees Who Gave to This Candidate." http://herdonl.sdrdc.com/cgi-bin/can_give/H6CA27124

————. 1998d. "Lisa Bergman Hughes: Committees Who Gave to This Candidate." http://herdonl.sdrdc.com/cgi-bin/can_give/H8CA46013

Fetzer, Joel, and J. Christopher Soper. 1997. "California: Between a Rock and a Hard Place." Chap. 9 in *God at the Grass Roots 1996: The Christian Right in the American Elections*, edited by Mark J. Rozelle and Clyde Wilcox. Lanham, Md.: Rowman & Littlefield.

Gerston, Larry N., and Terry Christenson. 1995. *California Politics and Government.* Belmont, Calif.: Wadsworth Publishing Co.

Gilbert, Christopher P. 1993. *The Impact of Churches on Political Behavior.* Westport, Conn.: Greenwood Press.

Hyink, Bernard L., and David H. Provost. 1998. *Politics and Government in California.* Menlo Park, Calif.: Longman.

Jeffe, Sherry Bebitch. 1998. "Feminization of California's Agenda." *Los Angeles Times*, 8 November, M1.

Los Angeles Times. 1998a. "Los Angeles Times Poll #416: 1998 Elections, September 12-17." Codebook and machine-readable datafile. Storrs, Conn.: Roper Center for Public Opinion Research.

Los Angeles Times. 1998b. "Los Angeles Times Survey #420: 1998 California Exit Poll." Codebook and machine-readable datafile. Storrs, Conn.: Roper Center for Public Opinion Research.

Marinucci, Carla, and John Wildermuth. 1998. "Gays, Right Snub Fong's Unity Tactic." *San Francisco Chronicle*, 28 October, A1.

Mecoy, Laura. 1998. "Dornan Defies GOP, Runs for House Seat." *Sacramento Bee*, 13 April, A1.

Morain, Dan, and Carl Ingram. 1995. "Hurtt's Spending Equals His Bold Conservative Agenda." *Los Angeles Times,* 24 November, A1.
National Association of Evangelicals. 1957. "Immigration Laws." Resolution 1957G. Available at http://www.nae.net/resolutions/archive/253.html
———. 1965. "Immigration Laws." Resolution 1965. Available at http://www.nae.net/resolutions/archive/192.html
———. 1993. "Refugee Resettlement." Resolution 1993C. Available at http://www.nae.net/resolutions/archive/27.html
———. 1995. "Compassion for Immigrants and Refugees." Resolution 1995B. Available at http://www.nae.net/resolutions/archive/23.html
Nollinger, Mark. 1993. "The New Crusaders—the Christian Right Storms California's Political Bastions." *California Journal,* January, 6–11.
Perry, Tony. 1998. "Social Issues Bring Out Differences." *Los Angeles Times,* 27 September, A3.
Pignatora, Anthony. 1998. "Adió, hypó crita: Harold Ezell goes to that Big Immigration Detention Center in the Sky." *OC Weekly,* 4 September, 11.
Purdham, Todd S. 1998. "In California Coast Race, the National Scandal Ebbs as the Local Issues Flow." *New York Times,* 27 October, A18.
Roll Call. 1998. "California Dornan Slams Sanchez on Abortion," 28 September.
Schrader, Esther. 1998a. "Dornan Pitches Self as 'True Latino': Garden Grove Republican Who Upset Many with Ballot-Fraud Allegations Now Is Courting Minority Vote." *Los Angeles Times,* 10 October, A1.
——— 1998b. "Rout by Dornan's Ex-Followers: Republicans, Vietnamese Who Aided Past Victories Vote for Sanchez." *Los Angeles Times,* 5 November, A14.
Shenon, Philip. 1999. "Clinton Renames Gay Philanthropist as Envoy." *New York Times,* 12 January, A8
Soper, J. Christopher. 1995. "California: Christian Conservative Influence in a Liberal State." Chap. 11 in *God at the Grass Roots: The Christian Right in the 1994 Elections,* edited by Mark J. Rozell and Clyde Wilcox. Lanham, Md.: Rowman & Littlefield.
Tobar, Hector. 1998. "In Contests Big and Small, Latinos Take Historic Leap." *Los Angeles Times,* 5 November, A1
Traditional Values Coalition. 1998. *California Voter's Guide: General Election.*
Warren, Jennifer. 1998. "Fong Fell Victim to Ad Strategy." *Los Angeles Times,* 6 November, A1.
Weintraub, Daniel M., and Mark Katches. 1998. "Lungren and Davis Face Off." *Orange County Register,* 24 September, A4.
Zipperer, John. 1995. "Immigration Debate Divides Christians (California's 1994 Proposition 187)." *Christianity Today,* 6 February, 42.

7

Answered Prayers and Mixed Blessings: The Christian Right in Florida

Kenneth D. Wald, Maureen Tartaglione, and Richard K. Scher

The election of 1998 may well have marked the final stage in Florida's transition to a one-party Republican state. By contrast with 1994, when the party's strong statewide showing was blemished by the loss of its gubernatorial candidate, or the 1996 election, in which the state voted for the Democratic presidential candidate, there were no such major disappointments on November 3, 1998. The election left the Republican Party in control of the governorship and with enlarged majorities in both houses of the state legislature, making Florida the first southern state since Reconstruction with Republican ownership of major statewide elective institutions. The GOP cemented its hold on Florida's congressional delegation by reclaiming fifteen of twenty-three seats. Although the Democrats salvaged some pride by winning half of the cabinet-level executive offices on the ballot, Republicans were heartened by their success in winning both of the open seats and by the strong rumors that one of the Democratic victors was soon to switch party affiliation. Apart from the mere fact of victory, the Republican ascendance was underlined by the stunning magnitude of the electoral margins. The Republican gubernatorial nominee, who had never held elective office, handily defeated his more experienced Democratic rival. The Republicans won twenty-one of their twenty-five state senate seats without opposition and similarly elected two-thirds of their state house members in uncontested races. Not a single one of the congressional Republicans drew an opponent who finished within 10 percent of the winner's vote total. The election of 1998, which did so much damage to Republican hopes nationwide, had no apparent downside for the GOP in the Sunshine State.

In politics, great victories often contain the seeds of future defeats. That may well turn out to be the hidden story lurking in the pro-Republican Florida blizzard of '98. As generations of political scientists have observed, politics in the United States is by nature an exercise in coalition building. Our two-party system and diverse social structure force winning political parties to fashion electoral majorities from a range of groups with different and sometimes conflicting policy agendas. Samuel Lubell (1965) best captured this reality decades ago when he used a celestial metaphor to describe the political system. In this model, a dominant "sun party" defines the terms of political debate through its latent electoral majority but must be constantly watchful of defections to the minority "moon" party.

Lubell's model seems to fit the evolution of party politics in Florida. Over the years, the once dominant Democratic moon cracked and fragmented, providing the Republicans with accretions that allowed it to win occasional elections. In 1998, the Democratic moon appeared to disintegrate and the Republican Party assumed the solar position in the Florida party system. However, the political dynamism that brought about this planetary realignment has not suddenly abated. Even as the Florida Republican party has been growing to parity with the Democrats, it has had to learn to deal with the political tensions of managing a heterogeneous electoral base, a problem rarely encountered when the GOP was a small and homogenous minority. The problem is more acute now that the Republicans have more to lose.

In Florida as elsewhere, the rise to power of the Republican Party has been heavily fueled by the political mobilization of evangelical Protestants. The party's most spectacular growth has been among what are often described as social conservatives, former Democrats found in the towns and countryside of northern Florida and migrants to some of the new suburbs in central Florida. We perceive this constituency as both a political resource and a political problem for the Republican Party in Florida. The votes and energy of evangelicals have augmented the Republican majority in the electorate, providing its base constituency. In that sense, the support of the evangelicals has answered the prayers of state Republicans for majority status. Yet the policy agenda of social conservatives produces a continual source of tension that threatens to drive away other groups no less central to the Republican coalition. The term "mixed blessing" in our title conveys this double-edged reality.

This chapter develops that theme in three sections. We begin with a brief overview of the political culture and structure of the Sunshine State, highlighting both the opportunities and pitfalls that confront the conservative Christians who have entered Florida politics. The next section reviews the role of social conservatism in the gubernatorial, legislative, and local contests on the 1998 ballot. We also pay careful attention in this part of the chapter to the contribution of religious forces to ballot referenda initiated as part of the constitutional revision process in 1998. In an attempt to foretell how the 1998 results may alter patterns of state politics, the third section looks at the role that conservative Christians have been playing in governance during the 1990s. In the conclusion, we return to the discussion of opportunities and barriers, reiterating our belief that Christian conservatism is both bounty and liability for Florida's new Republican ascendancy.

The Context

Throughout much of this century, Floridians have tended to keep religion and politics in separate spheres. Indeed, politics in this state have been decidedly secular, even when issues involving moral questions (such as abortion rights or prayer in the schools) have arisen.

Perhaps nowhere can the line between the sacred and the profane in Florida politics be better seen than in the history of political campaigns. Only once in the state's history did an overtly religious campaigner succeed in gaining office. Sidney J. Catts, an itinerant Baptist minister, ran for governor as a renegade Democrat in 1916. An electrifying personality and demagogue, Catts took full advantage of the widespread, virulent anti-Catholic sentiment that Thomas E. Watson and the Guardians of Liberty had stirred up in the rural Baptist Panhandle of the state (where most of the population at that time lived). Catts claimed that the Catholic Church had pumped some $180,000 into Florida to defeat him. He also had his campaign manager dress up as a Catholic priest and go from town to town in the rural areas, making vicious anti-Catts speeches. It was negative campaigning at its worst, but it was effective; Catts won the governorship easily (Colburn and Scher 1981, 66–67).

The success of Catts's campaign was probably attributable to the nativism and xenophobia that characterized rural Florida in the World War I era. What is both interesting and revealing about the Catts campaign is that it was never repeated. Rarely have candidates for public office in Florida attacked religious groups. Even in the recent past, when such appeals have become more common elsewhere, public officials holding deep religious convictions have generally not flaunted them or used them in a political context. Both Governors Reubin Askew and the late Lawton Chiles were men who cherished their Christian faith, but the electoral campaigns and administrations of both were decidedly secular. Indeed, Governor Bob Martinez's enthusiastic endorsement of the antiabortion movement was thought to have been a major factor in his resounding reelection defeat (to Chiles) in 1990.

The decidedly secular character of Florida politics rests on its political culture, its social profile, and the state's twentieth-century history.

Political culture, a concept well known to political scientists, refers to the fundamental beliefs and attitudes toward government and politics—more specifically, to the roles they should play in the lives of residents, the relationship between the public and private sectors, and so forth. Students of Florida politics, beginning with V.O. Key (1949) have long noted the highly "individualistic" nature of the state's political culture, in which it was literally "every man for himself." Later, Kirkpatrick Sale (1975) commented on the "cowboy culture" characterizing the sunbelt that Florida anchors on the east. Other scholars have observed that a "moralistic" political culture that might prove fertile for injecting religious elements into politics presumes a certain level of collective consciousness and community spirit, neither of which is well developed in Florida (Elazar 1984; Scher 1998). Indeed, the state has more often been likened to a crowd of anonymous strangers than viewed as an organized, cohesive social entity.

Florida's demography and historical development have also militated against the development of a religious strain in its politics. In 1916, when Catts ran and won, the state was still very rural, and many parts of peninsular Florida were almost completely uninhabited. Indeed, as late as 1940, Florida was still the least populous of all the southern states. Once the floodgates opened during and after World War II, however, Florida's population mushroomed.

Two aspects of the massive population growth in the state conditioned the subsequent fate of conservative Christianity in politics. First, the growth was highly pluralistic and cosmopolitan. Though immigrants were overwhelmingly white, they were not uniformly Anglo-Saxon or Protestant. Very quickly Florida developed Catholic and Jewish populations substantially greater in size and proportion than other southern states. The cosmopolitan religious demography of Florida coupled with a relatively lower level of religious affiliation militated against any significant role for religion in public life (Wald and Scher 1997). Among Florida Republicans voting in primaries in the 1990s, fewer than a third identified themselves with the religious right, a figure much lower than that of other southern states (Wald and Scher 1997, 82).

The presence of a large ethnic population, especially Hispanics, is further evidence of Florida's diverse and cosmopolitan demography. Hispanics now constitute about 14 percent of the state's total population. While concentrated in southeast Florida, Hispanics have diffused widely throughout the state. Cubans, the single largest group of Hispanics in Florida, continue to be robustly Catholic and Republican. They are also uncomfortable with the evangelical Protestant religiosity characterizing much of the Christian Right. Their presence in the Republican Party has helped prevent the takeover of the GOP by Christian conservatives that has occurred in other southern states. Indeed, the recent appointment of a Cuban-American attorney as chair of the state Republican Party can be interpreted as a signal that the GOP is likely to remain anchored in a secular style of politics.

The fundamentally urban/metropolitan character of immigrant settlement—the second critical aspect of the state's demographic transition—also had significant political implications for the linkage between religion and politics. In 1940, Florida was inhabited by a mere 2 million people. By 2000, it will have 15.5 million inhabitants—a growth rate of 675 percent. The population growth has not been evenly distributed around the state but clustered in urban areas. By 1990, fully 85 percent of the population resided in urban areas, making Florida one of the most urban/metropolitan states in the nation.

As evidenced by the Catts victory in 1916, Florida once had a political culture and style based on ruralism and small-town life, one often thought to be conducive to demagoguery and racial/religious appeals (Key 1949; Scher 1997, chap. 3). But this culture was simply swamped in the 1940s by the hordes of northern and midwestern migrants for whom the folk styles of traditional southern politics meant nothing. Though Florida cities have hardly been free of bigotry or hate crimes, it is reasonable to conclude that the metropolitan environment is generally more hospitable to social diversity and tolerance. In sum, then, the avalanche of new residents in Florida, particularly their decidedly urban/metropolitan residential character and ethnic diversity, has proven to be a significant stumbling block for social conservatives. The core of the movement is found among a relatively small group of white Protestant evangelicals located primarily along the I-4 corridor that runs across the geographic middle of the state, with another significant concentration in the Panhandle area. We shall now examine the role of this group in the 1998 campaigns.

The 1998 Campaign

The Governor's Race

In 1994, John Ellis "Jeb" Bush accomplished something that few of the Republican gubernatorial nominees in the South managed to do that year. He lost. True, Bush was competing against an icon of Florida politics, Lawton Chiles, and the Republican was seeking his first statewide office. Moreover, Bush came very close to winning, finishing with some 49 percent of the vote and losing by fewer than 64,000 votes out of more than 2 million cast. On the other hand, Bush enjoyed a huge advantage in financial resources, benefited from universal name recognition, and had the benefit of a united party that looked forward to taking the governorship for just the third time in the twentieth century. Nonetheless, Bush lost amid a GOP tidal wave that swept Republicans into power in statehouses across the South and to sweeping gains in Florida. The initial explanation for this striking defeat was a last-minute telephone blitz by the state Democratic Party. Worried senior citizens, told that Bush would threaten their Social Security benefits, were said to have turned out in huge numbers, swelling the Democratic vote in the state's most populous counties.

Only later did Bush concede that his defeat was in large measure due to his own campaign. Given the narrowness of the electoral margin, it may well have been that Bush's determined overtures to religious conservatives cost him the governorship in 1994. In that campaign, he ran as a right-wing Republican seeking the support of the most conservative members of the Florida electorate. The most visible sign of his outreach to the right was the choice of State Representative Tom Feeney as his running mate. Feeney, a leader of the Christian Right in the Republican ranks, may have helped Bush secure the nomination in a Republican primary where an estimated 40 percent of voters were religious conservatives, but his extreme positions came back to haunt the Republican ticket in the general election. Feeney damaged Bush's chances by allowing Democrats to paint the Republican nominees as religious extremists and, perhaps more seriously, to raise questions about Bush's judgment in naming such a weak nominee for lieutenant governor. Beyond appointing Feeney as a sign of obeisance to the Christian Right, Bush did virtually nothing to reach out to other constituencies in the diverse Florida electorate, ignoring blacks, Jews, and other important voter groups. The thrust of the 1994 effort was symbolized by the concluding event of the campaign, a mass rally at an evangelical Protestant church in the staunchly conservative Panhandle section of the state.

The different outcome of the 1998 race certainly owes something to the circumstances of the campaign. In 1998, Bush faced Lieutenant Governor Kenneth "Buddy" MacKay, a candidate with a distinguished governmental career but nothing like the political skills of the retiring Lawton Chiles. Whereas the Democrats had been united four years earlier, in 1998, the party was bitterly divided and the MacKay campaign never caught fire.

But the biggest change from one campaign to the next was in Jeb Bush (Judd 1998; Navarro 1998; Neal 1998). Stylistically, Bush evolved from a wooden candidate who seemed nearly comatose in the 1994 televised debates to a confident and relaxed performer who dominated the 1998 platform. Beyond style, Bush's issue emphasis also shifted dramatically. The candidate who four years earlier, in his own words, was "swinging on a vine with a knife in my teeth, giving Tarzan yells," ran in 1998 as a centrist whose most often invoked adjective was "compassionate" (Dyckman 1998). The Bush who by his own admission said he had "nothing to offer" blacks in 1994 gained considerable mileage in 1998 by founding a charter school in an inner-city neighborhood of Miami. The candidate evolved from wanting to "blow up" the state department of education in 1994 to making public education his priority in 1998. By contrast with 1994, when his antiabortion position was center stage, Bush never talked about the issue in 1998. Welfare mothers, told by the 1994 Bush campaign to find husbands, were promised domestic violence shelters and more vigorous enforcement of child support judgments in 1998. Rather than select another Christian Right stalwart for his running mate in a repetition of the disastrous Feeney nomination of 1994, Bush initially selected a progressive woman who was part of the Republican's pro-choice wing. When that candidate had to withdraw because of ethics issues, Bush overlooked several Republican legislators with Christian Right ties and replaced her with the secretary of education, a man who had gained a reputation as a strong advocate of public education. Bush ran his entire campaign as an advocate of diversity and pledged to appoint an administration that captured the full range of the state's heterogeneous population. In a striking contrast to the event that ended his 1994 campaign, Bush spent the final day of his second campaign in black urban churches (Wallsten 1998). Together with a much more favorable set of political circumstances, these changes from the 1994 campaign strategy enabled Bush to prosper in a year when many of the most conservative GOP gubernatorial candidates fared badly in the South.

When asked about the transformation, Bush spoke of learning from 1994 not to tie himself so closely to social conservatism and ascribed some softening to his new membership in the state's largest faith community, Roman Catholicism. However much Bush's outreach strategy was explicable in terms of the state's political demography, it clearly represented an attempt to distance the candidate from the religious right, a striking contrast from 1994, when the candidate and the movement were locked in a tight embrace. The lack of effort to harness Christian conservatives in 1998 was evident in acts of both omission and commission. In August, Bush missed a large "Faith and Families Gala" sponsored by the Christian Coalition in Orlando. At an appearance in Ft. Lauderdale a few weeks earlier, Bush welcomed representatives from the Log Cabin Republicans, a gay and lesbian caucus within the party (Broward Log Cabin Club 1998). He told caucus leaders that he did not discriminate on the basis of sexual orientation and had hired qualified gays and lesbians to serve in his campaign. That approach directly challenged the strong antigay mentality of Republican evangelicals. Bush could afford to take a cavalier approach to social conservatives because he faced no primary opposition and was considered the front runner almost from the moment he conceded the 1994 contest.

The issue that most immediately threatened this pluralist strategy was the perennial debate over school prayer. In 1996, the legislature had authorized prayers at "voluntary" school events such as sporting contests and graduation. Although the prayer was supposed to be nonsectarian, the fact that students would have control raised the specter of highly sectarian prayers that would offend religious minorities. Governor Chiles, himself a devout Presbyterian, issued a ringing veto message in which he affirmed religious pluralism and decisively rejected the bill. To those who wondered about Bush's commitment to religious diversity, the bill was a major issue in 1998. The Christian Coalition, the major lobbying organization of the Christian Right, left little doubt that it would repass the bill in the next legislative session and that it expected Governor Bush to sign it. Yet pledging to do so would surely undermine the candidate's promise to avoid divisiveness and sectarianism.

Bush responded to the issue with studied equivocation. He never raised the issue in public. When the Democratic nominee handed him the vetoed bill during a televised debate and asked point-blank if Bush would have signed it, the Republican nominee refused to answer, promising to study the bill and to veto any legislation that went beyond "voluntary" prayer. During an interview with the editorial board of one of the state's largest daily newspapers, Bush similarly avoided taking a position. Indeed, according to a witness to the interview, he showed an almost palpable physical aversion to even reading the text that had been prepared for him (Dyckman 1998). This position was not lost on many Jewish voters, who took it as evidence that Bush would sign similar legislation as part of his obligation to religious conservatives in the Republican Party.

Bush did raise another potential issue with religious implications, the question of school vouchers. After his 1994 defeat Bush had helped found a charter school, a private educational institution receiving public funds, and he advocated a larger program of school vouchers for parents of poor children. Bush attempted to defuse the religious dimensions of the proposal both by circumscribing the benefit—limiting it strictly to people in poverty—and making a confusing distinction between funding religious schools but not religious instruction (Hegarty 1998). Despite these efforts, the issue raised concerns about using public dollars to fund private sectarian education. This issue never gained prominence during the campaign, although it is likely to play a significant role in forthcoming legislative sessions. Nor did Bush's embrace of churches as social service providers raise much concern even though it could involve sending public money to religious organizations that would be released from state licensing requirements.

Bush's strategy of electoral pluralism met with a positive response from many voter groups. Owing both to his determined outreach and to the ill-considered decision by Democrats in the Florida House to depose their speaker-elect, a black state legislator, African American elites were much more favorable to Bush than to any previous Republican nominee. In perhaps an even stronger sign of his electoral reach, Bush also secured endorsements from a number of prominent Jewish activists. State Senator

Ron Silver of Miami, an influential Jewish Democrat, endorsed the GOP nominee after reporting that Bush had given him private assurances that he would not support a school prayer bill. The *Jewish Journal* of Palm Beach, the state's largest newspaper targeted to Jewish voters, also broke with tradition to endorse Bush over his Democratic rival (Fiedler 1998b).

The extent of Bush's appeal across a broad range of voter groups is evident from the preelection polls reported in table 7.1[1] When we compare the proportion of voters who had intended to support Jeb Bush with the data on voter support for Republicans in general (bottom part of the table), two things become clear. First, Bush ran ahead of the Republican ticket among virtually all voter groups in 1998. Bush was more popular than his party among blacks, Jews, and the nonreligious, groups that probably scorned him in 1994, but also among the more Republican-oriented Catholics and mainline and evangelical Protestants. The pluralist electoral strategy apparently managed to convert some groups who generally avoided Republican candidates and, in all probability, had stayed away from Bush in droves four years earlier. Second, Bush did not seem to hurt himself among evangelicals by his less ardent pursuit of social conservatives in the 1998 campaign. Certainly no candidate would be displeased to earn three-fourths of the intended vote from such a significant electoral bloc. But the 1998 vote pattern, impressive in its pro-Bush magnitude, sets up a distinct challenge for the new governor that falls into the mixed-blessings category. To the extent Bush repays evangelical support by endorsing conservative social policies, he risks alienating the broad and inclusive coalition that supported his election. Yet delivering on the social issues that dominate the Christian Right agenda threatens to activate the same backlash that undermined his first run for the governorship in 1994.

Other Statewide Offices and the Legislature

What was the story below the top of the ticket? Religious appeals and impact appear to have been distinctly muted elsewhere on the ballot. That was certainly true for the six cabinet-level positions on the 1998 ballot. Members of the cabinet are elected concurrently with the governor but run in separate elections. In recent years, partisan politics have entered cabinet races strongly, adding an additional complexity to the traditional role that powerful and well-heeled interest groups have played in influencing their outcomes. Given the Christian Right's close ties to the Florida Republican Party, is there evidence that it played a key role in the vote tallies that GOP candidates received in the 1998 elections?

In the Republican cabinet primaries, no candidates can be tied with certainty to the Christian Right. Both Faye Culp (for commissioner of education) and Fred Dudley (a former state senator running for attorney general) were very conservative Republicans, and both courted the

Table 7.1 Vote Intention for Major Public Offices by Religious Affiliation

Date of Survey	Major Religious Groups					Entire Sample
	African Americans	Jews/ Nonaffiliates	Catholics	Mainline Protestants	Evangelical Protestants	
Percentage of Decided Voters Supporting Republican for Governor						
January	11	26	51	66	75	52
March	11	40	60	60	82	57
May	13	33	57	65	70	57
July	33	40	58	63	70	57
September	15	48	66	70	73	62
October	21	37	54	60	74	55
Percentage of Decided Voters Supporting Republican for U.S. Senate						
January	10	15	28	35	59	32
March	4	20	22	33	40	27
May	0	15	31	28	39	27
July	5	17	28	24	41	25
September	7	23	26	29	46	29
October	3	15	32	32	50	31

Table 7.1 (Continued)

Percentage of All Voters Supporting Republican for Attorney General

March	8	19	18	29	30	23
May	0	9	30	27	27	23
July	10	15	30	21	37	24
September	0	18	22	28	40	26
October	0	22	22	26	40	25

Percentage of All Voters Supporting Republican for Insurance Commissioner

March	9	15	32	25	36	26
May	9	19	33	29	30	28
July	13	19	28	25	34	25
September	7	17	32	39	42	32
October	6	20	35	30	39	30

Percentage of All Voters Supporting Republican for Education Secretary

September	20	42	49	53	63	50
October	14	41	57	58	71	55

Table 7.1 (Continued)

Date of Survey	African Americans	Jews/ Nonaffiliates	Catholics	Mainline Protestants	Evangelical Protestants	Entire Sample
			Major Religious Groups			

Percentage of All Voters Supporting Republican for Agriculture Secretary

Date of Survey	African Americans	Jews/ Nonaffiliates	Catholics	Mainline Protestants	Evangelical Protestants	Entire Sample
September	3	14	22	27	34	23
October	9	14	28	26	37	26

Percentage of All Voters Supporting Republican for Secretary of State

September	7	25	42	45	44	38
October	0	23	46	44	56	41

Percentage of All Voters Supporting Republican for Comptroller

October	6	28	47	51	59	45

Percentage of All Voters Supporting "More Republicans Than Democrats"

January	10	13	32	42	55	34
March	2	20	32	36	45	31
May	9	22	34	41	43	35
July	9	22	41	37	61	37
September	3	26	36	41	56	38
October	3	28	41	45	58	41
Weighted N	30–50	86–118	102–162	174–225	95–120	500–628

coalition at its summer convention, but both lost very badly in their primaries to more moderate, essentially secular Republicans.

In the Republican secretary of state primary, former state senator Kathleen Harris handily defeated the incumbent, Sandra Mortham, 61 percent to 39 percent. Harris received a combined score of 93 percent in the 1997 and 1998 Christian Coalition legislative ratings while she served in the senate. However, there is no evidence that Harris won because of her high coalition approval score. Rather, Mortham turned out to be a flawed candidate, dumped by Jeb Bush as his 1998 running mate because of ethical improprieties and lapses in judgment. Public opinion data (not shown) provide no evidence that Mortham did badly among Christian conservatives and suggests that her perceived personal failings drove the electorate.

In the general election there is evidence that factors other than the Christian Right largely determined the outcomes. As table 7.1 shows, most Republican candidates were preferred by evangelical Protestants but not at levels beyond what would be expected given the partisan orientation of that voter group. Harris easily defeated Democrat Karen Gievers, an attorney and child advocate from Miami, by 54 percent to 46 percent; Gievers never could shake the liberal, south Florida label pinned on her by the well-financed Harris. David Bludworth, a secular Republican, never had a chance against the popular Democratic Attorney General Bob Butterworth, losing 60 percent to 40 percent; Butterworth had successfully managed the state's lawsuit against tobacco companies that ended not long before the election. The Republican incumbent comptroller, Bob Milligan, easily won reelection with 61 percent of the vote against a political unknown; Milligan is a moderate Republican with no known ties to the Christian Right. Republican Tom Gallagher swamped his Democratic opponent, former Speaker of the Florida House Peter Wallace, 57 percent to 44 percent; Gallagher is a secular, moderate Republican. In the race for commissioner of agriculture, the Republican Party gave no support to its candidate, and indeed tried to talk him out of the race after the Democratic incumbent, Bob Crawford, endorsed Jeb Bush (Talev 1998).

At one point it appeared that a religious element might be injected into the race for treasurer, which pitted incumbent Democrat Bill Nelson against former state representative Tim Ireland (whom Nelson had defeated for treasurer four years earlier). In what was regarded as the nastiest race this election season in Florida, Ireland conducted what one observer called a "scorched earth campaign" (Kaczor 1998). Questions of integrity and character were raised on both sides, but the campaign hit a low point when Ireland raised questions of anti-Semitism by Nelson, alleging that the incumbent had failed to go after banks that were cheating Holocaust survivors. Newspapers and other commentators were almost unanimous in condemning Ireland for this "spurious and unfair allegation" against a candidate who had been among the leaders in pressing Swiss banks to compensate the victims of Hitler. It later came out that one of the organizations making the charges was a Washington front for Republican activists. It is true that Ireland had a tendency on the campaign trail to talk about doing "the Lord's work." But most observers regarded him as a moderate Republican, and they ascribed his abysmal campaign to political ineptitude, bad advice, poor judgement, and uncouth manners. Even if the Christian conservatives did support him, it was to no avail; he lost badly, 57 percent to 44 percent.

At the congressional level, Florida's Washington delegation remained unchanged following the election. This meant that the Republican House incumbents most favored by the Christian Right—Representatives Charles Canady, Dave Weldon and Joe Scarborough—faced no serious opposition in their reelection bids. But the same pro-incumbent, anticompetitive environment that protected these candidates also helped to preserve the seats of Democrats who were targeted in a few House races. Florida's senior senator, Bob Graham, exploited his moderate voting record in the Senate to win his third term by an overwhelming margin.

In 1996, Christian conservatives' efforts to mobilize evangelical Christian voters helped the Republican Party gain control over both state legislative chambers. But the Republican tidal wave that swept the legislature brought with it a riptide for Christian conservatives, who saw their influence erode as more and more Republicans filled legislative seats. By 1998, the Christian Coalition and similar groups had little if any impact on Florida's 1998 legislative races. Once in office, Republicans no longer openly courted the conservative Christian bloc.

The Christian Coalition, in particular, was active throughout each campaign season, attempting to get out the conservative Christian vote, raise the salience of Coalition priorities in the minds of the voters, and ordain sympathetic candidates as carriers of the "family values" scepter. However, as far as we could determine, neither its mobilizing nor agenda-setting efforts determined the outcome of any 1998 Florida race at the state legislative level.

Continuing an effort begun in 1994, the Christian Coalition distributed 2 million voter guides in 1998. As in previous elections, the guides were customized for each race to highlight Coalition issues upon which the candidates differed. Some issues, such as "Banning Partial Birth Abortion," appeared on the scorecards of each candidate seeking a congressional or the gubernatorial seat. "Stop funding of Planned Parenthood" appeared only on the scorecard comparing Republican Congressman Lincoln Diaz-Balart (who favored it) to his Democratic challenger, but "Raising Federal Income Taxes" did not, though it was included on every other. Diaz-Balart scored favorably by Coalition standards on every issue included on the scorecard (Dozier 1998). Low-scoring candidates often complained that the Coalition manipulated the guides to show favorites in the best possible light and to denigrate others. The Coalition has been accused of taking public statements out of context to infer an issue stance. One state legislative candidate who said she would have voted for an ordinance prohibiting discrimination against homosexuals was listed as favoring "special rights to homosexuals" (March 1997).

Incumbency was by far the best predictor of outcomes for the 45 of 120 state representatives who drew challengers in 1998. Only four contested seats changed hands. Three of the four losing incumbents, two Republicans and one Democrat, were social conservatives. Each had scored above 90 percent on Coalition scorecards for votes cast during both the 1997 and 1998 legislative sessions. The fourth incumbent who lost, first-term Democrat Mary Fischer, had scored less than 30 percent on Coalition priorities in 1998, but these votes were not central to the campaign. Fischer found herself "burdened by a political millstone of a husband," the mayor of St. Petersburg, who was struggling to mollify frustrated local constituents (Nohlgren 1998).

Republicans won nine of twelve open seats, representing a net gain of four seats. However, it is doubtful that any of the Republicans won because they were more socially conservative than their predecessors. At least two were considerably less so. Pat Patterson, a Republican who won his bid to replace a conservative, outraged his district's party elders when he refused to unconditionally support school vouchers or adopt a pro-life stance (Poertner 1998). In another district, a Republican supported by the socially conservative leader of the house was soundly defeated in the primary by a more moderate Republican (Griffin 1998).

A similar picture emerged in the state senate races. All challenged incumbents were returned to office. In two open seats, a moderate Republican narrowly won the seat vacated by "Chain Gang Charlie" Crist, who unsuccessfully ran for the U.S. Senate. A liberal Democrat and second-generation politician overwhelmingly won the other.

Constitutional Revision

Every twenty years, according to article XI of the Florida Constitution, the state must convene a Constitution Revision Commission (CRC) for the purpose of reviewing the existing constitution and suggesting revisions that are put to the voters. Membership on the CRC is composed of the state attorney general and citizen representatives chosen by the governor, the speaker of the house, the senate president, and the chief justice of the state supreme court. In 1997, along with the usual collection of lawyers, the commission included six and possibly seven social conservatives chosen by Daniel Webster, speaker of the Florida House of Representatives and a close ally of the Christian Coalition.

Webster's appointees were not a monolithic group but varied considerably in their visibility and effectiveness. One individual, a former president of Florida State University, was a well-respected scholar and academician who brought substantial professional prestige to the commission. Another, a former gubernatorial candidate, was an exceptionally astute politician who was skilled in debate and possessed the ability to frame complex issues in ways that looked centrist but in fact were generally compatible with Christian Coalition views. This member caused considerable concern among his more moderate, secular colleagues because he could make the conservative social agenda look palatable. At the other extreme, one Webster appointee was described as a "loud-mouth" by colleagues, and another was regarded as a liability to conservative Christian causes because of a frequently shrill, hard-edged approach to debate. A number of the other Webster appointees played quiet or secondary roles during commission deliberations.

The process by which the CRC worked—permitting proposals to be considered on several different occasions until the final phase of deliberations—and the open discussion of proposals offered some advantages to the social conservatives. Examination of the CRC record indicates that conservative Christians had a limited agenda but one that they pushed very hard. Space prevents a detailed examination of each of their proposals, but they can be grouped into a few categories:

- *Abortion.* Conservative Christians offered several proposals for a constitutional ban on all abortions. One of the most far-reaching of such proposals specifically disallowed the "right of privacy" section of the Florida Constitution to cover abortions.[2] It is precisely the privacy clause that provides constitutional protection for Florida women's freedom of choice on this matter. Another proposal would have constitutionally defined abortion as murder. The social conservatives sought constitutional language that defined life as beginning at the moment of conception and sought to extend the right of privacy to unborn fetuses in order to ensure their development in the womb to full term.
- *Parental Rights.* Social conservatives pushed hard for constitutional language that guaranteed parents full supervision over their children against intervention by the department of children and family services to protect "at risk" children. One proposal would have made parental rights sovereign over all other rights concerning children. Other proposals included language requiring parental consent on all medical procedures for children under eighteen years of age, another attempt to limit abortion.
- *Family.* As part of their effort to protect families, conservative Christians proposed making divorce more difficult and wanted the consti-

tution to define marriage explicitly as a legal union of "one man/one woman."

- *Government.* Christian conservatives, including the Christian Coalition, actively sought to defeat proposals that would have moved Florida toward a "merit system" of appointive judges. They evidently felt that they could have a stronger impact on the state's judiciary (many of whom were apparently too liberal for them) by retaining the election of judges. They also proposed eliminating that portion of the state bar's judicial canon prohibiting judges from speaking out on issues of the day or revealing their personal and political beliefs on public questions. Social conservatives argued that voters had a right to know how judges might decide cases involving moral questions, presumably those involving abortion rights, parental consent, and the like. They also opposed a plan to appoint (rather than elect) the state education commissioner by a newly created (and gubernatorially appointed) state school board. Though conservatives framed their argument largely in terms of public accountability, it seems clear they were concerned that removing the office from electoral appointment would diminish their influence over public education.

- *Public Education.* Revision 6 of the CRC declared the education of children a "fundamental value" for all Floridians, and made provision of "a high quality" public education system a "paramount duty" of the state. Christian conservatives opposed this proposal on a number of grounds. Some felt that this was a legislative, not a constitutional, matter. Other were concerned that such language might have a deleterious impact on major portions of their educational agenda, including home schooling and tuition vouchers for private schools. Still others simply opposed the idea on the grounds that the revision would require the state to spend more money on a school system they felt was a hopeless failure.

How successful were the Christian conservatives in pushing their agenda during commission deliberations? They were not successful at all. They lost every one of their votes on eliminating or reducing abortion rights, defining the origin of life, and parental rights. Their efforts to stop cabinet reform and derail the state's commitment to public education were handily defeated by fellow commissioners, who put those proposals on the ballot. The only area in which they had any success was allowing for local option in selection of trial court judges. However, their attempts to create term limits for judges or remove the ethics canon preventing judicial candidates from speaking out on issues all met with failure.

The commissioners representing conservative Christians had even less luck with the electorate. All the proposals they resisted on the commission passed easily. As table 7.2 shows, evangelical voters were not distinct

Table 7.2 Vote Intention on Constitutional Amendments by Religious Groups

Date of Survey	Major Religious Groups					Entire Sample
	African Americans	Jews/ Nonaffiliates	Catholics	Mainline Protestants	Evangelical Protestants	
Percentage of All Voters Supporting County Option in Judicial Appointments						
March	38	24	34	23	19	27
May	28	43	45	48	48	46
July	43	37	41	32	40	37
September	50	49	68	60	53	57
October	57	60	50	54	59	55
Percentage of All Voters Supporting Cabinet Reduction						
March	28	20	38	30	18	28
May	33	34	36	33	39	35
July	50	25	34	35	34	34
September	42	34	43	41	32	38
October	29	35	36	37	34	35

Table 7.2 (Continued)

	Percentage of All Voters Supporting Longer Waiting Period for Gun Sales				
May	61	81	80	66	73
July	70	77	76	78	75
September	71	72	71	73	72
October	60	76	74	70	71
	Percentage of All Voters Supporting Redefinition of "Natural Person"				
July	60	67	65	61	61
September	63	58	65	54	55
October	80	70	73	68	68
Weighted N	30–50	86–118	102–162	174–225	95–120	500–628

from other voters on cabinet reform or local option for trial judges, both of which they supported handily in spite of the objections of the conservative commissioners. Evangelicals did prove much less supportive than other religious groups of one proposal that Webster's appointees had vehemently resisted. They had urged voters to oppose Revision 9, which guaranteed equality under the law to "female and male alike." To Christian conservatives, this language looked like a form of feminism and a backdoor route to sanctioning same-sex marriages. The Christian Coalition and the Florida Family Association established a special group called "Fairness for All Floridians" to oppose this revision. Nonetheless, it passed by more than 66 percent of the popular vote.

Why did the Christian Coalition and its allies not have a greater impact on the CRC and the ensuing electoral campaign? They were certainly visible, vocal, and active in pushing their agenda. Part of the reason lay with the CRC commissioners themselves. With one exception, they were regarded as ineffective spokespersons. More significant, however, advocates of the social conservative position seemed generally unable to find ways to make their positions attractive to secular conservatives and cautious moderates. Because they tended to frame arguments narrowly rather than broadly, it was difficult to expand the range of their appeal. In this regard, Christian conservatives who failed to practice the politics of inclusion by presenting their ideas in a way that others could find helpful/attractive/politically advantageous actually hurt their own cause. Thus, their basic constituency base did not grow during the campaign, and they were left as a distinct minority. Finally, though this is difficult to prove, it may well be that most of their fellow commissioners, and ultimately the voting public, were uncomfortable with the injection of quasi-religious moral dimensions into what they perceived as the fundamentally pluralistic and secular undertaking of constitutional revision. Indeed, the conclusion is inescapable that though the Christian Coalition and its allies blew a great deal of smoke during CRC deliberations and in the ensuing political campaign, their influence on the outcome of constitutional reform during 1997–1998 in Florida was virtually negligible.

Local Politics

Earlier studies of the Christian Right in Florida found limited success for the movement at the local level, especially when it ran stealth campaigns in nonpartisan contests (Wald 1995; Wald and Scher 1997). In more recent years, local candidates affiliated with the Christian Coalition and related organizations have raised their levels of visibility and, in some cases, actually came out of the closet to run openly as conservative Christians. The fate of these candidates largely reaffirms the findings from earlier research.

Perhaps the most prominent such example came in Pinellas County (St. Petersburg and Clearwater), in the Tampa Bay area. In 1998, David Caton of the Florida Family Association, a longtime opponent of gay rights, sought to dismantle Largo High School's Gay and Lesbian Alliance (GASA), a support group for gay students. The student group, which had existed for some eighteen months, was supported by both the school board and the principal (Beeman 1998; Barry 1998). Caton decided to target one of the three school board members whose positions were up for election. Linda Lerner, a Democrat, GASA defender, and mother of an openly gay child, became the major focus of Caton's efforts. Lerner's Republican opponent told the Florida Family Association that he opposed school curricula that taught students to use condoms and other devices to prevent the spread of the AIDS virus. In spite of Caton's efforts to unseat Lerner, she won reelection relatively easily.

In 1996, as in earlier elections, religious conservatives were once again ousted from a county school board. Republican candidates representing Christian Coalition positions, a majority on the Lee County (Ft. Myers) school board, had sought to impose a conservative Christian agenda on school policy and curricula. These included abstinence-based health sciences programs, teaching creationism in science classes, and establishing Bible study classes devised by a group close to Pat Robertson. In the course of imposing this agenda they fired the school superintendent, who protested their policies, and forced out the board's attorney, who raised legal questions about the majority's actions. In the end, however, they overreached themselves. GOP voters threw out two of the conservative Christian board members in the 1998 Republican primary and runoff elections, replacing them with more moderate candidates, who ultimately succeeded to the board (Fiedler 1998a).

The Christian Right in Florida Governance

What will be the governmental impact of the new Republican majority, augmented in major ways by religious conservatives? We can get some idea by examining the evolution of governance in Florida since the Christian Right has become a political presence.

Although the house and governor's office remained barely Democratic, it was very clear even in 1995–1996 which way the political winds were blowing. The 1995 and 1996 legislative sessions were marked by levels of partisan acrimony not previously seen in Florida. But though Governor Chiles and Democrats were shoved around a bit by increasingly muscular Republicans, the gridlock and sharp right-wing turns that some pundits and analysts predicted would characterize Tallahassee politics really did not materialize in any significant way.

Following the fall elections in 1996, when the Republican Party held a majority in both houses of the Florida Legislature for the first time since Reconstruction, the focus shifted toward the emerging Christian Right values and influence in the legislature ("Blessed Is the Veto Pen" 1997). In particular, the new speaker of the Florida House, Daniel Webster, was a central Florida Republican closely tied to the Christian Coalition. Though Webster stated that he would give all legislative proposals a fair hearing and would not push an exclusively conservative social agenda, some of his early actions suggested otherwise. In his initial organizational session following the elections, Webster invited his personal pastor to lead the house in prayer. Since in the past such prayers had generally been nonsecretarian, non-Christians found the pastor's invocation offensive; Webster's response was that if they didn't like the prayers, they could skip them and come later to the sessions. More tellingly, Webster, in a major overhaul of house procedure, established a series of "policy councils" led in the main by legislators sympathetic to a conservative Christian agenda. These councils were empowered to pass judgment on proposals emanating from house committees to ensure that they were compatible with Webster's legislative wishes. Furthermore, any number of observers and analysts of the Florida Legislature noted that John Dowless, the Florida Christian Coalition's executive director, had unlimited access to Webster's office, and several individuals thought that he had actually opened a branch office of his own in the speaker's chambers.

Thus, as the 1997 legislative session opened, there was considerable uncertainty about how far and how fast the Christian Coalition and its supporters would push their programs. The coalition announced a ten-point legislative agenda for the Florida Senate, and an eleven-point one for the house. There was substantial overlap between the two agendas. The major items on both included banning partial-birth abortions, prohibiting same-sex marriages, providing tuition vouchers for parents of private school students, opposing distribution of contraceptives in public schools, permitting religious references in American history displays, and chemical castration for sex offenders. Both agendas also supported a package of bills known as the "Women's Right to Know" act that required medical personnel to provide women with information about abortions, including alternatives to it, and mandated a twenty-four-hour waiting period before a woman could obtain an abortion. Beyond these core priorities, the Christian Coalition also supported bills that forced prisoners to work on chain gangs; raised additional hurdles before state social service workers could remove children from abusive households; established "character education" in the schools; and, in an echo from 1996, allowed students to be led in prayer at organized events (Wallsten 1997).

How successful were social conservatives in pushing their agenda? At one level, it appears that they did well. The legislature did indeed ban partial-birth abortions and implement a twenty-four-hour waiting period for abortions. The so-called American Heritage amendment (permitting religious materials in school historical displays), chemical castration, and defense-of-marriage bills also passed. The Coalition lost on school vouchers, school prayer, chain gangs for prisoners, and contraceptives in public schools. Governor Chiles vetoed the partial-birth abortion ban.

A closer look reveals that some of the social conservative successes were modest. Passing the partial-birth abortion ban and defense-of-marriage proposals was their biggest achievement because of the controversy surrounding those issues. But the American Heritage history amendment was so watered down that it achieved almost unanimous support in both houses of the legislature. Several of the other, relatively minor bills also favored by the Christian Coalition, including scholarships for adopted foster children and establishing faith-based ministries in prisons, were so noncontroversial that they too passed with unanimous support.

In 1998 the Christian Coalition announced a more ambitious agenda, building on some of the work done earlier. The major proposals included overturning the governor's veto of the ban on partial-birth abortions, an act to minimize government intrusion on religious activity, requiring couples to complete counseling before a divorce decree could be issued, granting a week of sales tax relief for clothing purchases, and imposing term limits and elections on all judges. The voucher proposal was resurrected and the abortion issue took a new twist when the coalition proposed creating a "Choose Life" specialty license plate.

As in the previous session, the conservative Christian agenda had a mixed fate. The most publicized success was overturning the governor's veto of the ban on partial-birth abortions. Social conservatives also succeeded in the marriage preservation act and the Religious Freedom Restoration Act, although the latter bill had a wide range of support in the religious community. The parental notification of abortions for minors passed but was vetoed by Governor Chiles. Tax relief also passed, but it too received support far beyond that of social conservatives because of the state's flush financial condition and the scheduling of the week-long tax relief period just before primary elections.

The Christian Coalition received its greatest defeat on a proposed constitutional amendment requiring parental consent for abortions for minors. Though it passed the senate, to the surprise of conservative Christians it died in the house, where it failed to receive the 60 percent vote needed to get it on the ballot (Smith 1998). Spokespersons for the Christian Coalition were angry and upset at the proposal's failure in the very chamber they thought would be most hospitable to it. Indeed, they publicly stated that no antiabortion bill was as important to them as this constitutional amendment, and they vowed revenge in the November elections; they expressed their greatest wrath at Republicans who they felt had abandoned them. Given the very high rate of incumbency reelection to the Florida House outlined elsewhere in this chapter, however, it appears that their threats were more idle than real.

Conservative Christian groups also lost on school vouchers and a bill to limit the powers of the department of children and family services to remove children from abusive homes. (In some respects, the legislature actually enhanced the capacity of the department to intervene on behalf of at-risk children). The legislature approved the "Choose Life" license plate, but the governor vetoed it. Neither of the constitutional amendments on judicial reform ever got out of committee.

The Christian Coalition's scorecard of senate and house members, discussed earlier, rates members of the legislature based on their votes on the ten or so measures most important to the organization. Presumably these results are passed along to members and allies in order to show which legislators are friends of the conservative Christian agenda and which are not. An examination of the 1997 and 1998 scorecards is revealing.

Legislators' scores can range from 100 percent (voted with the Coalition's position on each measure) to zero. No committee or procedural votes are included, and the measure includes very few votes on proposed constitutional amendments. The house average was 69 percent. However, the data reveal a sharp partisan split between house Republicans (88 percent) and Democrats (49 percent). In contrast to conventional wisdom, which holds that the Florida Senate is a more moderate body than the house, the senate's overall score was 79 percent, with Republicans voting with the Christian Coalition on 93 percent of its proposals and senate Democrats on 60 percent of the measures. Women legislators, especially in the Florida House, score lower than their male counterparts regardless of whether they are Republicans or Democrats.

What accounts for these numbers? Does the Christian Coalition really have the political clout that it suggests, especially among Republicans and males? It is true that in recent years the Florida Republican Party has sought to acquire for itself a more conservative mantle than it has had in the past. It is also true that in some aspects of abortion reform the coalition succeeded in securing some of its major goals. However, its attempt to raise the issue to constitutional status has so far come to naught. It should also be said that its major achievement of banning partial-birth abortions is relevant to only a minuscule number of medical procedures, and the actual impact of parental notification will not be known until these matters are litigated. The Christian Coalition also hindered educational reform by insisting that all movement in this direction include voucher programs, and they convinced Speaker Webster to derail a major educational reform measure in 1998 because there were no voucher provisions in it.

But several considerations lead to the conclusion that the figures cited are actually misleadingly high. In the first place, they assume that all the

Coalition's agenda items were of equal importance and significance to them. As the previous discussion shows, this was not the case. In some instances of high-priority items, such as certain aspects of abortion-rights reform, school prayer, weakening the department of children and family services, reinstatement of chain gangs, and educational vouchers, the Coalition either lost or found its measures vetoed. Only one of Chiles's vetoes—on partial-birth abortions—was overturned. In addition, some of the measures were so watered down that they became sufficiently inoffensive to foster levels of support far beyond that provided by Christian Coalition allies; the American Heritage history proposal was an example. In other instances, the Coalition ranking was inflated by including bills with universal appeal such as those requiring premarriage or divorce counseling, lowering the cost of marriage licenses, providing scholarships for foster children, tax breaks on clothes for school, and faith-based prison ministries. Next, the senate figures may actually say more about the size of the Republican majority in that body (twenty-four to sixteen) than about the power the Christian Coalition exerts in it. Finally, although it is difficult to prove, there is anecdotal evidence that some Democrats, in particular, voted with the Christian Coalition position on some inoffensive bills to keep the organization off their backs in the 1998 elections (Wald and Scher 1997).

In sum, prior to the 1998 election, the religious conservatives had some narrow legislative successes in limited areas of public policy. When they were able to limit the scope of debate, such as in banning partial-birth abortions and requiring that information be given to women contemplating an abortion, they were successful. As debate widened to include more controversial areas, such as school prayer, educational vouchers, prison chain gangs, and judicial reform, they were less successful.

These same considerations apply to the role of the Christian Right in the 1999 Florida legislative session. Following the inauguration of Governor Bush, and with the Republican Party holding solid majorities in both legislative houses, social conservatives held high hopes that the limited gains secured in the two previous legislative sessions would be advanced dramatically. During January and February of 1999, news stories reported that various factions of social conservatives were ready to roll when the legislature convened in March (Elmore 1999).

Those who anticipated a social revolution misread the political tea leaves. Governor Bush's inaugural address, as well as his first state of the state speech, was moderate to conservative in tone and content, articulating none of the major agenda items of social conservatives with the exception of his educational reform package, which included school vouchers.[3] As the session began, neither Senate President Toni Jennings nor the new House Speaker, John Thrasher, expressed any commitment to the Christian Right agenda; both are moderate, secular Republicans.

Indeed, as the session came to an end, it was clear that the Christian Right had secured only two modest gains: passage of bills authorizing the state to issue "choose life" license plates[4] and requiring doctors to notify the parents of minors seeking abortions. Both bills are subject to constitutional challenge, with a high degree of probability that the parental notification bill will not pass judicial scrutiny because of Florida's "right to privacy" amendment. Governor Bush made it very clear to legislators that he did not want to see a school prayer bill on his desk, and a proposal introduced by social conservatives languished during the session. Republican legislators also shot down a number of abortion bills, virtually all of them in committee before they ever got near chamber floors. Governor Bush's tuition voucher bill did pass—it is the first in the nation to provide vouchers on a statewide basis, including potentially to religious schools—but it would be inaccurate to say that its success was a result of pressure by the Christian Right. Bush built a substantial coalition on behalf of the measure, a minor part of which consisted of social conservatives.

At the end of the session, social conservatives were upset (Hollis 1999a). John Dowless of the Florida Christian Coalition indicated his extreme disappointment that the group's agenda had not received more attention and that his organization's success was so limited. He stated that "next year"—an election year—would be theirs. Whether or not social conservatives, including the Christian Coalition, can deliver on these threats seems highly problematic, as the political problems contributing to the inability of these groups to forge wide-ranging political coalitions in the legislature will not have disappeared. The "blessing" of Christian Right support for the GOP is mixed because of the very real danger that its legislative priorities could polarize the party, causing the new Republican ascendancy to collapse. Though the threat was averted during the 1999 session, the underlying tension remains very much alive.

Conclusion

In an analysis of the 1996 Florida elections, Wald and Scher (1997) emphasized the obstacles to Christian Right influence posed by an array of formidable opponents. In their discussion of the forces blocking or slowing the movement, the authors included the Republican Party, the very vehicle through which the Christian Right hoped to exercise power. The limited policy success of the movement in the Florida Legislature and in the 1998 constitutional revision process seems to have validated that conclusion. With the apparent emergence of the Republican Party as the new majority party in Florida, it is even more timely to discuss how the Christian Right is likely to fare vis-à-vis the GOP.

We began this chapter by invoking Lubell's model of sun and moon parties, suggesting that the ascendant Republicans are a fragile majority made up of various groups that could come apart under the weight of internal stresses. The Christian Right is one of the components that helped the GOP build majority support among the state's voters. Yet it is also a force that either could find itself disappointed by the moderation of the majority it helped elect or, if it prosecutes its claims vigorously, could become a source that drives away other elements of the majority coalition.

The dangers of close association with the movement were most apparent in the gubernatorial campaign where Jeb Bush kept his distance. In 1994, Bush embraced the Christian Right in his campaign team and message. By 1998, Bush did not openly disassociate himself from the movement but clearly kept it at arm's length. This did not seem to diminish the support of traditionalist Christians at the polls, but it may well have accounted for tensions when leaders of the movement pressed Governor Bush to support their legislative initiatives. Although Bush did push successfully for a limited voucher program and parental notification of teenagers seeking abortion, the major school prayer and abortion restrictions favored by social conservatives were denied gubernatorial support (Hollis, 1996b). The Christian Right also faces a renewed problem from other constituencies within the Republican Party. The leaders of both the senate and house are probusiness Republicans who have shown little commitment to the agenda of social conservatism. The state party chair and national committee representatives have always expressed a certain wariness of the evangelical activists. Cuban-Americans, who continue to play a leading role in the state party, remain unenthusiastic about the evangelical fervor of their colleagues within the state GOP. In a sign of growing concern among moderate party leaders, the outgoing secretary of state announced plans to create a foundation "to counteract the influence of the religious right" in the Republican Party by raising policy issues other than abortion and increasing primary turnout by moderate voters (Associated Press 1998).

All these signs of internal dissension reinforce our belief that the Christian Right is too big for the Republican Party to ignore but too controversial for it to embrace wholeheartedly. The next four years will determine whether the alliance of convenience between a large party and a narrow social movement can withstand the forces of political reality.

NOTES

We gratefully acknowledge Jim Kane, who generously provided us with the *Florida Voter* surveys for 1998, and Linda Chappetto, who procured the Christian Coalition scorecards.

1. Jim Kane of the *Florida Voter* collected the data for tables 7.1 and 7.2. In this statewide telephone survey using random digit dialing and random selection of respondents within households, the sample was restricted to adult residents who indicated they were registered voters. Samples were weighted to conform to the known demography of the registered electorate. (The final preelection sample was drawn from the voter register and was not weighted.) Assignment to religious traditions was based on a set of questions. The first asked voters to label themselves as Traditional Protestant, Evangelical Christian, Catholic, Jewish, nonaffiliated or other. In the tables, Jews and the nonaffiliated form a single category while Catholics and African Americans had their own classification. The Evangelical Protestant category includes all white respondents who selected the Evangelical option in the first question and self-described Traditional Protestants who considered themselves born-again Christians and who reported weekly attendance at religious services.
2. Article 1, Section 23, of the Florida Constitution, the "Right of Privacy," reads in part, "Every natural person has the right to be let alone and free from government intrusion into his private life."
3. The governor repeatedly refers to them not as vouchers, but as "opportunity scholarships."
4. These license plates had actually been available for more than a year, but were produced under private auspices. The new bill authorized the state to produce them.

REFERENCES

Associated Press. 1998. "Mortham Wants to Move GOP to Center." Associated Press State and Local Wire, 20 October.

Barry, Rick. 1998. "David Caton Jousts with Obscurity." *Tampa Tribune,* 4 April.

Beeman, Kathleen. 1998. "Student Group Draws Protest." *Tampa Tribune,* 3 April.

"Blessed is the Veto Pen, For It Can Stop Webster." 1997. *Palm Beach Post,* February.

Broward Log Cabin Club of Florida. 1998. "Florida's Log Cabin Republicans Guests at Bush Rally." Press release issued 25 June.

Colburn, David, and Richard K. Scher. 1981. *Florida's Gubernatorial Politics in the Twentieth Century.* Tallahassee: University Press of Florida.

Dozier, M. 1998. "Churches Raising a Voice in Politics; Voter Guides Spark Legal, Ethical Debate." *Sun-Sentinel,* 1 November.

Dyckman, Martin. 1998. "On School Prayer, Bush is Equivocal." *St. Petersburg Times,* 29 September.

Elazar, Daniel. 1984. *American Federalism: A View from the States.* 3rd ed. New York: Harper and Row.

Elmore, Charles. 1999. "Religion, Abortion Bills Face Bush Call." *Palm Beach Post,* 14 February.

Fiedler, Tom. 1998a. "Christian Coalition Loses Big in Lee County School Race." *Miami Herald,* 6 September.

———. 1998b. "Jews or Christian Coalition: Is Bush Choosing Sides?" *Miami Herald,* 11 October.

Griffin, M. 1998. "Religious Right Might Be Left Out." *Orlando Sentinel,* 18 October.

Hegarty, Stephen. 1998. "The Voucher Experiment." *St. Petersburg Times,* 19 October.

Hollis, Mark. 1999a. "Social Right Wing Struggles This Year." *Lakeland Ledger,* 30 April.

———. 1999b. "GOP Control Not Godsend for Religious Right," *Gainesville Sun,* 6B.

Judd, Alan. 1998. "Then, Now: Bush Changes." *Gainesville Sun,* 27 October.

Kaczor, Bill. 1998. "Nelson Defeats Ireland in Race for Insurance Commissioner." Associated Press, 4 November.

Key, V. O., Jr. 1949. *Southern Politics.* New York: Vintage.

Lubell, Samuel. 1965. *The Future of American Politics.* 3d ed. New York: Harper and Row.

March, W. 1997. "Christian Coalition Forms Spanish Group." *Tampa Tribune,* 25 October.

Navarro, Mireya. 1998. "Chastened by Loss, Jeb Bush Looks Unbeatable in Florida." *New York Times,* 12 May.

Neal, Terry M. 1998. "Centrist Platform Propels GOP in Florida." *Washington Post,* 14 November.

Nohlgren, S. 1998. "Fischer Name Proved to Be a Liability in House 52 Race." *St. Petersburg Times,* 8 November.

Poertner, B. 1998. "House Candidate Pat Patterson Scoffs at Talk That He's a Liberal." *Orlando Sentinel,* 9 September.

Sale, Kirkpatrick. 1975. *Power Shift.* New York: Vintage.

Scher, Richard K. 1997. *Southern Politics in the Twentieth Century.* 2d ed. Armonk, N.Y.: M.E. Sharpe.

———. 1998. "Florida: An Example of National Building?" In *Amid Political, Cultural and Civic Diversity: Building a Sense of Statewide Community in Florida,* edited by Lance deHaven-Smith and David Colburn, 187–216. Tallahassee: Florida State University, Florida Institute of Government.

Smith, Adam C. 1998. "Bill's Defeat Angers Christian Lobbyists." *St. Petersburg Times,* 6 May.

Talev, Margaret. 1998. "Republicans Take Strong Hold of Cabinet." *Tampa Tribune,* 4 November, 5.

Wald, Kenneth D. 1995. "Florida: Running Globally and Winning Locally." In *God at the Grass Roots,* edited by Mark Rozell and Clyde Wilcox, 19–46. Lanham, Md.: Rowman & Littlefield.

Wald, Kenneth D., and Richard K. Scher. 1997. "Losing by Winning? The Odyssey of the Religious Right in Florida." In *God at the Grass Roots 1996: The Christian Right in the American Elections*, edited by Mark Rozell and Clyde Wilcox, 79–98. Lanham, Md.: Rowman & Littlefield.

Wallsten, Peter. 1997. "Church Meets State." *St. Petersburg Times,* 16 February.

———. 1998. "Campaigning to the Wire, Bush Tells Churches of a 'New Florida.'" *St. Petersburg Times,* 2 November.

8

Alabama 1998: Luck Runs Out for GOP and Christian Right as Democrats Gamble on the Lottery

Harold W. Stanley and Christian Grose

An understanding of the fortunes of the Christian Right in the 1998 Alabama elections turns largely on the fortunes of Republican incumbent governor Fob James.[1] A state such as Alabama should provide fertile ground for candidates conveying a Christian conservative message. Although national studies find that a substantial majority of voters oppose Christian Right themes and messages (Buell and Sigelman 1985, Sigelman, Wilcox, and Buell 1987), Alabama was one state in which the Christian Right had reason to feel strong. James, the Christian Right's standard bearer in the 1994 gubernatorial election, had pulled out a come-from-behind victory over an incumbent Democrat partly because of a higher turnout among religious conservatives. A week before the election, James trailed the incumbent by 10 percent in most polls. A massive grassroots mobilization campaign by groups such as the Christian Coalition pushed James to victory by just 1 percent (Sack 1998a). Moreover, the previous Republican governor, Guy Hunt, elected in 1986 and 1990, had strong ties to the Christian Right.

One defensible perspective of Alabama politics extrapolated from recent Republican Party growth envisions that Republicans might dominate the political landscape for years to come. In 1996 Republicans had taken Alabama at the presidential level and swept all seven major statewide races up for election (Stanley 1998).

In Alabama the rise of the Republican Party had not resulted in the infighting similar to that which had characterized the Democratic Party for decades. Alabama's GOP was identified as one southern state party with comparatively low levels of intraparty factionalism (McGlennon 1998).[2] In other states, confrontation between the Christian Right and other Republican groups inhibited consolidation of the Christian Right within the Republican Party (Green 1995; Wald 1995). Within Alabama, prospects for consolidation rather than confrontation looked brighter, leaving the Christian Right positioned to gain even greater influence within the Alabama Republican Party.

Political Background: Governor James and Religion in Politics

Forrest Hood "Fob" James, a former All-American Auburn football star running back who was named after two Confederate generals, ultimately lost his bid for reelection in 1998, but he pulled out a renomination win that many thought in doubt. This renomination win was due in large part to the mobilization of Christian Right support. Well-known Christian Right figures, prominent among them Ralph Reed, cast their lot with James in his reelection bid. Reed's newly formed Century Strategies political consulting firm was hired by James as his chief campaign consultant. Although Alabama voters turned James, a candidate and incumbent governor who identified with the Christian Right, out of office, it would be a mistake to interpret his loss solely as a rejection of the Christian Right. Some values and principles of the Christian Right still have a strong resonance in the state although the candidate most linked to the Christian Right, in the context of the 1998 election, did not prevail.

James had served as governor earlier, elected in 1978 as a Democrat. Indeed, he had served in the 1970s on the state Republican executive committee, but statewide Republican prospects in the late 1970s were such that anyone seeking to gain election was well advised to run as a Democrat.[3] James had, as a Democratic governor, endorsed the Republican Ronald Reagan for president in 1980. James ran unsuccessfully as a Democrat for governor in 1986 and again in 1990.

In 1986 Democrats divided disastrously between Bill Baxley and Charles Graddick for governor. The resulting legal wrangle alienated voters from the Democratic nominee, allowing the election of Guy Hunt, the first Republican candidate to win the governorship this century. Hunt was reelected in 1990 with 53 percent of the vote. Hunt was later charged by the Democratic attorney general with misuse of personal campaign funds and convicted. Jim Folsom, the Democratic lieutenant governor, became governor in 1993.

In 1994 James, having switched back to the Republican Party, won the Republican nomination and ultimately edged out the unelected Folsom for governor in a tight contest. This was the third straight Republican gubernatorial victory in Alabama.

Early in his term, James had been commended for "getting more done without trying so hard in his second stint as Alabama's governor" (Smith 1996). James found his voice in a weekly radio talk show, enabling politically effective public outreach as he talked to and took questions from Alabama citizens. James gave high-profile support to school prayer, judicial display of the Ten Commandments, opening court with prayer, and the teaching of creationism. James claimed that his office had received thousands of messages following his defense of hanging a replica of the Ten Commandments in a circuit courtroom, and that "98 percent were in favor of the governor" (Duin 1997). Though such support gave great visibility to religious conservative positions, some thought that this grandstanding, reminiscent of Governor George Wallace's demagoguery on the race issue, served to distract James and voters from the more pressing problems facing the state and contributed to a less than positive state image. As one Republican primary voter noted, James "comes from a George Wallace tradition of goobers" (Manuel 1998a). Indeed, business conservatives among the Republicans found the James positioning on such issues counterproductive. And they found his record wanting on more familiar issues such as tort reform.[4]

More memorable were James's controversial antics, including his lambasting of the theory of evolution by parading around a stage during a speech to the state board of education with his back hunched over in an attempt to mimic a monkey. At one bill signing, James commented that the bill requiring a moment of silence in the schools that he was about to sign "wasn't worth the damn paper it was printed on." He thought the microphones were off; they were on, picking up his remarks for a much larger audience than James intended (Hotline 1998).

James's general positions on the issues were not out of sync with those of the majority of Alabama voters, though those issues that James emphasized were not quite as salient as he may have assumed. A 1998 survey of Alabamians asked respondents to rank a variety of issues in order of importance. School prayer, a key issue for James, was identified as an important issue, though three other issues were ranked higher by most respondents. Forty-eight percent of those polled said that education was the number one issue facing Alabama, an issue that would be promoted by James's general election opponent in the 1998 campaign (Associated Press 1998a).

James's positions did resonate with Christian conservatives, though. Not only did he take high-profile stands in defense of actions that blurred the line between church and state, but he also participated regularly in events sponsored by Christian-oriented organizations during his term. Right before Christmas in 1997, a makeshift nativity scene was set up by the Association for Judeo-Christian Values on the grounds of the state capitol to promote the importance of school prayer. Speaking at a rally there, James declared that the battle for prayer in school "is not going away, today, tomorrow, forever" (Smith 1997b). James also participated in other events in defense of school prayer with Christian Right leaders such as Ralph Reed and Pat Robertson throughout his term.

The James record had other problem spots. He had also promised educational reforms in 1994, but many concluded he failed to deliver. His get-tough-on-crime 1994 campaign stance led him to reimpose chain gangs for Alabama prisoners in 1995, but he backed off from this the next year in the settlement of a federal court suit. Several members of the James administration left the team and bitterly attacked James as chief executive. In what struck many as an unnecessarily reactionary step, James seceded from the National Governors Association, claiming it was a waste of time and money. James also suggested that state workers look to the chain restaurant the Waffle House as a model to improve their public service. Why the Waffle House? "They're all good. That's the thing I like about it. There ain't no surprises" (Sack 1997).

The 1998 Republican Primary

James's bid for reelection was indeed a troubled one. He failed to gain the majority required for nomination in the Republican primary. The required runoff deepened fissures within the Republican Party between religious and business conservatives, pitting James against Winton Blount III, a wealthy businessman and former chair of the Business Council of Alabama. James had defeated Blount for the Republican nomination in 1994. This runoff opposition deepened James's dependence on support from the Christian Right.

In the Republican primary, former Republican governor Guy Hunt, removed from office in 1993 but since pardoned, drained some religious conservative support from James. An analysis revealed that Hunt's role in the primary did serve to undercut James's evangelical support. In table 8.1, an analysis of votes by county reveals that Hunt appeared to be the main benefactor of religious conservatives' support. The percentage of the vote received by each serious Republican primary candidate is regressed using percentage of evangelicals in the county, the median income of the county, and an indicator variable designating whether the county is part of a metropolitan area. The measure of evangelicals comes from Bradley et al. (1990) and has been used in prior aggregate studies of the Christian Right and state elections (Bullock and Smith 1997). While the majority of Alabamians identify themselves as Christian (Bradley et al. 1992), there are vast distinctions in the intensity of support for the

Table 8.1 The 1998 Republican Primary for Governor and Evangelical Voter Support

Independent Variables	Percentage of Vote for James	Percentage of Vote for Blount	Percentage of Vote for Hunt
Percentage of Evangelicals in county	0.038 (0.080)	−0.251 (0.072)*	0.231 (0.057)*
Median county income	−0.00099 (.00024)*	0.0014 (0.0002)*	−0.00046 (0.00016)*
County in metropolitan Area	3.228 (3.625)	−6.77 (3.27)*	2.380 (2.596)
Constant	74.703 (5.090)*	12.835 (4.64)*	11.144 (3.645)*
R^2	0.227	0.421	0.237
F	6.17*	15.26*	6.53*
n	67	67	67

*These variables are statistically significant at the .05 level.

Christian Right between evangelical and mainline Protestants (Green et al. 1998). Thus, only the percentage of evangelicals is included in the regression as this religious group is the Christian Right's primary constituency and generally is the most intensely supportive of Christian Right candidates (Rozell and Wilcox 1996).

As demonstrated in table 8.1, the percentage of evangelical voters in a county was significant in Hunt's primary totals.[5] The inclusion of the income variable is an attempt to capture economic conservative sentiment, and the metropolitan area variable is introduced as a control (see Bullock and Smith 1997).

As expected, Blount, as the probusiness candidate, did his best in high-income counties. Interestingly, the evangelical variable was also significant with Blount, though it indicated that those counties with high levels of evangelicals did not support him. James, during his term as governor and during the campaign, presented himself as a populist and a defender of religious conservatism. His populist rhetoric may have worked, as the income variable was also significant in the James equation, in the direction of lower income. Evangelical voters did not prove to be significant in the percent of vote that James received by county.

The 1998 Republican Runoff

With Hunt out of the race, James's strategy was to bring religious conservatives back into his primary coalition for the upcoming runoff. Although Hunt endorsed Blount in the runoff, religious conservative voters backed James.

James's campaign leading up to the runoff focused its resources on the mobilization of Christian conservative voters. Three direct mailings highlighting the support of James Dobson, Jerry Falwell, and Pat Robertson for James were sent to 90,000 people who had attended rallies supporting Etowah County Circuit Judge Roy Moore's display of the Ten Commandments in his courtroom.

James also struck a populist chord in the runoff. He ran advertisements criticizing his opponent's patrician heritage. James's criticisms even included Blount's portly figure, calling him a "fat monkey." James's wife, Bobbie, went one step further, declaring that Blount was a "big, fat sissy." Allegations circulated again as they had in 1994 that Blount was driving the car in a 1969 accident in which his first wife died (Wyman 1998).

In a highly unusual political move, both James and Blount sought support for the runoff from Birmingham Mayor Richard Arrington, a black Democrat. Democrats had no runoff contests, and since Alabama has no party registration, the prospects of erstwhile Democrats voting in the Republican runoff loomed large. An Arrington endorsement might possibly move a critical margin of black Democrats to vote for and nominate a more favorable Republican candidate for governor. Some suspect James sought Arrington's support simply as a ploy to encourage Blount to seek that support and to find out what Arrington might be seeking in return. Ultimately, Arrington backed Blount, encouraging his supporters to vote in the runoff, and James's campaign forces charged that nominating and ultimately electing Blount would give Arrington great power statewide. Some campaign flyers portrayed Arrington aides with Afros (taken from decades-old photographs), thus injecting race into the runoff.

Some analysts conclude that even though Arrington's endorsement of Blount did increase Blount support among black voters, greater numbers of conservative white voters were moved to back James, netting James an advantage from the Arrington endorsement (Beiler 1998). Some discuss Arrington's endorsement as indicating the vitality of the race issue in Alabama politics. Even if this is correct for James's runoff win, the question arises as to why James did not return to the issue in the general election when running against Don Siegelman, whose black support was far more pronounced.

An analysis of the aggregate voting patterns in the runoff demonstrates that James's populist and religious appeals were key to his victory and that the Arrington endorsement may not have been important in motivating black voters across the state. In table 8.2, James's percentage of the vote by county is regressed with the same independent variables used earlier (percentage of evangelicals, median income, and metropolitan area). An additional independent variable, the black population percentage in each county, is included to measure whether James lost black support as a result of Arrington's endorsement of Blount. Both higher levels of evangelicals and lower levels of income were significant in predicting James's percentage of the vote by county. The percentage of blacks did not prove to be significant, though this variable does not completely capture the extent to which Arrington may have motivated black voters in his home base of Birmingham and Jefferson County.

The costs of the runoff campaign drained James's coffers, positioning him poorly for the run-up to the general election. By contrast, Don Siegelman had a sizable campaign war chest and no serious primary opposition for the Democratic nomination. Siegelman approached the general election politically and financially prepared. In fact, Siegelman ended up outspending incumbent James $7 million to $6 million.

The bruising primary and runoff also widened fissures within the Republican Party. Christian Right activists are typically more conservative than the religious voters they claim to represent and are also more conservative than the Republican Party and general electorate as a whole (Buell and Sigelman 1985; Green and Guth 1987; Guth and Green 1987; Sigelman et al. 1987). The greater the influence of the Christian Right on

Table 8.2 1998 Republican Primary Runoff for Governor between James and Blount

Independent Variables	Percentage of Vote for James
Percentage of evangelicals in county	0.242 (0.103)*
Median county income	−0.0010 (0.0003)*
County in Metropolitan area	3.250 (3.345)
Percentage of blacks in county	−0.128 (0.069)
Constant	79.328 (8.914)*
R^2	0.368
F	9.02*
n	67

*These variables are statistically significant at the .05 level

the nomination, the greater the risk that the Republican nominee is out of step with the general electorate (Bullock and Grant 1995; Swisher and Smith 1997). The role of the Christian Right in the 1998 Alabama gubernatorial nomination lends some support to these findings. James relied on Christian Right mobilization to beat Blount in the runoff. This positioned him to the right of center for the upcoming general election and deepened the divide between Alabama's social and economic conservatives. Siegelman, on the other hand, was not forced to move leftward in order to win the Democratic Party's primary.

The 1998 General Election

Siegelman, the incumbent lieutenant governor, had run successfully for different statewide offices on four previous occasions, losing only once, in the 1990 Democratic gubernatorial runoff.[6] Not only did Siegelman have the funding and the experiences of several statewide election victories, but he had an issue that put James on the defensive and on which James never found his footing. Siegelman proposed a lottery whose revenues would go for education expenditures. This had previously been an alluring, winning issue in Georgia and would also prove to be such in South Carolina in 1998.

Siegelman's skillful use of the lottery issue can be analyzed using the theoretical context of "wedge" issues. A wedge issue is one introduced by an opposing candidate or party in order to break up the other candidate or party's potential coalition of supporters. Wedge issues in southern politics have typically been those related to race. In recent years, Republican candidates have injected racial issues in an attempt to divide black and white Democratic voters, sometimes succeeding. Glaser (1996) points out that Republican candidates who are successful at using race as a wedge do so without highlighting the issue too much. Similarly, Edsall and Edsall (1991) claim that the race issue was used as a wedge to divide the Democratic coalition that originated with the New Deal.

A wedge issue can also be viewed in the context of Riker's "heresthetic." Riker (1990) explains that a successful political heresthetician can separate "voters into a new majority-minority division that is advantageous to him or her" (51). Prior to 1998, the equilibrium in Alabama politics appeared to be one of Republican control via a coalition of economic and religious conservatives. The gubernatorial elections of 1986, 1990, and 1994 all resulted in the victory of the Republican candidate. In fact, in 1997, many political commentators were wondering if Alabama was heading into a period of extended Republican dominance. Bob Ingram, a political commentator, following the 1996 Republican electoral successes in the state, declared that "Republicans have gone from an oddity to a majority" (Ingram 1996). Cotter and Stovall (1998) pointed to Alabama's booming economy and the fact that more Alabamians believed the state was heading in the "right" direction as evidence that James "should have had an easy walk to the GOP nomination."

Despite the Republican Party's limited intraparty factionalism leading up to 1998, some suggested that Siegelman's lottery proposal was a "wedge" issue that could exacerbate preexisting fissures within the Republican coalition (Sack 1998a). The lottery proposal appealed to economic conservatives for its ability to increase spending on education without the need to raise taxes. For those opposed to the lottery on moral grounds, Siegelman would reply that "we've already got a lottery," referring to two lotteries in neighboring states. Rather than sending Alabama dollars out of state, Siegelman's campaign sought to capture that money for Alabama education. Siegelman crusaded to "keep those hundreds of millions of dollars that are leaving Alabama" (Sack 1998b).

Just as the Democratic biracial coalition had been plagued for decades by Republican issues that drove a wedge between black and white Democratic voters, with the lottery proposal Republicans found themselves on the receiving end of a wedge issue. Republican economic conservatives were more open to the lottery's ability to raise education funds without taxes, whereas religious conservatives opposed the lottery on moral grounds.

The initial public response to Siegelman's lottery proposal seemed muted, and James may have misinterpreted how much this issue resonated with Alabama voters. In his speeches early in the campaign, Siegelman would receive more applause when he spoke about issues such as crime than when he mentioned the lottery. Democratic State Senator Lowell Barron remarked that the lottery was "like a wet-dry referendum" and that "Nobody wants their neighbor to know how they are going to vote" (Rawls 1998).

James, vulnerable on his education record, never found an effective response to Siegelman's lottery proposal. According to Brad Moody, "James never had a campaign saying, 'I've been a good governor. This is why you ought to re-elect me,'" and thus his general election campaign was mostly reactions to Siegelman's proposals (Sher 1998). In the middle of his term as governor, he actually announced that the state's public school system had been "fixed" following the passage of one of his reform measures related to removing mobile classroom units (Cotter and Stovall 1998). Near the end of the race, James offered a counterproposal that included the creation of new college scholarships paid for with existing state money in a last-ditch effort to stop the bleeding on the education issue.

Given his reliance on Christian conservatives as a core support group, James was compelled to come out against a lottery. The state's leaders of the Southern Baptist Convention, Alabama's largest religious denomination, publicly opposed the lottery (Rudin 1998). Patrick Cotter and James Stovall said that James's "opposition to the idea of a lottery, while it may have heartened some of his hard-core Christian conservative supporters, put him on the wrong side of this issue with two-thirds of the electorate" (Cotter and Stovall 1998). Given the unpopularity of raising taxes among Republicans in particular and voters in general, James had no convincing proposal with which to counter Siegelman's education lottery proposal. Democratic pollster Geoff Garin declared that Siegelman "completely dominated the high ground as the education candidate" (Walsh 1998).

Siegelman actually claimed that some religious voters favored his lottery proposal. "Southern Baptists have children and they want the best for their kids" (Sack 1998b). William Stewart, a political scientist at the University of Alabama, observed: "I don't think they're [the voters] saying they didn't support his agenda—protecting the Ten Commandments or school prayer—but they were just focusing on a lottery, which Don Siegelman was able to articulate so well" (Manuel 1998b).

The dynamics of the campaign favored the Democratic challenger as well. Siegelman had television advertisements running a month before James unveiled his advertisements. In Siegelman's advertisements, he stuck to his message promoting the lottery, extolling its success in increasing education funds in neighboring Georgia. He also focused on noncontroversial issues that were able to highlight his professionalism in contrast to James's more colorful populism.

James's positive campaign advertisements attempted to highlight his record in his first term, as his slogan "More Fob!" suggested. But James's depleted war chest following the Republican primary and runoff allowed Siegelman to define his opponents' record without an effective response from James. Siegelman said that "more Fob" would be "like asking for more disease or famine" (Sack 1998c).

Eventually James did air advertisements, some of which focused on the negative aspects of introducing a lottery in Alabama. One of James's general election commercials featured a cockfight while the announcer attacked Siegelman's contributions from the gambling industry, claiming that Siegelman would "let his gambling friends sneak other games of chance into Alabama behind his lottery" (Sack 1998a). James, in speeches, would often refer to Siegelman's lottery proposal as the "crap game" (Cason 1998). Another James advertisement showed a likeness of Siegelman, his nose growing like Pinocchio's, allegedly because of his excessive lying.

The general election campaign was framed primarily by Siegelman and his promotion of the lottery. The populist and religious rhetoric that saw James through to victory in the runoff primary may have hurt him during the general election campaign when he derided the lottery as immoral. Most important, James never established his own message. After the election, Marty Connors, a GOP activist and candidate for the GOP state party chair stated, "We reacted to Don Siegelman and we deserved to lose for that reason" (Associated Press 1998h).

Exit polls furnish insights into the patterns of the vote in the 1998 general election. Comparing 1998 with the earlier James win in 1994 can be particularly instructive. Table 8.3 displays each group's share of the voters at the polls in 1994 and in 1998. Group turnout was essentially similar in both elections. Within the span of four years, though, more affluent voters made up a larger share of the voters: those with family incomes of $50,000 or more made up 27 percent of the voters in 1994, 37 percent four years later. Whites not identifying with the religious Right seem to have declined from 67 to 60 percent, but this decline may be more apparent than real. (The decline is perhaps attributable to a shift in how missing data were handled—in 1998 6 percent of whites are not categorized as either identifiers or nonidentifiers, whereas in 1994 all whites are so categorized.)

In terms of how groups cast their votes (table 8.4), the striking conclusion is that James did less well overall. James gained a majority of the vote from only four groups: those opposed to a state lottery (85 percent), Republicans (84 percent), whites identifying with the religious Right (70 percent), and white men (53 percent). James lost political independents, a critical swing group, since neither party's identifiers command a majority of the voters. The importance of the lottery issue is underscored in these exit poll results. Of the people at the polls, 56 percent favored a state lottery, and Siegelman got 88 percent of their votes. Simple arithmetic

Table 8.3 Voter Turnout for the 1994 and 1998 Gubernatorial Election (Percentage)

Voter Category	1994 %	1998 %
White men	49	47
White women	51	53
Race		
Whites	79	79
African Americans	20	19
Age		
18–29	13	13
30–44	32	31
45–59	27	30
60 or older	27	27
Income		
Less than $15,000	16	14
$15,000–30,000	30	21
$30,000–50,000	27	27
$50,000–75,000	17	21
$75,000–100,000	5	9
Over $100,000	5	7
Education		
No high school	11	9
High school graduate	32	29
Some college	25	28
College graduate	20	22
Postgraduate	12	12
Party identification		
Democrat	44	46
Republican	30	29
Independent/other	26	25
White identifying with the Christian Right	33	34
White not identifying with the Christian Right	67	60
State lottery		
Favor	—	56
Oppose	—	41

Sources: 1994:http://cnn.com/ELECTION/1998/states/AL/polls/AL94GH.html and 1998: . . ./G/exit.poll.html.

Notes: "—" indicates not available.

Voters totaled 1,317,842 in the 1998 general election, 1,201,969 in the 1994 general election http://www.sos.state.al.us/election/1998/ggov98.htm and . . ./1994/GOVERNOR.HTM.

shows that lottery supporters gave Siegelman a near majority of the vote (49.26 percent). Though this does not prove the lottery issue decided the election—many of these voters may have decided to back Siegelman for other reasons and the lottery issue simply reinforced a vote decision reached on other grounds—it is still an impressive figure.

Leaders vying to become the state's GOP chair following the November election concurred with the evidence from the exit polls. Paul Haughton, one of the unsuccessful candidates for party chair, said that the Republicans "made the lottery a gambling issue. Hell, the lottery isn't a gambling issue. The Democrats made it a hope issue, and they won." ("GOP Took Misstep" 1999). The elected state Republican leader following the 1998 elections was Winton Blount, the same man James defeated in the Republican runoff. Blount promised to reunify the Republican Party of Alabama and win back the governor's chair in 2002.

Conclusion

Although the 1998 gubernatorial election in Alabama was a setback for the Christian Right, it would be a mistake to interpret this defeat as the demise of the movement. A battle for the Republican nomination accentuated fault lines in the Republican coalition between business and religious conservatives. James was financially depleted after the nomination battle and in a position from which he needed not only to shore up support among business conservatives but also to appeal to centrist voters. Siegelman, his Democratic opponent, thwarted James with a strategically savvy emphasis on the lottery for education. Despite his emphasis on issues dear to religious conservatives, James was unable to go beyond a religious conservative base to patch together levels of support that he garnered in 1994. The challenge for business conservatives now leading the state Republican Party will be to consolidate religious conservatives within the party, minimize confrontation, and mount an outreach capable of amassing a winning coalition.

After the 1998 election, disappointment ran deep among Christian conservatives. Roy Moore, the judge whose display of the Ten Commandments in his courtroom was championed by James, concluded that the Christian Right had been dealt a blow with Siegelman's defeat of James: "I'm disappointed that the people would seem to choose darkness instead of what I consider light" (Manuel 1998b). The battle had been lost but not the war, and Christian conservatives were not retreating from the field of battle. Ralph Reed looked beyond the loss to urge perseverance: "[R]eligious conservatives have got to . . . resist the impulse for self-flagellation . . . [and] we should recognize that this is a long-term, 30- to 40- year struggle" (Baxter 1998).

Table 8.4   Fob James's Support in the 1994 and 1998 Gubernatorial
General Elections: Exit Polls (Percentage of Voters)

Category	1994 %	1998 %
All voters (election results)	50	42
White men	63	53
White women	61	48
African Americans	8	5
Age		
18–29	41	37
30–44	53	38
45–59	49	44
60 or older	56	47
Income[a]		
Less than $15,000	34	34
$15,000–30,000	42	34
$30,000–50,000	63	40
$50,000–75,000	55	43
Education[a]		
High school graduate	48	40
Some college	51	45
College graduate	51	39
Postgraduate	58	42
Party identification		
Democrat	20	13
Republican	86	84
Independent/other	61	43
White identifying with the		
Christian Right	76	70
White not identifying with		
the Christian Right	37	26
State lottery		
Favor	—	12
Oppose	—	85

Sources: 1994: http://cnn.com/ELECTION/1998/states/AL/polls/AL94GH.html
and 1998: http://cnn.com/ELECTION/1998/states/AL/G/exit.poll.html.
   Note: "—" indicates not available.
   [a] Income categories above $75,000 and education categories below high school
were not reported because of the small number of respondents in these categories.

NOTES

1. Statewide races in 1998 other than governor and lieutenant governor generated limited interest. The reelection bid of Republican U.S. Senator Richard Shelby was a foregone conclusion, generating no serious opposition. In fact, Shelby's general election opponent, Clayton Suddith, mortgaged his pickup truck in order to pay his qualifying fee for the campaign (Anthony 1998). The day after the 1994 general elections, in which the Republicans captured a majority in the House of Representatives and James returned to the governor's chair as a Republican, Senator Shelby announced his switch from the Democratic to Republican Party.

2. There have been notable exceptions to the Republican Party's generally low levels of factionalism centering around religious issues. In a 1980 Republican primary race, a moderate incumbent congressional representative, John Buchanan, was challenged and defeated by Albert Lee Smith, the head of Alabama's John Birch Society at the time. The Moral Majority weighed in on the side of Smith. Crucial to Smith's victory was his criticism that the incumbent had not focused enough on defending prayer in school (Smith 1997a).

3. Another statewide Democratic official elected in 1978, Attorney General Charles Graddick, had served as a Republican county committeeman in the mid-1970s.

4. In contrast to James's conservative stances on religious issues, Bill Pryor, the Republican attorney general during the latter portion of James's term, struck a more moderate stance on the school prayer controversy. In accord with James, he appealed portions of a district court ruling not allowing prayer in Alabama public schools, but he distanced himself from James by agreeing with other parts of the district court ruling discussing the separation of church and state. Pryor went on to a fairly easy general election victory. The Republican lieutenant governor nominee, Steve Windom, was backed primarily by business interests and was able to eke out a general election victory as well.

5. The denominations classified as evangelical are Assembly of God; Christian and Missionary Alliance; Church of God of Anderson, Indiana; Church of God of Cleveland, Tennessee; Church of the Nazarene; Foursquare Gospel; Independent Charismatic and Noncharismatic churches; Lutheran, Missouri Synod; Pentecostal Church of God; Presbyterian Church of America; Reformed Presbyterian; Southern Baptist; Wesleyan.

6. The 1990 Democratic gubernatorial runoff led Siegelman to cross swords with Joe Reed, a prominent black political figure in Alabama and second in command at the Alabama Education Association. (Paul Hubbert, Siegelman's runoff opponent, headed the Alabama Education Association.) The bad blood engendered from that 1990 contest lingered

through 1998. Siegleman did not have the black political leadership of the state firmly in his corner during the 1998 general election campaign, but he did garner the black vote—95 percent of the black vote, which made up 19 percent of the voters, a percentage comparable to that in recent Alabama elections.

REFERENCES

Anthony, Ted. 1998. "Scenes from the Edge of Election Day." Associated Press, 4 November.

Associated Press. 1998a. "AEA Poll Finds Support for Erasing Interracial Marriage Ban." *Associated Press State and Local Wire,* 1 December.

———. 1998b. "Three Want to Be Chairman of GOP." *Montgomery Advertiser,* 7 December, 1C.

Baxter, Tom. 1998. "On Politics, Election '98." *Atlanta Journal and Constitution,* 5 November, 1K.

Beiler, David. 1998. "Bama Bash: '90s Style." *Campaigns & Elections,* October/November.

Bradley, Martin B., Norman M. Green, Jr., Dale E. Jones, Mac Lynn, and Lou McNeil. 1992. *Churches and Church Membership in the United States, 1990.* Atlanta: Glemnary Research Center.

Buell, Emmett H., Jr. and Lee Sigelman. 1985. "An Army That Meets Every Sunday? Popular Support for the Moral Majority in 1980." *Social Science Quarterly* 66: 426–34.

Bullock, Charles III and John C. Grant. 1995. "Georgia: The Christian Right and Grassroots Power." In Mark J. Rozell and Clyde Wilcox, eds., *God at the Grassroots: The Christian Right in the 1994 Elections.* Lanham, Md: Rowman and Littlefield.

Bullock, Charles III and Mark C. Smith. 1997. "Georgia: Purists, Pragmatists, and Electoral Outcomes." In Mark J. Rozell and Clyde Wilcox, eds., *God at the Grassroots, 1996: The Christian Right in the American Elections.* Lanham, Md: Rowman and Littlefield.

Cason, Mike. 1998. "Hopefuls Argue Lottery Proposal for Education." *Montgomery Advertiser,* 7 October, 1A.

Cotter, Patrick R., and James G. Stovall. 1998. "Siegelman Brilliantly Blended Lottery and Education." *Montgomery Advertiser,* 8 November, 9A.

Duin, Julia. 1997. "Governor Flouts Judiciary Over Prayer; James Supports Judge Posting 10 Commandments." *Washington Times,* 28 February, A2.

Edsall, Thomas Byrne, and Mary D. Edsall. 1991. *Chain Reaction: The Impact of Race, Rights, and Taxes on American Politics.* New York: W.W. Norton and Co.

Glaser, James M. 1996. *Race, Campaign Politics, and the Realignment in the South.* New Haven: Yale University Press.

"GOP Took Misstep, Haughton Believes." 1999. *Montgomery Advertiser,* 11 January.

Green, John C. 1995. "The Christian Right and the 1994 Elections: An Overview." In *God at the Grass Roots: The Christian Right in the 1994 Elections,* edited by Mark J. Rozell and Clyde Wilcox, 1–18. Lanham, Md.: Rowman & Littlefield.

Green, John C., and James L. Guth. 1987. "The Christian Right in the Republican Party: The Case of Pat Roberston's Supporters." *Journal of Politics* 50: 150–65.

Green, John C., Lyman A. Kellstedt, Corwin E. Smidt, and James L. Guth. 1998. "The Soul of the South: Religion and the New Electoral Order." In *The New Politics of the Old South: An Introduction to Southern Politics,* edited by Charles S. Bullock III and Mark J. Rozell, 261–76. Lanham, Md.: Rowman & Littlefield.

Guth, James L., and John C. Green. 1987. "The Moralizing Minority: Christian Right Support Among Political Contributors." *Social Science Quarterly* 67: 598–610.

Hotline. 1988. "Governor Report: Alabama: Expletive Deleted," 30 April.

Ingram, Bob. 1996. "Historic Alabama Republicans Rise to Dominance." *Montgomery Advertiser* 12 November, 10A.

Manuel, Marlon. 1998a. "James Cruises Past GOP foe in Alabama Runoff." *Atlanta Constitution,* 1 July, A1.

———. 1998b. "Lottery Appeal Captured Middle." *Atlanta Journal and Constitution,* 5 November, 3K.

Marlowe, Gene. 1998. "Democrats: 'Party Is Back in South'; They Didn't Have to Wince at the Map." *Richmond Times-Dispatch,* 5 November, A1.

McGlennon, John. 1998. "Factions in the Politics of the New South." In Robert P. Steed, John A. Clark, Lewis Bowman, and Charles D. Hadley, eds., *Party Organization and Activism in the American South.* Tuscaloosa: University of Alabama Press.

Rawls, Phillip, 1998. "Highlights and Low Lights from the Campaign Trail." Associated Press, 8 November.

Riker, William H. 1990. "Heresthetic and Rhetoric in the Spatial Model." In *Advances in the Spatial Theory of Voting,* edited by James M. Enelow and Melvin J. Hinich. Cambridge, England: Cambridge University Press.

Rozell, Mark J., and Clyde Wilcox, 1996. *Second Coming: The New Christian Right in Virginia Politics.* Baltimore: Johns Hopkins University Press.

Rudin, Rabbi. 1998. "Election Confounded the Political Pundits." *Stuart News/Port St. Lucie News* (Fl.), 14 November, D2.

Sack, Kevin. 1997. "Alabama G.O.P. Governor Sees a Different South." *New York Times,* 29 August, A1.

———. 1998a. "3 G.O.P. Candidates for Governor Face Trouble." *New York Times,* 22 October, A1.

———. 1998b. "2 Democrats Hope Support for Lottery Will Help Break G.O.P. Grip on South." *New York Times,* 29 September, A1.

———. 1998c. "Democrats Buck 20-Year Trend, Faring Well in Once 'Solid' South." *New York Times,* 4 November, A1.

Sher, Andy. 1998. "Lottery Issue Turns Out a Good Bet for Democrats." *Chattanooga Times,* 9 November, A1.

Sigelman, Lee, Clyde Wilcox, and Emmett H. Buell, Jr. 1987. "An Unchanging Minority: Popular Support for the Moral Majority, 1980 and 1984." *Social Science Quarterly* 68: 876–84.

Smith, Gita M. 1996. "Second Chance: Easy Does It: Fob James Appears to Be Getting More Done Without Trying So Hard in His Second Stint as Alabama's Governor." *Atlanta Journal-Constitution,* 28 January.

Smith, Gita M., 1997a. "Lawmakers to Join Alabama Rally for Public Prayer." *Atlanta Constitution,* 11 April, D1.

Smith, Gita M. 1997b. "Alabama Nativity Scene Tests Limits: Governor Finds Room at Capitol for Manger." *Atlanta Journal-Constitution,* 1997 December, 4A.

Stanley, Harold W. 1998. "Alabama: Republicans Win the Heart of Dixie." In *The New Politics of the Old South: An Introduction to Southern Politics,* edited by Charles S. Bullock III and Mark J. Rozell, 67–84. Lanham, Md.: Rowman & Littlefield.

Swisher, Ray, and Christian Smith. 1997. "North Carolina: Jesse's Last Stand? The Christian Right in the Elections." In *God at the Grass Roots: The Christian Right in the American Elections,* edited by Mark J. Rozell and Clyde Wilcox, 67–78. Lanham, Md.: Rowman & Littlefield.

Wald, Kenneth D. 1995. "Florida: Running Globally and Winning Locally." In *God at the Grass Roots: The Christian Right in the 1994 Elections,* edited by Mark J. Rozell and Cyde Wilcox, 19–46. Lanham, Md.: Rowman & Littlefield.

Walsh, Edward. 1998. "An Endorsement of Pragmatism: In Choosing Governors, Voters Rejected Ideological Appeals." *Washington Post,* 5 November, A40.

Wyman, Hastings. 1998. "Alabama: Runoff Pits Rightwing Against Business/GOP Moderates." *Southern Political Report,* 16 June, 1–2.

9

Michigan 1998: The "Right Stuff"

James M. Penning and Corwin E. Smidt

Although sharp electoral conflict is nothing new in Michigan, the 1998 primary and general election campaigns proved to be among the most bitterly fought in recent memory, featuring fierce partisan battles for control of the statehouse, state legislature, supreme court, and a host of lesser offices. The campaigns involved political characters such as Geoffrey Feiger, former attorney for Dr. Jack Kevorkian ("Dr. Death") and among the most colorful and outspoken gubernatorial candidates in Michigan history, as well as heated debate in "Kevorkian country" over Proposal B, a ballot proposal to legalize assisted suicide in the state.

When the dust of the election finally settled, both parties could claim a measure of success, although Republicans clearly did better overall than did Democrats. The GOP could take satisfaction in Gov. John Engler's thumping reelection victory over Geoffrey Feiger and in successful efforts to regain control of both the house of representatives and the Michigan Supreme Court. Thus, for the first time since 1928, Republicans control the governor's office, the supreme court, and both houses of the state legislature. On the other hand, the Democrats could take comfort in the election of Jennifer Granholm to succeed Michigan "institution" Frank Kelly as attorney general. Moreover, the Democrats surprised the pundits by winning three of eight seats on governing boards of state universities; in past years the party dominating state elections has almost invariably won the vast majority of governing board seats.

The 1998 election results indicate that the ideological pendulum of Michigan politics has, once again, swung back to the right, reversing some of the Democratic Party gains of 1996. Yet, this movement represents political evolution rather than revolution. For the most part, the Michigan electorate exhibited satisfaction with Michigan's booming economy and current political leadership as Feiger's call for radical change fell on deaf ears. And voters, in overwhelming numbers, rejected the assisted suicide proposal. In addition, wherever possible, voters reelected incumbents; no incumbent running for U.S. House, state house, or state senate lost his or her bid for reelection. Changes that did occur were due as much to institutional imperatives (e.g., term limits) and idiosyncratic factors (e.g., candidate personalities) as they were to voter demands for new political faces.

Still, we cannot discount the impact of advocacy groups such as those associated with the Christian Right on the election results. Certainly Michigan's major Christian Right groups were highly active in 1998. Moreover, leaders of these groups claim considerable electoral success. The purpose of this chapter is to analyze the 1998 elections in Michigan. We assess what role groups associated with the Christian Right played. What factors have contributed to the rise of these groups in Michigan? How active have the groups been? And what impact have they had in Michigan politics, particularly in 1998? To answer these questions, we begin by examining the geopolitical and historical context of the 1998 election. We then discuss the emergence of Christian Right groups in Michigan politics, their historical evolution, and their organizational structure. We conclude by examining the impact of the Christian Right on the 1998 election outcomes within the state.

The Political Context

The Partisan Context

During the early years of this century, Michigan could be accurately classified as a one-party Republican state. But the Great Depression stimulated a revival of the Democratic Party in Michigan that transformed the state into a partisan battleground.[1] Today, Michigan's two major parties are rooted in differing patterns of social class, race, ideology, and region. Michigan's GOP finds its primary bases of support among small businesspersons, farmers, and suburban professionals. It also receives substantial support from conservative Protestants and traditional middle-class WASPS. In contrast, the core of the Michigan Democratic Party is organized labor, particularly the powerful United Auto Workers Union and the Michigan Education Association. The party also receives considerable support from university liberals, blue-collar workers, Roman Catholic ethnics (particularly Irish and Polish ethnics), and African Americans.

The Geopolitical Context

To a greater extent than most other states, Michigan "is driven by the politics of place" (Browne and VerBerg 1995, 270). GOP support tends to be concentrated in the more prosperous agricultural regions, in the small and medium-sized cities of west Michigan (Grand Rapids, Holland, Kalamazoo), and in the suburban ring of counties (e.g., Oakland and Macomb) surrounding the city of Detroit. The Democratic Party finds its greatest support in Wayne County (Detroit), in the cities of the I-75 corridor (Ann Arbor, Saginaw, Pontiac, Flint, Bay City), and in the more economically depressed Upper Peninsula. Though Michigan is divided into eighty three counties, roughly three-quarters of all the votes cast within the state are cast within the seventeen most populous counties (discussed below). Generally, one or two counties serve as the major anchor(s) of a particular congressional district, though not every populous county falls fully or neatly within one of the state's sixteen congressional districts.

Term Limits

Starting in 1998, term limits have begun to shape election outcomes for state legislative races. Michigan has one of the most stringent term-limit laws of any state. Out of 110 state house seats, 64 had no incumbent candidates running for reelection because the state representative had served the maximum six-year limit.[2] The impact of term limits has important consequences strategically. Primary elections have become much more competitive, with multiple candidate races. In 1998, for example, there were 21 house districts in which 5 or more candidates were competing for the party's nomination, and two such districts had eleven competing against one another. This situation serves as a double-edged sword for political organizations wishing to support candidates that reflect their political perspectives. On the one hand, term limits provide groups with new opportunities to seek the nomination of favored candidates as well as the potential to enjoy a considerable return on the unit of resource invested in the candidate in such highly competitive races. On the other hand, with so many competitive races at the nomination stage, group resources can become easily depleted—limiting the resources available for shaping the general election campaign.

The Christian Right

The Evolution of the Christian Right

Over the past decade, a variety of Christian Right groups have been formed in Michigan, and they have become increasingly active, particularly in the Republican Party. In 1988, for example, supporters of the Reverend Pat Robertson threw the Michigan GOP into chaos with their aggressive efforts on his behalf, which resulted in a split between the Christian Right supporters of Robertson and the more moderate supporters of George Bush (Smidt and Penning 1990). In fact, the state Republican convention split into two groups—a regular convention dominated by Bush delegates and a rump convention dominated by Robertson's supporters (Penning 1994, 329). The resulting ill will has taken a long time to dissipate. Still, according to one recent study, Michigan's GOP state organization exhibits a "substantial" level of Christian Right strength within its ranks (Persinos 1994, 22).

The decade of the 1980s helped to set the stage for the proliferation and growth of many political organizations with ties to conservative Christians. Four factors, in particular, should be noted: (1) the impact of the Reagan revolution, (2) the candidacy of Pat Robertson, (3) the changing political agenda, and (4) the changing rhetoric of the Christian Right. First, though the Reagan administration did not implement many of the policy objectives of conservative Christians, one important legacy of his administration was that power began to shift back to state governments. Accordingly, Christian Right leaders began to view organizational decentralization as the key to political success. Not only was it desirable to create organizations built from the precincts upward, but also these organizations needed to be given considerable local autonomy.

According to Ralph Reed, former national director of the Christian Coalition, it was Robertson's presidential campaign in 1988 that served as "the political crucible" for the proliferation of many of these local Christian Right groups (Reed 1994, 193). This was certainly true in Michigan. Some of the organizations that arose in the wake of the Robertson candidacy have direct ties to his presidential campaign; others have little direct relationship but arose in a political climate that existed following his statewide efforts. Of the four major statewide Christian Right organizations described below, three originated with or after Robertson's candidacy.

A third reason for the growing success of Christian Right organizations is their development of a broader political agenda. Initially, the abortion issue dominated the agenda of conservative Christians. But as the political context changed, more issues were included. Euthanasia, the rights of homosexuals, pornography, sex education in schools, charter and home schools, and gambling have become issues of concern to the pro-family movement. The Christian Right is also beginning to speak to various economic issues, particularly issues related to taxation. With such a proliferation of issues, Christian Right organizations have been able to develop unique functions and particular issue niches. For example, while some organizations focus primarily upon issues related to abortion and euthanasia, others address policy issues related to the family or traditional values, such as the teaching of "creationism."

Finally, a fourth reason for the continuing success of the Christian Right is its changing political rhetoric. To a large extent, the Christian Right has replaced its earlier language of moralism with the language of liberalism (Moen 1997). Rather than framing public policy issues in moralistic, sectarian terms, they have moved to recast many of their arguments in terms of the language of rights, freedom, and equality that is associated with liberal democratic thought. This approach was evident with regard to discussion of Proposal B, in which opponents of B avoided "culture war" terminology and used explicitly secular language and argumentation through their advertising campaign of "B is bad legislation."

The Organizations of the Christian Right

Several major organizations play a prominent role in Christian Right efforts within the state of Michigan. Except for the first organization, all have been created within the last decade.

Right-to-Life of Michigan (RTLM)

Begun in the late 1960s, RTLM is one of Michigan's most powerful interest groups—well led, well focused, well financed, and well organized. Indeed, *Detroit News* reporter Charlie Cain recently asserted that the organization "now rivals organized labor as a power on the state's political scene" (Cain 1997a, 1). To anyone familiar with the tremendous power of organized labor in Michigan politics, that is a remarkable comparison.

One indicator of the group's power is the tremendous support it enjoys among Michigan politicians. Not only does RTLM enjoy the backing of Michigan's (Roman Catholic) governor, John Engler, but majorities in both houses of the state legislature also support it. As one would expect, RTLM's influence is particularly great within the GOP.[3]

A second indicator of the political clout of RTLM is its success in achieving the nomination of favored candidates both in primary elections (used to nominate legislative and gubernatorial candidates) and at the state convention (used to nominate candidates for certain statewide offices such as board of education). Not since Governor Milliken's 1978 campaign has a pro-choice Republican been nominated for governor. Moreover, the defeat of Judy Frey, a pro-choice candidate for a Republican nomination for the Michigan Board of Education in 1996, indicates that many Republicans still employ an abortion litmus test in selecting nominees. According to the *Detroit News*, "if you're a Democrat [in Michigan], it's nearly impossible to win your party's nomination without labor's blessing. And if you're a Republican, Right to Life's endorsement carries comparable weight" (Cain 1997a, 1).

A third measure of RTLM's political clout is its ability to help favored candidates win general elections. Of course, abortion is only one of many factors influencing vote choice, a fact recognized by RTLM officials. According to Barb Listing in Cain's Detroit News article, "People vote on a variety of issues. Ours is one they feel strongly about. If there is a difference between candidates on the abortion issue, we can make a difference; if abortion is the only difference we can make a bigger difference" (Cain 1997b, 3). Although measuring the exact impact of RTLM is exceedingly difficult, it is clear that the organization has had good success in those races where it has endorsed candidates. In 1998, for example, 83.3 percent of RTLM-endorsed candidates won. This included 89.3 percent of state senate candidates, 82.5 percent of state representative candidates, and 81.3 percent of judicial candidates. Because of term limits, RTLM placed greater emphasis upon primary nominations in 1998. This strategy may well have paid important dividends, as there was a gain of eleven pro-life seats in the house and a gain of one in the senate.

A fourth indicator of RTLM's clout is its ability to influence public policy. RTLM has successfully mounted voter initiative drives to end tax-paid abortions for poor women (1988) and require parental consent for minors seeking abortions (1990). In addition, RTLM has worked successfully within the state legislature. In 1998, for example, RTLM led a successful effort to block legislation that would have permitted advanced nurse practitioners to dispense prescription drugs without the supervision of a physician.[4]

Several factors help to account for the political clout of RTLM. The first is its organization. Like most single-issue organizations, RTLM has had little difficulty in establishing clear objectives and maintaining its focus on those objectives. All its activities are directed toward achieving a relatively narrow pro-life agenda, enabling it to use a pro-life screen to distinguish friends from foes.

Not only has RTLM established clear objectives, but it has also developed a remarkably complex organizational structure.[5] RTLM maintains its state headquarters in the city of Wyoming, a suburb of Grand Rapids, and also works closely with 120 affiliate organizations located across the state. In addition, it attempts to coordinate its activities with national right-to-life organizations. RTLM is organized into fourteen semi-autonomous regional affiliates, each of which elects one member to the state board of directors. Twenty additional voting board members are selected on an at-large basis (Smidt and Penning 1997, 118). State and affiliate organizations are linked not only by newsletter and telephone but also by a computer network. RTLM employs a staff of approximately fifty-five persons, including seven field workers (who coordinate the work of the local affiliates), a PAC director, and a Lansing lobbyist. The organization maintains an in-house telephone center and has recently established a "life media" department to create pro-life television advertisements (Listing 1997).

According to RTLM president, Barb Listing, the organization is rapidly growing. Listing reports that "when I became president [in 1981], we didn't even have a computer and kept a list of maybe 50,000 households on index cards" (Cain 1997b, 2). Today RTLM maintains a computerized mailing list of 200,000 donor households (up 40,000 over the past two years) and 500,000 households are listed as pro-life (Smidt and Penning 1997; Listing 1997). RTLM's annual budget today exceeds $3 million. In addition, RTLM's PAC, headed by Larry Galmish, allocates approximately $300,000 to candidates in election years.

A second factor that helps to account for RTLM's clout is its skilled leadership. The organization has enjoyed a long period of stable, skilled leadership under the direction of President Listing, a person with a mild demeanor but outstanding organizational ability and a high level of commitment to her cause. The *Detroit News* (Cain 1997b, 2) labels her a "soft-spoken tiger." One measure of the increasing sophistication of the organization under Listing's leadership has been its growing ability to make common cause with like-minded groups and successfully operate within the regular processes of the Michigan political system. In this sense, although RTLM remains relatively inflexible in the pursuit of its pro-life agenda, it demonstrates its commitment to cultural pluralism.

Thus, even though RTLM is not officially tied to any church and welcomes support from all pro-life people, it has been able to work well with such church-related groups as Baptists for Life, Lutherans for Life, and the Michigan Catholic Conference.[6] RTLM has also worked closely with other groups opposing assisted suicide (Listing 1997). At times, RTLM has even made common cause with its opponents. Former State Representative, Maxine Berman, a Democrat from Southfield, reports on a 1994 budget debate in which she and Listing became allies. The house approved, by a two-to-one margin, an amendment to deny additional payments to a client who bore another child. Berman was amazed that Listing supported the amendment since it was likely to increase the number of abortions. According to Berman, "We split up the list of those who voted to cut off welfare benefits; I called the pro-choice people and she called the pro-lifers" (Cain 1997b, 3).

Finally, RTLM's political influence can be attributed to the commitment of its followers. Abortion is, of course, an emotional issue. Perhaps as a result, the organization has demonstrated its ability to generate a tremendous amount of political activity from its supporters on relatively short notice. Even RTLM opponents recognize and give grudging respect to this. According to Howard Simon, former executive director of the American Civil Liberties Union of Michigan, "There is a lot to admire and learn from Right to Life about dedication and an ability to organize and whip up their troops into some little army." As The *Detroit News* reports, "hundreds of thousands of dedicated foot soldiers have proven they can mount statewide petition drives with surprising ease" (Cain 1997d, 2).

Michigan Family Forum (MFF)

Though the Michigan Family Forum (MFF) is also a relatively strong organization, it is not in the same league politically with RTLM. MFF, headquartered in Lansing, was founded in April 1990 as a nonprofit research and education organization (Michigan Family Forum 1997b) with a 501(c)3 Internal Revenue Service status. As a 501(c)3 organization, MFF is limited by IRS regulations that prohibit it from devoting a "substantial part of its activities" to influencing legislation. Thus, unlike RTLM, MFF does not employ paid lobbyists or sponsor a political action committee.

MFF was originally organized to function as a "family policy council" associated with the national organization Focus on the Family. Nevertheless, it is neither legally nor financially tied to the national Focus on the Family organization that is led by psychologist James Dobson, whose radio program is aired on over 1,450 radio stations across the United States. The Colorado Springs-based Focus is a parachurch organization that seeks to promote traditional family values based on biblical teachings. Focus on the Family is loosely associated with the Family Research Council in Washington, D.C., headed by former Reagan official Gary Bauer. The links between the national Focus organization and MFF are more psychological than structural. The two organizations promote a similar agenda and generally share common objectives, but they do not share funds or attempt to integrate their organizational structures.

MFF was founded as an organization "dedicated to serving Michigan's individuals and families by encouraging government to perform its proper and unique roles" (Michigan Family Forum 1997c, 1). By "proper and unique roles," MFF means, essentially, limited government, but a government that nevertheless promotes a pro-family agenda. According to MFF literature, government can't do everything. Government by itself cannot solve all of our culture's vexing problems, nor should it. Our problems need attention and input from all facets of society, each playing their appropriate roles: from strong families, from active churches and civic organizations, and, of course, from government (Michigan Family Forum 1997c, 2).

By its own admission, MFF began as a rather disorganized and unfocused group, with diffuse goals and a rather unsophisticated approach to Michigan politics. However, much has changed over the past seven years. Under the direction of MFF's first executive director, Randall Hekman, a former probate court judge who resigned from the bench to head the organization, MFF evolved into a highly sophisticated organization. According to the MFF, "Since Michigan Family Forum opened its doors in April of 1990, its focus has evolved and sharpened with increased experience in the governmental process" (Michigan Family Forum 1997b, 1). MFF's current executive director, Mike Harris, a former Kansas state senator, reports that MFF's pro-family agenda focuses primarily on social issues but also includes a few economic issues such as tax breaks for families (Harris 1997). MFF's agenda is articulated most clearly in its recent publication "A Formula for Success: A Series of Recommendations for the 89th Legislative Session" (Michigan Family Forum 1997a), in which MFF made a large number of recommendations to the state legislature.[7]

Pursuing such a large policy agenda has its drawbacks in that it limits the organization's ability to target its resources very effectively. This, in part, helps to explain why RTLM has been more politically effective than has MFF. However, one should also note that as a 501(c)3 organization, MFF is not as free to pursue a policy agenda as is RTLM.

Although MFF struggled early on with a small staff and limited budget, the MFF executive director reports that MFF has grown into an organization that employs eleven people full-time and has an annual budget of over $1 million. In addition, MFF maintains a mailing list of 15,000 individuals (13,000 families).

MFF's five-member executive board meets monthly to set policy and review operations, and a larger advisory board meets semiannually to provide vision. In addition, MFF has established a Research and Public Policy Department as well as a Community Input Department, which provides training sessions for MFF supporters and sponsors the Michigan Prayer Network (a group linked by a telephone tree, e-mail, and regular mail that prays for the success of MFF's policy objectives). The Community Input Department is also associated with MFF's Physicians' Research Council, a group of physicians that aims at developing and supporting MFF's policies in such medical areas as assisted suicide, cloning, medical insurance, HMOs, and hospice care.

MFF utilizes a variety of methods and strategies to promote its pro-family educational agenda. First, it distributes Info-Paks—materials that contain research, essays, and articles on a variety of family-related issues. Second, MFF publishes LegiService—a monthly newsletter that provides analyses of eight to twelve key issues each month along with the voting records of state legislators on two or three family-related issues. Third, it publishes voter guides in election years to assist voters in assessing candidates for local, state, and national office. In 1998, for example,

MFF sent questionnaires to all candidates for the state legislature, Congress, governor, courts of appeal, and the supreme court. It distributed over a million guides in the fall elections, up from the 500,000 distributed in the 1996 election. To assist in distributing the voter guides, MFF has created a network of volunteers across the state, working particularly closely with churches and pastors. Finally, MFF distributes a variety of research publications designed to bolster support for pro-family legislation. It has recently established a new communications department and become increasingly sophisticated in using the media. Executive Director Mike Harris reports that he speaks frequently on various Michigan radio stations. In addition, MFF regularly issues press releases to Michigan newspapers (which editors, hungry for copy, frequently print as news stories). Nevertheless, Harris notes that MFF's focus continues to be on grassroots organization rather than on use of the mass media.

MFF leaders understand the rules of American politics and have become increasingly sophisticated at working within the system.[8] According to MFF, the organization approaches its political task "not through an abrasive, take-no-prisoners manner, but with a calm, winsome, persuasive style, based on quality support and information" (Michigan Family Forum 1997 c, 2). On the other hand, MFF has made only limited efforts to cooperate with other Christian Right organizations.

Citizens for Traditional Values

Another Lansing-based Christian Right organization is Citizens for Traditional Values (CTV), whose origins can be traced to Rev. Pat Robertson's 1988 presidential campaign. CTV was organized in 1986 as the Michigan Committee for Freedom and quickly became involved in the Robertson campaign, but the Robertson forces withdrew their national people from the organization after Robertson's defeat. This left the Michigan Committee for Freedom in a shambles—leaderless, without direction, and deeply in debt from the Robertson campaign.

At that time, the board of directors of the Michigan Committee for Freedom hired James Muffett, former director of Pat Robertson's campaign in Vermont, to head their organization. It proved to be a wise decision. Muffett moved quickly and effectively to eliminate the organization's $200,000 debt. In 1990 the organization filed as a 501(c)4 organization and a year later changed its name to Citizens for Traditional Values.

Under Muffett's leadership, CTV has established a clearly defined mission statement and set of objectives. CTV's four "guiding principles" are (1) "preserving the influence of faith and family as the great foundation of American freedom embodied in our Judeo-Christian heritage," (2) "protecting our God-given right to life, from conception through every stage of life," (3) "promoting a free enterprise philosophy of government which includes freedom from excessive taxation and government regulation," and (4) "providing the means by which parents can obtain educational freedom and strive for academic excellence in the instruction of their children. Ultimate responsibility for a child's education lies with the parents" (Citizens for Traditional Values 1997a, 1).

In many ways, these guiding principles parallel those endorsed by MFF, although CTV tends to take a more explicitly free-market approach to economic issues and to give economic issues a bit more emphasis. Like MFF and unlike RTLM, CTV has adopted a rather broad policy agenda. Indeed, its literature (Citizens for Traditional Values 1997b, 1–2) encourages supporters to interrogate candidates for public office on a large number of policy issues relating to "faith and family," the "proper role of government," and "education."[9]

Just as with the MFF, CTV's pursuing of such a large and broad policy agenda can limit the overall effectiveness of the organization. As a result, CTV has tended in recent months to focus on certain key issues such as educational freedom and affirmative action. And it has achieved at least a limited degree of legislative success. Michigan Senate Majority Leader Dick Posthumus has called CTV "the most underrated political organization in Michigan in relation to the amount of impact" generated. And former Michigan speaker of the house, Paul Hillegonds, reported that "without the help of Citizens for Traditional Values, many of the important legislative reforms that the House passed in 1993 might never have been passed" (Citizens for Traditional Values 1997a, 4).

Over time, CTV has developed a fairly complex organizational structure, though its structure is not as complex as that of RTLM or MFF. In seeking to develop a distinctive identity, CTV chose to eschew becoming a mass-based membership organization with a high profile. Rather, as James Muffett put it, the organization chose to adopt a "servant" rather than a "confrontational" mode (Smidt and Penning 1997, 119). Accordingly, it has chosen not to affiliate or identify itself with any national organization such as the Christian Coalition or Focus on the Family but instead has chosen to remain an independent organization focusing primarily on state elections and policy. Currently, a six-to-eight-person board of directors governs CTV.

In 1993, CTV created the Foundation for Traditional Values (FTV), a 501(c)3 tax-exempt, nonprofit organization that serves as the educational component of the organization. FTV, housed in the same building as CTV, publishes its own newsletter, *Liberty Lamp,* quadrennially, giving special attention to education issues. Among FTV's activities are promoting a summer "Student Statesmanship Institute" and distributing a variety of educational books and tapes. FTV has also produced an extensive "Community Action Pack" that provides detailed information for parents who wish to "conduct an investigation" of their local school board, teachers, textbooks, and curricula. In addition, it provides detailed information on how to run for school board positions.

CTV has also established a separate PAC to assist candidates running in selected legislative districts. However, its primary electoral activity in elections is to produce voter guides targeting key races. The first state-wide election in which the organization mounted an extensive effort occurred in 1992. In an effort to use its resources efficiently, CTV mailed questionnaires to 110 candidates for public office to determine whether they deserved support. After analyzing the responses, CTV decided that although 64 candidates were worthy of support, the group would use its limited assets strategically, targeting only seventeen of the most competitive races. Within those districts, CTV conducted voter registration drives in churches, distributed 10,000 to 20,000 voter guides per district, and organized "phonathons" targeted to specific churches (Smidt and Penning 1997, 119–29). Similarly, in 1996 and again in 1998 CTV limited its electoral activities to targeting fifteen "key races" (Muffett 1997). Like MFF, CTV makes a special effort to mobilize church members, its natural constituency. Indeed, one of CTV's brochures contains detailed answers to the question "Why should Christians vote?"

CTV's decision to target only a limited number of races no doubt reflects its relatively small size and budget. Compared with RTLM or even MFF, CTV is exceedingly small. For example, CTV currently has a staff of four persons, including Executive Director Muffett, and FTV currently has a staff of only two, including Political Director Jeff Visscher. And whereas FTV has a relatively modest annual budget of $200,000, CTV itself operates on a minuscule $50,000.

Christian Coalition of Michigan

There is little doubt that, at the national level, the Christian Coalition is among the most important and well publicized of the Christian Right organizations. But that isn't necessarily the case at the state or local levels. In some states, the organizational strength and activity level of the Christian Coalition varies tremendously from one local chapter to the next (Berkowitz and Green 1997), while in others, including Michigan, the Christian Coalition is exceedingly weak across the entire state.

Like CTV, the Christian Coalition of Michigan (CCM) traces its heritage in part to the Michigan Committee for Freedom. But it wasn't until 1991 that CCM was officially created as a tax-exempt, nonprofit organization. As such, CCM cannot endorse candidates, although contributions to the group are tax deductible. Its activities must be primarily educational rather than partisan. Thus, like CTV, CCM has devoted itself to such "nonpartisan" activities as distributing voter guides for election campaigns.

The CCM remains relatively independent of the national organization, free to articulate its objectives as it sees fit. In practice, this has meant that its president and board of directors have felt relatively free to establish and pursue their own agendas—agendas that have changed with each change in leadership. This is not necessarily undesirable, for, as former CCM Field Director Tom McMillin points out, it has permitted CCM to concentrate on certain state-specific issues such as the actions of the Michigan State Board of Education. It can be undesirable, however, in that it can waste resources as objectives change and can create a degree of confusion as well. Moreover, as agendas have changed with changes in leadership, CCM has failed to articulate a clear and consistent set of objectives to Michigan citizens.

State autonomy for CCM has also produced considerable friction between the state and national Christian Coalition organizations. According to the *Detroit Free Press,* the national Christian Coalition organization recently became "*very* unhappy with its highly independent and sometimes unpredictable Michigan leadership" (McDiarmid 1997, 1). Indeed, the national organization was so upset that in May 1997, Ralph Reed quietly paid a visit to Michigan, seeking to round up replacements for both CCM president, Nancy Cherry of Warren, and the entire CCM board of directors. Reed, accompanied by the national coalition's field director D. J. Gribbin, stopped in Grand Rapids, Lansing, and Detroit to discuss possible leadership changes with prominent Michigan Christian Coalition supporters, including state GOP chair, Betsy DeVos.

Explained CCM board member and veteran McComb County political activist Harry Veryser, "They want a bigger operation in terms of both membership and money and they want more control. . . . Frankly, Nancy [Cherry] has been too independent for them" (McDiarmid 1997, 1). Constance Cumbey, CCM attorney, agreed with Veryser, complaining that "the whole thing is about big power, big money. . . . They want Michigan to surrender its autonomy." Gribbin disputed these claims, although he acknowledged that there is significant state-national disagreement (McDiarmid 1997, 1).

Presently, Jack Horton is the temporary CCM chairperson. Horton is a former state representative from the Grand Rapids area (the western side of the state) who had to leave the house because of term limits. CCM maintains an exceedingly small mailing list of 10,000 persons (Brand-Williams 1997, 2), although it boasts 55,000 "contributors"—people who have contributed time or money (Smidt and Penning 1997, 121). Although CCM hires two paid staffers during election years, in other years CCM maintains no paid staff whatsoever. The CCM is currently organized on a county basis, although leaders hope to add city and even township chapters.

To date, CCM has focused on federal rather than state or local races. Its primary political activities have involved publication of election year voter guides and publication of a monthly newsletter. Though CCM claims to be a statewide organization, for organizational and strategic reasons it has tended to focus its attention on areas close to its headquarters. This makes sense because it helps CCM to use its limited resources in a populous area of the state and because no other Christian Right organization is headquartered in eastern Michigan.

Of the various Christian Right organizations examined here, CCM has tended to be least accepting of the norms of cultural pluralism. CCM leaders interviewed for this chapter tended to be quite wary and somewhat hesitant about responding. Indeed, this wariness even extends to its national headquarters. For example, former CCM field director and head of Pat Buchanan's 1996 presidential campaign in Michigan, Tom McMillin, asserted that there is a distinct lack of trust in the national Christian Coalition organization among CCM members. According to McMillin, "We need to develop bonds of trust. . . . Trust is so huge. People continually ask whether they are giving their time to an organization they can trust" (McMillin 1997).

The 1998 Elections

The 1998 elections in Michigan tended to center on two matters, the gubernatorial race and Proposal B, a proposal to legalize assisted suicide in Michigan. Though not directly associated, the two campaigns were indirectly tied together in some important ways. Not only had the Democratic candidate for governor, Geoffrey Feiger, served as the defense attorney for Jack Kevorkian, the person most responsible for bringing the issue of assisted suicide to public attention, but in both campaigns religion played a notable role.

The Gubernatorial Race

After winning the Democratic Party nomination in the party's primary in mid-August, Feiger found his campaign to be dogged by several problems. First, Feiger, who had contributed nearly $1.25 million to his own primary campaign, had to spend valuable time in late August and early September mending fences with big labor, which had backed one of his opponents in the Democratic primary. Feiger, who attempted to portray himself in his primary campaign as a "populist," advancing the cause of the weak and powerless, had to apologize to those labor and party leaders he had slammed in the primary, as he needed their support in the general election campaign to defeat Engler.

Second, Feiger's campaign was never able to neutralize the impact of several acid remarks he made prior to his candidacy (see, for example, Steinfels 1998). Feiger, in comments to a *Washington Post* reporter in 1996, had portrayed Jesus as "just some goofball that got nailed to the cross." But this religiously offensive remark was not Feiger's sole transgression. When asked several years previously why Jack Kevorkian sought a permit to carry a concealed weapon, Feiger had quipped that one reason "was to protect himself from nuts like Cardinal Maida," the Roman Catholic Archbishop of Detroit. Feiger was also quoted as calling Pope John Paul II "some [expletive] who's wearing a hat three feet tall." And in early 1996, after Orthodox rabbis issued a statement condemning assisted suicide as contrary to Jewish teaching, Feiger compared the Orthodox rabbis to Nazis.

Not surprisingly, Feiger was engulfed in religious controversy from the very beginning of his general election campaign. On September 3, 1998, the Anti-Defamation League demanded a public apology from Feiger for his earlier comments concerning the Council of Orthodox Rabbis of Greater Detroit. Feiger countered the next day with the announcement that he had received the endorsement of the Michigan Clergy United and that the largely black Ecumenical Ministers Alliance, a political action committee that represented some one hundred Detroit pastors and churches, would endorse him the following day. But in speaking before the Ecumenical Ministers Alliance, Feiger contended that Engler was "offering money and benefits in the form of charter schools to black ministers in return for their endorsement or silence." In response, other black pastors lashed out at the contention that their votes could be bought: "Does he really believe that ministers, pastors, reverends and other religious leaders, that the African American churches would betray their flock for 30 pieces of silver and a charter school?" ("Black Ministers Blast" 1998, A25).

Early Engler ads painted Feiger as being out of touch with the people of Michigan. The GOP spent $750,000 on a devastating September television commercial publicizing the controversial religious comments made by Feiger. Engler, as a Roman Catholic, subtly used this religious controversy to bolster his campaign when he stated in a television ad: "We all love our state and want to keep Michigan in the mainstream, not the extreme" ("Catholic Church Anchors" 1998, 1).

For his part, Feiger contended that the remarks were taken out of context and that they did not fairly or accurately reflect his beliefs about religion. He also expressed deep regret for any pain or offense he might have caused by such remarks. Still, Feiger never seemed able to dull his sharp tongue. He called his fellow Democrat, Detroit Mayor Dennis

Archer, a "slow learner" when Archer wouldn't meet with him and said that the Democratic candidate for attorney general, Jennifer Granholm, seemed "almost hysterical" when she took issue with some of the key planks of Feiger's anticrime agenda. Remarks such as these made it easy for Engler to win points on the credibility issue.

Money also played an important role in the gubernatorial race. Because of Feiger's large personal contributions to his primary race, he was ineligible to receive matching public money for the general elections campaign—but he was free to raise and spend unlimited funds on the race. Although Feiger spent well over another $3 million of his own money on the general election campaign (Luke 1998), he never managed in the eyes of most voters to achieve the status of a credible candidate. In the end, Engler received 1.86 million votes (62.4 percent) to Feiger's 1.12 million votes (37.6 percent).

Engler, as shown in table 9.1, captured a majority of votes in each of Michigan's seventeen largest counties—except for Wayne county (Detroit)—though he barely carried Genesse county (Flint). In eleven of the seventeen counties, Engler's percentage of the vote exceeded the percentage he won in his reelection campaign of 1994—a year in which the GOP dominated election returns in Michigan as well as nationally. In fact, in only three of these seventeen largest counties did Engler's vote total fall below the 60 percent margin.

Other State Races

A major conflict also developed over control of the Michigan House of Representatives. Since the 1990 state reapportionment, control of the house has shifted hands almost every election. In the 1994 election, Republicans were able to garner a one-seat majority in the 110-member house, only to lose control to the Democrats in 1996. The 1998 election reversed the GOP losses, giving the party a 58–52 majority. But the Democratic losses were not confined to the house. The GOP also increased its control of the Michigan Senate by winning an additional senate seat (where it now enjoys a 23–15 margin) and captured control of the Michigan Supreme Court for the first time since 1948, giving the GOP a 4–3 margin.[10]

Although, as noted above, the Christian Right worked exceedingly hard in the 1998 election, it is unclear to what extent Christian Right organizations may have shaped these electoral outcomes. More than likely, their efforts served as a contributing, though not necessarily a decisive, factor. Although the Christian Right tended to support GOP candidates and oppose Democratic candidates, Feiger's candidacy probably had a greater negative impact on Democrats in 1998. A telling illustration of how other Democrats sought to distance themselves from Feiger was a

Table 9.1 Percentage Voting Republican in Two-Party Vote for Governor
(Seventeen Largest Counties)

County	1994 %	1998 %
Bay	60	61
Berrien	72	73
Calhoun	63	67
Genesee	50	51
Ingham	55	60
Jackson	70	67
Kalamazoo	60	68
Kent	74	77
Livingston	76	74
Macomb	70	67
Muskegon	60	61
Oakland	66	66
Ottawa	83	85
Saginaw	60	63
St. Clair	70	64
Washtenaw	54	57
Wayne	43	43

campaign brochure of Chuck Busse, a Democratic candidate for the state house from Warren, who sought to link his Republican opponent, Jennifer Faunce, to Feiger.

On the other hand, Democratic congressional candidates were fairly insulated from Feiger's candidacy. Nor was there any significant Christian Right impact evident in the congressional races across the state. All incumbent house members easily won reelection. As can be seen from table 9.2, the percentage of votes going to GOP candidates in each of the sixteen congressional districts has not varied greatly over the past decade. In fact, the closest race for an incumbent in 1998 occurred in the Tenth Congressional District, where Representative David Bonier received 55 percent of the vote. In view of such margins of victory, it is hard to contend that Christian Right activity in any of these races provided the necessary votes to ensure victory.

Proposal B

Proponents of Proposal B generally contend that "big money" led to its defeat. It is true that those who favored the proposal spent most of their money in the effort to get the proposal on the ballot, and opponents of the

Table 9.2 Percentage Republican Votes of Total Congressional Votes Cast (by Michigan Congressional District)

Congressional District	1998 Winner	1992 %	1994 %	1996 %	1998 %
1	Stupak (D)	44	42	27	40
2	Hoekstra (R)	63	75	65	69
3	Ehlers (R)	61	74	69	73[a]
4	Camp (R)	63	73	65	91[a]
5	Barcia (D)	38	32	28	27
6	Upton (R)	62	73	68	70
7	Smith (R)	88[a]	65	55	57
8	Stabenow (D)	46	52	44	39
9	Kildee (D)	45	47	39	42
10	Bonior (D)	44	38	44	45
11	Knollenberg (R)	58	68	61	64
12	Levin (D)	46	47	41	42
13	Rivers (D)	43	45	41	40
14	Conyers (D)	16	17	12	11
15	Kilpatrick (D)	17	14	10	10
16	Dingell (D)	31	40	36	31

[a]Indicates race had no Democratic Party candidate.

bill raised five times as much money as proponents. During the last weeks prior to the election, the airwaves were full of ads against Proposal B.

The group working for the defeat of Proposal B, Citizens for Compassionate Care, was composed largely of religious groups, and religious voters were more likely to oppose the proposal than were nonreligious voters (Bullard 1998). The Roman Catholic Church was among the most outspoken opponents of Proposal B. Archbishop Maida of Detroit, whom Fieger had earlier called a "nut," was particularly active. Maida not only mailed a get-out-the-vote letter to more than 800 priests, but he sent videotapes opposing Proposal B that were to be played at all 310 churches in the Metro Detroit archdiocese. Furthermore, he arranged for the *Michigan Catholic* newspaper, which had included special reports opposing assisted suicide, to be sent free to nearly 360,000 families (Cain 1998).

In all, the Roman Catholic Church pumped over $2 million into securing the defeat of Proposal B (Golder 1998). In the end, these mobilization efforts appeared to pay dividends. Whereas Roman Catholics constituted 27 percent of the Michigan electorate in 1994, they constituted approximately 31 percent in 1998, according to exit poll data

(Golder 1998). Still, the coalition opposing Proposal B was not limited to Roman Catholics; it included evangelical Protestants, Michigan Right to Life, and many medical and business groups, including the state medical society, the state hospice association, and a disability rights group.

The debate surrounding Proposal B was cast almost entirely in secular terms. Obviously, advertisements warning, "B is bad legislation" were much more conducive to building broad coalitions to defeat the proposal than statements proclaiming that assisted suicide is sin, or declaring the wrath of God against Jack Kevorkian would have been.

In the end, many "nonreligious" voters joined with religious voters in opposing Proposal B. What the Michigan election revealed is that it is easier to sell the basic notion of assisted suicide than it is to sell a complex statute translating that idea into law. What Michigan voters were asked to approve was a 12,000-word initiative. Serious questions were raised over whether the proposal provided too few procedural safeguards or too many. Many Michigan voters, for example, appeared to be disturbed by the fact that the proposal included no requirement that family members be notified of a patient's decision to seek assisted suicide. Obviously, arguments about individual cases and personal autonomy and self-determination are one thing, but concrete proposals that seek to cover thousands of cases are something else. In the end, Proposal B received less than 30 percent of the votes cast.

Conclusion

Several conclusions emerge from this look at the Christian Right in Michigan. First, the 1998 election results indicate that Michigan voters were generally not seeking radical change. Rather, they exhibited considerable satisfaction with the economic and political status quo. Every incumbent congressional candidate easily won reelection. In addition, voters soundly rejected the "radical" Proposal B that would have legalized assisted suicide in the state. And voters gave incumbent Governor John Engler a landslide victory over the radical populist, Geoffrey Feiger.

A second conclusion is that the political changes that did occur tended to be in a more conservative direction. Hence, we label this chapter the "Right Stuff." When voters were forced to select new officials, because of either term limits or voluntary retirements, they tended to favor Republicans. The GOP regained control of the state house of representatives and added one seat to its majority in the senate. To some degree, then, the rightward drift of 1998 has offset the leftward drift of Michigan politics in the 1996 presidential election. These pendulum swings, if you will, continue a pattern of political competition in the state that goes back twenty years or more.

However, in the third place, all was not lost for the Democrats. They were able to retain sizable minorities in both houses of the state legislature. They did well in various races for university boards of regents. Perhaps most important, they were able to win the election of rising star Jennifer Granholm to the office of attorney general. Many observers in the state expect Granholm to make a serious run for the governorship in the near future, especially since incumbent Governor John Engler must leave office in four years as a result of term limits.

Fourth, given the fact that (1) most incumbents seeking reelections won and (2) most incumbents enjoyed large margins of victory, one might conclude that the Christian Right played a major role in the 1998 election. However, this conclusion might be premature. For one thing, term limits have shifted electoral battlegrounds, especially for legislative seats, from general elections to primary elections. And it was in the numerous hotly contested primary races that the Christian Right focused much of its attention in 1998 and arguably achieved its greatest successes. In addition, it is easy to forget that as late as mid-summer 1998, public opinion polls indicated that Proposal B stood a good chance of winning voter approval. It took an energetic fall campaign by members of the Christian Right to turn things around.

Finally, the 1998 election in Michigan reveals that, like its national counterpart, the Christian Right in Michigan is closely tied to the Republican Party and to political conservatism. Though the rightward drift of the state's electorate in 1998 clearly worked to the Christian Right's advantage, that may not always be the case. The cyclical nature of Michigan politics suggests the need for Christian Right leaders and organizations to seek as broad a coalition as possible to ensure organizational stability and long-term political success. The fight over Proposal B suggests one possible way to do this. The anti-B coalition united conservatives from the ranks of both evangelical Protestants and Roman Catholics. The challenge of the future, however, will be to overcome mutual suspicions and forge coalitions that can unite over issues characterized by less dramatic appeal.

NOTES

1. For a discussion of the history of political parties in Michigan, see Smidt and Penning (1995).
2. State senators will feel the law's impact in 2002, when thirty out of thirty-eight senators will be forced to retire after serving their current four-year term of office.

3. Bill Ballinger, editor of a widely read Michigan political newsletter, was a Republican state senator when *Roe v. Wade* was decided. According to Ballinger, "Ironically, at the time Senate Republicans were more pro-choice than Democrats, many of whom were Roman Catholics with a strong, anti-abortion view" (Cain 1997c, 3).

4. RTLM feared that "liberal" nurses would be more likely to prescribe the "abortion drug" RU-486 than would more "conservative" physicians.

5. RTLM is structured as a 501(c)4 organization for most purposes. This means that, under IRS regulations, it is permitted to function as an advocacy group, lobbying government officials to achieve its policy ends. However, under 501(c)4 regulations, contributions to the organization are not tax deductible. As a result, RTLM has also established three legally separate 501(c)3 organizations. These three organizations—an education fund, a legal defense fund, and an endowment fund—are legally required to avoid direct lobbying of government officials. Rather, their primary focus is educational, and contributions to these three organizations are tax deductible.

6. Even though RTLM is officially secular, it draws the vast majority of its members and supporters from socially conservative Catholics and evangelical Protestants. Thus, there are empirical grounds for including RTLM among the Christian Right organizations discussed.

7. Among the legislative proposals that MFF labeled as "essential" were those pertaining to alcohol and tobacco use (tougher standards for drunk driving, payment to victims' families, and labeling of alcoholic beverages for pregnant women); governmental affairs and economics (ensuring the constitutional validity of legislation and including family impact statements in legislation; exempting used automobiles from the sales tax); human life issues (permitting civil and criminal charges to be filed against someone who causes death or injury to a fetus; banning assisted suicide); education (improving statewide testing); family law (waiting period and counseling in divorce cases, establishment of child support trust funds in custody cases); adolescent health (protecting teenage girls from predatory sex offenders); and public indecency (limiting minors' access to pornography). Besides these essential recommendations, MFF included a large number of "additional" recommendations in each of these categories.

8. It is clear that MFF leaders, at least, see it this way. In a 1996 interview, MFF Research Director, Don Jarvis, asserted that MFF has been growing more influential in the [Michigan] legislative process (Smidt and Penning 1997, 132 f).

9. These broad categories include "faith and family" issues such as religious freedom, gambling, pornography, drugs, parents' rights, gay rights, abortion, and crime; "proper role of government" issues such as personal liberty, property rights, welfare reform, prison reform, gun control,

excessive taxation, government spending, health care, and governmental regulation; and "education" issues such as local control, schools of choice, charter schools, sex education, abstinence, school prayer, parental control, and school funding.

10. After the general election, a Democratic member of the supreme court announced his resignation, enabling Engler to appoint another Republican to the court. As a result, the GOP now enjoys a five-to-two majority on the court.

REFERENCES

Berkowitz, Laura, and John C. Green. 1997. "Charting the Coalition: The Local Chapters of the Ohio Christian Coalition." In *Sojourners in the Wilderness: The Christian Right in Comparative Perspective,* edited by Corwin E. Smidt and James M. Penning, 57–72. Lanham, Md.: Rowman & Littlefield.

"Black Ministers Blast Fieger's Claim that Backing of Engler Was Bought." *Grand Rapids Press,* 10 September, A25.

Brand-Williams, Oralandar. 1997. "Many Skeptical of Christian Coalition's Pledge to Diversify." *Detroit News,* 4 February.

Browne, William, and Kenneth VerBurg. 1995. *Michigan Politics and Government.* Lincoln: University of Nebraska Press.

Bullard, George. 1998. "Religious Unity Key to B's Defeat." *Detroit News,* 5 November.

Cain, Charlie. 1997a. "Right to Life: In 25 Years, Michigan's Group Gains Enough Political Clout to Rival Unions." *Detroit News,* 2 March.

———. 1997b. "25 Years of Michigan Right to Life: Group Pushes Medical Issues With Lawmakers." *Detroit News,* 2 March.

———. 1997c. "25 Years of Michigan Right to Life: Key Events in the History of Michigan's Debate Over Abortion and Assisted Suicide." *Detroit News,* 2 March.

———. 1997d. "25 Years of Michigan Right to Life: 'Little Old Catholic Ladies' Find Their Bully Pulpit." *Detroit News,* 2 March.

———. 1998. "State's Assisted Suicide Vote Attracts Spotlight." *Detroit News,* 19 October.

"Catholic Church Anchors His (Engler's) Life." 1998. *Detroit Free Press,* 14 September.

Citizens for Traditional Values. 1997a. "A Voice for Your Values." Brochure. Lansing, Mich. Citizens for Traditional Values.

———. 1997b. "From the Pews to the Polls: Candidates and Campaigns." Brochure. Lansing, Mich.: Citizens for Traditional Values.

Golder, Ed. 1998. "Polpourri '98." *Grand Rapids Press,* 4 November, D4.

Harris, Michael. 1997. Interview. Michigan Family Forum Headquarters, Lansing, Mich; 30 October.

Listing, Barbara. 1997. Interview. Right-to-Life of Michigan Headquarters, Wyoming, Mich., 1 December.

Luke, Peter. 1998. "Feiger Still Bankrolls his Campaign for Governor." *Grand Rapids Press,* 24 October, A2.

McDiarmid, Hugh. 1997. "Christian Coalition Pushes to Change Its Michigan Leadership." *Detroit Free Press,* 13 May.

McMillin, Tom. 1997. Telephone interview. 15 December.

Michigan Family Forum. 1997a. "A Formula for Success: A Series of Recommendations for the 89th Legislative Session." Lansing, Mich.: Michigan Family Forum brochure.

———. 1997b. "About MFF." http:www.mfforum.com/about.thml. 26 November.

———. 1997c. "The Voice of Hope for Michigan Families." Lansing, Mich: Michigan Family Forum brochure.

Moen, Matthew. 1997. "The Changing Nature of Christian Right Activism: 1970s–1990s." In *Sojourners in the Wilderness: The Christian Right in Comparative Perspective,* edited by Corwin Smidt and James Penning, 21–37. Lanham, Md.: Rowman & Littlefield.

Muffett, James. 1997. Interview. Headquarters, Citizens for Traditional Values, Lansing, Mich., 30 October.

Penning, James M. 1994. "Pat Robertson and the GOP: 1988 and Beyond." *Sociology of Religion* 55 (fall). 327–344.

Persinos, John. 1994. "Has the Christian Right Taken Over the Republican Party?" *Campaigns & Elections* 15 (September): 20–24.

Reed, Ralph. 1994. *Politically Incorrect: The Emerging Faith Factor in American Politics.* Dallas: Word Publishing.

Smidt, Corwin, and James M. Penning. 1990. "A Party Divided?: A Comparison of Robertson and Bush Delegates to the 1988 Michigan Republican State Convention." *Polity* 23 (1): 127–38.

———. 1995. "Michigan: Veering to the Right." In *God at the Grass Roots: The Christian Right in the 1994 Elections,* edited by Mark J. Rozell and Clyde Wilcox, 147–68. Lanham, Md.: Rowman & Littlefield.

———. 1997. "Michigan: Veering to the Left?" In *God at the Grass Roots, 1996: The Christian Right in the American Elections,* edited by Mark J. Rozell and Clyde Wilcox, Lanham Md.: Rowman & Littlefield.

Steinfelds, Peter. 1998. "Mixing Religion and Politics." *New York Times,* 8 August.

10

Washington: Christian Right Setbacks Abound

Andrew Appleton and Michael Buckley

Introduction

In 1996, the activism of the Christian Right in the political realm was most obviously manifested in the election campaign for governor. That year, a Christian Right activist and supporter, Ellen Craswell, won the Republican nomination for the governorship and subsequently lost to Gary Locke, the Democratic nominee, in the general election. Craswell's capture of the Republican nomination was at the time a real breakthrough for the grassroots mobilization of the Christian Right in the state of Washington; however, her inability to challenge Locke more closely in the general election signaled the limits of the organizing capacity of the Christian Right (Appleton and Francis 1997).

The midterm elections of 1998 offered another opportunity for the Christian Right to flex its political muscle and to catapult the ambitions of the movement onto the national political stage. The most keenly watched race in Washington in 1998 was that involving the incumbent Democratic senator Patty Murray; many observers in the state saw the race as shaping up to be a litmus test of the durability of the Gingrich/Republican revolution. Murray was elected in 1992 on the coattails of Bill Clinton and at the time was seen as offering a rather different and fresh perspective on the role of politician. Billing herself as a "mom in tennis shoes," Murray positioned herself as a champion of common folk and common sense, albeit with a distinctly liberal flavor. By 1998 the problems of the president and the perception that Murray had become too liberal for the state electorate meant that her seat was widely regarded as vulnerable.

187

Thus the Senate race in Washington State became another fascinating gauge of the influence of the Christian Right in the political process. Again, the same challenges existed for the grassroots mobilization of the Christian Right as in 1996, albeit in a different political climate: the need to act cohesively, the winning of the Republican nomination, and then the attempt to build a winning coalition with moderate Republicans in the general election. As we will argue in this chapter, the outcome was not dissimilar to that of 1996; despite many favorable circumstances, the Christian Right in Washington remains incapable of rallying enough support to beat even a weak opponent in a statewide election.

The 1998 elections in the state of Washington also offered another arena in which to observe the extent of the influence of the Christian Right in state politics. In common with many other western states, Washington has a process for amending state law through both initiatives and referenda. The general election of 1998 saw five different measures on the ballot (four initiatives and one referendum) that called for citizens to cast a yes or no ballot. One of these measures, I-200, was a relatively moderate version of an anti-affirmative action law (modeled in part after proposition 187 in California). Another, I-694, was an initiative that would lead to a ban on partial-birth abortions, a hot-button issue for the Christian Right in the election year (at the national level, the right wing of the Republican Party attempted to pass a partial-birth abortion ban but failed).

The comparison of the fate of these two initiatives serves as another litmus test for the ability of the Christian Right to mobilize the general electorate behind their agenda. The impetus for I-200 did not come out of the Christian Right of the party, whereas I-694 was one of the flagship issues of that same Christian Right. The extent to which either of these two initiatives could assemble support across the ideological spectrum would serve as an interesting indicator of the possibilities and limits to political action. The Christian Right was hoping that I-694 would be a potent means to reenergize the abortion debate and to turn moderates against the prevailing climate of legal abortion. By choosing an issue that had such powerful imagery and such potential to touch individual emotions, the Christian Right hoped to score an important statewide victory.

In this chapter we will describe and analyze the Senate campaign of 1998 that pitted Patty Murray against a challenger from the Christian Right, Linda Smith, and the dynamics of the vote on I-694. It is our contention that both events signaled the incapacity of the Christian Right to appeal to a moderate vote that was the linchpin of the 1998 election (as much on a national as a state level). Indeed, the 1998 election showed that the activism of the Christian Right is a clear liability for the Republican Party in the state in terms of general election outcomes; we do not foresee any change in this scenario in the near future. Before analyzing these particular components of the 1998 elections, however, we will turn to a brief examination of some of the important elements of the political environment in Washington state, which both stimulate and circumscribe the limits of political and party activism.

The Political Environment

As has been pointed out elsewhere, the institutional environment of Washington state is one that facilitates political activism on the part of insurgent groups (Appleton and Depoorter 1997; Appleton and Francis 1997). The key aspect of the electoral system (adopted by voter initiative in 1935) that provides incentives for grassroots activism is the so-called wide-open or blanket primary. This system allows voters to participate in the primary process with no partisan restrictions (prior partisan declared affiliation, etc.). Thus insurgent movements can take advantage of the openness of the primary system to run candidates challenging the orthodoxy of the party organizations and mobilize highly energized voters to swamp the perennially low turnout of the party regulars.

Added to the electoral mechanism of the wide-open primary is the heavy regulation of party organizations in the state. Historically, the same antiparty sentiments that bequeathed the particular form of primary election to the state also resulted in a tight web of state law shaping and governing the internal processes of the parties themselves. In addition, the structure of the party organization that is effectively prescribed by the law is one that vests a disproportionate share of power in rural county organizations. The parties of the state are decentralized in nature (Nice, Pierce, and Sheldon 1992), and this decentralization allows the more rural, less populous, counties of the state to have a major sway over the direction of the central party organizations. In the modern party era, the state parties (both Democratic and Republican) have had to cope with important splits between the rural and more urban county organizations that have manifested themselves at the level of the central party organizations.

It is in this environment—with a wide-open primary system, decentralized party organizations, and a disproportionate influence in the party political process accorded to rural counties—that grassroots activism has ebbed and flowed in the state of Washington. Though not all activism in the state is of the insurgent variety (indeed, far from it), the institutional environment is one that magnifies the potential for such insurgency and makes it a rational strategy on the part of those wishing to shift the balance of political forces. The modern party era, as alluded to above, has been characterized by repeated instances of challenges to the control of the central party organizations by established political elites.

The Republican Party in the state has already experienced these kinds of factional/ideological disputes repeatedly in the modern era. In the 1960s, the party organization faced a vigorous and sustained challenge from the John Birch Society that was strongest in the eastern part of the state. As pointed out elsewhere (Appleton and Francis 1997), this insurgency failed to wrest control of the central party organization from the moderate wing of the party, but it was a harbinger of the shift to come. In the 1990s, the party organization became the battleground for sustained conflict between moderates, social conservatives, and the Christian Right.

The 1992 party convention exposed these often-bitter struggles to a wide audience. Effectively, the Christian Right emerged for the first time with the upper hand in the organization of the party and controlled the agenda of the convention. The state delegation to the national convention was heavily tilted in favor of the Christian Right, and the ground was being prepared for the attempt of Christian Right activists to use their party base to win electoral office. Without question, the ideological and organizational battles were divisive (Appleton and Francis 1997), and this may in part account for the relatively poor showing of the Republican Party in national and statewide elections in 1992.

Given the apparent negative impact of the 1992 Christian Right insurgency on the general election, a fragile truce was brokered for the 1994 convention and elections (Appleton and Francis 1997). Although it is hard to disentangle the effects of intraparty processes from the more general dynamic of the protest vote of 1994 against the Democratic majority in Congress, Washington state actually experienced the largest swing in the composition of its congressional delegation of any state in the union. From a House delegation that was majority Democratic, the party of defeated speaker Thomas S. Foley was reduced to holding just two of the nine seats allocated to this state. In many ways, 1994 seemed to herald an important lesson for the Christian Right; that is, it could be on the winning side in an election but only if it moderated its public image and presented a visage of unity and coalition with moderate Republicans. Unfortunately for the aspirations of the Christian Right, this lesson was to be lost with the gubernatorial campaign of Ellen Craswell in 1996, which reignited the tensions between the different factions of the party and brought the less palatable image of the Christian Right once again to the fore (Appleton and Francis 1997).

The 1996 election in the state of Washington represented a major setback for the aspirations of the Christian Right movement (Appleton and Francis 1997). The experiences of the 1992, 1994, and 1996 election campaigns all pointed to the growing institutionalization of the movement in the primary elections as an electoral force with which to be reckoned. Indeed, by the time Linda Smith declared her candidacy for the Senate seat to be contested in 1998, it was seen as less than surprising that she would both seek the nomination and eventually obtain it. Yet these elections also demonstrated, each with a different outcome emanating from different electoral dynamics, that the Christian Right had a problem building effective coalitions with moderate Republicans and shoring up the centrist vote. Thus the most obvious questions, from the perspective of the campaign observer in 1998, were two: Could the Christian Right once again dominate the important primary processes? And if so, could the movement build the necessary bridges with moderate voters to finally win a statewide office?

As we will demonstrate, the answers in brief are yes and no. In placing Linda Smith's name in nomination and successfully winning the state primary, the Christian Right proved that it had become a reliable electoral force in primary elections. Despite bitter struggles of the past or maybe because of them, the central party organization is either unwilling to challenge the predominance of the Christian Right in the primary process or incapable of doing so. However, in an electoral climate that cried out for moderation and appeals to the center, the Christian Right did exactly the opposite in the general election. Far from being able to mobilize moderate voters and pull them away from the siren song of the Clinton agenda, the Christian Right's presence in the general election seems to have either demobilized moderate Republicans or pushed them into the grateful arms of the Democratic Party. Either way, the 1998 election demonstrates the fundamental incapacity of the Christian Right movement in the state to present itself with a more moderate and broader voter appeal. Once again, the activist base and ideological instincts of the Christian movement prevented the party from picking up a seat that many thought was highly vulnerable. In the end, we would argue, the victory of Patty Murray was as much due to the efforts of the Christian Right as to her own voter appeal.

Equally, the dismal failure of I-694 to live up to the expectations of its sponsors shows that the Christian Right in the state seems incapable of finding an emotive issue drawn from its activist agenda that can pull moderate voters into its fold. The astonishing rapidity with which the initiative qualified for the ballot seemed to presage a potential breakthrough for the agenda of the Christian Right—indeed, many observers thought that it was possibly the most likely initiative to pass. In the end, the electorate rejected the ballot proposition by a substantial margin while approving I-200 (ending affirmative action) by almost exactly the same differential. This, we argue, clearly shows that the willingness of moderates to support popular issues coming from the social conservative wing of the Republican Party does not translate over to issues more closely identified with an activist religious agenda. In the end, the defeat of I-694 was a blow for the future hopes of the Christian Right in the state of Washington.

The 1998 Election

The general election of 1998 was noteworthy in several respects in the state of Washington in comparison with other elections in recent years. First, voter turnout was exceptionally high for a midterm election: 62 percent of the registered electorate cast a vote for at least one ballot item in the November contest. This represented the highest turnout in a midterm election since 1982 (particularly given that voter registration numbers have risen in recent years in the state of Washington). Of those ballots cast, fully 47.5 percent were cast in the form of absentee ballots, another record for a midterm election. The mobilization of the electorate mirrored the turnout in the September primary elections, in which almost 35 percent of the registered voters of the state participated. In that contest, a staggering 60 percent of the ballots cast were absentee.

The U.S. Senate Race

The 1998 U.S. Senate race in Washington State provides an excellent example of the limits of the Christian Right's appeal to Washington voters. Linda Smith, the Republican candidate, ran a grassroots campaign based on Christian values, campaign finance reform, antitax proposals and a general outsider populist agenda. This style and substance are similar to those of many traditional Christian Right candidates (Johnson and Bullock 1991).

She inherited the leadership of the Christian Right from Ellen Craswell, the Republican candidate for governor in 1996. Unlike Craswell, Smith was seen as more mainstream and presented what many thought a legitimate chance to elect a conservative Christian candidate to statewide office. However, like Craswell, Smith ultimately lost the election and by a larger margin than her predecessor.

Linda Smith: Background and Political Career

Smith was born Linda Ann Simpson on July 16, 1950; she was raised by her mother and stepfather in a lower-middle-class household, where lack of money was always a concern. She spent her childhood in La Junta Colorado with three brothers and sisters. Her mother was not overly religious, but her maternal grandparents were and often took Linda to the Assembly of God Church. The combination of little money and frequent church attendance had a lasting impact on her. According to her husband, Vern Smith, these early influences provided her with the strength and convictions to pursue her conservative Christian agenda (Serrano 1998a).

Married soon after high school, Vern and Linda Smith settled in Hazel Dell, Washington, located near Vancouver, in southwestern Clark County. Her interest in politics began after a tax increase forced her to lay off employees at the H&R Block tax preparing company she managed. Religion continued to be important to the Smiths, as they became active members of the Glad Tidings Assembly of God Church. Combining early life experiences of little money and the importance of religion, Smith's political agenda included cutting taxes and conservative social issues. The impetus for her decision to run for the state legislature may have been her opposition to increasing taxes on small businesses, but her political philosophy was founded on conservative Christian values.

Smith's political career began in 1983, when she was elected to the state house of representatives, a post she held until 1987, when she was elected to the state senate. In 1994 Smith left the state senate when she was elected to the United States House of Representatives from the Third Congressional District, a traditionally Democratic area of southwestern Washington. She was elected again in 1996 after a difficult campaign against political novice Brian Baird. In 1998 she decided to run for the United States Senate against Patty Murray, one of the more liberal members of the Senate, according to ranking organizations.

From her election to the state house of representatives in 1983 until her defeat in the 1998 U.S. Senate race, Smith pursued a socially and fiscally conservative agenda. Her early proposals included legislation banning anyone under eighteen from having sex and ending no-fault divorce. Not one to be limited to the legislative process, Smith took issues directly to the people with two initiatives. The first, initiative 134, proposed campaign-finance reform that set statewide contribution limits to campaigns. Initiative 601 proposed spending limits on campaigns (Serrano 1998b).

In addition to supporting tax cuts and campaign finance reform, Smith was consistent with the Christian Right on most issues. She campaigned against abortion, gun control, gay rights, and assisted suicide and supported initiative 200 (repealing affirmative action). She received high conservative ratings from groups that rank elected officials according to how they vote on pending legislation. For example, the National Abortion Rights Action League ranked Smith 0 out of 100 on a scale of 0 to 100, with 0 being the most conservative. Liberal groups ranked Smith similarly: the American Civil Liberties Union, 8; League of Conservation Voters, 0; AFL-CIO, 8. Using a similar scale but with 100 as the most conservative, the National Right to Life Committee ranked her 96; the U.S. Chamber of Commerce, 100; the Christian Coalition, 100; and Private Property Voters, 100 ("How They See Her" 1996).

Beyond her conservative agenda, Smith is also well known for being independent and somewhat abrasive. Both qualities endeared her to voters frustrated with candidates from the Democratic and Republican parties who appeared more conventional. Her style gained the attention of Ross Perot in 1996 and prompted him to offer her the vice presidential spot on his Reform Party ticket. Though she declined Perot's invitation, her political outsider, populist approach made many in the Christian Right feel her appeal was broad enough to attract voters outside the group. Another sign of Smith's potential broad appeal was her ability to win the Third Congressional District. Democrats had held the seat for thirty-four years prior to Smith's election in 1994, and the percentage of registered voters in the district favored the Democrats.

On the basis of her previous political success (Smith had never lost a campaign), her core support of conservative Christians, and her populist appeal, she decided to run for the U.S. Senate. Before challenging incumbent Patty Murray in the general election, Smith had to get the nomination of the Republican Party. Though she was a two-term member of the House of Representatives, Smith's endorsement from fellow Republicans was not certain. Her independence (she voted against Newt Gingrich for Speaker of the House, calling him a fat little boy) alienated many in her own party. Senate Majority Leader Trent Lott, when asked who he would support as the Republican nominee for U.S. Senate in Washington, indicated his preference for Dunn. Republican United States Senator Slade Gorton noted that any "candidate had to be a Republican team player," a reference to Smith's independent ways. George Nethercutt, the Republican house representative from Washington's Fifth Congressional District, was more direct when he stated that he would support Dunn over Smith (Gimaldi 1997).

The Primary

Smith's populist independent style benefited her in Washington, where voters have weaker party attachments than their counterparts in other states (Nice, Pierce, and Sheldon 1992). Also favoring Smith was the blanket primary, which allows voters to vote in all party primaries simultaneously. As a result, Smith could attract voters from more than the Republican Party. She, more than her main Republican challenger, benefited from this arrangement, as supporters of Christian candidates are often from a wide range of socioeconomic backgrounds. Research suggests that Christian Right candidates draw support from "rural residents, low wage earners, the aged, the poorly educated, nativists, conservatives, and Republicans" (Johnson and Bullock 1991, 176).

Linda Smith's main opponent in the primary was Chris Bayley, a millionaire Harvard-educated lawyer and former King County prosecutor. Almost a political unknown, Bayley had been in private business since leaving his prosecutor's job in the late 1970s. His ideological background suggested that he was a moderate Republican. Bayley's personal style also differed significantly from Smith's; soft-spoken, articulate, and choosing his words carefully, he was more traditional.

Although Bayley's moderate style may have been a positive trait in the general election, traditionally more conservative members of the party have controlled Republican primaries in Washington. This includes the Christian Right, whose members have high turnout rates that are inflated during primaries because of the low overall voter turnout (Gray, Jacob, and Albritton 1990; Fiorina and Peterson 1998). During Ellen Craswell's bid for the governorship in 1996, 66 percent of the vote went to those candidates who identified themselves as conservative or Christian Right candidates ("Race for the Senate" 1998).

Smith also had the advantage of being a member of the House of Representatives. Though she did not pursue fundraising opportunities as most incumbent politicians do, she did have name recognition. Instead, she decided to run a grassroots campaign, collecting small sums of money from 35,000 individuals known as "Linda's army." Smith refused to take soft money or corporate donations from political action committees.

On the issues Bayley and Smith provided Republican voters with a choice between a conservative Christian Republican and a moderate Republican. Smith opposed funding for the National Endowment for the Arts; Bayley favored it. Smith opposed most free trade legislation; Bayley supported free trade. Both were on record as opposing abortion, though Bayley's position was not as clear as Smith's. They both opposed gay rights and gun control and favored Initiative 200.

Smith's strategy worked for the primaries. She soundly defeated Bayley by a two-to-one margin, though preelection polls predicted the race would be closer. Bayley in his concession speech seemed generally shocked by the outcome, but as noted above, a low turnout usually favors ideologues on the right or left of the political spectrum. In this case, turnout was about 35 percent giving the conservative Christian Smith and her army a distinct advantage.

Table 10.1 shows the overall state turnout rates. Table 10.2 shows how all the candidates did in the 1998 primary. As noted above, as a result of the blanket, or wide-open, primary system, Patty Murray appeared on the same primary ballot as Smith and her main opponent.

Table 10.1 Voter Participation in the 1998 Washington State Primary

Total registered voters	3,082,341
Total ballots cast	1,087,650
Statewide turnout	35.29%

Source: Secretary of State, Washington.

Table 10.2   Primary Election Results, U.S. Senator of Washington State

Candidate	Votes	Percentage
Hanson, Warren E. (R)	22,411	2.15
Murray, Patty (D)	**479,009**	**45.86**
Amundson, Thor (D)	10,905	1.04
Stokes, James Sherwood (D)	5,989	0.57
Mover, Mike The (RFM)	6,596	0.63
Medley, Robert Tilden (D)	3,350	0.32
Vernier, Harvey (D)	3,882	0.37
Smith, Linda (R)	**337,407**	**32.31**
Bailey, Nan (SW)[a]	3,709	0.36
Bayley, Chris (R)	**155,864**	**14.92**
Thompson, Steve (RFM)[b]	3,371	0.32
Marshall, John (R)	9,662	0.93
Jackson, Charlie R. (RFM)	2,234	0.21

Source: Secretary of State, Washington
[a]SW, Socialist Worker's Party
[b]RFM, Reform Party of Washington State

The General Election

The November general election for the U.S. Senate in Washington drew national attention for a number of reasons. It was the only woman-versus-woman election in the country and only the third in U.S history. In addition, both Smith and Murray portrayed themselves as populists, though from different perspectives. Smith remained faithful to the course that had guided her throughout her political career, relying on her status as an outsider, underdog, and populist. In doing so, she retained her solid base of religious conservatives. In addition, she continued to make campaign finance reform her central issue. Murray's strategy was to portray herself as a populist from the left who remained close to the people, concerned about education, jobs, and the environment.

The approach to raising money taken by both candidates would be one of the more important factors deciding the outcome of the election. Murray accepted PAC and soft money. Smith continued to refuse PAC and soft money, instead relying on a grassroots campaign that collected donations from individuals and small businesses, though she did take money from the Republican National Committee, which receives much of its funding from large corporations, including the tobacco industry. Murray did not let this apparent double standard go unnoticed.

On the issues, Murray and Smith presented a stark contrast. Smith re-mained true to the issues that had been important throughout her

political career and had appealed to her conservative Christian supporters. In addition to advocating campaign finance reform, Smith campaigned against abortion, gay rights, the National Endowment for the
Arts, and most environmental policies and taxation. Murray, a former
state senator from Shoreline County with a long record of supporting liberal democratic issues, opposed Smith on each of the above topics and
made education the central issue of her campaign. Smith attacked
Murray for taking money from large corporations and being a traditional
tax-and- spend liberal and career politician. Murray countered by portraying Smith as a right-wing extremist pursuing a religious agenda.

The outcome of the election highlighted the limits of the Christian
Right in Washington state. Mirroring the 1996 gubernatorial race that
pitted religious conservative Ellen Craswell against moderate Democrat
Gary Locke, the 1998 U.S. Senate race produced similar results, though
Smith lost by a larger margin than Craswell (see table 10.3). Locke's mar-
gin of victory was 58 to 42 percent; Murray's margin was 59 to 41.

The outcome of the election was especially frustrating for Republicans
who had believed Murray was beatable. According to Republican Secretary of State Ralph Munro, "These are huge losses. Patty Murray is the
most beatable Senator in the nation. I hope sooner or later the party will
listen to solid advice from the middle" (Postman and Serrano 1998). Political observers' prediction that Chris Bayley would have had a better
chance against Patty Murray because he was not a member of the Christian Right may have been correct. The similarities between Craswell and
Smith are striking. Both represented the Christian Right, presenting a
moral message combining religion and politics. Their stances on the issues were almost identical. Smith received the endorsement of Craswell
and consulted with her before deciding to run for the Senate. Both did
well in their respective primary races, which reflected the commitment of
the Christian Right to turn out. In the general election, when turnout increased, the Christian Right and Smith and Craswell suffered. In 1998,
turnout for the primary was 35 percent; in the general election it was 62
percent. Craswell and Smith received just over 40 percent of the vote in
the general election. Thus, unless turnout is low, the Christian Right and
their candidates, though committed, vocal, and participatory, appear to

Table 10.3 General Election Results, 1998, Washington State

Ticket for U.S. Senate	Votes	Percentage
Murray, Patty (D)	1,103,184	58.41
Smith, Linda (R)	785,377	41.59

Source: Secretary of State, Washington.

have limited appeal and are destined to remain a minority in the state of Washington.

The Initiatives

Although the number of initiatives and referenda in 1998 was not historically high, it was noteworthy that there were three high-profile initiatives on the ballot that had received a lot of regional and even national attention. The political system of Washington allows for initiatives to be placed on the ballot by the gathering of signatures; referenda can be moved either by citizen demand (the signature process) or by decision of the legislature. Four initiatives and one referendum were at issue in 1998: I-200, I-688, I-692, I-694, and Referendum 49. Of these, I-200, I-692, and I-694 garnered the most attention. The first of these measures attempted to halt state participation in affirmative action programs, I-692 would have allowed the medical use of marijuana, and I-694 was an attempt to eliminate the procedure popularly known as partial-birth abortion.

Ending abortion has been a goal of the Christian Right since the Supreme Court decision making it legal in the 1973 *Roe v. Wade* case. Arguing that abortion is murder, right-to-life supporters have attempted to limit or stop abortion using multiple means. Proponents of choice with regard to abortion argue that women have a constitutionally protected right to privacy when making decisions regarding their bodies. In 1973 the U.S. Supreme Court agreed with pro-choice advocates, ruling that women have the right to end a pregnancy. The ruling was not absolute, however, since it found that a woman's right to privacy may be outweighed by the state's interest when the fetus is potentially viable.

Washington's history on the issue of abortion predates *Roe v. Wade*. In 1970 Washington legalized abortion, becoming only the third state to do so. In 1984 the voters defeated an initiative that would have denied state funding for abortions. And in 1991 Washington voters passed Initiative 120 (the Reproductive Privacy Act), writing into state law the same rights enunciated by the U.S. Supreme Court in *Roe v. Wade*. Limiting access to abortion was again put to the voters of Washington in 1998 in the form of Initiative 694, the partial-birth abortion initiative, or what doctors call "intact dilation and extraction."

The 1998 Washington State legislature considered a similar bill, supported by the Christian Right, but its sponsors decided to kill it after it passed the house and was revised and weakened in the senate. Believing they had the support of the majority of the Washington voters, advocates of a ban on late-term abortions collected the necessary 193,904 signatures to place it on the ballot in November.

The speed and number of signatures gathered encouraged supporters of the ban that they had a chance to limit abortions. The Monroe-based

Committee to Stop Infanticide needed only six weeks to collect 220,658 signatures and did not use paid signature gatherers to accomplish this task. In addition, this number represents a near state record for valid signatures collected (Varner 1998). Much of the credit for the rapid pace of signature gathering goes to clerics who allowed petitioners to solicit outside churches and to the direct participation by some churches, including the Catholic Church, in the dissemination of information about the initiative.

Initiative 694 stated, "Shall the termination of a fetus's life during the process of birth be a felony crime except when necessary to protect the pregnant woman's life?" (Office of the Secretary of State 1998) This measure, the fourth time an abortion issue had been before state voters, would have made it a felony for doctors to perform an abortion once a woman's "cervix has dilated, the amniotic sac ruptured, and the fetus has entered the birth canal." (Office of the Secretary of State 1998). Supporters of I-694, the Committee to Stop Infanticide, argued that this type of abortion was so heinous it should be outlawed. Citing evidence of the occurrence for elective, not medical, reasons and of doctors lying about the frequency of the procedure, the proponents of the initiative (led by Dr. Robert Bethel, a family physician from Poulsbo, Washington) hoped to persuade voters to approve I-694. This was not Bethel's first foray into politics; he had worked as a volunteer for Ellen Craswell's gubernatorial campaign in 1996. In the tradition of the Christian Right, Bethel's campaign to limit abortion was grassroots in style. The committee raised $50,000, most of it in $100 and $200 donations.

Opponents of I-694 argued that of the 27,000 abortions performed in Washington state in 1996, none were partial-birth as defined by the initiative. In addition, they claimed the law was poorly written and could be interpreted more broadly, placing greater limits on abortions. Citing the language of I-694, opponents argued that it did not use medical terminology and thus doctors would not know what procedures were within the scope of the law. They also argued that I-694 was simply was not necessary. Initiative 120, the Reproductive Privacy Act passed in 1991, made abortion a crime if the fetus was viable except in cases where the mother's life or health was in danger (Charbonneau and McGough 1998). In a somewhat ironic twist, Bethel claimed that I-120 was also poorly written, allowing doctors and patients to end a pregnancy for such reasons as depression or lack of money (Varner 1998). Ultimately, opponents of I-694 argued the initiative would allow the state, not doctors and patients, to decide when an abortion was legal. In addition, they argued this was only the first step in an attempt by the Christian Right to end abortion completely. Supporters of I-694 did not deny the latter claim, acknowledging that their primary goal was ending all abortions.

As was the case with the candidates running on a conservative religious agenda, support for I-694 peaked at just above 40 percent (see table 10.4); the initiative did not pass, again highlighting the limits to the Christian Right's effectiveness in the state of Washington. For the fourth time since 1970 Washington state voters chose not to limit abortion. Commenting on their loss, supporters of I-694 believed their inability to show one partial-birth abortion had been performed in Washington proved fatal. Their ad campaign included a nurse commenting on the horrors of the procedure, but it was later revealed that she was from Ohio. Though disappointed, supporters of I-694 vowed to fight on, contemplating lobbying the U.S Congress for a ban on late-term abortions.

In contrast to the fate suffered by I-694, it can be seen from table 10.5 that I-200 (the ending of state affirmative action programs) fared significantly better (indeed, it passed by the same margin—58 to 42 percent—by which I-694 was defeated). What is significant is that the gap between the vote for the project initiative of the Christian Right (I-694) and the citizen initiative that emanated from the social conservative wing of the Republican Party (I-200) was greatest in the most populous counties—precisely those areas where Smith had done relatively poorly. According to one Republican strategist, Smith's showing in King County (the most populous county in Washington) was "beyond terrible"; there she received 31 percent of the vote (Nelson 1998a). In fact, in all but one of the most populous counties (Yakima) the Republican candidate and I-694 lost. In addition, in all but four counties there were different levels of support for Linda Smith and I-694. Both Smith and I-694 won seventeen out of thirty-nine counties, most with a population under 15,000. What this suggests is that the moderate constituency that failed to rally behind the partial-birth abortion initiative was willing to cast its vote for I-200 to end state affirmative action programs. The latter vote is more surprising given the opposition of the relatively popular Democratic governor, Gary Locke.

Thus it seems clear from these figures that the activism of the Christian Right behind the candidacy of Linda Smith and the passage of I-694 had definable and clear contours. The relatively clear victory of Smith in the primary and the extraordinarily quick gathering of petition signatures for I-694 demonstrates that this activism is determinant in low-salience, highly partisan political contexts. However, when issues of public concern are placed before the general electorate, or when a statewide office

Table 10.4   Initiative 694 (Partial Birth Abortion)

Outcome	Votes Cast	Percentage
Yes	802,376	42.85
No	1,070,360	57.15

Source: Secretary of State, Washington.

Table 10.5 Results for Smith and Selected Referendum Measures in the 1998 General Election (Votes Cast as Percentage of Registered Voters)

County	Smith	I-694	Difference (Smith I-694)	I-200
Adams	32	31	1	38
Asotin	21	20	1	28
Benton	32	32	0	40
Chelan	34	30	4	41
Clallam	32	31	1	44
Clark	30	30	0	39
Columbia	37	33	4	44
Cowlitz	28	31	−3	41
Douglas	32	30	2	40
Ferry	35	34	1	50
Franklin	36	36	0	41
Garfield	38	41	−3	48
Grant	36	36	0	44
Grays Harbor	22	27	−5	37
Island	31	28	3	41
Jefferson	28	25	3	41
King	19	20	−1	29
Kitsap	28	31	−3	41
Kittitas	33	32	1	44
Klickitat	31	30	1	40
Lewis	37	32	5	41
Lincoln	36	32	4	44
Mason	27	26	1	40
Okanogan	35	28	7	43
Pacific	23	25	−2	38
Pend Oreille	33	36	−3	51
Pierce	25	27	−2	37
San Juan	27	20	7	40
Skagit	28	27	1	39
Skamania	32	32	0	43
Snohomish	25	26	−1	35
Spokane	27	28	−1	37
Stevens	31	28	3	38
Thurston	25	25	0	36
Wahkiakum	36	35	1	52
Walla Walla	30	31	−1	39
Whatcom	28	28	0	35
Whitman	20	21	−1	28
Yakima	30	32	−2	42

is at stake, the presence of the Christian Right serves to either demobilize moderate conservatives, push them toward the opposing fold, energize the liberal electorate, or do all three. For moderate Republicans who support a centrist candidate, the process is a frustrating one, for they are often defeated in the primary by the more vocal yet smaller Christian Right, only to see the candidate representing their party defeated in the general election. The clear concordance between the fate of Linda Smith and that of I-694 signals the incapacity of the Christian Right in the state of Washington to pass the bar that leads to state office.

The Christian Right in Washington state is a vocal, committed participatory group that appears to be a permanent minority. Washington state's system of blanket primaries and initiatives rewards and encourages minority groups in the early stages of the electoral process. This does not hold true in the general election if turnout is relatively high, and in Washington this is usually the case (Nice, Pierce, and Sheldon 1992). The more moderate candidate or position on an issue is more likely to win.

The defeat of Bob Williams in 1988, Ellen Craswell in 1996, Linda Smith, and Initiative 694 may reflect a more fundamental problem for the Washington state Republican Party. Many moderate Republicans stated publicly that abortion should be dropped as a core Republican issue and that they need to nominate moderate candidates. Brett Bader, a GOP political consultant, noted after the 1998 election, "I'm a pro-life conservative, but as far as I'm concerned, [initiative] 694 closed the debate on that issue. It's absolutely vital that Republicans get control of their nominating process and nominate viable, strong candidates who can win" (Nelson 1998a). Thus, it is not only the Christian Right that lost but also the Republican Party, since it failed to elect its candidate in two elections that many felt were winnable. As long as this small but participatory group exists within the party and the nominating process remains unchanged, the ability of the Republican Party to nominate candidates with a legitimate chance to win will remain suspect.

One possible solution to the problem of a vocal minority may be the creation of a separate party by the Christian Right. However, the 1998 election suggests this may not be the panacea moderate Republicans might hope for. Bruce Craswell, Ellen's husband, ran as an American Heritage party candidate for the U.S. House of Representatives in the First Congressional District. His message, like his wife's, was based on core conservative values. Though his supporters were most likely not all Republicans, conservative independents often take from the Republicans more than the Democrats. Table 10.6 reveals the importance of the division within the Republican Party between social conservatives and the Christian Right. If Rick White, the Republican candidate, had received Bruce Craswell's support, he would have won the election with just over 50 percent of the vote.

Table 10.6   Votes for U.S. Representative First Congressional District

County	Jay Inslee (D)	Rick White (R)	Bruce Craswell (AH)
King	55,047	47,213	4,786
Kitsap	19,487	17,349	3,399
Snohomish	38,192	35,344	5,652
Total votes	112,726	99,910	13,837
Percentage of vote	49.77	44.12	6.11

Source: Secretary of State Washington.

Conclusion

Once again, the story from the state of Washington is one that reflects the presence of a permanent minority of highly visible and highly active Christian Right political activists. The experience of the 1990s—the abortive election campaign of 1992, the fragile peace of 1994, the fiasco of 1996, and the indifference of 1998—demonstrates that the Christian Right in this part of the Pacific Northwest has proved incapable of accommodation with the political mainstream or even the moderate wing of the Republican Party. Given the repetition of essentially the same dynamics in at least three of the four most recent general elections in the state (if not all four), it seems fairly safe to conclude that the problems facing the Christian Right in its attempt to penetrate the politics of the state are systemic. In our analysis, these systemic aspects are twofold.

In the first instance, the *ideological* environment of the 1990s is not one that favors the accession to power of the activist Christian Right. Though this may not appear obvious on the surface, given the rightward shift of the the electorate, the Christian Right seems, in the state of Washington, to be incapable of making the overtures to the center that would be necessary to build a broad electoral coalition. Here the experience of I-694 is the most instructive. The partial-birth abortion debate, as we have suggested, is one that is highly emotional and definitely at the most difficult end of the spectrum for supporters of abortion rights to defend. Though physicians may debate technical aspects of the procedure, the notion that a viable fetus on the cusp of independent life would be aborted is one that seemed sure to galvanize public reaction. Yet in the election, the public decided by a sixty-to-forty majority that such a procedure should not be sanctioned by the state. Without a doubt, the failure of the moderate and centrist right to support the ballot measure demonstrates the lack of appeal of the ideological pretensions of the Christian Right.

204 0 PRAYERS IN THE PRECINCTS

The second factor placing the Christian Right in a situation of permanent minority status is the *electoral and institutional environment.* There is little or no incentive for the Christian Right to build coalitions with the social conservatives or moderates in the primary process, for the institutional mechanisms of the state primary process facilitate activist insurgency and even encourage it. Thus, where the Christian Right triumphs in the intraparty phase of the electoral process, it is a triumph that is predicated on defeating opposition forces rather than building coalitions. Even though there is an inevitable shoring up of Republican support for candidates like Ellen Craswell and Linda Smith on the eve of the general election, both candidates began with such disadvantages created by the extreme positions they took in the primaries that they were simply unable to credibly portray a more moderate face. It is hard to imagine that the activism of the grassroots citizen alliances associated with the Christian Right will produce any candidates who are by temperament and training more moderate.

Thus, to conclude, there is little change in the broader dynamics of the Republican dilemma in the state of Washington. The Christian Right is far from a spent force in electoral politics in the state. The same issues that dominated the agenda in 1996—abortion, homosexual rights, etc.—will inevitably come up again and again. The simple fact is that the Christian Right is buttressed by a network of local activist communities based in churches and sects, out of the purview of the general public. The airwaves are filled disproportionately with the message of the Christian Right, and in the rural communities where church and AM radio are still an integral part of the way of life, the message of the movement remains strong and present. However, the possibility that the Christian Right will achieve some unforeseen breakthrough in statewide politics seems very remote. How the Republican Party will continue to live with this dynamic is another matter and one that preoccupies many moderate Republicans in the state.

REFERENCES

Appleton, Andrew, and Anneka Depoorter. 1997. "Washington." In *State Party Profiles. A 50-State Guide to Development, Organization, and Resources,* edited by Andrew Appleton and Daniel S. Ward. New York: Congressional Quarterly.

Appleton, Andrew, and Dan Francis. 1997. "Washington: Mobilizing for Victory". *God at the Grass Roots, 1996: The Christian Right in the American Elections,* edited by Mark J. Rozell and Clyde Wilcox. Lanham, Md.: Rowman & Littlefield.

Charbonneau, Christine, and Peter McGough. 1998. "Voters shouldn't be fooled by deceptive Initiative 694." *Seattle Times,* 29 October.

Fiorina, Morris P., and Paul E. Peterson. 1998. *The New American Democracy.* Needham Heights, Mass.: Allyn and Bacon.

Gray, Virginia, Herbert Jacob, and Robert B. Albritton. 1990. *Politics in the American States.* 5th ed. Glenview, Ill.: Scott, Foresman/Little, Brown Higher Education.

Grimaldi, James V. 1997. "Linda Smith to Run for Senate." *Seattle Times,* 9 May.

"How They See Her." 1996. *Seattle Times,* 9 October.

Johnson, Loch, and Charles S. Bullock III. 1991. "The New Religious Right and the 1980 Congressional Elections." In *"Do Elections Matter?"* edited by Benjamin Ginsberg and Alan Stone. New York: M. E. Sharpe.

Nelson, Robert T. 1998a. "Conservatives Still Sticking with GOP." *Seattle Times,* 17 September.

———. 1998b. "Republicans Seek Answers after Big Losses." *Seattle Times,* 5 November.

Nice, David C., John C. Pierce, and Charles H. Sheldon, eds. 1992. *Government and Politics in the Evergreen State.* Pullman, Wash.: Washington State University Press.

Office of the Secretary of State of Washington. 1998. Complete Text of Initiative 694.

Postman, David, and Barbara Serrano. 1998. "Big Victories for Murray and I-200." *Seattle Times,* 4 November.

"Race for the Senate." 1998. *Seattle Times,* 7 June.

Serrano, Barbara A. 1998a. "Murray, Smith: Populist Opposites." *Seattle Times,* 25 October.

———. 1998b. "Smith Continues to Go Her Own Political Way." *Seattle Times,* 10 September.

Varner, Lynne K. 1998. "Initiative 694's Abortion Ban Is the Latest Battle in a War." *Seattle Times,* 2 August.

11

Minnesota 1998: Christian Conservatives and the Body Politic

Christopher P. Gilbert and David A. M. Peterson

For nearly two decades Christian conservative activists have worked assiduously to take effective control of the state Republican Party. Progressing from political outsider status to significant positions of power within the party structure, Christian conservatives realized a pivotal victory with the elections of November 1998. At long last Republicans wrested control of the Minnesota House of Representatives from the Democratic-Farmer-Labor (DFL) Party, which had held power almost continuously since 1974.

But it seems that for Christian conservatives in Minnesota, success never comes without a price. Over the years, the religiously motivated wing of Minnesota Republicans has gained small victories and lost major battles; Christian Right successes in pre-November events have not always translated into November triumphs. November 1998 added a different twist to this trend. Though a Christian Right-dominated Republican Party won the great battle for the state house, nobody took much notice because of the remarkable gubernatorial victory of Reform Party candidate and former professional wrestler Jesse "The Body" Ventura.

Our chapter outlines the activities of the Christian Right during the 1998 election cycle, described in the context of Minnesota's unique electoral system. We provide a brief overview of the Christian Right's successes and failures in the 1990s, as well as an empirical analysis of 1998 voting patterns. Finally, we discuss the role of Ventura's candidacy in the Republican takeover of the state house. We conclude that though two decades of hard work and political organizing helped bring Minnesota's Republicans (including the Christian conservative wing of the party) to the brink of success, the ultimate credit for their state house takeover belongs to Jesse Ventura, a most unwitting and unwilling accomplice to such an event.

Structural Considerations

Minnesota's political parties operate under a party caucus-convention system that culminates in official party endorsements of candidates for the September primary election.[1] Since a very small proportion of the electorate attends the county caucuses (usually about 1 percent), a small and well-organized group of individuals can have a disproportionate impact on the decisions of their party. The endorsement process begins in late February or early March when all three major parties hold precinct caucuses, open to every party member who chooses to attend, to pick delegates for the county conventions a few weeks later. These conventions in turn select delegates to the state and congressional district conventions, held in late May or early June. Each caucus and convention endorses candidates for the various local elections: the county conventions endorse for local and county offices, state representatives, and state senators; district conventions endorse congressional candidates; and the state convention chooses the endorsed candidates for statewide offices.

These endorsements pertain only to each party's primary election, and candidates who are not endorsed are free to contest the primary in September. The endorsement carries with it the financial and organizational support of the party, as well as considerable free publicity from coverage of the caucus-convention season. Party support includes contributor and membership lists, sample ballots, poll data, and access to the party booth at the state fair in late August.

For many local candidates a viable campaign without the benefits of party endorsement is hardly possible. However, at the statewide level the endorsement has become increasingly irrelevant as a vehicle to victory. Tradition holds that unendorsed candidates should not contest the primary, but recent elections have seen a reversal of this trend and a corresponding reduction in the importance of the party endorsement. The 1994 Republican race for governor is the prototypical example of both the importance and limitations of the endorsement. Allen Quist gained the Independent Republican endorsement with little difficulty at the June convention (see the next section) but was trounced by Governor Arne Carlson in the September primary.

The Background, 1974–1994

Given the reputation of Minnesota voters for political knowledge and sophistication, most national analysts professed absolute shock at Jesse Ventura's gubernatorial victory. In fact, throughout the twentieth century Minnesota's political scene has witnessed numerous electoral and social movements operating through and around the two-party system to win elections and govern effectively. The DFL Party is one by-product of this trend, forming just after World War II, when significant electoral successes by the Farmer-Labor Party led Democrats to the merger table (Gilbert et al. 1999, 46).

Though most of this movement-based activity has centered on ideas from the political left, in the 1980s the same caucus-convention process that opened the door for old movements became the vehicle for a new movement that sought to reform politics on moral grounds. Well before the Christian Coalition began to develop grassroots organizations and to exploit the multiple centers of political power in the United States, Christian conservative activists could be found doing the very same thing in Minnesota, gaining strength within the Republican Party and forming a reliable core constituency for several prominent conservative officeholders (Haas 1992). The track record of Minnesota's Christian Right activists at the polls, however, is decidedly mixed throughout this period of organization and institutionalization.

Minnesota's Republican Party is best understood as two distinct entities, whose differences were for many years captured in the party's name. The old label Independent Republican, or IR (adopted during the Watergate years and dropped in 1995), stood for two competing political ideologies—a primarily secular constituency advocating moderate to progressive social policies combined with fiscal restraint (the "I" side), and the increasingly Christian conservative-dominated "R" wing that stressed a social agenda centered on opposition to abortion and the restoration of traditional values and family structures.

The conflict between the party's two wings has remained intact, though a few notable Republicans have successfully melded or have overcome the schism. For example, the most visible and arguably most influential Minnesota Republican of the 1980s and 1990s was Vin Weber, who represented the Second Congressional District (southwestern and south central Minnesota) for twelve years. Weber became a member of the House minority leadership, and following his retirement in 1992 he has played prominent roles in developing strategies for the national Republican Party and the 1996 Dole campaign. Articulate and politically savvy, Weber understood the importance of combining the party's two wings in order to advance any agenda, including the Christian conservative agenda he adopted in Congress. Weber's leadership and an existing set of pro-life activists and organizations within the state provided the foundation for the strong emergence of the Christian conservatives in the 1990s, a fact that Weber (who is not himself a Christian conservative) has publicly acknowledged numerous times (Schmickle 1996; "The State Republican Convention" 1996).

If Vin Weber stands as an example of how Christian conservatives can work effectively within the state Republican Party, the eight-year governorship of Republican Arne Carlson demonstrates that Christian conservatives can also be left behind if they are unwilling to compromise. A former state auditor, Carlson won the 1990 gubernatorial election after a peculiar series of events brought down the IR's original nominee, who was a Christian conservative himself, just three weeks before the election.[2] The pro-choice, pro-gay rights Carlson defeated DFL incumbent Rudy Perpich in the general election (Hoium and Oistad 1991); coupled with the loss of a U.S. Senate seat to the DFL, Christian conservatives thus found 1990 to be a near disaster. After a shaky beginning to his governorship, Carlson gained public respect, and his tough dealings with the DFL-controlled legislature led to unparalleled economic prosperity in Minnesota.

Carlson's success as governor must be understood in the context of some significant IR failures during his tenure in office. In 1992, by which time Christian conservatives had gained control of the IR party apparatus and hence control over candidate endorsements and party resources, electoral successes were decidedly mixed. Despite having a strong Christian conservative and well-known candidate running to replace Vin Weber, Weber's Second District seat was lost to the DFL by 569 votes (Barone and Ujifusa 1993, 690–91). This result plus the weak performance of President Bush in Minnesota (33 percent in the state) led many moderate Republicans to warn of the impending doom brought on by the increased influence of the Christian conservatives, who responded in turn by exerting even more influence over the party (Smith 1992, 1993).

Internal difficulties within the IR Party took center stage in 1994. At the precinct caucuses in early March, Christian conservatives turned out in large numbers to support the gubernatorial bid of former state legislator Allen Quist, who essentially wrapped up the party endorsement over Governor Carlson that first night.[3] The sizable advantage of Christian conservatives at these caucuses also kept a number of prominent Republicans from becoming delegates to the county and eventually the state convention.[4] Eventually Quist's candidacy would peter out. Carlson soundly defeated him in the primary, a victory due partly to good economic times but also to an anti-Quist backlash among moderate voters.[5] Carlson went on to swamp DFL candidate John Marty in the general election, winning reelection by a record margin (Whereatt 1994).

On the positive side of the 1994 ledger, first-term U.S. representative Rod Grams won a close, bitter race for the open U.S. Senate seat vacated by fellow IR David Durenberger. Grams benefited from his perfect 100 percent congressional rating from the Christian Coalition and the fact that moderate and independent voters did not connect Grams strongly to the Christian conservative movement.[6] Another candidate strongly supported by Christian Right groups, former state legislator Gil Gutknecht, won his bid to replace moderate DFLer Tim Penny in the First District. Gutknecht's connections to the Christian Right and his endorsement of the Contract with America were considered essential to his victory.

The Immediate Background: 1996–1998

Entering the 1996 elections, the main mission of the Minnesota Republican Party was to defeat incumbent Paul Wellstone, perhaps the most liberal member of the U.S. Senate. The GOP primary race had the potential to be yet another "I versus R" battle within the party, but in fact the Christian Right never came close to defeating former Senator Rudy Boschwitz, who had lost to Wellstone in 1990 after a series of campaign missteps (McGrath and Smith 1995).

Boschwitz had won election to the Senate in 1978 (defeating incumbent Wendell Anderson with 57 percent of the vote) and 1984 (58 percent) (Smith 1996h). He was considered a conservative by the standards of his era in the Senate, but despite this record he conflicted on several fronts with Minnesota's Christian conservatives: Boschwitz was Jewish; he had distanced himself from Jon Grunseth's troubles back in October 1990; and his Senate voting record also included opposition to the school prayer amendment, support for funding the National Endowment for the Arts, and support for the 1982 and 1990 tax increases (Smith 1996j). Realizing this dissonance, Boschwitz chose the route pioneered successfully by Arne Carlson in 1994: he did not bother seeking the convention endorsement actively, declaring that he would run in the September primary regardless (Schmickle 1996; Smith 1996a).

The favored candidate of GOP Christian conservatives was Bert McKasy, a former state legislator and commerce commissioner. To court Christian Right GOP support McKasy had hired several staff members from the 1994 Quist campaign (deFiebre 1996b). But Christian conservatives perceived McKasy as less than committed to their agenda; he had never campaigned on a strong social issues platform in the past and he had worked previously for moderate Republicans Carlson and former U.S. Senator David Durenberger. Moreover, McKasy was an undistinguished campaigner and never developed a coherent, visible ad campaign in the weeks leading up to the state convention (Baden 1996b).

The final, fatal blow to the McKasy campaign came from within. A third GOP contender, Monti Moreno—a political newcomer, evangelical Christian, former Golden Gloves boxer, and hairdresser by trade—made his mark in the race by distributing photocopies of AIDS awareness pamphlets that included graphic illustrations of gay sex, which he claimed came from a high school sex education class.[7] In passing out this literature he would point out that McKasy had voted to legalize sodomy as a state legislator in 1983 (Smith 1996k).

Moreno succeeded in splitting the Christian Right wing of the party, which led to a disastrous June convention. Instead of endorsing McKasy, which most observers considered an inevitable outcome (Smith 1996d, 1996g,) after fourteen ballots spanning two days the delegates finally decided to endorse no one at all (deFiebre 1996a). Without the support of the party to give him a needed boost for the primary, and more than forty points behind in the preprimary polls, McKasy withdrew from the race (Baden 1996a) and cleared the way for Boschwitz to win the primary with more than 80 percent of the vote (Baden 1996c).

The June Republican convention also nominated a conservative slate of delegates to the GOP National Convention in San Diego. This group was notable for two reasons. First, it was without exception pro-life and socially conservative and included the leaders of the state's three most influential Christian Right groups: the Minnesota Concerned Citizens for Life (MCCL), the Minnesota Christian Coalition (MNCC), and the Minnesota Family Council (MFC) (Smith 1996i). Second, the group's support for presumptive nominee Bob Dole was lukewarm at best. Only 52 percent of Minnesota delegates were "very favorable" toward Dole, versus 72 percent of all delegates (Smith 1996i). The clear first choice of Minnesota delegates, according to a *Star-Tribune* survey, was Texas Senator Phil Gramm, who had exited the race months before. Allen Quist, who helped organize the original effort for Gramm, publicly backed Pat Buchanan after Gramm withdrew from the race, and Alan Keyes also enjoyed significant support (Smith 1996b). Overall, the San Diego delegation may have been the best indicator of the dominance of Christian conservatives in Minnesota.

Given the fractiousness of the 1996 convention season, perhaps it is not surprising that Christian conservatives were generally disappointed in the November results. In the U.S. Senate race Paul Wellstone won a surprisingly decisive victory over Rudy Boschwitz (Ragsdale 1996). Among other factors, Boschwitz was hurt by the inability of the Christian conservatives to match Wellstone's mobilization efforts on election day (Gilbert and Peterson 1997, 199–200).

The presidential race in Minnesota was more or less conceded by the Republicans from the outset. While Bill Clinton made frequent trips to the state throughout his presidency, Bob Dole hired "one lone operative" to staff his St. Paul headquarters and made but one personal appearance during the race. Not surprisingly, Clinton gained a decisive victory in November.

Rather than focusing on presidential politics, Christian Right activists directed resources to congressional and state legislative races, with modest success. The national office of the Christian Coalition was a decisive factor in the First Congressional District (southeast) race, helping first-term GOP incumbent Gil Gutknecht win reelection by a four-point margin.[8] In the Sixth District (northern Twin Cities suburbs) Minnesota's other first-term representative, Democrat Bill Luther, defeated Republican Tad Jude, who abandoned his 1994 focus on social issues and lost Christian conservative support as a result. Finally, the race in the Seventh District pitted three-term DFL incumbent Colin Peterson against first-time candidate Darrel McKigney, a former MFC legislative director and aide to Vin Weber and Rod Grams (Smith 1996e). The Seventh District covers the northwestern region of Minnesota, an area more socially conservative than the rest of the state. Peterson fit the district well, frequently deserting congressional Democrats on spending and social issue votes; he swamped McKigney by gaining over two-thirds of the vote (Smith 1996e).

At the state legislative level the Christian Right hoped to capitalize on its significant gains of 1994, when eleven Christian right-backed candidates won seats (Baden 1994). The 1995–96 legislative session was marked by a series of scandals within the house DFL caucus, leaving a tight 68–66 DFL margin heading into the 1996 elections. Consistent with the other results in November 1996, the Republicans were shocked to discover that not only did they fail to retake the house, but many of the Christian conservatives who had stormed into office in 1994 were defeated, leaving a 70–64 DFL majority in place (Whereatt 1996). This is perhaps the most surprising of any of the election results. Christian conservatives usually have the biggest organizational advantage at the local levels, as demonstrated in 1994. This time, the dominant pro-DFL voting pattern of the state, buoyed by strong showings from Clinton and Wellstone at the top of the ticket, emerged again to overcome any organizational advantages held by the Christian Right.

The 1998 Gubernatorial Election: Winning the Issues, Losing the Governor's Chair

Minnesota Republicans entered 1998 with high hopes of holding the governorship. Arne Carlson was voluntarily leaving office after two successful terms. The state had record low unemployment and a budget surplus exceeding $2 billion for the second time in three years. Carlson enjoyed his highest approval ratings (over 60 percent), and the GOP felt a worthy successor had been found in the mayor of St. Paul, Norm Coleman. From the perspective of Minnesota's Christian conservatives, Coleman was a definite improvement. In 1996, three years into his first term as St. Paul's mayor, Coleman left the DFL Party and easily won reelection in 1997 as a Republican. Shortly thereafter he announced his candidacy to succeed Carlson. Coleman had been consistently pro-life and supportive of economic growth, so in many ways he fit more naturally with the GOP agenda. He was certainly a better fit with the Christian Right wing of the party, and he courted this group effectively through the caucus process.

Coleman's main competitors for the party endorsement were Allen Quist and Lieutenant Governor Joanne Benson, who had received Governor Carlson's support. All three candidates agreed prior to the June convention that the endorsed candidate should run unopposed in the September primary, thus making the convention the real decision-making body. Despite Benson's strong organizing efforts and Quist's lingering appeal to the most ardent Christian Right delegates, Coleman swept to the endorsement on the fourth convention ballot (Smith 1999).

As we have noted earlier, recent Republican state conventions have tended not to benefit the party greatly, and even this successful convention backfired somewhat, though not because of anything done by Christian conservatives. Since there was no race on the Republican side, the DFL gubernatorial primary in the September race received all the attention of the state's political media, with the sons of three prominent DFLers and two other well-known candidates running.[9] Out of this pack, state Attorney General Hubert "Skip" Humphrey emerged with a surprising and clear victory. Moreover, a poll published just after the election showed Humphrey with a twenty-point lead over Norm Coleman; Reform Party candidate Jesse Ventura had 10 percent support in this mid-September poll, reflecting a clear and emerging base of support for the Reform Party in Minnesota (Gilbert et al. 1999, 103–06).

In the end, the story of the 1998 Minnesota gubernatorial election has little directly to do with the Christian Right and its actions in support of Norm Coleman. Yet Jesse Ventura's victory is so remarkable that it deserves attention, if only to point out the obvious: a minor party candidate in U.S. politics can win only if everything goes right for his campaign and almost nothing goes right for his opponents. Despite their long track records of electoral success and strong records of achievement in office, neither Humphrey nor Coleman said or did much to excite Minnesota voters about their candidacies. By contrast, Jesse Ventura became a phenomenon: his plain speaking resonated with the public; his contrasting background to two career public servants appealed especially to disaffected nonvoters as the perfect example of what ailed modern politics; and his campaign advertising team developed a brilliant series of television spots using "Jesse Ventura action figures" and scenes of the candidate touring the state in a motor home.

With each succeeding poll Ventura's standing grew, Humphrey's lead shrank, and Coleman's percentage moved slowly upward to parity with Humphrey. Most preelection polls had the race too close to call between the major party candidates, but on November 3 it was Ventura who emerged with 37 percent of the vote to Coleman's 34.5; Humphrey faded badly to third with 28 percent. Exit polls revealed that Ventura won for three major reasons. First, he capitalized on a base built by Ross Perot and other Reform Party candidates in previous elections, good for about 10 percent of the vote. Second, he undercut the bases of support for both major party candidates, running even with Humphrey among women (the Minnesota gender gap mirrors the national advantage that women have given Democrats in recent years) and even or ahead of Coleman among voters stressing economic growth and tax relief (Coleman's main issues). Finally, an estimated 12 percent of voters showed up only to vote for Jesse Ventura. This remarkable turnout boost made the difference in what would otherwise have been a narrow Coleman victory over either opponent.

For Norm Coleman, the gubernatorial results reflected a small victory for the party's conservative platform, though this is obviously overshadowed by the final result. Minnesota voters did not believe Coleman to be too conservative, although he fared poorly among moderate voters (behind both opponents). Nor did Minnesota voters connect Coleman in a negative way to the Christian Right wing of the state GOP, which worked hard to turn out Christians for Coleman and for state house candidates (Hallonquist 1998). In many respects, Coleman won the battle of ideas in this election, and to the extent that he represented ideas palatable to Christian conservatives this was a solid triumph.

1998 State Legislative Elections: The Christian Right Wins One

The lone success for Christian conservatives in the 1998 Minnesota elections (except for some low-level statewide offices) was the Republican Party's reclaiming majority status in the Minnesota House of Representatives for the first time since 1987. Going into the election, the DFL held a 70–64 seat majority; thus a three-seat gain would switch party control, and this possibility was widely discussed throughout the campaign (only the state house was contested in this election; the state senate remained solidly DFL).

Most analysts predicted that all but twenty of the seats were certain for the incumbent. Of those uncertain seats, five were held by retiring Democrats, seven by retiring Republicans, and eight by incumbents running for each party. The House DFL caucus seemed to have the superior campaign organization with seventeen full-time staff working some of the marginal races throughout the state (Spano, Leary, and Janecek 1998).

But in the general election, the Republicans won seventy-one seats, taking firm control of the house.

In the aftermath of the election, Christian conservative organizations, including the Minnesota Family Council, claimed responsibility for the takeover of the house. Their explicit argument was that despite the loss of the governor's race and stability in the state's congressional delegation (all eight incumbents won reelection), the Republican Party was indebted to Christian conservatives for gaining control of the house. GOP executive director Tony Sutton specifically credited the mobilization efforts of conservative organizations (Hallonquist 1998).

These claims come mostly from party and organization leaders, who have a vested interest in being perceived as effective. Unfortunately, their claims are not directly testable, and though their story seems plausible, there are some alternative explanations for the GOP state house victories. First, the Republican gains could simply have been the result of a secular trend in partisanship within the state. That is, the results were not due to the specific campaign tactics of the Republican Party or any Christian conservative organization, but rather were the eventual and logical outcome of changes in the composition of the electorate. Certainly, get-out-the-vote efforts may have helped, but this argument suggests the Republicans would have taken control one way or another.

The second alternative explanation for the Republican takeover is that it was a by-product of the huge turnout boost caused by the Ventura candidacy. Minnesota had a tremendous level of turnout in 1998, the highest in the nation. Many of these voters turned out solely to vote in the gubernatorial election. Of course, the governor's race was not the only race on the ballot, and most of these voters voted for other offices, including the local house of representatives. Further, Ventura's issue positions clearly did not fit neatly with voters of either party. He was socially liberal but fiscally conservative, as were many of his supporters. Which party they voted for in the house races is an open question.

Both of these counterhypotheses hold that the local house races were at least partially determined by statewide concerns. How likely is this? Though it is generally believed that local races are affected by statewide or national concerns, there is an additional reason to expect to find such a link in Minnesota. Heading into the 1998 election then-House Minority Leader Steve Sviggum attempted to make control over the chamber a central issue in the house races. During the late summer and early fall, he challenged then-Speaker of the House Phil Carruthers to a series of debates about each party's vision for state government. This strategy clearly mimicked the Contract With America's nationalization of congressional campaigns in 1994, and the results suggest that statewide factors probably played a role in determining the outcomes of the statewide races.

The long-term trend in Minnesota politics is a move toward partisan parity in the state. Table 11.1 presents the aggregate percentage of the popular vote received by the DFL for Minnesota House races from 1974 through 1998. Clearly, being the plurality winner in the total vote does not guarantee that the party will be the majority in the house. In four of these thirteen elections, the DFL received a minority of the votes but won control of the house; the only previous Republican victory (1984) also fits this circumstance. On the basis of table 11.1, we can say that as early as 1994, the Republicans apparently became the majority party among Minnesota House voters, but they could not win control until the third election contested under these conditions.

The clear explanation for this disparity is the drawing of the district boundaries. This is usually a contentious issue, and the lines for the 1990s were no exception. At the time, the legislature was unified under DFL control while Republican Arne Carlson was governor. The plan that came out of the legislature clearly benefited the Democrats and was widely expected to be vetoed by Carlson. In perhaps the biggest mistake of his administration, Governor Carlson took longer than his three-day deadline to veto the bill and it became law. The elections of 1994 and 1996 provide some evidence for the accusations of unfair boundaries. In each case, the Democrats held the majority, despite receiving less than 50 percent of the total vote.

Although the district lines for 1998 were identical to those for 1996, the gerrymandering that had occurred earlier in the decade was losing some of its impact. Specific portions of the state, especially the outer suburbs of

Table 11.1   State House Voting for the DFL Party, 1974–1998

Year	DFL Percentage of Total Vote	No. of DFL Seats (out of 134)
1974	59.5	103
1976	59.1	101
1978	51.0	67
1980	49.4	70
1982	55.9	78
1984	50.9	66
1986	54.1	83
1988	52.5	80
1990	53.0	80
1992	54.2	87
1994	47.2	71
1996	48.5	70
1998	47.5	63

the Twin Cities, underwent a dramatic increase in population. These changing dynamics and urban sprawl altered the demographic makeup of some key swing districts. Instead of being mostly agricultural and rural (and thus expected to vote DFL), a handful of districts became largely suburban, and wealthy suburban at that. At least four of the seats the Republicans gained in the House came from these changing swing suburban districts (Sweeney and O'Connor 1998).

Though some of these gains may have stemmed from Christian conservative activism, it is likely that the electoral changes would have occurred with or without the active groups. The voters moving into these districts are upper-middle-class citizens building large homes in the (current) outermost ring of the suburbs. Though there is no direct evidence one way or the other, it is likely that these voters were motivated more by economics than by Christian conservative social agendas. Thus, at least some of the changes stem more from changing demographics, and economic demographics at that.

Our second hypothesis for a cause of the Republican gains in the house is that they constitute an offshoot of the Ventura victory. As outlined earlier, the Ventura campaign was unlikely to attract Christian conservatives. He was extremely liberal on social issues; one of the few issue stands he took during the campaign was weak support for legalizing prostitution. More important, Ventura appealed to voters who were disconnected from the political process. Christian conservatives in Minnesota have been mobilized in recent elections by the candidates, Republican Party organization, and independent political organizations (Gilbert and Peterson 1995, 1997). Republican gubernatorial candidate Norm Coleman had been working to court and mobilize Christian conservatives ever since he switched from the Democratic Party in 1997. Thus, voters who turned out to support Ventura are unlikely to fit the profile of the Christian conservatives.

How the Ventura voters cast their ballot for lower offices is an open question. The commercial exit polls did not ask voters about their votes for the state house. The only data that exist are the aggregate election returns. Of course, making inferences about individual-level behavior from this aggregate data is problematic. Standard inferences are subject to aggregation bias because of the well-known ecological fallacy (Robinson 1950; Achen and Shively 1995). A recent advance in cross-level inference developed by King (1996) provides some degree of certainty in the estimates, but even this "solution" is not perfect (Freedman et al. 1998). Thus, the specific point estimates should not be taken too seriously, but the general pattern of results does provide some evidence for how Ventura voters behaved in lower-level elections and thus, by inference, how much relative impact Christian conservative activism had on the results.

We begin the analysis of the Ventura voters with a standard ecological regression. Though this approach does have some limitations (Achen and Shively 1995), the standard regression approach allows us to control for multiple influences in a single model. The data for these models are collected at the level of house district. The dependent variable is the percentage of the two-party vote for the Republican candidate.[10] The three independent variables included in the model are the share the Republican candidate received in the 1996 house election, the percentage of the vote in the district for Ventura, and the percentage in the district for Coleman. The expectation is that both the lagged dependent variable and the Republican share in the gubernatorial election will be positively related to the 1998 Republican house candidate's share.

The key question is how Ventura's share relates to the house outcome. The results in table 11.2 suggest that Ventura's performance is statistically related to how well the Republican house candidate fared. When we control for the historical performance of Republicans in the district and the relationship with Republican voting in the gubernatorial election, Ventura's vote share exerts a significant, positive relationship.

As noted earlier, these results are suggestive but could suffer from biases induced by the aggregation of individual-level voting behavior. To help rectify this potential difficulty, we utilize King's method of ecological inference (EI) to analyze the same data. A detailed discussion of the method is beyond the scope of this chapter (see King 1996 and Burden and Kimball 1998 for a detailed description). It is sufficient here to note that the method produces an estimate of the percentage of Ventura voters who voted for the Republican house candidate in each district. These estimates can then be aggregated to get a single statewide estimate of the proportion of Ventura voters who supported the house Republican candidate.

The specification of the model estimated includes a single covariate. King advises including covariates if the researcher believes that there is

Table 11.2 Republican Share of State House Vote by District, 1998 (OLS results)

Variable	Coefficient (Standard error)
Constant	−0.15 (0.08)[a]
Republican share, 1996	0.55 (0.07)[a]
Ventura vote	0.23 (0.11)[a]
Coleman vote	0.90 (0.18)[a]
Number of cases	134
R-squared	0.68

[a] = Significant at .01 level.

some other factor that will alter the relationship between the two variables of interest. In this case, the covariate included is the percentage of voters in the district that registered the day of the election. As discussed earlier, a sizable portion of all 1998 voters (around 13 percent) registered at the polls on election day, and most of these voters were mobilized by Ventura's candidacy. It is plausible that those voters who registered on election day may behave differently than those who had registered previously.

The first set of EI results is presented in table 11.3. The first column presents the estimate and standard error of the statewide proportion of Ventura voters who voted for the Republican house candidate. The second column is the same proportion for all other voters. Two conclusions are evident. First, Ventura supporters voted disproportionately for the Republican house candidate. Though this estimate aggregates out all of the differences across the districts, it does appear that the general trend was for Ventura voters to vote Republican in the lower-level elections. The second conclusion stems from the proportion of the voters who supported one of the two major-party gubernatorial candidates. Approximately 40 percent of the two-party gubernatorial voters supported the Republican candidate. This is especially striking considering that the Republican gubernatorial candidate received a larger share of the vote than the DFL candidate did. It seems that many of the voters who supported Coleman then supported the Democrat (often an incumbent) for state house.

Though the results in table 11.3 suggest an overall pattern, the table results obscure the differences across the districts. Certainly some districts should have more or less Republican house voters than others, and the simple average ignores this. Fortunately, King's technique makes it possible to produce a histogram of the proportion of each group of gubernatorial voters who supported the Republican house candidates. Figure 11.1 presents these histograms. For each histogram, a dash along the X-axis denotes one house district, the X-axis is the proportion who voted Republican, and the Y-axis is the density estimate. The specific values along the Y-axis are not important; what matters is the relative difference. Ventura voters behaved in a more uniform manner than major party voters did. This is not surprising. The major-party voters consist of two pools,

Table 11.3 Statewide Support for Republicans

	Ventura Voters	Other Voters
Mean	0.7205	0.4028
Standard error	0.0475	0.0282

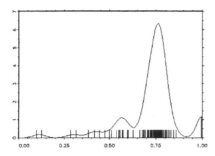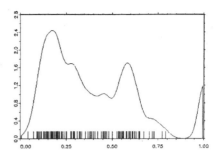

Figure 11.1   Density Plots for Ventura and Major-Party Voters

Coleman and Humphrey voters. How they behave in the district should depend on the relative mixture of the two pools.

The final way to examine the evidence from this method is to ask, what if Ventura voters had behaved differently? Would control of the house have changed if Ventura voters had either not turned out or split their votes evenly in the house elections? This is simple to test. The method produces an estimate and standard error for the proportion for each of the districts. The district-level estimates indicate that had the Ventura vote been unrelated to Republican house vote, the Republicans would have won only around sixty three seats, eight fewer than they did win, and not enough to take control of the house.

Although these results are not conclusive about the role of the Christian conservatives in the Republican takeover of the state house, they do suggest that the Republican Party's success stemmed largely from the Ventura candidacy. Though Ventura may have cost the party the governor's mansion, he, and not Christian conservatives, was also responsible for the Republican takeover.

Lessons

The story of Christian Right influence in Minnesota remains one of limitations. Although activists played a large role in mobilizing voters to support the Republican state house takeover, our statistical analysis reveals that an outside factor was more important in pushing the GOP over the top. Further, one of the first acts of the new house speaker, Steve Sviggum, was to deemphasize the social agenda that motivated Christian Right activists to work with and through the Minnesota Republican Party in the first place (Whereatt 1998). Hence the long-awaited acquisition of the state house majority will not translate into immediate or significant advances in the legislative agenda long sought by the Christian Right cause in Minnesota.

Christian Right organizations have succeeded in Minnesota by forming coalitions with broader cross-sections of the Republican Party, a strategy favored by pragmatic politicians like Vin Weber but at odds with the ideological fervor that leads many Christian Right activists to engage in politics in the first place. Though the 25 to 30 percent of the electorate affiliated with Christian conservative causes is necessary for Republicans to win statewide elections, the state's voters remain more likely to support political moderates (Arne Carlson) or even outsiders (Jesse Ventura) than strongly identified Christian conservatives. Clearly, Christian conservatives will be mobilized and involved in Minnesota state politics no matter who runs for office under the Republican banner. There is no viable alternative for their electoral interests and none is likely to arise. When conditions are favorable—low turnout in midterm or special elections, weak DFL opponents, low-visibility activities like delegate selection, or targeting of state legislative districts in the Twin Cities suburbs—the potential for success will be high. But the lack of legislative progress on restricting abortion rights, promoting vouchers for private schools, and denying benefits and legal protections to gays and lesbians will continue to frustrate the Christian Right for the foreseeable future.

NOTES

1. For an overview of the evolution of this system and significant events of the 1970s, see Marshall 1980.
2. The gubernatorial candidate endorsed by the IR party, Christian conservative Jon Grunseth, was initially accused of sexual improprieties with a teenage girl. Then came allegations that he had engaged in a nine-year extramarital affair. Just three weeks before the general election, he withdrew from the race (Barone and Ujifusa 1993, 681; Hoium and Oistad 1991).
3. Carlson saw the writing on the wall and made only a half-hearted attempt to organize for the endorsement, choosing instead to save his resources for the primary election.
4. This group included the previously acceptable Cal Ludeman and the venerable Harold Stassen (Triggs 1994).
5. Quist had nearly as many votes as the successful IR gubernatorial primary candidate in 1990, but still lost by nearly two to one to Carlson.
6. For a detailed discussion of this phenomenon, see Gilbert and Peterson 1995, 174–82.
7. Moreno was by far the most colorful candidate in the race. In an effort to raise campaign funds he challenged an equally colorful local figure— Jesse Ventura, who was at this time a radio talk show host—to a boxing match. Additionally, in December 1995, he told a local weekly newspaper

that the IRS was controlled by the Rockefeller and Rothschild families (Smith 1996k).

8. The Minnesota chapter of the Christian Coalition is a relatively weak organization. MNCC has been distributing voter guides for congressional and local races since its founding in August 1994, but it has a far lower profile than the older and better organized MCCL and MFC.

9. The DFL primary candidates were Hubert "Skip" Humphrey, son of the late senator and vice president; party endorsee Mike Freeman, son of former governor and U.S. agriculture secretary Orville Freeman; Ted Mondale, son of the former vice president; Mark Dayton, former state auditor and heir to the department store chain fortune; and State Senator Doug Johnson, who was the only social conservative among the five.

10. No Reform Party candidate gained more than 16 percent in any state house race; in fact the candidate winning 16 percent ran unsuccessfully as a Republican in 1996.

REFERENCES

Achen, Christopher H., and W. Phillips Shively. 1995. *Cross Level Inference.* Chicago: University of Chicago Press.

Baden, Patricia Lopez. 1994. "Religious Right Sees Its Influence in IR House Wins." *Minneapolis Star Tribune,* 23 November.

———. 1996a. "McKasy Ends His Quest for Senate Nomination." *Minneapolis Star Tribune,* 24 July.

———. 1996b. "McKasy Exudes Confidence in Uphill GOP Senate Battle." *Minneapolis Star Tribune,* 3 July.

———. 1996c. "Primary, Polls Rouse U.S. Senate Campaigns." *Minneapolis Star Tribune,* 12 September.

Barone, Michael, and Grant Ujifusa. 1993. *The Almanac of American Politics 1994.* Washington: National Journal, Inc.

Burden, Barry C., and David C. Kimball. 1998. "A New Approach to the Study of Ticket Splitting." *American Political Science Review* 92: 533–44.

deFiebre, Conrad. 1996a. "GOP Backs No Senate Candidate." *Minneapolis Star Tribune,* 2 June.

———. 1996b. "The Race to Face Paul Wellstone." *Minneapolis Star Tribune,* 29 February.

Freedman, D. A., S. P. Klein, M. Ostlund, and M. R. Roberts. 1998. Review of "A Solution to the Ecological Inference Problem." *Journal of the American Statistical Association,* 93, no. 444: 1518–22.

Gilbert, Christopher P., and David A. M. Peterson. 1995. "Minnesota: Christians and Quistians in the GOP." In *God at the Grass Roots: The Christian Right in the 1994 Elections,* edited by Mark J. Rozell and Clyde Wilcox, Lanham, Md.: Rowman & Littlefield.

———. 1997. "Minnesota: Christian Conservatives Confront Their Limitations." In *God at the Grass Roots, 1996: The Christian Right in the American Elections,* edited by Mark J. Rozell and Clyde Wilcox. Lanham, Md.: Rowman & Littlefield.

Gilbert, Christopher P., David A. M. Peterson, Timothy R. Johnson, and Paul A. Djupe. 1999. *Religious Institutions and Minor Parties in the United States.* Westport, Conn.: Praeger.

Haas, Cliff. 1992. "Life of the Party: Issues and Ideas Man Vin Weber Sets His Sights on Reviving GOP." *Minneapolis Star Tribune,* 22 November.

Hallonquist, Sarah. 1998. "In Year of Mavericks, DFLer Mike Hatch Finally Wins." *Minneapolis Star Tribune,* 5 November.

Hoium, David, and Leo Oistad. 1991. *There Is No November.* Inver Grove Heights, Minn.: Jeric Publications.

King, Gary. 1996. *A Solution to the Ecological Inference Problem.* Princeton, N.J.: Princeton University Press.

Marshall, Thomas R. 1980. "Minnesota: The Party Caucus-Convention System." In *Party Renewal in America: Theory and Practice,* edited by Gerald M. Pomper. New Brunswick, N.J.: Eagleton Institute of Politics.

McGrath, Dennis, and Dane Smith. 1995. *Professor Wellstone Goes to Washington: The Inside Story of a Grassroots U.S. Senate Campaign.* Minneapolis: University of Minnesota Press.

Ragsdale, Jim. 1996. "Wellstone Wins Big in Senate Rematch." *Saint Paul Pioneer Press,* 6 November.

Robinson, William S. 1950. "Ecological Correlation and the Behavior of Individuals." *American Sociological Review* 15: 351–57.

Schmickle, Sharon. 1996. "It's a Different GOP for McKasy and Boschwitz." *Minneapolis Star Tribune,* 3 June.

Smith, Dane. 1992. "Tuesday's IR Losses Bound to Bring Changes in Strategy." *Minneapolis Star Tribune,* 8 November.

———. 1993. "Carlson Must Speak Softly and Carry the IR Right." *Minneapolis Star Tribune,* 13 September.

———. 1996a. "Boschwitz Would Buck Party, Run in Primary." *Minneapolis Star Tribune,* 10 April.

———. 1996b. "Buchanan Wins Support from Quist and Others Who Had Backed Gramm." *Minneapolis Star Tribune,* 17 February.

———. 1996c. "Decision on GOP Abortion Plank Pleases State Delegation." *Minneapolis Star Tribune,* 7 August.

———. 1996d. "GOP Backs No Senate Candidate." *Minneapolis Star Tribune,* 2 June.

———. 1996e. "McKigney Wins GOP Backing in 7th." *Minneapolis Star Tribune,* 28 April.

———. 1996f. "Moreno Vows to Stick to His Guns." *Minneapolis Star Tribune,* 4 July.

———. 1996g. "Republican State Convention." *Minneapolis Star Tribune,* 30 May.

———. 1996h. "Rudolph Ely Boschwitz: Believer in the American Dream." *Minneapolis Star Tribune,* 24 October.

———. 1996i. "State Delegates Will Be on the Right at GOP Convention." *Minneapolis Star Tribune,* 4 August.

———. 1996j. "The Race to Face Paul Wellstone." *Minneapolis Star Tribune,* 28 February.

———. 1996k. "Zealous Young Candidate Stirs Up Senate Race." *Minneapolis Star Tribune,* 27 April.

———. 1999. "Coleman Is the GOP's Choice." *Minneapolis Star-Tribune,* 20 June.

Spano, Wy, D. J. Leary, and Sarah Janecek. 1998. "The Battle for Control of the Legislature." *Politics in Minnesota* 17: 3–6.

"The State Republican Convention." 1996. *Minneapolis Star Tribune,* 1 June.

Sweeney, Patrick, and Debra O'Connor. 1998. "House: GOP Claiming a Slim Majority After 14 Years." *St. Paul Pioneer Press,* 4 November.

Triggs, Mike. 1994. "Zombie Conservatives Decimate IR Faithful." *Minneapolis Star Tribune,* 12 April.

Whereatt, Robert. 1994. "Governor Hands DFL Its Biggest Defeat." *Minneapolis Star Tribune,* 9 November.

———. 1996. "DFL Speaker Battle Begins." *Minneapolis Star Tribune,* 7 November.

———. 1998. "Republicans Weigh Agenda Ideas" *Minneapolis Star-Tribune,* 10 December.

12

After the Flood: The Kansas Christian Right in Retreat

Allan J. Cigler and Burdett A. Loomis

Outside the Topeka Ramada Inn the cold January rain continued. Inside, the faux New Orleans decor of the convention area seemed even seedier than usual, as wastebaskets collected water from the leaking roof. But the winter rain could not dampen the spirits of moderate Kansas Republicans, who were about to recapture formal control of their party. Former GOP chair and gubernatorial primary candidate David Miller was nowhere to be seen, although later that night he and a band of social conservatives would set up their own competing Republican organization. Lobbyist and long-time party stalwart Pete McGill plopped into a chair and approvingly watched the proceedings. Former Senator Bob Dole surfaced, as he regaled the veterans' lunch crowd (average age, sixty-plus) with a mix of humor and patriotism.

For the moment, at least, all was right with the world for old-line Republicans who had supported Nancy Kassebaum, Governor Bill Graves, and dozens of traditional party candidates over the years. As of 1999, the Christian Right was on the defensive in Kansas—but Republicans still had to address the issue of a divided party as they planned for elections in 2000 and beyond.

Although there has been a long history of populist, moralistic politics in Kansas, their contemporary presence dates to 1974, when Senator Dole and his supporters used the abortion issue to fend off a serious challenge to his reelection by Democratic Representative Bill Roy (a physician who had performed some abortions). But the politics of abortion played little role in Kansas politics until the 1980s (see Cigler and Loomis 1997 for more background). Indeed, the overall trends in Kansas social politics from the late 1970s through the late 1980s were distinctly liberal. That is, Kansas finally modernized its liquor laws, adopted a lottery, and allowed parimutuel wagering on dog and horse races. It is not coincidental that all these policies were designed to fill the state's coffers in a time of economic weakness.

One offshoot of such new policies was the growth of many highly focused interest groups representing both particular economic interests (the Kansas Greyhound Owners Association) and specific social concerns (Kansans for Life). The political landscape of Kansas had changed; not only had the number of single-interest groups increased, but they had moved beyond lobbying into electoral politics (Cigler and Kiel 1993). In 1990, after a wild legislative session in which a handful of social conservatives made life miserable for Mike Hayden, a traditional Republican governor, State Representative David Miller ran as the lieutenant governor candidate as part of a team that narrowly lost to Hayden in the GOP primary election (Loomis 1994). Hayden may well have lost his reelection bid as a result of crossover Republican votes for Joan Finney, a pro-life Democrat.

Miller left the legislature after 1990, but he did not disappear from public life. Rather, for the remainder of the decade, from several different positions (including Republican Party chairman), he would oppose the traditional Republicanism of Hayden, Dole, Kassebaum, and eventually Bill Graves, the most popular governor in Kansas history. Although the Republicans generally dominate Kansas electoral politics, state and local party organizations have always been weak (Mayhew 1986). Traditionally, the parties have played only modest roles in recruiting candidates, who "are pretty much on their own in running for office" (Grumm 1967, 51). The Republican organization has been open enough that concerted special-interest efforts to win control have a real chance for success.

The Christian Right Ascendant: Organizational and Electoral Victories

The 1989 legislative session and the 1990 gubernatorial campaigns were mere preludes to the battle for the Republican Party that began in 1991–92 and continued through 1999. By the early 1990s key figures in the Christian Right, such as David Miller, became convinced that Kansas politics would change only when religious activists, social conservatives, and pro-life supporters could gain control of the state Republican Party. Throughout the state, but especially in Wichita and suburban Kansas City (Johnson County), a concerted grass roots effort sought to dominate the party. Since precinct positions often went vacant and were filled by appointment, in many precincts finding the right candidate was enough to assure victory. Traditional Republicans did react to the social conservatives' efforts, but too little and too late.

Johnson County presents a vivid example of how the Christian Right altered the Republican Party at the local level (Sullinger 1996). In 1990 there were 330 candidates and 10 contested races for precinct committeeman/woman in Johnson County; this rose, respectively, to 487 candidates and 94 contested races in 1992, 759 and 221 in 1994, and 935 candidates and 343 contested races in 1996. Both Kansans for Life and various evangelical churches, especially the Full Faith Church of Love West, played major roles in developing slates of candidates and working to turn out conservative Republicans at precinct caucuses. At the same time, these same activists were successful in winning numerous local offices (particularly school board seats) and a substantial number of seats in the state legislature. In 1994, Bob Dole's candidate for chair of the state party (and the incumbent state chairman) chose not to run for re-election rather than face certain defeat. Rather, with Christian Right adherents firmly in control of the party, David Miller was elected state chairman—despite the opposition of long-time incumbent senators Dole and Nancy Kassebaum, as well as the newly elected governor, Bill Graves, who had won in a landslide. Two Republicans—Todd Tiahrt and Sam Brownback—won U.S. House seats in 1994 with the enthusiastic support of the Christian Right. The tide was rising.

Although the Christian Right in Kansas includes any number of groups and churches, some with national affiliations (e.g., the Christian Coalition and the Eagle Forum), antiabortion groups, and especially Kansans for Life, have stood at the center—and have provided much of the electoral muscle. In the early and mid-1990s, first David Miller and then Tim Golba served as head of Kansans for Life and used this position to recruit candidates for office, train them, and organize volunteer efforts to elect them. All in all, they succeeded. With the election of 1996, Christian Right-backed Republicans had won a Senate seat (Brownback), three of the state's four U.S. House seats (including Jim Ryun, former world record holder in the mile and a highly committed religious conservative), about half of the state senate's GOP majority, and more than half of the Republican majority in the state house of representatives (Farney 1996). The Christian Right had become the most consistently powerful force in the state. In particular, antiabortion forces, led by Kansans for Life, demonstrated the capacity to do very well in Republican primaries—a great asset in a Republican state.

Despite the electoral successes of the Christian Right and its takeover of the state GOP organization, most Kansans (including Republicans) did not share the movement's views on issues like abortion and the content of school curricula. In general election campaigns, therefore, the

Christian Right has adhered to low-profile strategies—often focusing on get-out-the-vote (GOTV) efforts such as phone banks—and has downplayed many social issues. Moreover, because social conservatives have never captured the governorship, their electoral successes have not led to many major policy changes. Still, the Christian Right in Kansas approached the 1998 elections with a great deal of confidence—with high hopes to win clear control of the state house of representatives and, most important, to capture the governor's seat, held by Bill Graves (see Beinhart 1998). And the challenger would be Graves's nemesis, David Miller, the sitting chair of the Republican party.

The Last Hurdle: The Decision to Challenge the Republican Governor

Despite the Christian Right's success at taking control of the Republican state party organization and electing a clear majority of state house members committed to a conservative social agenda, the movement's leaders remained frustrated in their attempts to change state policy on fundamental issues such as abortion. The focus of their resentment centered upon Bill Graves, the state's Republican governor.

Graves, a fiscal conservative with a distaste for moral issues intruding on the political agenda, had been elected governor in the 1994 Republican landslide. After shrugging off a social conservative challenge in the Republican primary, then-Secretary of State Graves won an overwhelming 30-percentage point victory over a well-regarded Democratic opponent, U.S. Representative Jim Slattery.

As governor, Graves proved to be no friend of the Christian Right. He was staunchly pro-choice; during his first term he had even worked closely with Democrats to thwart efforts to strengthen the state's antiabortion laws. He was adamant in his opposition to school vouchers and prayer in schools. After his first two years in office, relations with Christian Right Republicans were so strained that Graves was not in regular communication with David Miller, the Republican state chair, and representatives of the governor were not welcome at executive committee meetings of the state party.

The bad blood between Graves and Christian Right forces was exacerbated by Graves's actions in the 1996 elections. When Senator Robert Dole resigned his seat in mid-May to pursue the presidency, Representative Brownback, a favorite of the Republican right, announced his candidacy almost immediately. The governor took his time in selecting an interim Senate appointment and finally made a decision that was perceived to be an affront to Christian Right elements within the party. He chose his lieutenant governor, Sheila Frahm, a former state senate majority leader and fiscal conservative who supported abortion rights, to replace Dole on an interim basis. Graves then endorsed and campaigned for Frahm prior to the August primary, disregarding the pleas of Republican chair Miller to remain neutral.

Despite an early advantage in the polls, Frahm proved unable to translate the powers of holding office into electoral advantage. Brownback was better funded and his campaign more professionally run. The Christian Right vigorously supported Brownback with money and manpower. Both Kansans for Life and the Christian Coalition distributed voter guides throughout the state, often to church congregations; their grassroots effort in a low-turnout primary was widely viewed as a major factor behind Brownback's 55 percent to 42 percent upset and later an easy victory in the general election. To many among the leadership of the Christian Right, Brownback's victory was evidence that the moderate wing of the Republican Party was in retreat and that Graves was potentially vulnerable to a challenge if he sought reelection in 1998.

But the Kansas economy was on the side of the governor. As in most states during the 1990s, the Kansas economy, despite weakness in agriculture commodity and energy prices, was the best in decades; unemployment was under 4 percent and increasing tax revenues had created a large budget surplus. When the legislative session began in January 1998, both increases in state expenditures and tax cuts seemed possible. The session started with the governor's proposing a $170 million tax cut, the fourth consecutive year taxes were to be decreased.

Social conservatives in the party remained unsatisfied, and tensions between the Christian Right and pro-Graves moderates soon turned public. Early in the session chairman Miller wrote a letter to Republican legislative leaders complaining that taxes were not being cut deeply enough (he believed a $300 billion tax cut was in order) and that state spending was rising too rapidly. Miller claimed he was "truly shocked" to see that the governor had proposed a 15 percent spending increase during the last two budget sessions. "That is not Republican," he claimed.

The pressure for a primary challenge from the right to Graves mounted. Early in the session, Steve Abrams, a Christian Right proponent and a member of the state board of education, declared his candidacy, although his bid was not taken seriously by most observers. In late March Miller made his move, calling a meeting attended by sixty conservative Republicans in Salina to discuss whether Graves should face a challenge from the party's social conservative wing. The meeting was widely viewed as a prelude to a Miller campaign. The heat was on the governor.

Graves's legislative agenda moved to the right. Claiming the state budgetary scenario was even more favorable than when the session started, Graves enthusiastically supported an expansion of his initial tax proposal and eventually signed into law a $246 million cut, the largest single tax cut in state history. Even more surprising, Graves, who in his first election campaign in 1994 had pledged he would not seek further restrictions in the state's abortion laws, signed a new abortion law despite opposition from many of his own supporters. The new law prohibited the late-term abortion procedure called dilation and extraction, termed "partial-birth abortion" by abortion opponents. The legislation also increased abortion reporting requirements for physician and removed from present state law severe or life-threatening deformity or abnormality as a reason for late-term abortions. Essentially, third-trimester abortions were eliminated for any reason except to save the life of the mother.

The reaction of pro-choice advocates was immediate. The director of ProChoice Action League and a Graves supporter said that she was "Shocked. I'm horrified. I'm also outraged" (Petterson 1998a). Reminding the governor of his 1994 promise, she indicated she believed Graves had "signed what I believe is the most restrictive bill to hit any governor's desk in this country" (Petterson 1998a). The governor, in an effort to prevent a primary challenge, had clearly risked alienating his core moderate Republican constituency by signing the abortion bill.

Despite the policy victories on the tax cut and abortion, the Christian Right was not appeased. At a news conference after the governor's signing announcement, the lobbyist for Kansans for Life said she was pleased that Graves had taken "this small step," but noted that Graves had previously fought attempts by abortion opponents to enact "any more meaningful legislation," and contended that "even the law's partial-birth abortion ban is filled with exceptions" (Petterson 1998a).

While still sitting as the Republican chair, Miller finally announced in early May that he had decided to challenge Graves in the August primary. A few days later Abrams withdrew from the primary contest and replaced Miller as state chair. Miller began his campaign by proclaiming, "We in America and we here in Kansas are in a moral crisis. Our founding Fathers admonished us that only a virtuous people can remain free. I am deeply concerned that if we do not heed that admonition, our entire culture may be lost" (Kraske 1998). Reconciliation between social conservatives and moderates had become impossible. The differences between Graves and Miller were personal as well as ideological. In the words of one Miller ally, "everyone has become so angry and bitter that it's just like a divorce" (Kraske 1998).

The 1998 Republican Gubernatorial Primary

Miller understood from the beginning that unseating Graves was a formidable task. According to polls taken during the legislative session,

Graves's approval rating exceeded 80 percent. The governor had over $1 million in ready campaign funds at the end of the session, while Miller had done little fund-raising. Still, the challenger remained undaunted. "My odds of winning are not the issue that concerns me. The future of our children and our families is the reason I must make this race" (Toplikar 1998).

In Miller's view, the race was "a battle for the heart and soul of the Republican Party" (Kraske 1998). The campaign was to be about a series of issues, economic as well as moral, including educational choice to allow parents to send their children to the schools of their choosing (including home school and charter school options), preservation of the small family farm, paycheck protection from unions who endorse candidates, and the right to carry a concealed weapon, as well as tax cuts. Campaign strategy was to focus on a grassroots campaign that would energize the Christian Right base, providing victory in an expected low turnout August primary.

The first big campaign event occurred the first weekend of June when the Miller campaign held a "Restoring Kansas Values Rally" and fund-raiser in Wichita, attended by an estimated four thousand supporters. At the rally, red, white, and blue bunting decorated the stage and a church choir performed. Featured speakers included 1996 Republican presidential contender Alan Keyes and one of the most influential national figures in the conservative Christian movement, Focus on the Family founder James Dobson. While endorsing Miller, Dobson chastised Graves for his position on same-sex marriage. Though Graves had signed a bill prohibiting same-sex marriages in 1996, he opposed including such issues on the legislative agenda and was quoted as saying afterwards that "I thought the best thing to do was get it signed and be done with it. Why whip all the ultraconservatives up into a lather over this thing?" (Hanna 1998). The rally was probably the high point of Miller's campaign, garnering much press attention.

The Miller campaign confronted a number of obstacles. Funding was crucial since Miller, though prominent in Republican Party organization circles, was a virtual unknown statewide and needed money to buy the media time to increase his name recognition. Miller also hoped he would get the endorsement of and campaign help from U.S. Representatives Tiahrt, Ryun, and Snowbarger as well as Senator Brownback, all of whom, at least partially, owed their previous electoral successes to Christian Right grassroots activists. Such endorsements never materialized, as the elected officials remained neutral in the primary.

Miller also faced a mobilized moderate wing of the Republican Party. The devastating losses faced by moderates in the 1994 and 1996 elections and the loss of control of the state party had led to organized efforts to counteract the perceived extremism of the Christian Right. Most

prominent was the Mainstream Coalition, a new organization made up
primarily of fiscally conservative but socially cosmopolitan Republicans
and religious leaders in eastern Kansas, with a full-time executive director; it aimed to challenge social conservatives at the precinct level in order to retake the party. Fearing that a low turnout election would
strengthen Miller's chances, the Mainstream Coalition ran an aggressive
get-out-the-vote campaign in areas deemed likely to support Graves.
Even Democrats were encouraged to change their registration just for
the August primary in order to turn back the Miller challenge.

Graves took the Miller campaign seriously, spending $1.6 million dol-
lars in the primary, a record for a Kansas primary. Saying little about his
opponent, the governor emphasized his record on taxes and the state's financial health in a statewide television advertising campaign.

Miller attempted to overcome his image as a single-issue, antiabortion
candidate in his statewide appearances (especially in the three televised
debates) by emphasizing economic issues, pledging to never raise taxes,
to freeze state spending levels, to replace the progressive Kansas income
tax with a flat tax rate, and to initiate a $6.6 billion highway building plan,
with funding to come not from bonds or new taxes but from redirecting
state lottery proceeds. But it was Miller's comments accusing the governor of accepting "blood money" from a Wichita doctor noted for per-
forming abortions that seemed to attract press coverage (Dvorak 1998).

In the end Miller raised only $400,000 to spend on his campaign, which
limited his efforts to move beyond his base. The campaign concentrated
on radio advertisements in the rural areas in the state and television ads
in the Wichita area, a hotbed of Christian Right activism. Ads in support
of Miller or against Graves were common on Christian radio stations
throughout the state. With the exception of the Wichita area, little advertising was done in the mainstream media in the major population centers
of the state, especially the corridor from Topeka to the Kansas City
suburbs.

Miller's stiff and overly serious demeanor made it difficult for him to
relate to the state's non-Christian Right voters. His pious, self-righteous
style, which included saying grace aloud over meals, even in restaurants
with strangers at the table, drew negative comments from a press not ac-
customed to a candidate's emphasizing his or her religious convictions
publicly (Shields 1998).

Polls taken during the campaign suggested Kansans, including Republicans, were relatively pleased with the status quo. Moral issues, while
divisive, were not dominant. Among Republicans, while forty-seven
percent believed that state regulation of abortion should be more
restrictive, an equal percentage indicated it should be either less
restrictive or left as is. But when asked a general question about what
issues would be most important in determining their votes, only four

percent of respondents indicated abortion, while another thirteen percent indicated other social issues (Carpenter 1998).

Fifty-eight percent of respondents, on the other hand, indicated economic issues or education were the dominant issues. The performance of state government under Graves received high praise as well. Eighty-three percent of Republicans surveyed agreed with the statement that "Kansas is on the right track and provides effective and efficient government" (Carpenter 1998).

In such a climate the Miller campaign could make no inroads. A month before the election, a statewide poll indicated that 66 percent of those surveyed had a favorable opinion of the governor, whereas only 15 percent had an unfavorable opinion. Miller had a favorable reading of 11 percent; 5 percent had a negative view of Miller. Fully 50 percent of those surveyed did not even recognize Miller's name (Petterson 1998b)!

Well before the returns were in on August 6 the election was a foregone conclusion. Miller had basically quit campaigning two weeks before the election. Graves received 73 percent of the vote to Miller's 27 percent, a humiliating defeat for the individual most observers believed to be the unchallenged leader of the Christian Right in Kansas.

Miller took his defeat hard. The election left him "deeply disappointed by the people who abandoned the cause" (Ferguson 1998). He refused to endorse Graves in the general election, as he labeled the governor's campaign "deceitful" (Ferguson 1998). Nor did the former state chairman attend the traditional party unity breakfast two days after the primary, claiming that such events were seen by the public as not "genuine," but merely "phony photo ops" (Ferguson 1998). There would be no reconciliation.

Further Setbacks for the Christian Right

Republican Representative Vince Snowbarger won his initial election to his suburban Kansas City seat in 1996. A former state house of representatives majority leader, he was not like many of the fire-breathing conservatives that won election in 1994. But he was conservative, very conservative. The *National Journal's* measure rated him as the sixth most conservative member of the U.S. House in the 105th Congress (1997–98). The Third District of Kansas had sent Republicans to Congress since 1960, but they had been social moderates and fiscal conservatives in the tradition of this suburban setting. However, the district had changed over time, with a strong Christian Right element becoming prominent in the southern third of the district (Beinhart 1998). In 1996 Snowbarger capitalized on this trend to win the Republican primary and then, by five percentage points, the general election.

His fairly narrow margin and his conservatism made him an immediate target of Kansas Democrats, who succeeded in recruiting the single strongest potential candidate, Dennis Moore, a former district attorney in Johnson County, the most populous and wealthiest area in the district. Moore had excellent name identification, raised almost a million dollars, and ran a strong campaign. Snowbarger raised little early money and relied heavily on national GOP funds for his support. Moore, a moderate Democrat, won by out-organizing Snowbarger and by wining 17 percent of the Republican vote (Loomis 1998).

The Christian Right, which had proved crucial two years earlier, simply did not supply the needed energy or resources in 1998. Although the data are sketchy here, the Miller debacle did reduce the enthusiasm of the social conservatives. Moreover, Snowbarger, like the two other social conservatives in the Kansas House delegation, remained neutral in the Graves-Miller primary. This cost the incumbent some support—perhaps more among activists than among voters. In the general election, 75 percent of the Third District voters supported Graves in the general election, while just 48 percent backed Snowbarger. In part, at least, Snowbarger was simply too socially conservative for the district, and in the first few months of the 1999–2000 election cycle, no Christian Right candidate moved forward to challenge the moderate Moore.

Less prominent, if no less significant, than the Snowbarger defeat was the evolution of the Kansas House of Representatives, where the Christian Right had held a clear edge within the Republican majority in 1997–98. As the house organized for its 1999 session, a moderate Republican coalition won control of the chamber—leaving twenty to thirty social conservatives in a minority position, to the extent that they began to caucus together, much like the original "rebels" had done a decade earlier.

Reorganization of the GOP and the Christian Right

After Miller's defeat in August, social conservatives did not immediately relinquish control of the state party apparatus. All precinct committee members were selected in the primary, and although moderates apparently had the votes to assert control over the state party, it was not until after the general elections that county parties were to be reorganized and the leadership chosen; only then, in January, would a new state committee select its leadership. State committee chair Steve Abrams decided to remain in office, and the state GOP executive director, Jim Van Meteren, who had left his party post in May to become Miller's campaign chairman, returned to his previous position after the primary. Relations between the Graves camp and the Kansas Republican State Committee simply did not exist during the general election campaign.

Soon after the general election, various county committees throughout the state met to select their leadership, as well as delegates to the January state party reorganization meeting. Battles within various counties were heated, particularly those in Third District, where Snowbarger had lost his reelection bid. Especially galling to the social conservatives in the district was the fact that four of the moderates elected in August as Republican precinct committee members had been on a list of 431 Republicans released by Democrat Dennis Moore as his supporters (called RINOs—Republicans in Name Only—by the social conservatives). An aborted attempt was made by Abrams to change the Republican State Committee constitution by forbidding any person holding a position within the party from voting for the party's offices or participating on any party committee if he or she endorsed an opposition party's candidates during a general election (Altevogt 1998). Graves indicated his opposition to the measure and the issue was dropped.

The new state organization was finally constituted the last weekend in January. Moderates reclaimed the party by electing Mark Parkinson, a former state legislator and the hand-picked choice of Graves, by an 84–50 margin over his social conservative opponent. All twenty-nine votes from the Fourth Congressional District, home of Representative Todd Tiahrt and a hotbed of Christian Right activism, went to Parkinson's opponent. Moderates also elected the other three statewide party officials and regained command of the state executive committee (Kraske 1999). The new treasurer reported that only $577 remained in state party coffers when the moderates took control.

Parkinson was quick to assert his leadership. In a thinly veiled message to the strong antiabortion faction within the party, he noted that "never again while I am chairman will a single-issue group take control of the party" (Ferguson 1999). The social conservatives did not accept defeat quietly. Even before the January state party meeting, when they knew they would be ousted from the party leadership, Abrams and Van Meteren worked closely with Miller supporters and antiabortion group leaders to chart a new direction for social conservatives.

On Kansas Day, the anniversary of the state's admission to the Union in early February 1861, about a hundred prominent social conservatives met in Topeka and approved the bylaws of the Kansas Republican Assembly, a new statewide organization affiliated with the National Federation of Republican Assemblies, with chapters in forty-three states. The meeting was deliberately held at the same time Governor Graves was giving a speech at an official Republican Kansas Day celebration. No legislators or statewide Republican officials attended the assembly's event.

According to Van Meteren, the decision to create a new organization was the result of recognition among social conservatives that the movement had to expand beyond its narrow antiabortion base; "Everyone, including Kansans for Life, got together and agreed that for the good of the movement there needed to be another organization established to represent all conservative issues" (Sullinger 1999a). The group envisioned itself as an umbrella organization that would unite activists concerned with gun-control laws, property rights, high taxes, and home schooling, as well as abortion. According to Tim Golba, influential Kansas for Life official and one of the new group's founders, a major aim of the assembly was to again recapture the Republican Party starting at the precinct level (Sullinger 1999b). In fact, there was a recognition that antiabortion policies and activists simply represented an inadequate base for building a majority coalition within the Republican party.

Not all social conservatives were in agreement that an alternative Republican organization was a good idea. Parkinson made some efforts to mend fences with those social conservatives who remained active in the party. He appointed the chairwoman of the Sedgwick County (Wichita) Republican Party, a Graves opponent, to a position on the state executive committee and sought to talk personally with party officials from all of the state's 105 counties. More significant, in the Kansas House of Representatives, the speaker worked diligently to bridge gaps between social conservatives and moderates—with substantial success.

In the end, reconciliation remains an elusive task, at least outside the legislature. In Parkinson's initial meeting with social conservatives in Wichita after his election as state chair, one party official said he was quite willing to work with Parkinson until he "betrays the conservative cause" (Sullinger 1999a). Another indicated, without a trace of irony, that she would follow his leadership as long as he was "doing God's will" (Sullinger 1999a). The tensions are unlikely to diminish in the near future. The revision of the party platform was among the first orders of business for the newly selected state party leadership.

The existing state party platform, adopted in January 1998, was anathema to the moderates (Kansas Republican Party 1998). The document reflected a mix of populist economic ideas, libertarian notions concerning the role of government, and extreme moral stances associated with the Christian Right. A federal flat tax was advocated, the privatization of many government functions was encouraged, and the capital gains tax was to be phased out. The document advocated the "return of control" over the nation's public lands to the states and supported the Constitution's "takings clause." Provisions in the Brady Bill on gun purchase, as well as restrictions on semiautomatic weapons, were to be repealed. Even soil conservation efforts (in an agrarian state) were to be voluntary rather than supervised by the federal government.

In addition, the official Republican platform, drafted by members of the Christian Right, declared that abortion under any circumstances was to be forbidden, gay rights were to be curtailed, and efforts to sanctify heterosexual marriage were to be given high priority (including the elimination of no-fault divorce). The current trends in public education were to be challenged: school vouchers were advocated, and the teaching of evolution was to be presented as "theory, not fact." Home schooling was to be given a high priority, with little regulation by the state. The document advocated the establishment of English as the official language of Kansas. The platform represented the principles on which Miller had based his primary campaign. However true to the Christian Right's preferences, these preferences remained far from the mainstream of Kansas politics—even Kansas Republican politics.

The Election-Organization Connection: Limits of the Christian Right

It could be argued that, nationally speaking, it doesn't matter very much who governs Kansas. But Kansas, although a small state, has had a way of becoming the battleground for larger national issues. It was the spectacle of "bleeding Kansas" that helped ignite the Civil War. It was *Brown vs. Board of Education,* in Topeka, that signaled the end of school segregation. In recent years Kansas, which has relatively permissive abortion laws, has become a flashpoint for antiabortion protests and social issues generally.

"Issues and divisions are what elections are all about," says [David] Miller.

"They're what politics is all about." (Farney 1998)

"For the party to be a governing party, the party must govern for all the people." (Moderate Republican San Diego Mayor Susan Golding)

In 1998, and on toward 2000, most Kansas Republicans—in and out of office—turned away from Miller's conflictual definition of politics. Rather, as Republican governors across the country demonstrated (Solomon 1999), governing effectively meant playing down or recasting conflicts. In Kansas, David Miller and, less blatantly, Representative Vince Snowbarger emphasized highly conservative positions that invited conflict within their own party. Likewise, the Republican organization defined itself in narrow, conflict-oriented terms. And they reaped what they sowed. Miller, who had operated effectively within the Kansas legislature as an antiabortion activist and as the chair of the state party, proved wildly, even foolishly, optimistic in assessing his chances for unseating a most popular governor. Moreover, his overwhelming defeat led to the

Christian Right's loss of control over the state GOP as well as discouraging many activists who did not work as energetically on Snowbarger's behalf as they had in the past. Like social conservatives across the country, the Christian Right in Kansas must reassess its tactics and prospects in a state where traditional Republicans have regained their footing after a decade of difficult challenges.

Not surprisingly, the internal factionalism within the movement has intensified, and the word that best describes the situation is "disarray." The challenge to the sitting Republican governor by David Miller, the movement's champion and the Republican state chair, outraged not only moderates but many social conservatives as well. Elected officials sympathetic to the movement, in particular, believed efforts to capture the governorship should have been delayed until 2002, when the popular Graves would be ineligible for reelection. The Miller campaign not only proved to be embarrassing to the cause but also contributed to activating the moderate wing of the party, as pro-Graves supporters campaigned at the precinct level to regain control of the party organization.

The 1998 experience of the Kansas Christian Right illustrates the difficulties faced by a movement based on unwavering principles and the application of litmus tests when it confronts the realities of statewide electoral politics, where accommodation and coalition building are the order of the day. Taking over a party organization and winning local, low-profile elections is possible for a dedicated band of activists who operate quietly. Winning statewide elections, in contrast, typically entails a political strategy in which a candidate moves from the role of factional leader to leader of a grand party coalition. Movement leaders like Miller, who so skillfully engineered the takeover of the party in the early 1990s, have yet to accept the reality.

Consequently, the purists among the Christian Right have become more and more estranged from Republican elected officials, even those recruited from or sympathetic to the movement. In 1998 such officeholders took note of the lack of Christian Right backing for Representative Snowbarger, a movement supporter with a thoroughly conservative voting record in Congress, because he did not endorse and work for Miller in the gubernatorial primary, even though most observers believed it would have been political suicide for him to have done so. Sensing the moderate tone of the Kansas electorate, officeholders like Senator Sam Brownback, with strong movement credentials, have toned down their social conservative rhetoric, deemphasized abortion as a political issue, and made extra efforts to cooperate with the moderates now in charge of the state Republican Party. Even dedicated social conservatives like U.S. Representative Todd Tiahrt and Jim Ryun have distanced themselves from the organizational efforts to create a Kansas Republican Assembly as an alternative to the Republican State Committee. Nor have Christian

Right adherents in the Kansas State Legislature affiliated themselves with the assembly.

Another reality the movement faces is a simple lack of money. It remains unclear whether the Kansas Republican Assembly will be anything more than a paper organization. In the 1998 gubernatorial primary, the Graves forces prevailed in part because of their financial resources. Statewide campaigns are about money, media, communications, and professionally run candidate organizations. The Christian Right wing of the party does not possess the connections to tap into the vast networks of business-sponsored campaign funding sources that underlie modern campaigns. To the purists politics is about principle, not money. As much as anything else, that perspective may limit their reach in this part of the heartland.

REFERENCES

Altevogt, John. 1998. "Responsibility Requires Loyalty." *Kansas City Star,* 2 December, B6.

Beinhart, Peter. 1998. "Battle for the 'Burbs." *New Republic,* 18 October, 25–29.

Carpenter, Tim. 1998. "Poll Gives Graves Big Edge." *Lawrence Journal World,* 11 July, A1.

Cigler, Allan J., and Burdett A. Loomis. 1997. "Kansas: The Christian Right and the New Mainstream of Republican Politics." In *God at the Grass Roots, 1996: The Christian Right in the American Elections,* edited by Mark J. Rozell and Clyde Wilcox, 207–22. Lanham, Md.: Rowan & Littlefield.

Cigler, Allan J., and Dwight Kiel. 1993. "Kansas Representation in Transition." In *Interest Groups in the Midwestern States,* edited by Clive Thomas and Ronald Hrebenar, 163–78. Ames: Iowa State University Press.

Dvorak, John A. 1998. "Graves, Miller Exchange Abortion Charges." *Kansas City Star,* 29 June, C11.

Farney, Dennis. 1996. "With Many Hot Races, Politics Is Now Putting Kansas on the Map." *Wall Street Journal,* 25 September.

———1998. "Kansas Republicans Are Bitterly Split into Two Camps." *Wall Street Journal,* 24 April, 24.

Ferguson, Lew. 1998. "Battle for Heart of GOP Swings to Middle." *Lawrence Journal World,* 9 August, 5B.

———1999. "GOP Rift Produces Slim Win for Chair." *Lawrence Journal World,* 31 January, A2.

Grumm, John G. 1967. "The Kansas Legislature: Republican Coalition." In *Midwestern Legislative Politics,* edited by Samuel Patterson. Iowa City: Institute of Public Affairs, University of Iowa.

Hanna, John. 1998. "Campaigns Continue to Exchange Barbs Over Same-Sex Marriage Bill." *Lawrence Journal World,* 11 July, A1.

Kansas Republican Party. 1998. *1998 Republican Party Platform.* http://www.Ksrepublicans.org/Platform98.html.

Kraske, Steve. 1998. "Miller Enters GOP Race for Governor." *Kansas City Star,* 6 May, C1.

———1999. "Parkinson to Lead Kansas GOP." *Kansas City Star,* 31 January, B1.

Loomis, Burdett A. 1994. *Time, Politics, and Policy: A Legislative Year.* Lawrence: University Press of Kansas.

———. 1998. "Kansas 3rd District: The 'Pros from Dover' Set Up Shop." Prepared for the "Money, Media and Madness: Inside the 1998 Elections" conference sponsored by the Center for Congressional and Presidential Studies, Washington, D.C., American University, December 4.

Mayhew, David. 1986: *Placing Parties in American Politics.* Princeton: Princeton University Press.

Petterson, John. 1998a. "Graves Approves Abortion Limits." *Kansas City Star,* 28 April, A1.

———. 1998b. "Poll Cites Graves' Big Lead in Race." *Kansas City Star,* 11 July, A1.

Shields, Mike. 1998. "Miller Preaching Morals on Crusade Through State." *Lawrence Journal World,* 12 July, A1.

Solomon, Burt. 1999. "The Other, Softer GOP." *National Journal,* 20 February, 454–59.

Sullinger, Jim. 1996. "Precinct Positions Seen as Important Amid Party Division." *Kansas City Star,* 14 June, 1C.

———. 1999a. "GOP's New Leader in Kansas Visits Party's Conservative Camp." *Kansas City Star,* 12 February, B6.

———. 1999b. "Kansas Conservatives Regroup." *Kansas City Star,* 26 January, B1.

Toplikar, David. 1998. "Miller Begins Crusade to Be Next Governor." *Lawrence Journal World,* 6 May, A1.

13

Illinois: Moral Politics in a Materialist Political Culture

Ted G. Jelen

The state of Illinois would initially seem very unpromising territory for the Christian Right, or for the assertion of moral issues generally in political discourse. Traditionally, Illinois has been regarded as a state with an individualist political culture, in which issues involving economic matters, real estate, and public works predominate (Royko 1971; Barone and Ujifusa 1997). Illinois has historically been dominated in Cook County by an active Democratic organization (popularly termed "the Machine") that has been based on patronage and economic incentives for activists and voters alike, with corresponding Republican organizations at various locations in the "collar counties" surrounding Chicago and "downstate" (Rakove 1975; Royko 1971). There also exist Democratic strongholds in the southern third of the state, an area that some have argued constitutes a cultural extension of the border states of Kentucky and Missouri. Much of the political history of Illinois has been animated by conflict over the distribution of such material resources. Despite court rulings in the 1980s limiting the power of local governments to hire and fire public employees (Jelen 1994), issues such as the location of new airports, sports stadiums, and highways have dominated the political conversation in the Land of Lincoln.

Moreover, the last quarter of the twentieth century has witnessed a rise in the salience of racial politics in the city of Chicago and the surrounding suburbs. Some analysts (Royko 1971; Grimshaw 1992) have suggested that a tacit arrangement to maintain racial segregation has motivated the actions of many public officials throughout most of the twentieth century. Others (Jelen 1994; Kleppner 1985) have chronicled the political empowerment of African Americans during the past two decades, which may have culminated in the election of Harold Washington as mayor of Chicago in 1983. Since that time, race has been a constant, public source of cleavage within the Democratic Party of Illinois, and the racial issue has posed both challenges and opportunities for the GOP.

Thus, the political culture of Illinois can legitimately be characterized as one of "real estate and race." These two issues, which are often related, form much of the political agenda in the Prairie State. To an extent unusual in the United States, Illinois politics has been driven by the assertion of material interests rather than of abstract values. As the late Mayor Richard J. Daley is said to have observed about political reformers, "What trees do they plant? What buildings do they put up?" (Royko 1971, 15). Nevertheless, the elections of 1996 and 1998 manifested what might be termed "lifestyle issues" in a manner most unlike typical Illinois politics. In particular, the issue of abortion has exposed cleavages between and within the political parties. Moreover, the formal Democratic and Republican organizations appear to have lost a good deal of control over the nominating process, which has presented entrepreneurial candidates with opportunities to raise nontraditional political concerns in Illinois elections.

To a considerable extent, the insertion of moral issues into Illinois political discourse has taken place most recently in the last two elections for the United States Senate. It is to the candidacies of Republican Senate candidates Al Salvi and Peter Fitzgerald that attention is now turned.

Senate Elections, 1996–1998

The 1996 Senate election in Illinois was contested over an open seat, vacated by the retirement of Paul Simon. The general election race pitted a moderately liberal Democrat, U.S. Representative Richard Durbin, against socially conservative Republican Al Salvi. In the general election, Durbin defeated Salvi, 56 percent to 41 percent, with most of the balance going to the Libertarian candidate.

Among the most interesting aspects of this election was the Republican primary. Governor James Edgar persuaded Lt. Governor Bob Kustra to seek the GOP nomination for U.S. Senate. Kustra, who had publicly announced and then reversed a decision to retire, appeared to lack enthusiasm for a statewide campaign. In a populist, anti-incumbent period, Kustra's campaign emphasized his experience and his academic credentials (he is a former university professor). Running against Kustra was Al Salvi, an attorney making his first run for public office. Salvi, who financed his campaign with over a million dollars of his own money, emphasized the issue of tax cuts, but also made quite clear his conservative positions on abortion and gun control. Salvi defeated Kustra in a closely fought primary. Salvi may have been aided by a major snowstorm on primary day in the southern half of the state, which apparently limited turnout in Kustra's home region. By contrast, Democratic Representative Richard Durbin won the Democratic nomination rather easily over former state treasurer Pat Quinn (bearer of a venerable name in Chicago political history).

In the general election, Durbin emphasized his pro-choice position on abortion and attacked Salvi for his ties to the tobacco industry and his opposition to a ban on assault weapons. As in the primary, Salvi emphasized the issue of taxes, but again was quite explicit in his opposition to legal abortion and gun control. Aided by a Salvi gaffe late in the campaign, and by Bill Clinton's coattails, Durbin won the Senate seat rather easily (Barone and Ujifusa 1997).

As table 13.1 indicates, self-identification as a member of the Christian Right was a powerful predictor of the Senate vote in 1996. While Salvi maintained a ten-point lead among all Protestants (with Durbin achieving a comparable lead among Catholics), his lead among whites who identify with the Christian Right was a staggering forty-one points. Durbin's support among Christian conservatives was just below 30 percent, with Salvi attracting 70 percent of self-identified religious conservatives.

Similarly, the abortion issue was of great importance in the Illinois Senate race in 1996; support for Durbin decreased monotonically, as respondent attitudes on abortion became more pro-life. Clearly, the 1996 Senate race was contested in large part on the basis of conservative religious identification and social issues. Salvi's ability to wrest the GOP nomination from Robert Kustra had a great deal to do with setting the issue agenda in this race.

A similar phenomenon occurred in the Illinois Senate election of 1998, which pitted one-term incumbent Carol Moseley-Braun (the first African American woman to serve in the U.S. Senate) against attorney and political neophyte Peter Fitzgerald. Once again, a major part of the story is the Republican primary, in which Fitzgerald narrowly defeated state comptroller and long time Republican stalwart Loleta Didrickson. As in 1996, a moderate Republican, who had received a good deal of support from the state Republican organization and GOP Governor Jim Edgar, was defeated by a socially conservative political amateur. As was the case in 1996, the insurgent Republican Senate candidate was a man of substantial means, who ran an essentially self-financed campaign. Also, in a manner similar to Al Salvi's, Peter Fitzgerald made tax reform the centerpiece of his campaign, although he also took a strong pro-life position on the abortion issue, opposing legal abortion even in cases of rape or incest. Fitzgerald supported tuition tax vouchers (long a favored position of the

Table 13.1 Religion, Abortion Attitudes, and Voting, Illinois Senate
Election, 1996

Issues	Durbin (D) %	Salvi (R) %
Religion (Caucasian respondents):		
Protestant	44	54
Catholic	53	44
Christian Right? (17% of Caucasian respondents)		
Yes	29	70
No	61	35
Abortion should be		
Legal in all cases	70	29
Legal in most cases	65	32
Illegal in most cases	36	61
Illegal in all cases	33	66

Source: VRS Surveys, CNN.com. Percentages may not add to 100% because of
the presence of minor party candidates.

Christian Right), although he was generally supportive of gun control
(Kemper 1998).

It is not clear why Fitzgerald was able to defeat Didrickson (who had
won statewide election to the office of comptroller). As was the case with
Kustra in 1996, Didrickson ran a relatively lackluster campaign, emphasizing her moderation and experience and suggesting that nominating a
woman candidate might offset a presumed Democratic advantage
among female voters (see Jelen and Wilcox 1996). In the end, two factors
were likely decisive. First, Fitzgerald's willingness to spend "whatever it
took" (Kemper 1998) was obviously an enormous advantage. Fitzgerald's
ability to dominate the airwaves during the primary season was a severe
handicap to Didrickson. Second, without a serious contest for the Republican nomination for governor, the Republican turnout in the March
primary was very light, which may have provided an advantage for an insurgent candidate of strong views on lifestyle issues.

Carol Moseley-Braun's reelection bid was plagued by a number of
problems, which ultimately proved insurmountable. Moseley-Braun was
a rather unlikely senator, having won the seat in 1992 under unusual circumstances. She gained the Democratic nomination in a closely contested primary between incumbent Alan Dixon and millionaire Alfred
Hofeld, receiving approximately 38 percent of the primary vote. In the
general election, she ran successfully against a lackluster Republican,
Richard Williamson (Barone and Ujifusa 1997). The lack of a more

credible GOP candidate was widely attributed to the generally held belief that Illinois would be difficult terrain for Republican candidates in
1992 because of President Bush's relatively low approval ratings. Further,
most observers expected Dixon to be renominated, and Dixon was regarded by most observers as virtually unbeatable (Jelen 1994).

During the 1992 campaign, Carol Moseley-Braun had been charged
with failure to account adequately for campaign funds, misuse of campaign funds for personal purposes, and misrepresenting her net worth to
obtain a spot in a publicly financed nursing home for her mother (Jelen
1994). In the 1998 general election, Fitzgerald consistently pointed out
that Moseley-Braun was under investigation by both the Internal Revenue Service and the Federal Election Commission (Kemper and
McRoberts 1998). Despite the fact that the IRS eventually dropped its
investigation of Moseley-Braun's finances, she was never able to overcome the negative impression generated by these problems.

Further, while a United States senator, Carol Moseley-Braun made several well-publicized visits to Nigeria, where dictator General Sani Abacha
hosted her. Moseley-Braun was widely criticized for her association with a
Third World tyrant and for failing to condemn the alleged human rights violations of the Nigerian regime (Kemper and McRoberts 1998).

In the general election, political newcomer Peter Fitzgerald defeated
Moseley-Braun by a margin of 51 percent to 47 percent. To a very large extent, the election was contested on the basis of Moseley-Braun's personal
morality and on the issue of abortion. Moseley-Braun characterized Fitzgerald's opposition to virtually all legal abortions as "scary," while Fitzgerald charged Moseley-Braun with favoring partial-birth abortions. Each
candidate for the U.S. Senate attempted to characterize the other as an
"extremist" on the abortion issue (Kemper 1998; Kemper and McRoberts
1998).'Despite the fact that Moseley-Braun ran unopposed in the Democratic primary, she was far behind for most of the general election. A late
surge, occasioned in part by several visits to the state by Hillary Clinton,
closed the gap, but Fitzgerald prevailed on election day.

It is instructive to examine the geographical distribution of the Illinois
Senate vote in 1998. Moseley-Braun carried only five counties, including
Cook County and four very small counties in the extreme southern section
of the state. Within the city of Chicago, Moseley-Braun carried forty-seven
of the city's fifty wards. She lost two predominantly Republican wards on
the city's northwest side and largely Polish American Twenty-third Ward
on the southwest side. Within Cook County outside the city limits,
Moseley-Braun carried four traditionally African American townships to
the south of Chicago and traditionally liberal bastions in the north and
west suburbs. She carried west suburban Oak Park, and the North Shore
communities of Evanston (which contains Northwestern University) and
Skokie (a predominately Jewish suburb). Moseley-Braun was unable to

replicate her strong 1992 showing in the rest of the greater Chicago area and ran very poorly downstate ("Election 98" 1998).

Although the 1998 election was largely a referendum on Carol Moseley-Braun, issues of religion and personal morality appear to have been decisive in the outcome. The effects of abortion attitudes and identification with the Christian Right on the 1998 Illinois senate election can be seen in table 13.2.[1] These data are remarkably similar to those reported in table 13.1, except that in 1998 the Democratic candidate did not do as well among voters who did not identify with the Christian Right, or with those who hold pro-choice attitudes. Durbin ran twice as well as Moseley-Braun among Christian Right identifiers and ran ahead of Moseley-Braun among respondents across categories of the abortion issue. While support for both Durbin and Moseley-Braun varied directly with voter attitudes toward abortion, Durbin ran better among abortion liberals, moderates, and conservatives.

Clearly, Carol Moseley-Braun was a considerably weaker candidate than Dick Durbin and had some difficulty in carrying her ideological base among white voters. Nevertheless, Moseley-Braun did achieve a majority among white voters who did not self-identify with the Christian Right. If her vote among this large (77 percent) group of white voters had been combined with her near-unanimous support among African Americans, Moseley-Braun, despite all her difficulties, would have been re-elected rather easily had it not been for the four-to-one advantage

Table 13.2 Religion, Abortion Attitudes, and Voting, Illinois Senate Election, 1998

Issues	Moseley-Braun (D)	Fitzgerald (R)
Religion (Caucasian respondents only)		
Protestant	32	65
Catholic	30	69
Jewish	66	34
Christian Right? (13% of Caucasian respondents)		
Yes	15	83
No	52	46
Abortion should be legal		
In all cases	61	37
In most cases	50	47
In few cases	31	67
Never	25	72

Source: VRS Surveys: CNN.com. Percentages may not add to 100% due to rounding.

Fitzgerald gained among supporters of the Christian Right. Though many factors contributed to the outcome of the 1998 Senate election in Illinois, Fitzgerald's victory over Carol Moseley-Braun is one for which the Christian Right may (perhaps legitimately) claim credit.[2]

Perhaps the most interesting aspect of the last two Senate races in Illinois is the fact that in both cases voters in the Republican primaries rejected experienced, moderate candidates, who had at least the tacit support of a very popular Republican governor. Though it is not possible to examine this conjecture with available data, it may well be that the GOP electorate in Illinois is becoming more ideological on social issues and less "pragmatic" or moderate. Conversely, it may also be that Republican elites in Illinois place less emphasis on elections for the U.S. Senate than for other races, such as governor or attorney general. In a competitive two-party state such as Illinois, it is unlikely that any U.S. Senator will achieve sufficient seniority to attain a leadership position in the upper chamber. Since the days of Democrat Scott Lucas and Republican Everett Dirksen, no Illinois Republican has attained a position of party leadership in the United States Senate. Lacking either substantial power at the federal level or patronage-type influence within the state, it may be that a seat in the U.S. Senate is not as important to Illinois party leaders as are other offices. If this is the case, it may follow that Senate elections provide opportunities for more "value-based" candidates to contend seriously in Republican primaries and in general elections.

The Race for Governor, 1998

The retirement of James Edgar from the Illinois governorship provided the Democratic Party with an opportunity to win the office for the first time in two decades. Democratic hopes were dashed, however, as Republican George Ryan, who had held the office of secretary of state, defeated five-term U.S. Representative Glenn Poshard 51 percent to 47 percent. Ryan thus became the third consecutive Republican governor in the highly competitive state of Illinois.

In contrast to the Senate races described above, the Democratic primary for governor was the more interesting and competitive nomination contest. Whereas Ryan won the GOP nomination with 86 percent of the vote against token opposition, the Democratic primary contained three credible, well-known, and experienced candidates. Roland Burris, who was the first African American to win statewide office in Illinois (state comptroller and attorney general), was generally considered the preelection favorite. He was opposed by Associate Attorney General John R. Schmidt, a white liberal who enjoyed strong support among the affluent "Lakefront Liberals" who inhabit the North Shore of Lake

Michigan in Chicago and its northern suburbs, and downstate U.S. Representative Glenn Poshard. In a closely contested primary, Poshard won with just over 38 percent.

The fact that three professional public officials were able to contest the Democratic primary speaks volumes about the decline of party organizations in Illinois, and in particular in Cook County. In the heyday of machine politics in Chicago, it might have been anticipated that Burris, given his proven ability to win statewide elections and his long-standing loyalty to the party, would have received the support of the Democratic organization and, indeed, of the mayor of Chicago. In the post-machine politics of 1998, Mayor Richard M. Daley (the son of the late Mayor Richard J. Daley) maintained highly visible neutrality, to the consternation of some of Burris's supporters. The lack of a strong preprimary organization permitted three highly credible candidates to contest the gubernatorial primary. Such intraparty anarchy would have been virtually inconceivable in an earlier era.

Representative Glenn Poshard was an unusual statewide candidate for Illinois. A Southern Baptist, Poshard holds a Ph.D. in education from Southern Illinois University. Prior to his gubernatorial campaign, he represented the Nineteenth Congressional District in Illinois, which approximately covers the southeastern quadrant of the state. Poshard represented a primarily rural district, which borders southern Indiana and Kentucky. In the House of Representatives, Poshard took generally liberal positions on economic and labor issues but rather conservative positions on social issues (Pearson 1998). For example, while in Congress, Poshard voted to override President Clinton's veto of the ban on partial-birth abortions and opposed the ban on assault weapons.

Despite strong support from organized labor, Poshard's general election campaign was uphill from the start. A major problem for Poshard was funding. Poshard imposed a limit on the size of the contributions he would accept and challenged George Ryan to do the same. Ryan predictably declined without comment (Pearson 1998). Moreover, Poshard's pro-life and anti-gun control positions cut him off from the financial support a Democratic candidate could normally expect from the North Side liberals, and from organizations such as NOW and Planned Parenthood. Poshard's support among labor unions was not nearly sufficient to offset these disadvantages.

In the general election, Poshard was able to carry Cook County narrowly, as well as approximately thirty smaller counties in the southern third of the state ("Election 98" 1998). In essence, Poshard was able to reconstruct his congressional base, but he made a relatively poor showing among northern liberals and African Americans (18 percent of whom voted for Ryan). In the city of Chicago, Poshard carried most wards but lost three Republican wards on the northwest side of the city. Perhaps more tellingly, he also lost six lake-front wards on the North Side. The votes and financial support of this area are generally regarded as crucial to any Democratic candidate for statewide office. Most observers regarded the gun-control issue as the most important determinant of the outcome.

To what extent did religious or moral issues contribute to Poshard's defeat? As table 13.3 shows, the socially conservative Poshard made a fairly respectable showing among Christian Right voters, comparable to Durbin's performance in 1996. However, Ryan also led among voters who did not identify with the Christian Right, and among whites in all major religious groups in Illinois.

The political costs of Poshard's social conservatism (and particularly his pro-life stance on the abortion issue) can be seen most clearly in these data. Unlike Moseley-Braun, Rep. Poshard lost badly among Illinois Jews, a group with a long-standing tradition of social liberalism. Moreover, Poshard failed to realize any substantial gains as a result of his conservative views on abortion. Unusual for a Democrat, Poshard carried only a bare majority of pro-choice voters and did not carry a majority in any other category of abortion attitudes. Indeed, Poshard's losses among pro-choice respondents were compensated with few if any gains in other categories. For example, among pro-life voters, Ryan ran only two points behind senatorial candidate Fitzgerald. Among pro-choice voters, Moseley-Braun ran ten points ahead of Poshard. Poshard ran five points

Table 13.3 Religion, Abortion Attitudes, and Voting, Illinois Gubernatorial Election, 1998

Issues	Poshard (D) %	Ryan (R) %
Religion (Caucasian respondents):		
Protestant	40	59
Catholic	32	67
Jewish	34	62
Christian Right? (13% of Caucasian respondents)		
Yes	31	67
No	47	50
Abortion should be legal		
In all cases	51	46
In most cases	45	51
In few cases	38	62
Never	28	70

Source: VRS Surveys, CNN.com. Percentages may not add to 100% because of the presence of minor party candidates.

behind Moseley-Braun among voters who thought abortion should be legal in most cases, and only seven points ahead among voters who believed abortion to be permissible in only a few cases. Perhaps more revealingly, if Poshard's showing in 1998 is compared with Durbin's victorious effort in 1996, it can be seen that Poshard ran nineteen points behind Durbin among strong pro-choice voters, and twenty among moderate pro-choice respondents. Conversely, Poshard in 1998 ran only two points ahead of Durbin among moderate pro-life voters, and only five points among respondents who thought that abortion should never be legal.

Thus Representative Poshard, as well as the Illinois Democratic Party, paid a heavy price for Poshard's social conservatism, and particularly for his conservative position on abortion. This suggests that there exist substantial limits to the ability of Democratic candidates to maneuver across the hazardous terrain of social or moral issues. If the 1998 Illinois campaign for governor is in any way typical, there are some votes to be gained by a Democratic shift to the moral right, but such votes can be won only at great risk and substantial cost.

Conclusion

The Senate elections of 1996 and 1998, as well as the gubernatorial election of 1998, serve to illustrate the limits and potential of moral politics in Illinois in the immediate future. The nominations of Republican Senate candidates Salvi and Fitzgerald and Democratic gubernatorial candidate Poshard indicate quite clearly that formal party organizations no longer dominate Illinois politics as in the past. To this extent, Illinois appears to be catching up with other states in terms of the decline of party machines and the corresponding importance of candidate-centered election campaigns. Increasingly, candidates for statewide office in Illinois are self-recruited and responsible for their own fund-raising efforts. This trend in turn implies that candidates need no longer concern themselves with the maintenance of party organizations, and therefore may have more discretion over the issue agendas they present to the electorate. Put another way, if the party cannot or will not deliver resources to individual candidates, the candidates have no obligation or incentive to provide resources (understood as patronage, public works, or government expenditures) to the party. Thus, candidates in the post-machine era of Illinois politics have a relatively high level of discretion in setting their own issue agendas. The decline of party organizations in Illinois appears to have created a public space within which issues such as abortion, school prayer, and gun control can be contested.

Second, the Christian Right in Illinois appears to have a modest, but occasionally crucial, role in determining the outcomes of elections.

Although just over 10 percent of the Illinois electorate identifies with the Christian Right, religious conservatives appear to have created a niche for themselves in the Republican Party. In the past two Senate elections in Illinois, politically inexperienced social conservatives defeated well-known and reasonably popular candidates in the GOP primaries. Moreover, the data for 1998 show that the Christian Right can take a great deal of credit for Fitzgerald's victory over Carol Moseley-Braun. As table 13.2 indicates, Moseley-Braun held a slight but significant majority among even white voters who did not identify with the Christian Right. Peter Fitzgerald owes his Senate seat to the virtually unanimous support he received among white religious conservatives.

The influence of the Christian Right contains both long-term and short-term components. In this regard, it is instructive to compare Christian Right support for Fitzgerald and Ryan. The Republican candidates for Senator and governor in Illinois in 1998 both received large majorities from voters who reported identifications with the Christian Right. Two-thirds of religious conservatives supported Ryan for governor, and over four Christian Right voters in five reported casting a vote for Fitzgerald. Thus, a large portion of the Christian Right support enjoyed by Republican candidates seems attributable to possible realignment among certain groups of evangelical Christians (Kellstedt 1989; Kellstedt et al. 1994). The governor's race in Illinois, which pitted a moderate Republican against a socially conservative Democrat, illustrates that there is relatively little opportunity for Democrats to make inroads among Christian Right voters. To a large extent in Illinois, as elsewhere, religious conservatives are becoming an important and stable component of the Republican coalition.

Nevertheless, a certain proportion of the Christian Right does appear responsive to short-term forces unique to particular campaigns. A small but substantial number of Christian Right identifiers apparently voted for Fitzgerald for the Senate and crossed over to vote for Poshard for governor. Though this may not be a large group of voters, Fitzgerald's narrow victory suggests that even small groups can be decisive in closely contested elections. However, Poshard's relatively high level of support among religious conservatives does appear to have been rather costly. As noted earlier, Poshard was handicapped by his relative inability to raise money from groups of social liberals normally inclined to support Democratic candidates. Poshard's poor fund-raising efforts among such groups as the National Organization for Women and Planned Parenthood, as well as his self-imposed limits on campaign contributions, hurt his effort quite seriously. Further, as table 13.3 suggests, Poshard ran astonishingly poorly among Jews, who constitute a traditionally liberal group on many social issues (Cook, Jelen, and Wilcox 1992). Thus, Glenn Poshard's campaign for governor illustrates quite clearly the dilemma faced by socially conservative Democrats: there are relatively few votes to be gained by shifting to the right on issues of personal morality, and a substantial price to be paid among certain traditional Democratic constituencies. The fact that Poshard was unable to offset these losses with popular and financial support from other Democratic groups such as organized labor is quite revealing. Even in Illinois, liberals for whom social issues are very salient are a key component of the Democratic coalition, who can be ignored only at great risk.

Finally, the limited data on which this chapter is based suggest that the Christian Right in Illinois has substantial potential to form a genuinely ecumenical coalition. Some analyses of earlier manifestations of the Christian Right have suggested that the political strength of moral conservatives is often limited by the effects of religious particularism (Jelen 1991; Wilcox 1992; Green 1993). Religious differences between Protestants and Catholics, or between different groups of conservative Protestants, have historically limited the ability of theologically diverse groups of moral conservatives to form political coalitions. More recent accounts of religious political activism have argued that the effects of particularism are a problem with which contemporary Christian conservatives must contend (Reed 1994). The results of the elections in Illinois suggest that Catholic candidates such as Salvi and Fitzgerald can do quite well among self-identified members of the Christian Right. As small as the Christian Right appears to be in Illinois, its size and influence may not be limited by interdenominational or theological differences. If moral or lifestyle issues gain prominence on the political agenda in future elections, the Christian Right in Illinois exhibits substantial potential for growth and for influencing the outcomes of elections in this pivotal state.

Thus, the elections of 1996 and 1998 suggest that the Christian Right remains a minor force in Illinois politics. However, the small size of this religious component of the Illinois electorate should not conceal either its potential to determine the outcomes of close elections or its possibilities for growth and expansion. The importance of moral issues in the 1998 election and the countermobilization that Poshard's social conservatism occasioned illustrate the importance of such issues even in a traditionally materialistic political culture such as that of Illinois. In the Land of Lincoln, as elsewhere, the personal is becoming political.

NOTES

1. At this writing, the raw data from the Voter Research Services Exit Polls are not generally available. Data presented here are drawn from cross-tabulations made available by the Cable News Network (cnn.com).
2. Of course, it is quite possible that Didrickson would have defeated Moseley-Braun even more handily.

REFERENCES

Barone, Michael, and Grant Ujifusa. 1997. *The Almanac of American Politics: 1998.* Washington, D.C.: National Journal.

Cook, Elizabeth Adell, Ted G. Jelen, and Clyde Wilcox. 1992. *Between Two Absolutes: Public Opinion and the Politics of Abortion.* Boulder, Colo.: Westview Press.

"Election 98." 1998. *Chicago Tribune,* 5 November sec 2, p. 5.

Green, John C. 1993. "Pat Robertson and the Latest Crusade: Religious Resources and the 1988 Presidential Campaign," *Social Science Quarterly* 74: 157–68.

Grimshaw, William J. 1992. *Bitter Fruit: Black Politics and the Chicago Machine, 1931–1991.* Chicago: University of Chicago Press.

Jelen, Ted G. 1991. *The Political Mobilization of Religious Beliefs.* New York: Praeger.

———. 1994. "Carol Moseley-Braun: The Insider as Insurgent." In *The Year of the Woman: Myth or Reality?,* edited by Elizabeth Adell Cook, Sue Thomas, and Clyde Wilcox, 71–86. Boulder, Colo.: Westview Press.

Jelen, Ted G., and Clyde Wilcox. 1996. "A Tale of Two Senators: Female Candidates in the United States Senate in Illinois, 1990–1992," *American Review of Politics* 17: 299–310.

Kellstedt, Lyman A. 1989. "Evangelicals and Political Realignment." In *Contemporary Evangelical Political Involvement: An Analysis and Assessment,* edited by Corwin E. Smidt, 99–117. New York: University Press of America.

Kellstedt, Lyman A., John C. Green, James L. Guth, and Corwin E. Smidt. 1994. "Religious Voting Blocs in the 1992 Election: The Year of the Evangelical?" *Sociology of Religion* 55: 307–26.

Kemper, Bob. 1998. "Fitzgerald Keeps to the Right, Though Occasionally He Veers." *Chicago Tribune,* 5 November, sec 1, p. 20.

Kemper, Bob, and Flynn McRoberts. 1998. "Moseley-Braun Trails in Tight Race." *Chicago Tribune,* 4 November, sec 1, pp. 1, 24.

Kleppner, Paul. 1985. *Chicago Divided: The Making of a Black Mayor.* DeKalb, Ill.: Northern Illinois University Press.

Pearson, Rick. 1998. "GOP Retains Lock on Top State Office." *Chicago Tribune,* 4 November, sec 1, pp. 1, 12.

Rakove, Milton. 1975. *Don't Make No Waves. . . . Don't Back No Losers: An Insider's Analysis of the Daley Machine.* Bloomington: Indiana University Press.

Reed, Ralph. 1994. *Politically Incorrect.* Dallas: Word Publishing.

Royko, Mike. 1971. *Boss: Richard J. Daley of Chicago.* New York: Signet.

Wilcox, Clyde. 1992. *God's Warriors: The Christian Right in the Twentieth Century.* Baltimore: Johns Hopkins University Press.

14

New York, New York: Start Spreadin' the News

Robert J. Spitzer

New York State would seem to be a particularly inhospitable political environment for serious Christian Right political activity. New York is, by reputation and fact, one of the most politically liberal states in the nation—a fact revealed not only by the political views of its residents but by the behavior of its representatives and by the state's public policies (Wright, Erikson, and McIver 1987; Colby 1994). The state's party enrollment has favored the Democrats since the 1950s. In 1998, Democratic enrollment stood at 4.9 million, compared with about 3.1 million Republicans. Further, New York Republicanism has composed the most liberal wing of the party, from Tom Dewey and Nelson Rockefeller to George Pataki, the current governor. Even so, New York's political landscape has long included prominent and influential conservative political movements, including an active Conservative Party (Stonecash 1998).[1] The 1998 elections witnessed a continuation of conservative pressure, incorporating new efforts by Christian conservative activists.

This chapter will examine some conservative elements of state politics that constitute Christian Right appeals—specifically, New York's unique Right to Life Party (RTLP), which in turn provided a critical springboard for the other focus of this chapter, the congressional campaigns of conservative Christian activists Randall Terry and James Pierce. The electoral activities of the RTLP, and of activists like Terry and Pierce, are impossible to understand without first noting two key facts about the New York State political landscape: its diversity and its unique electoral system.

The Diversity That Is New York

Non-New Yorkers often consider the state to be synonymous with New York City, an observation that not only rankles upstaters but also is far from true. As Liebschutz (1998, 10) notes, "demographically and geographically, New York is not one but many states." Liebschutz divides the state into ten subregions, each with distinctive traits. The congressional district in which Randall Terry ran, the Twenty-Sixth, coincides closely with the Southern Tier region; the Thirty-First District, in which James Pierce ran and which lies directly west of the Twenty-Sixth, sits in the Western New York region. Both of these districts, which hug the straight east-west border with Pennsylvania, share many of the social traits of the region that forms the northern portion of Appalachia, including a prevalent rural-agricultural base, persistent economic stagnation, a conservative Republican-leaning electoral base, and a strong Protestant fundamentalist strain. These particular regional traits thus suggest a more fertile political grounding for conservative Christian activity.

State Election Law

The second trait of state politics pertinent to this analysis is the state's unique electoral structure. Through decades of intentional and unintentional change, New York has developed a hybrid multiparty system that has the effect of cultivating and preserving a coterie of stable minor political parties (Scarrow 1983; Spitzer 1987). Two features of state election law fortify minor parties. The first is the method by which parties obtain official recognition. According to state law, a political party may establish an automatic ballot line for all New York elections by running a candidate for governor who receives at least 50,000 votes on that party line in the general election. If this threshold is reached, the party is guaranteed a ballot position in all New York elections for the next four years, until the next gubernatorial election. In comparison with the ballot access laws of other states, New York's is one of the more demanding. Despite this fact, however, determined and organized third parties can endure in New York where they cannot in most other states because of a second key feature of state law—the cross-endorsement rule. This provision of the law says simply that parties may nominate candidates already endorsed by other parties. The candidate's votes are then added together from all the lines where his/her name appears. This cross-endorsement process has yielded numerous so-called "fusion candidacies" that are today a routine feature of state elections. Indeed, after the 1998 elections, no fewer than six minor parties maintained such official ballot recognition.[2]

These minor parties exert influence by trading access to their lines for ideological support or patronage extracted from major party candidates who are anxious to have their names appear on the ballot as often as possible. On the other hand, the minor parties can seek to punish candidates with whom they disagree either by fielding candidates to publicize causes that receive little attention from the major parties or by attempting to siphon votes from major candidates (Spitzer 1997). Minor parties thus possess a kind of political currency that allows them to survive and influence state politics even though they lack what would otherwise be the one power that would doom them in most other settings—that is, the ability to elect candidates to office on their own.[3]

The Right to Life Party

The Right to Life Party (RTLP) entered New York's political fray in the 1970s, beginning inauspiciously during a book discussion group in the home of a Merrick, Long Island housewife. The party's grassroots beginning was prompted by attempts in the state legislature to liberalize the state's abortion law. Those attempts succeeded in 1970, and the concerns of these formerly apolitical individuals with antiabortion sentiments accelerated when the Supreme Court ruled in 1973 (*Roe v. Wade*) that women had a right to a safe, legal abortion (Spitzer 1984). Unlike New York's other minor parties, the RTLP is predicated on a single issue—that of opposition to abortion. The salience of this issue for a core of New York voters was evidenced when, in 1978, the RTLP succeeded in establishing its own line on the New York ballot after a brief attempt to work within the major parties (notably, party founder Ellen McCormack sought the Democratic party nomination in 1976). Gubernatorial candidate and party cofounder Mary Jane Tobin received over 130,000 votes with party cofounder McCormack running for lieutenant governor. Aside from fielding candidates in state races, the RTLP has also run minor party candidates for president. Unlike the state's other minor parties, however, the RTLP has operated under several handicaps.

First, as a single-issue party that is generally considered extremist and inflexible even within the right-to-life movement, it often drives away candidates (including many who consider themselves strongly antiabortion) who would otherwise jump at a chance to obtain an extra ballot line. One example of the party's perceived inflexibility was its refusal to endorse Ronald Reagan for president in 1980 and 1984, as party leaders considered his opposition to abortion to be insufficiently strong. The party has long feuded with other elements of the right-to-life movement, such as the national Right to Life Committee. Another example of the party's pariah status among potential allies was seen in Nassau County, a strongly Republican and conservative suburban county on Long Island. From 1981 to 1997, the county Republican Party formally barred any

Republican nominee from accepting the RTLP endorsement, regardless of the candidates' views on abortion. Such a move is unheard of in a state where multiple party endorsements are the norm. The ban was lifted in 1997 only because an RTLP endorsement of a Democrat helped that candidate upset a Republican to win a local election (Spitzer 1999).[4]

Second, New York State is one of the most strongly pro-choice states in the nation; thus, an RTLP endorsement is often considered a net liability, especially for a candidate who already has a major party endorsement (Spitzer 1987, chap. 2 and 3). This verdict is reflected in the RTLP's sometimes precarious fortunes. In the 1982 gubernatorial election, its candidate received just over 52,000 votes, putting the RTLP ballot position at fifth from 1983 to 1986 (parties are listed on the New York ballot according to gubernatorial votes received). This election dip caused RTLP leaders to seek a better-known gubernatorial candidate for 1986. After the Republican-Conservative gubernatorial nominee declined the endorsement, despite his own opposition to abortion, the RTLP turned to a Democrat, Nassau County District Attorney Denis Dillon, who waged a vigorous campaign and received 130,802 votes. In 1990, the RTLP turned to a Staten Island consultant and Republican, Louis Wein, who received about 137,000 votes. In the 1994 gubernatorial race, RTLP candidate Robert Walsh garnered 67,750 votes. In 1998, RTLP activist Tom Reynolds received 56,683 votes for governor.

A study of the RTLP's leaders and activists conducted in the 1980s found that the vast majority were either Catholic or fundamentalist Protestant. In general, the social and attitudinal characteristics of RTLP identifiers and leaders conformed closely to studies of other New Right groups motivated by social-issue concerns. Party leaders in particular revealed devotion to the antiabortion cause that eclipsed the desire to win more votes or elections. For example, they rated education of the public on the abortion issue to be a more important goal than winning elections (Spitzer 1987, chap. 3). The leaders' inner-directed behavior, focused on issue purity over compromise and coalition building, underscores their devotion to the antiabortion cause and their narrow electoral base.[5]

The RTLP's zenith year was 1980, when it endorsed candidates in more than three-fourths of all races for Congress, state senate, and state assembly, a total of two hundred elections alone. Since the mid-1980s, the party has fielded progressively fewer candidates for congressional, state legislative, and other contests. In 1996, according to the party, it endorsed a total of 107 candidates for all races throughout the state. Of those, 16 won election. This small number of endorsements and victories underscores the party's diminished reach as compared with the early 1980s. Voter enrollment in the RTLP has increased gradually. In 1980, it stood at 8,031. By 1986, it was 21,606. In 1991, it was 25,066, and in 1998, 50,600.

Most of these enrollees are found in suburban and upstate areas, as only 13,189 of the 1998 enrollees live in New York City.

In short, the RTLP has survived for over two decades in an electorally inhospitable environment because of New York's unique election law system, coupled with its ability to maintain the support of a zealous core of followers. Without question, the RTLP has followed a confrontational political strategy, emphasizing issue purity rather than a consolidation strategy emphasizing pragmatism and conciliation. This pattern conforms to Green's analysis (1997, 4), which predicts a confrontational style for Christian Right groups that exist in a more inhospitable political environment, as is the case with the RTLP in New York. It also parallels analysis of third-party behavior throughout American history, when minor party movements have followed either a "broad" political strategy emphasizing compromise, coalition building, and moderation, or a "narrow" strategy emphasizing issue purity and homogeneity (Spitzer 1987, chap. 1). This takes us directly to the 1998 congressional candidacies of Randall Terry and James Pierce.

1998 Congressional Races

The Twenty-Sixth Congressional District

In 1998, thirty-nine-year-old antiabortion activist Randall Terry ran a well-financed, high-profile campaign for Congress that represented the culmination of much of his political effort. The son of Rochester schoolteachers, Terry displayed a combination of religious and political activism after he embraced Christianity as a young man. After his religious conversion, he enrolled in Elim Bible Institute, graduating in 1981. He held a series of jobs in the Binghamton area, becoming a lay minister in the Church at Pierce Creek by 1983. When an abortion clinic opened in Binghamton sometime later, both Terry and his wife, Cindy (they have three children), mobilized in opposition, first applying the aggressive confrontational tactics for which he became well known. The organizational result was Operation Rescue, for which he gained national prominence. Formed by Terry in 1988, the organization adopted militant tactics to close abortion clinics, including sit-ins and blockades. Various civil and criminal prosecutions have been pursued against the group and its members. The group has since splintered (Bower 1994). Terry disassociated himself from the group as well, but not before finding himself serving several prison terms, including five months in prison for his involvement in an antiabortion protest at the 1992 Democratic National Convention held in New York City (Hannagan 1998).

While serving time in prison for blocking access to an abortion clinic in Wichita, Kansas, Terry (1993) wrote a book defending his actions and those of other protesters, arguing that he was bound by God's law, a higher law that superseded the wrongful government laws protecting abortion practices. A prolific author, Terry has also written books from behind prison bars on the formation of and justification for Operation Rescue (Terry 1988), a broader political analysis of those organizations that have supported abortion rights (Terry 1990), and two books that expand on his views concerning the relationship among his theological perspectives, various natural calamities, and civil governance (Terry 1995a, 1995b).

In 1992, Terry began a daily radio program, "Randall Terry Live," broadcast on various Christian radio stations. In 1996, he formed the Christian Leadership School, based at his home in Windsor, a small town in Broome County. By his own account, Terry traces his political awakening to his first vote in 1980 for Ronald Reagan. In the 1980s, Terry considered himself a hard-core, single-issue voter and activist animated solely by opposition to abortion. By the 1990s, however, Terry's interests had broad-ened to include issues like gun control, education, the economy, and taxation. "As my understanding of freedom and justice grew, I had to branch out" (Terry 1998). According to Terry, his leap to electoral politics was not an impulsive decision but had been planned since 1992. Terry's explanation for the sharp change in political tactics was his belief that officeholders hold ultimate political power, that most officeholders are "cowardly, compromised, or corrupt men" who are "thieves" that need to be pressured to do the right thing, and that "we've got to have the right people in office" (Terry 1998). As for Operation Rescue, Terry noted that it had accomplished its goal of pushing the country in a more pro-life direction and, according to Terry, helping to elect George Bush in 1988. Like other social movements to which Terry compared his, such as the civil rights movement, the progression from the streets to the ballot box was a logical step.[6]

Terry's 1998 run for the Twenty-Sixth Congressional District was part of a larger, coordinated effort to organize and encourage other Christian Right candidates. Terry organized a loose association of congressional hopefuls, dubbed the "Patrick Henry Men," composed of six evangelical Christian candidates around the nation seeking congressional seats (including fellow New Yorker James Pierce; a seventh recruit dropped out). One of the six, Joseph J. Slovenec, won a Republican primary in Ohio's Tenth District (part of Cleveland) but lost in the general election to incumbent Democrat Representative Dennis Kucinich by a margin of 67–33 percent. The rest dropped out or lost in primaries (Dao 1998).

Seeking to take advantage of the electoral opportunity afforded by the cross-endorsement system, Terry sought the Republican, Conservative, and Right to Life endorsements in the race against incumbent Democrat Maurice Hinchey. First elected in 1992, Hinchey took over a seat that had been held by a Democrat since 1974, but the district had been considered vulnerable to a Republican takeover by virtue of its Republican leanings (it had been a traditional Republican stronghold before 1974), and because Hinchey himself had won reelection by narrow margins.

Terry won the RTLP endorsement without opposition but was challenged for the Republican and Conservative nods by William "Bud" Walker, an apple farmer and radio station owner, who was the choice of most of the Republican establishment. In an unusual move, other prominent Republicans, such as Representative Gerald Solomon, spoke out during the primary on behalf of Walker and against Terry, and independently funded an ad campaign on Walker's behalf. In his letter supporting Walker, Solomon said, "I will continue to fight for conservative principles and against the Randall Terrys and David Dukes of this world" (Dao 1998). The chair of one county Republican committee in the district said that Terry "isn't a true Republican." ("Walker Wins Close One" 1998) A polished and articulate speaker with considerable experience at being in the public eye, Terry fought a well-financed and highly visible campaign, buttressed by a staff of ten plus about fifty volunteers, in which he emphasized economic issues (Dao 1998).

In a half-hour campaign video scripted by Terry, he blasted away at both political parties (while recognizing that election to office was nearly impossible without a major party endorsement), and at the modern welfare state, arguing that social ills including crime, poverty, illegitimacy, and immorality were the direct consequence of government programs. His platform called for elimination of the income tax (and repeal of the Sixteenth Amendment), property, and other land taxes, and the Social Security system and advocated campaigns against abortion, gay rights, gun control, government-regulated and financed schools, and child pornography. Tying these issues together were the themes of freedom and liberty "based on Christian ethics" and what Terry characterized as a natural affinity between Christianity and Libertarian economics ("Randall Terry" 1997; Dao 1998; Terry 1998).

Terry outspent Walker and another Republican challenger in the primary and by his count raised a campaign war chest of $1.2 million from around the country. Despite his financing edge, however, stiff Republican organization opposition took its toll, as Terry lost the Republican primary, garnering 35 percent of the vote to Walker's 53 percent. He also lost the Conservative primary to Walker, but by a narrower margin. Assessing the primary loss, Terry concluded that Walker had been beatable but that Terry's campaign had erred by ignoring Walker and not vigorously attacking him. "We should have buried him," Terry (1998) said. Running solely on the RTLP line, Terry continued to hammer away at his opponents and his campaign themes, but polled only 12,160 votes. Hinchey won by his widest margin ever, polling over 108,000 votes. Walker polled 54,776 votes.

On the matter of principle versus pragmatism, Terry was clear in asserting that the "populist economic message" was a winning message. Despite the disappointing showing, Terry is convinced that he will one day win election on the themes honed in his campaign. "People admire courage" and those who "hold out for principles," even though they may need to do so "creatively" at times. The national Republican losses in 1998, and those of the Christian Right, were attributable to faulty strategy on their part, Terry noted, in that they failed to find a consistent theme, and did not appreciate the value of a populist economic message that also includes an emphasis on moral and traditional family values. Terry said that polling done by his campaign had confirmed the power of such an approach. The Republican Party, he concluded, was "clueless, visionless, leaderless, and treacherous" for betraying the core of the party (Terry 1998).

Without denying the legitimacy of Terry's analysis of the problems with his campaign, it is also obvious that he continues to carry considerable political baggage. Though his right-to-life stance certainly resonates with many voters, the militancy of his style, held up to public view through media coverage of Operation Rescue and explicitly stamped "beyond the law" by the several judges who sentenced him to prison, was and is an undeniable turnoff to many potential supporters. His antitax, antigovernment message also has potentially great resonance with voters, but the extremity of his program, as seen especially in his proposal to privatize and voluntarize Social Security, strikes a sensitive nerve with most voters. Few programs are so enduringly popular as Social Security. Even on his radio show, Terry has encountered resistance when talking about ending Social Security (Nieves 1998). Finally, the blending of secular and sacred messages that invoke apocalyptic visions of the near future in the context of a political campaign does not sit well with voters of many—perhaps most—religious persuasions. In New York in particular, "religious-based politics" (Green et al. 1996, 2) is met mostly with suspicion, as are such assertions as the claim that natural disasters, AIDS, and riots are signs of God's judgment against a sinful nation (Sylvester 1993; Terry 1995a).

As for the future, Terry had not settled on any particular election race at the time of my interview with him, but he was clear that election politics was "what I want to do for the rest of my life." Even before election day, Terry said that he would be back in the year 2000 ("Invisible Man" 1998). He plans to recruit five hundred like-minded candidates to run for office in the year 2000, including twenty-five candidates for the House of Representatives around the country. "We're destined to be leaders," Terry said, because we have "the ideas and the character" to lead.

The Thirty-First Congressional District

Rev. James Pierce is senior pastor of the Love Church, located in Horseheads, near the city of Elmira. The Pentecostal pastor's affiliation to the church extends back eighteen years. Since 1992, Pierce has served as president and general manager of Lighthouse Media, Inc., which includes an AM radio station that broadcasts "issue-based programming" as well as Bible-based teaching and music. Pierce traces his political activism back to 1984, when he became involved in antiabortion activities in the local area. He has often spoken locally, has engaged in debates, and has been involved in the Southern Tier Crisis Pregnancy Center, an organization formed by one of Pierce's parishioners that steers pregnant women away from abortion. Like Terry, however, Pierce has broadened his involvement in other community activities, such as a local food bank, and in other issues, including teenage pregnancy, other family issues, and the economy (Perry 1998; Pierce 1998).

Though identified as one of Terry's Patrick Henry Men, Pierce downplayed the impact of this organization, calling it "borderline nonexistent." Pierce has known Terry since 1981 through church activities. Over the years, the two talked issues and strategies, but nothing more formal. Pierce announced his decision to seek the local congressional seat in May 1997. When asked why, Pierce said that he considered the House of Representatives to be patterned after the British House of Commons in that it was a body intended for "the common man to have a voice in government." After praying for a representative who "represented our values," Pierce finally decided to act.

Pierce's opponent, Republican Amory Houghton, posed a formidable challenge. First elected to the House in 1986 from a strongly Republican district, Houghton is the former head of Corning Inc., and one of the wealthiest members of the House. In the House, Houghton has behaved as an independent, supporting President Clinton more often than most Republicans. Most notably, Houghton was one of only four House Republicans to vote against all four articles of impeachment brought against President Clinton in December 1998. Even so, Houghton has always won reelection by wide margins.

In his 1998 campaign, the forty-one-year-old Pierce sought Republican, Conservative, and RTLP nods. Lacking Terry's financial and organizational resources, however, Pierce ran afoul of state requirements. Houghton's campaign challenged Pierce's nominating petitions, claiming various procedural irregularities. On appeal, Pierce was knocked off the Republican primary ballot. Though he planned to obtain the Conservative endorsement, his campaign never gathered enough signatures to qualify for the line, leaving him only the RTLP endorsement. In comparison with Terry's campaign, Pierce's possessed far fewer resources. Though he made a couple of visits outside of the state to raise money, most of his contributions came from within the district, he said, yielding a total campaign budget of about $75,000. Pierce relied heavily on help from his family (he is married with six children; his wife served as his treasurer) and local friends and associates for financial assistance and labor (Pierce 1998).

Pierce's campaign emphasized both economic and moral issues. Pierce railed against taxation, noting that half of wage-earners' income goes to taxes, which, Pierce argues, forces both parents in two-parent families into the workforce, a trend Pierce views with alarm. Aside from high taxes, Pierce campaigned for a minimalist government, including such measures as opposition to gun control. On election day, Pierce polled roughly the same vote as Terry, receiving 10,546 votes, compared with Houghton's 107,000 votes and 40,091 votes for Democratic nominee Caleb Rossiter.

Despite the disappointing showing, Pierce wasted little time in announcing his future intentions. Within twenty-four hours of Houghton's announcement that he would vote against Clinton's impeachment, Pierce announced that he would again seek Houghton's seat in the year 2000. That announcement garnered national attention. Though the Clinton impeachment inquiry mobilized many conservatives, Pierce's motivation extended beyond a narrow political calculus in that, like Terry, his views bridged the secular and the sacred. "Satan, knowing his time is short, is stepping up his efforts to destroy as much of humanity as he can" (Grann 1999).

When asked about the balance between principle and pragmatism, Pierce echoed Terry's philosophy. Sticking to one's guns is "a matter of honor and integrity," according to Pierce. He went on to say that he conceived of three approaches to representation: a finger-in-the-wind style, where representatives do whatever the people want; a conscience stand, where representatives do whatever they think best; and a third approach, where the representative establishes clear issue positions before the election and then follows those promises. Whereas the second and third approaches are similar, the third option, which Pierce extolled, underscored his unwillingness to hedge or compromise and emphasized his differences with Houghton, who noted that his votes against impeachment were based on conscience. Assessing national Republican reversals in the 1998 elections, Pierce faulted the Republicans for trying to "out-Democrat the Democrats" and for failing to keep their word after election. This, Pierce noted, was a survival tactic that backfired. "Principles work better," he noted (Pierce 1998).

Conclusion: If I Can Make It There, I'll Make It Anywhere

The RTLP and the congressional candidacies of Randall Terry and James Pierce have to date followed a remarkably similar trajectory. They have all pursued a confrontational political style in a larger political atmosphere generally hostile to their interests. At the same time, they have found political niches (Green 1997, 13) within the state's diverse political and social geography that have provided loyal, if limited, followings.

On the other hand, the RTLP continues to maintain its single-issue focus, which, along with its continued unyielding political style, certainly explains its slowly narrowing appeal. Both Terry and Pierce, however, have consciously broadened their platforms and appeals, while at the same time rejecting any move to the political center. Terry's efforts in particular are of interest because of his long-time public prominence, his highly controversial political past, and his ambitions not only for himself but also for a broader Christian Right movement. Terry's Christian Leadership School is designed precisely to train a new generation of Christian Right political activists and leaders, as is the Patrick Henry Men idea. Terry's activities encapsulate the three realms identified by Green (1997, 9) where such movements seek to maximize their influence: candidate recruitment, participation in the nominating process, and participation in general election campaigns. In New York, the third option is not foreclosed by failure in the second.

The most significant consequence of the activities described in this chapter may be to provide a kind of a "political friendly zone" to which bridges from similar organizations in other states may be extended. Beyond this, it is difficult to imagine that the efforts of Terry, Pierce, or the RTLP will yield anything like electoral success, beyond perhaps an occasional primary election win, anytime in the immediate future within the state's boundaries. The fact that Terry and Pierce polled virtually the same percentage of the vote (less than 7 percent), despite the huge differences in visibility and resources, supports the proposition that they are severely limited in the degree to which they can expand their electoral bases (although either candidate would have certainly polled more votes on a major party line).

Emblematic of the difficulty with this appeal is the case of New York Republican Senator Alphonse D'Amato, who was turned out of office in his bid for a fourth term in 1998. His natural social conservative tendencies were carefully sublimated in each of his reelection bids. Despite his close alliance with the RTLP (which endorsed D'Amato in each of his four races, although he faced a primary challenge in 1998), D'Amato championed the cause of gay rights in the Senate, soft-pedaled his opposition to abortion, and emphasized his nonideological commitment to bringing home the bacon for New York. Yes, the state as a whole is far more liberal than rural upstate communities. Nevertheless, D'Amato's rise and fall echoes a prevailing mistrust for the kind of hard-Right political appeals that resonate in some southern states and elsewhere around the country but that are simply alien to most New York political ears.

Ideological commitment, a hard core of true believers incorporating the ability to mobilize money and other resources, and the state's unique electoral system will continue to support the Christian Right efforts of the RTLP and aspirants like Terry and Pierce. Though the latter caused fits within the state's Republican Party, these efforts are simply unlikely under current conditions to establish much more than a foothold in Empire State politics. On the other hand, if the Christian Right could somehow take hold as a major force in liberal, cosmopolitan, streetwise New York, its national prospects would be bright indeed.

NOTES

I would like to extend my sincerest thanks to Mike Royce for helping me to arrange the interviews upon which much of this chapter is based, and for his thoughtful comments on many of the subjects raised here.

1. The Conservative Party was formed in 1962 in opposition to Nelson Rockefeller's more moderate Republicanism. Its traditional ideological basis has been more broadly conservative than that of the Right to Life Party, emphasizing fiscal rather than social conservatism. It has at times made cautious alliance with social conservatives in the state, but for the most part it has pursued a consolidation rather than a confrontation strategy.

2. The six parties, with dates of formation, are the Liberal (1946), Conservative (1962), Right to Life (1978), Independence (1994), Green (1998), and Working Families (1998). The two most recent entrants attracted the 50,000-vote minimum by using one of two standard techniques. The Green Party nominated a celebrity, acid-tongued actor "Grandpa" Al Lewis. The Working Families Party nominated a major party gubernatorial nominee, Democratic candidate Peter Vallone.

3. In a handful of instances, minor parties have beaten the major parties. In 1969, incumbent New York City Mayor John Lindsay was reelected on the Liberal Party line, defeating Democratic and Republican nominees. In 1970, the Conservative Party elected James Buckley to the U.S. Senate, defeating Republican and Democratic challengers. Such occurrences are, however, rare.

4. In 1995, for example, a Democratic-Independent candidate for Onondaga County Executive (the county in which Syracuse is located) was pressured by Democrats to drop his endorsement by the RTLP. Despite the fact that the candidate faced an uphill battle against a popular Republican incumbent, the Democratic challenger agreed to drop the RTLP endorsement because Democrats had a long-standing agreement, dating to 1981, that no Democratic candidate would also accept the RTLP line (Arnold 1995).

5. The party's goals are reflected in recent documents. According to its 1998 statement of purposes, the RTLP seeks to encourage passage of a consti-

tutional amendment to reverse *Roe v. Wade*. Lacking that, it supports any and all legislative efforts to restrict abortions, and similarly opposes any effort to promote euthanasia (mercy killing). Its nine-point program includes ending Medicaid-funded abortions, educational efforts to inform women about the consequences of abortion, parental notification for minors seeking abortions, an end to so-called partial-birth abortions, opposition to restrictions imposed on those who picket at abortion clinics, opposition to physician-assisted suicide, opposition to granting legal protections to surrogates who may be able to make life or death decisions over the ill, increased funding for groups that support women with troubled pregnancies, and ending public funding for groups that support abortion rights.

6. Terry rejects the label "Christian Right," saying that he is an "Orthodox Christian." Pierce also rejected the term, saying that he was just a citizen with religious faith who wants to influence politics. I use the term here because it is the term of currency, and because the general political bent of Terry, Pierce, and others can defensibly be characterized as of the political Right.

REFERENCES

Arnold, Jacqualine. 1995. "Party Lines Tug Executive Candidate." *Syracuse Post-Standard*, 16 June, C3.

Bower, Anne. 1994. "Did Operation Rescue Flower from Branch Ministries?—Part I." *The Body Politic* 4(May): 3–6.

Colby, Peter W. 1994. "New York State in Comparative Perspective." In *Governing New York State*, edited by Jeffrey M. Stonecash, John Kenneth White, and Peter W. Colby, 365–75. Albany, N.Y.: SUNY Press.

Dao, James. 1998. "Putting Aside Protest for Politics." *New York Times*, 27 July, B1.

Grann, David. 1999. "Going to Extremes." *New Republic*, January 4 and 11, 9–10.

Green, John C. 1997. "The Christian Right and the 1996 Elections." In *God at the Grass Roots, 1996: The Christian Right in the American Elections*, edited by Mark J. Rozell and Clyde Wilcox, 1–14. Lanham, Md.: Rowman & Littlefield.

Green, John C., James L. Guth, Corwin E. Smidt, and Lyman A. Kellstedt. 1996. *Religion and the Culture Wars*. Lanham, Md.: Rowman & Littlefield.

Hannagan, Charley. 1998. "Terry: Not One Cent for Clinics." *Syracuse Post-Standard*, 11 November, A1.

"Invisible Man." 1998. *Binghamton Press & Sun Bulletin*, 18 October, A7.

Liebschutz, Sarah F. 1998. "The Character of New York: Competition and Compassion." In *New York Politics and Government*, edited by Sarah F. Liebschutz, 1–21. Lincoln: University of Nebraska Press.

Nieves, Evelyn. 1998. "A Candidate Talks of Revolt on the Radio." *New York Times,* 24 May, A27.

Perry, James M. 1998. "New York Congressional Race Is Challenge for Centrist." *Wall Street Journal,* 18 June, A20.

Pierce, James. 1998. Telephone interview, 18 December.

"Randall Terry for Congress." 1997. Campaign videotape.

Scarrow, Howard. 1983. *Parties, Elections, and Representation in the State of New York.* New York: NYU Press.

Spitzer, Robert J. 1984. "A Political Party Is Born: Single-Issue Advocacy and the New York State Election Law." *National Civic Review,* July/August, 321–28.

———. 1987. *The Right to Life Movement and Third Party Politics.* Westport, Conn.: Greenwood Press.

———. 1997. "Multiparty Politics in New York." In *Multiparty Politics in America,* edited by Paul S. Herrnson and John C. Green, 125—37. Lanham, Md.: Rowman & Littlefield.

———. 1999. "The Right to Life Party." In *The Encyclopedia of American Third Parties,* edited by Ronald Hayduk, Immanuel Ness, and James Ciment. New York: M. E. Sharpe.

Stonecash, Jeffrey M. 1998. "Political Parties and Conflict." In *New York Politics and Government,* edited by Sarah F. Liebschutz, 63–79. Lincoln: University of Nebraska Press.

Sylvester, David A. 1993. "Brimstone from Foe of Abortion." *San Francisco Chronicle,* 15 July, A18.

Terry, Randall. 1988. *Operation Rescue.* Springdale, Pa.: Whitaker House.

———. 1990. *Accessory to Murder.* Brentwood, Tenn.: Wolgemuth and Hyatt.

———. 1993. *Why Does a Nice Guy Like Me Keep Getting Thrown in Jail?* Lafayette, La.: Huntington House Pubs.

———. 1995a. *The Judgment of God.* Windsor, N.Y.: The Reformer Library.

———. 1995b. *The Sword.* Windsor, N.Y.: The Reformer Library.

———. 1998. Telephone interview, 4 December.

"Walker Wins Close One Over Terry in Twenty-Sixth District." 1998. *Ithaca Journal,* 16 September, A1.

Wright, Gerald C. Jr., Robert S. Erikson, and John P. McIver. 1987. "Public Opinion and Policy Liberalism in the American States." *American Journal of Political Science* 31(November): 980–1001.

15

Maine: Which Way Should Life Be?

Matthew C. Moen and Kenneth T. Palmer

When motorists enter or leave the state, they are faced with an interstate sign that reads: "Maine: The Way Life Should Be." That chauvinism is partly a reflection of a political system that is unusually clean, civil, and moderate compared with those of many regions of the country. For example, Maine has a Clean Elections Act that regulates campaign spending in state legislative races. Moreover, in recent years virtually all candidates for federal office have signed a campaign code of ethics in which they pledge to refrain from negative campaigning (Maine Code of Election Ethics 1996).

The prevailing political culture is one of moderation, weak political parties, and a high proportion of independents (Palmer, Taylor, and LiBrizzi 1992). Against that backdrop, Maine has been a surprising battleground in recent years particularly over gay rights, pitting urban, coastal areas against more rural, inland areas. It is the only state in New England identified as having a "substantial" Christian Right influence, defined as having 25–50 percent strength within the state's Republican Party organization (Persinos 1994); it is also the only state in New England that currently lacks a law prohibiting discrimination on the basis of sexual orientation. This chapter tries to explain the anomaly of Maine's political culture with recent events and assesses the Christian Right's current impact and influence within the state.

Maine Politics

Maine is the only state in the contiguous United States that is bordered by only one other state (New Hampshire). Its unusual geographic isolation has traditionally insulated it from the pressures of urbanism, and it largely remains that way today, even with growth in its southern corridor. The four largest cities in Maine contain only 13 percent of the state's population. The rest of the population is scattered over a relatively wide geographic area (by eastern standards) in small towns, villages, and unorganized territories. International paper companies own vast tracts of land in the northern and western parts.

Maine was originally settled by bands of French Catholics and English Protestants, who constructed small, close-knit communities (Palmer, Taylor, and LiBrizzi 1992). One important consequence of this decentralized residential living pattern is a strikingly high rate of citizen participation in politics. Maine had the highest level of voter participation in the nation (64 percent) in the 1996 election cycle, even though Republican challenger Bob Dole did not seriously contest the presidential race. Maine routinely turns out a greater proportion of its citizens than almost all other states during presidential and midterm election cycles. It also frequently employs citizen referenda, which are a reflection of its egalitarian and participatory culture.

Historically, Maine's coastal waters were a battleground for English Protestant and French Catholic navies. The region was a district of Massachusetts until 1820, when it became a separate state. Sensitive to the long-standing ethnic and religious differences in the state, Maine's delegates to its constitutional convention deliberately tried to minimize future conflict. They adopted an absolute guarantee of religious freedom which makes "no distinction whatever . . . between Protestants and Roman Catholics, Christians and non-Christians" (Banks 1970). That guarantee was a clear departure from the Massachusetts Charter of 1780, under which Maine was governed. The charter required church attendance and the taxation of all citizens to support public worship and "Protestant teachers of piety." According to a Maine historian, the language written into the Maine Constitution reflected "the liberal attitude of most of those at the convention" (Banks 1970).

Yet Maine has also demonstrated interest in moral issues throughout its history. Temperance is a case in point. In 1846, Portland businessman Neal Dow authored legislation banning the sale and consumption of alcohol, well in advance of the modern temperance crusades (Gusfield 1963; Byrne 1985). He struck a deal in 1851—the year he was elected mayor of Portland—to enhance enforcement of temperance in return for supporting Hannibal Hamlin's candidacy for the U.S. Senate. Dow also created the Watchmen of Temperance, whose sole purpose was to ferret out information about hidden liquor stocks for public officials. His reputation plummeted, however, when his militia killed one person and injured several others in a melee over confiscated liquor stocks at city hall. Dow was legally absolved, but his political career ended.

Not surprisingly, Dow's temperance crusade was carried out with backing from religious groups, but it was not as pronounced as one might expect. Dow was not an especially religious man and his heavy-handed tactics as a citizen-politician offended many of the clergy. Asa Cummings, of the *Portland Christian Mirror*, for example, observed that Dow was attempting "to dictate [his views] to ministers and churches" (Byrne 1985). Dow's failure to win reelection as Portland's mayor actually typifies Maine's historic preference for political consensus and moderation. Those viewed as sharpening divisions within the electorate are not especially successful. State politicians have usually reconciled religious liberty with morality by approaching moral issues in a moderate fashion.

Because of a substantial Franco-American community (about 20 percent of the population) and approximately equal numbers of Protestants and Roman Catholics, Maine has always faced the danger of schism. In the nineteenth century, Protestant resentment against Irish immigrants caused Catholic churches to be burned and the nativist "Know Nothing" party to gain widespread popular support (Palmer, Taylor, and LiBrizzi 1992); in the 1920s, the Ku Klux Klan enjoyed a membership boom, and it played a minor role in a gubernatorial election. Yet the norm has been the separation of religious and political issues in state politics.

A principal reason for this separation has been the state's overwhelmingly centrist political tendencies, which have worked to discourage politicians from advancing sectarian or moralistic appeals. The heavy concentration of Franco-Americans in certain cities (Saco, Lewiston, and Biddeford) and particular regions (northern Aroostook County on the Canadian border) has further mitigated conflict. Franco-American politicians have generally been satisfied with exercising influence in those communities and retaining their regional seats in the state legislature (Palmer, Taylor, and LiBrizzi 1992). Unlike other New England states, where ethnic politics is regularly practiced on a statewide basis, Maine politics generally lacks such overtones. Few Franco-Americans have actively pursued the highest state offices, with none winning the governorship in the twentieth century.

Perhaps the most visible conflict between Protestants and Catholics, involving ethnic and regional differences, was over public transportation of parochial students. In *Everson v. New Jersey* (1947), the U.S. Supreme Court ruled that a state law allowing public school buses to carry pupils to sectarian schools did not breach the "wall of separation" between church and state. The Court reasoned that children not churches, benefited from the policy. Maine lacked established policies on this matter at the time, with several cities routinely offering bus service to parochial students. These services gained little attention in Franco-American communities, but they engendered sharp protest in Protestant communities following the *Everson* decision. The issue was particularly intense in the state capital of Augusta, where voters approved a nonbinding referendum in 1956 that allowed transportation of parochial students at city expense. The following year, the city council provided a small appropriation for the program, creating a legal challenge.

In *Squires v. Augusta* (1959), the Maine Supreme Court ruled by a 4–2 margin that publicly supported transportation of nonpublic students was illegal. Interestingly, the court found no conflict with the U.S. Constitution; instead, it reasoned that Augusta had exceeded its authority because neither the Maine constitution nor the state's education statutes gave local communities the power to bus students (in New Jersey, an authorizing statute existed). A majority of the justices argued that the state legislature could grant such a power to local communities. In a lengthy dissent, two of the supreme court's Catholic justices argued that communities already had a police power that allowed them to transport parochial school students. The Maine Supreme Court essentially diffused the issue, placing the onus on the state legislature, where the issue soon deflated (Sorauf 1977). This case is a telling description of the normal relationship between religion and politics in Maine.

The Christian Right in Maine

The Christian Right emerged on the national scene in the late 1970s, with groups such as Christian Voice and the Moral Majority (Moen 1989, 1992). Maine basically missed the first wave of activism by religious conservatives because its state elections around that time ran contrary to national trends. In 1974, most states were electing liberal politicians to office in response to the Watergate scandal; Maine replaced Democratic incumbent Peter Kyros in the First Congressional District with conservative Republican David Emery, and it elected Independent James Longley to the governorship. Longley campaigned on strongly conservative themes, such as reducing taxes and downsizing government, and he pursued very conservative policies during his tenure in office. Interestingly, the 1978 governor's race reversed the conservative direction, with the election of the Democratic candidate, but it, too, ran contrary to the larger national trends that presaged the Republican victories of 1980 (McIntyre 1979).

The 1978 gubernatorial race offered voters three distinctive choices: moderate Democrat Joe Brennan; conservative Republican Linwood Palmer; and conservative Independent Buddy Frankland, a well-known and charismatic Baptist minister. Frankland was opposed to abortion and gay rights, favoring a reduction in the University of Maine's state appropriation when its administration extended formal recognition to a homosexual student organization (Fisher 1978). He campaigned for governor on traditional conservative themes such as lower taxes and less government, receiving 25 percent of the statewide vote. Frankland cut deeply into Republican Linwood Palmer's base of support in eastern and northern Maine, assuring an easy victory for Democrat Joe Brennan.

Again in 1980, Maine and national election results diverged. As Republicans won control of the U.S. Senate for the first time in a generation and Ronald Reagan won the presidency, Democrats in Maine increased their number of seats in both chambers of the legislature.

Maine missed the first wave of Christian Right activism because of strong support for abortion rights, which denied religious conservatives a key mobilizing issue. One poll taken during the 1996 election cycle found that 70 percent of Maine people opposed a constitutional amendment to ban abortion (Campbell 1996), with those numbers reflected in the public arena. Maine has experienced almost no abortion clinic violence. Local communities such as Bangor passed ordinances that discouraged picketing by right-to-life groups—in some cases so restrictive that the courts disallowed them and they had to be rewritten (Saucier 1997). Every governor and every member of the congressional delegation since the late 1970s has been strongly pro-choice. It is instructive that pro-life forces felt it was necessary to bypass the political establishment to ban partial-birth abortions by gathering referendum signatures to place the abortion issue on the November 1999 ballot (Meara 1999). Usually right-to-life groups and Christian Right organizations have been tightly linked by the abortion issue (Berkowitz and Green 1997), but those connections are less important in a state with a strong pro-choice majority.

For the most part, religious conservatives have operated in relatively discrete organizations across the state, with limited success. Right-to-life organizations can claim few public policy successes, although a partial-birth abortion vote by citizen referendum holds more promise. Home schooling receives limited attention compared with funding levels for public education, with Governor Angus King (I) not even including exemptions for home schools in his 1997 educational standards for secondary schools.

The Maine Christian Civic League (MCCL)—the linchpin for organizing conservative churches in the state—cannot claim many victories. Originally founded in 1897 as a temperance organization, the MCCL was run for thirty years by a charismatic preacher from northern Maine named Benjamin Bubar (Higgins 1998a). The MCCL gradually expanded its agenda to incorporate issues such as sex education, abortion, gambling, and gay rights. Yet even as the Christian Right was coalescing nationally, the MCCL was moribund (Martin 1980). Few people attended its meetings, and its cooperative relationship with the Maine Department of Education to offer sex education programs in the public schools atrophied as its message of abstinence conflicted with secular messages of safe sex.

In the 198()s and 1990s, the MCCL was closely identified with the political aspirations of its executive director, Jasper Wyman, much as it had been with his predecessor, Benjamin Bubar. Wyman ran unsuccessfully as the Republican nominee for the U.S. Senate seat held by Democratic Majority Leader George Mitchell in 1988; he ran for the Republican nomination for governor in 1994, placing third in a crowded field. Following that loss, Wyman left Maine to work in the Prison Fellowship Ministry program.

During his tenure, Wyman pushed the MCCL to moderate some of its positions. He gradually changed his own antiabortion stance to a more neutral position, on the grounds that abortion would be solved in people's hearts rather than by politics. He criticized right-to-life organizations for "unreasonable and indefensible opposition" to birth control (Rawson 1995). He repudiated his support for a 1986 antiobscenity referendum aimed at restricting adult bookstores (Weinstein 1994). Following exposure to harsh antigay rhetoric, he called for compassion and tolerance (while remaining opposed to gay rights) in the midst of a hotly debated gay-rights referendum in 1995. Many bedrock conservatives blamed Wyman for weakening the positions of the MCCL on social issues in pursuit of his personal political goals. Wyman's successor even banned him from the MCCL office, changing the locks on the doors (Rooks 1995; Higgins 1998a).

Internal conflict is still affecting the MCCL. In 1998, the press reported that members of the MCCL board went to court to force Director Michael Heath to open the financial records of the organization, on the grounds that an accounting was long overdue (Higgins 1998b). Heath responded to their challenge at a board meeting by calling the local police department to remove them from the premises; subsequently, the MCCL released a report of an audit showing no financial improprieties ("Christian Civic League Says Audit OK" 1998). Publicity over the conflict, combined with withering editorials in state newspapers, pushed the MCCL into an uncertain financial standing, with the group failing to make its payroll on time on several successive occasions (Fisher 1998).

In September 1998, Heath announced that he was leaving the MCCL for the Washington-based Family Research Council (Higgins 1988c). Yet the planned relocation did not occur as scheduled. The following month Heath announced that his start date at the Family Research Council had been delayed and that the board members who made allegations of financial mismanagement had been removed from the MCCL board (Quinn 1998). The story became even more peculiar in 1999, when those ousted from the board returned with a court order to gain access to the MCCL computers. This time around, it was they who called the local police to enforce the court order (Higgins 1999). In yet another twist, the board members began working with an attorney on a "contempt of court" charge, claiming that critical information stored on a laptop computer had not been turned over by Heath when he was served with the court order (Higgins 1999). Heath lost his opportunity to work for the Family Research Council.

The Moral Majority never gained a widespread following in the state, despite a salient role for The Reverend Jerry Falwell in the 1980s, when he assumed temporary custody of Bangor Baptist Church following scandal involving the former gubernatorial candidate, the Reverend Buddy Frankland. The Christian Coalition seems to have a small organization in Maine, with low visibility and an "under construction" Web site as of January 1999. The Christian Right in Maine lacks the powerful groups and supportive networks that are in place in many other states (Rozell and Wilcox 1997).

One response of religious conservatives to their difficult political situation in Maine has been to appeal directly to the citizenry through referendum measures. The state has fairly low threshold requirements for gaining access to the ballot, with only 51,131 signatures required for a recent referendum measure (Vegh 1998b). Under Maine law, it is even legal to collect the signatures on petitions right in the precincts as voters leave the polls. The referendum approach allows religious conservatives to work outside a moderate, pro-choice Republican Party. It also promotes elections at odd times, when few measures are on the ballot and voter turnout is depressed.

In 1986, religious conservatives promoted an antiobscenity referendum, which arose from an ordinance approved by Portland voters inhibiting the growth of adult bookstores. The goal of the referendum measure was to apply the Portland ordinance statewide. However, educators successfully framed the referendum as an issue of censorship, even "book burning" (Rooks 1995). The referendum measure failed by a wide margin, but it set a precedent.

Amendment 1

In 1995, religious conservatives advanced an antigay rights referendum, the only one of its kind in the nation that year. Gay rights had been a hotly contested issue in Maine for years, going back at least as far as a vote in the state legislature against gay rights in 1977. Following that vote, gay rights advocates tried to pass a statute on seven separate occasions, never doing so until 1993 (*Portland Press Herald* 1998). That bill was vetoed by Republican Governor John McKernan, whose political situation required it (Rooks 1995). Prior and subsequent to McKernan's veto, communities such as Portland and Lewiston approved local ordinances prohibiting discrimination on the basis of sexual preference. The 1995 anti-gay-rights referendum was therefore an effort to supersede and prohibit future local ordinances through statewide vote.

A group called Concerned Maine Families, headed by Carolyn Cosby, gathered the required signatures to place the measure on the ballot. The referendum was patterned after "Amendment 2" in Colorado, which prohibited the extension of protected status to gay people; it passed with 53 percent of the vote, but it was struck down by the courts as unconstitutional (Morken 1994). The Maine referendum—known as "Amendment 1"—was more cleverly crafted. It prohibited the extension of the Maine Human Rights Act to any new classes, which made it prima facie, even if it was aimed at homosexuals in practice.

Powerful forces were arrayed against Amendment 1. Virtually every prominent politician in the state opposed the referendum, including popular Governor Angus King. He was joined by members of the state and federal legislative delegations, the Maine AFL-CIO, the Roman Catholic Diocese in Portland, the Maine Chamber of Commerce, and numerous human rights groups. Together, those opposed to Amendment 1 easily outspent those favoring it ("Gay Rights Funds Outstrip Anti-Gay Coffers 10 to 1" 1995). Although Amendment 1 opponents carried eleven of the sixteen counties in the state, they won by only a 54 percent to 46 percent margin in a fairly high-turnout election. The victors believed it was time to capitalize on the showing and pressed the state legislature to enact an antidiscrimination statute; those who had favored Amendment 1, on the other hand, pondered their chances in a rematch where voter turnout was lower.

The 1998 Referendum

In May 1997, the Maine Legislature amended the Maine Human Rights Act to make it illegal to discriminate against people on the basis of sexual orientation relative to employment, housing, access to public accommodations, and financial credit. Religious organizations were exempted from the provision. The bill passed by an overwhelming vote of 25–5 in the senate, but a much closer 82–62 margin in the house. Governor King had indicated before the legislature acted that he would sign such a bill, and he promptly did so. For the first time in Maine's history, both chambers of the legislature and the governor backed a gay rights bill.

Yet the issue was not settled. The Maine Christian Civic League challenged the statute through a "people's referendum." Under Maine law, opponents of a bill enacted into law may make it the subject of a referendum if they present the requisite number of signatures to a petition within six months. The MCCL rounded up approximately 65,000 signatures by November, forcing Governor King to set a date for a referendum. He chose February 10, 1998.

The eleven-week campaign over the people's referendum took place during two particularly severe winter months, with January bringing the worst ice storm in the state's history. Thousands of people lost power for many days, and Maine was officially labeled a federal disaster area. The storm undercut the effectiveness of a television campaign against the referendum by the well-financed political establishment simply because people lacked electricity. More important, the storm decreased interest in the referendum. Joe Cooper, of "Maine Won't Discriminate," the organization that successfully defeated the 1995 referendum, said about two weeks before the election: "So far there hasn't been much interest. A lot of people have been preoccupied with the storm" (Pochna and Nacelewicz 1998). Moreover, many voters believed that gay rights had been settled by the 1995 referendum vote and then by the 1997 statute. Polls showed majoritarian support for gay rights within the state, and few people expected a reversal.

Those favoring the referendum focused almost exclusively on turning out their people in a low-salience election. The petition drive had given them a tremendous advantage: they had identified approximately 65,000 voters who supported their position. Those favoring the referendum were much more clever in their approach this time around. They crafted a rather inverted referendum question, with "yes" actually being a vote against gay rights, and "no" a vote for gay rights. The referendum question created widespread confusion: "Do you want to reject the law passed by the legislature and signed by the governor that would ban discrimination based on sexual orientation with respect to jobs, housing, public accommodations, and credit?" Supporters rallied behind an equally clever organizational name, known as "Vote Yes for Equal Rights." Finally, they neutralized the Catholic Church in Maine, which was often critical to the results in the Franco-American community. The Catholic Church stood with gay rights organizations in 1995 because that referendum prevented the extension of rights to any new classes of people; in contrast, the 1998 referendum focused only on rights for gay people, and the Church's official position against homosexuality forced it into neutrality (Vegh 1998a).

When the votes were cast, the "yes" vote prevailed by 52 percent to 48 percent. The statute passed by the legislature and signed by Governor King was therefore overturned by the people's referendum. The election returns cut mostly across urban and rural lines. Eleven counties voted yes, with particularly big wins in eastern and northern Maine. In Presque Isle, situated in northern Aroostook County, for instance, the yes vote prevailed 1,119 (64 percent) to 618 (36 percent). In contrast, gay-rights supporters fared well along the southern coast and the larger towns, with Portland voting against the referendum by a margin of 12,232 (71 percent) to 4,963 (29 percent) votes. Subsequent analysis showed that the referendum did particularly well in the rural and urban Franco-American areas of the state, such as Lewiston/Auburn (Chapman 1998).

The vote was viewed as a stunning upset, but it reflected the continuing divisiveness of gay rights in Maine politics. In 1995 gay-rights forces won by 8 percent and in 1998 they lost by 4 percent. The issue remains unresolved by the 1998 returns, since slightly less than one-third of the eligible electorate turned out to vote in a state where polls show majority support for gay rights. The issue is bound to resurface.

The vote left Maine as the only state in New England without an antidiscrimination statute involving sexual orientation. Many national newspapers wrote sharply critical editorials. The *Boston Globe* lamented that "the state of Maine is the poorer for this particular people's veto," and the *New York Times* editorialized about "A Retreat on Gay Rights in Maine." State leaders warned that Maine might suffer through convention and tourism boycotts, but as summer arrived, those threats did not seem to materialize.

In the aftermath of the people's referendum, organizations favoring gay rights began a concerted effort to build political support for their side in the rural areas. They believed too much effort had been expended in the large towns and cities, a classic mistake in a state of small towns and villages. Civil rights groups also began establishing organizational structures in rural areas to counter the influence of conservative churches. One such group, known as the Maine Rural Network, was patterned after an organization in Oregon that tried to link gay rights with other empowerment issues such as homelessness and nuclear disarmament. In Aroostook County, in the northern part of the state, members of gay and lesbian groups joined local area Chambers of Commerce. A "Maine Speakout Project," launched in 1995, intensified its efforts to reach especially rural citizens on issues of tolerance and civil rights.

Another consequence of the 1998 referendum vote was that some communities passed contrary local ordinances. Both Portland and Long Island had local gay rights ordinances before the vote, and those two communities were soon joined by Bar Harbor, Orono, Camden, Sorrento, and South Portland. Yet not all of the local efforts succeeded. In Old Orchard Beach, a generally liberal town on the southern coast, a pro-gay rights ordinance lost by a large margin. Yet most observers agreed it was an idiosyncratic result that reflected resistance to the attempt by the gay community to recall a member of the city council who used derogatory language about homosexuals. For the most part, civil rights groups have prevailed locally in the wake of the statewide 1998 referendum, thereby preventing religious conservatives from advancing much beyond their victory.

The Future of the Christian Right in Maine

The 1998 passage of Amendment 1 may well have been the high-water mark for the Christian Right in Maine. Religious conservatives prevailed but in a low-salience election that ran contrary to a 1995 statewide referendum and a 1997 vote of the legislature on gay rights. Polls still suggest that most Maine citizens favor an antidiscrimination statute, and several local communities moved quickly to overturn the Amendment 1 vote.

The referendum process itself is currently under fire. We have already discussed the contravening 1995 and 1998 gay rights referenda; in the interim between those votes, two petitions filed with the secretary of state brought unfavorable publicity to the referendum process. One measure required that opposition to congressional term limits be displayed on future ballots for candidates seeking state legislative and congressional seats, despite the obvious unconstitutionality of such an act. Another measure capped property taxes. It did not gain ballot access when the secretary of state discovered bogus names and signatures on the enabling petitions, leading to indictment of the leader of the petition drive ("State Indicts Tax Activist on Charge of Petition Forgery" 1996). Other referenda in the 1990s involved Sunday retail sales, term limits, clear-cutting in the forests, clean elections, and widening the turnpike. A well-known Maine journalist provided perspective amidst the 1996 petition drives: "What used to be a selectively applied lawmaking tool has set loose a flood of petition drives concerning every half-baked idea that pops into some energetic advocate's head" (Brunelle 1996). His point is reinforced by the fact that measures permitting the medicinal use of marijuana and banning partial-birth abortions are likely to appear on the November 1999 ballot. When the 119th Maine Legislature (1999–2000) convened in January 1999, lawmakers filed more than a dozen bills to restrict citizen referenda. They may not withstand constitutional scrutiny, but bills are being promoted that would increase the required number of signatures on petitions, mandate that referendum votes occur on only primary or general election days, prohibit collection of signatures within 250 feet of a polling place, and require financial disclosure by the petition circulators (Meara 1999).

The Christian Right has relatively few alternatives to the referendum process. Weak political party structures in Maine make a takeover by religious conservatives simple in theory but less meaningful in practice. The reward is not commensurate with the effort. Then, too, the Maine Republican Party generally has been unsympathetic to strong conservatives. When Democrat Ed Muskie turned Maine into a competitive two-party state during the 1950s and 1960s, Republicans responded by electing Cyril Joly as state party chair. Joly had backed the presidential candidacy of Barry Goldwater in 1964, and he had strong conservative credentials (Palmer 1997).

This organizational shift to the political right hurt the Republican Party. It lost gubernatorial races from 1966 to 1982, and lost control of the state house of representatives in 1974 and the state senate in 1982 for protracted periods. In contrast, the GOP won with moderate congressional candidates, such as Olympia Snowe and William Cohen, running quite independently of the state party apparatus. The vivid contrast between the GOP's fate in state versus federal elections caused all three Republican members of the congressional delegation to write a letter in 1982 to all GOP state committee members, encouraging them to elect a moderate and experienced person to the post of state party chairperson. As a result, an experienced moderate named Lloyd Sewall became state party chairperson. He helped the Republicans win the governorship in 1986 for the first time in almost a quarter century (Palmer 1997).

Since the mid-1980s, moderates have been in control of the party structure, and they have turned back occasional efforts by conservatives to wrest control of the state chairmanship. One bit of telling evidence is that moderates inserted a provision in the 1984 state platform calling for an Equal Rights Amendment, in a year in which the national GOP refused to endorse the ERA. Along similar lines, the state party included a pro-choice plank in its 1988 platform, in stark contrast to the platform of the national GOP. Resistance to strong conservatives is also evident in tepid support from the state party for conservative candidates, such as Jasper Wyman, when they manage to win a nomination.

Local politics also lacks promise for the Christian Right. As part of a broader national effort in the 1990s, the Christian Right devoted attention to school board races. They thought it was possible to win those low-salience elections and thereby achieve policy objectives and train their supporters for higher office. The result was some scattered skirmishes over school board composition and policy. In Gardiner in 1991, for instance, religious conservatives pressured school officials to drop the *Impressions* reading series in their middle school. In Harpswell in 1994, religious conservatives fought to scuttle outcome-based education standards. In Palermo in 1996, religious conservatives gained control of the school board, and they used their power to eliminate sex education programs and guidance counseling. They also chose not to apply for federal grants for special and remedial education programs on the grounds that federal money brought federal interference (Chutchian 1996). Local citizens eventually forced the board to apply for the grants with a 150–20 vote at a public meeting. Amidst these controversies over school boards, a university professor authored a sharply critical report of Christian Right goals and tactics (Davis 1996). Despite these salient conflicts, however, the Christian Right's influence over school boards remains isolated and often ephemeral.

Finally, the Maine State Legislature lacks promise for the Christian Right. A small cadre of religious conservatives in the house often meets for an informal prayer breakfast, but this group constitutes only a small percentage of the membership (Moen and Palmer, 1997; Carrier 1999). Few religious conservatives serve in the legislature. Moreover, their agenda has limited appeal. In 1996 and 1998, the MCCL mailed issue-oriented questionnaires to state legislative candidates, gauging their congruence with the MCCL on issues such as abortion, gay rights, liquor sales, and gambling.

Table 15.1 is very revealing. In 1996, the MCCL sent out 314 questionnaires to candidates competing for the 151 seats in the Maine House of Representatives. A total of 225 candidates did not respond, either because they disagreed with the positions of the MCCL or because they did not wish to be identified with it. Of the 89 candidates who did respond, 60 supported two-thirds or more of the MCCL agenda, but only 30 of them were elected. In 1998, the MCCL mailed 277 questionnaires. Once again, only 87 responded. Of those respondents, only 46 supported two-thirds or more of the MCCL agenda, and only 29 of them were elected.

The picture is even less favorable in the state senate. In 1996, the MCCL mailed out 71 questionnaires to candidates chasing 35 senate seats, and it received only 21 responses. Of the 21 respondents, only 14 supported two-thirds or more of the MCCL agenda, and only 3 were elected. In 1998, the MCCL sent out 68 questionnaires. Again, few candidates responded. Of the 16 who did, only 6 supported two-thirds or more of the MCCL agenda, and only 3 were elected to office.

The political establishment is also substantially arrayed against the Christian Right. In the U.S. House, moderate-to-liberal Representative John Baldacci and liberal Tom Allen, both Democrats, hold safe seats. Neither drew a serious challenge in 1998. Maine also has two very moderate, pro-choice, Republican women senators in Olympia Snowe and Susan Collins. Senator Snowe seems to have a lock on her seat. Senator Collins hails from the more conservative northern part of the state, but she has had a very uneasy relationship with religious conservatives. When Collins ran for governor in 1994, social conservative Mark Finks

Table 15.1 Questionnaire Results

Year	Chamber	No. of Surveys	Responses	Supportive	Elected
1996	House	314	89	60	30
1998	House	277	87	46	29
1996	Senate	71	21	14	3
1998	Senate	68	15	6	3

filed a legal challenge to her residency because of service in a federal post outside the state of Maine. Collins eventually won the GOP nomination, but the controversy undermined her campaign, and she finished third in a three-way race involving Democrat Joe Brennan and victorious Independent Angus King. Subsequently, Collins came out against the antigay rights referendum of 1995; she also beat social conservative John Hathaway in 1996 to win the GOP primary for the Senate seat being vacated by her former boss, Senator William Cohen.

Governor Angus King can also be viewed as unsympathetic to the Christian Right. He is strongly pro-choice on abortion and favors gay rights. He worked more closely with Democrats than Republicans in the 118th Maine Legislature (1997–1998), and he seems headed that way in the current legislative cycle. He has enormous personal popularity in all regions of the state.

In short, opportunities for the Christian Right in Maine are limited. Moderates control the Republican Party. School board victories are narrow and often fleeting. The current Maine Legislature is even less sympathetic to the Christian Right than the previous one. Every member of the congressional delegation and the governor are pro-choice and favor gay rights. Learning from their defeat in 1998, gay rights advocates and more liberal activists are unlikely to be caught napping the next time a major initiative appears on the political horizon. In a different vein, the leading state organization of religious conservatives—the Maine Christian Civic League—is fighting an intense intramural battle.

The Christian Right can win victories in Maine given the right circumstances. The 1999 citizens' referendum on banning partial-birth abortions holds promise. However, the state's long-established traditions of moderate, nonsectarian politics present almost insurmountable obstacles to long-term success. For most Maine citizens, the "way life should be" varies from the way religious conservatives think it should be.

NOTE

The authors wish to thank Jason Libby for his excellent research assistance.

REFERENCES

Banks, Ronald F. 1970. *Maine Becomes a State*. Middletown, Conn: Wesleyan University Press.

Berkowitz, Laura A., and John C. Green. 1997. "Charting the Coalition: The Local Chapters of the Ohio Christian Coalition." In *Sojourners in the Wilderness,* edited by Corwin E. Smidt and James M. Penning, 57–72. Lanham, Md: Rowman & Littlefield.

Brunelle, Jim. 1996. "Voter Initiatives Taken Over by Professionals and Zealots." *Portland Press Herald,* 14 March.

Byrne, Frank L. 1985. "The Napoleon of Temperance," In *Maine: A History Through Selected Readings,* edited by David C. Smith and Edward Schriver, 244–53. Dubuque, Iowa: Kendall-Hunt.

Campbell, Steve. 1996. "Poll: Mainers on the Issues." *Portland Press Herald,* 29 September, A8.

Carrier, Paul. 1999. "Conservatives Push, But Uphill." *Maine Sunday Telegram,* 24 January, 1.

Chapman, Liz. 1998. "Most Area Voters: Gay Rights Wrong." *Lewiston Sun Journal,* 11 February.

"Christian Civic League Says Audit OK." 1998. Associated Press Wire Story, reprinted in the *Bangor Daily News,* 10 September.

Chutchian, Kenneth Z. 1996. "A Rude Awakening: Is It Democracy in Action or a Stealth Takeover?" *Maine Times,* 19–25 September, 2–5.

Davis, William E. 1996. "Impact of the New Religious Right on Public Schools." Monograph distributed by the College of Education, University of Maine.

Fisher, Frank. 1998. "Money Troubles for Civic League." *Bangor Daily News,* 9 September.

Fisher, Peggy. 1978. "Longley's Heir." *Maine Times,* 28 July, 14–15.

"Gay Rights Funds Outstrip Anti-Gay Coffers 10 to 1." 1995. Associated Press Wire Story, 2 November.

Gusfield, Joseph R. 1963. *Symbolic Crusade: Status Politics and the American Temperance Movement.* Urbana: University of Illinois Press.

Higgins, A. Jay. 1998a. "Civic League Struggles with Bubar's Legacy." *Bangor Daily News,* 24–25 October, 13.

———. 1998b. "Civic League's Schism, Continued." *Bangor Daily News,* 1–2 August, 13.

———. 1998c. "Heath Quits as Head of Embattled Christian Civic League." *Bangor Daily News,* 29 September, 1.

———. 1999. "Heath Faces Accusation of Contempt." *Bangor Daily News,* 27 January, B1.

Maine Code of Election Ethics. 1996. Developed by the Margaret Chase Smith Library, the Institute for Global Ethics, and the Margaret Chase Smith Center for Public Affairs, University of Maine.

Martin, Lucy L. 1980. "Maine's Premier Conservative Group: Has the Christian Civic League Gone Soft?" *Maine Times,* 7 November, 16–18.

McIntyre, Thomas J., with John C. Obert. 1979. *The Fear Brokers.* Boston: Beacon Press.

Meara, Emmet. 1999. "Battle Over Citizens Initiatives Headed for Legislature, Courts." *Bangor Daily News,* 20 January, 1–2.

Moen, Matthew C. 1989. *The Christian Right and Congress.* Tuscaloosa: University of Alabama Press.

————. 1992. *The Transformation of the Christian Right.* Tuscaloosa: University of Alabama Press.

Moen, Matthew C., and Kenneth T. Palmer. 1997. "Maine: Slow Growth in the Pine Tree State" In *God at the Grass Roots, 1996: The Christian Right in the American Elections,* edited by Mark J. Rozell and Clyde Wilcox, 223–37. Lanham, Md.: Rowman & Littlefield.

Morken, Hubert. 1994. "No Special Rights: The Thinking Behind Colorado's Amendment #2 Strategy." Paper delivered at the Annual Meeting of the American Political Science Association, New York, September 1–4.

Palmer, Kenneth T. 1997. "Maine." In *State Party Profiles: A 50-State Guide to Development, Organization, and Resources,* edited by Andrew M. Appleton and Daniel S. Ward, 132–38. Washington, D.C.: Congressional Quarterly.

Palmer, Kenneth T., G. Thomas Taylor, and Marcus A. LiBrizzi. 1992. *Maine Politics and Government.* Lincoln: University of Nebraska Press.

Persinos, John. 1994. "Has the Christian Right Taken Over the Republican Party?" *Campaigns & Elections,* September 21–24.

Pochna, Peter, and Tess Nacelewicz. 1998. "Low Voter Turnout Could Doom Gay-Rights Laws." *Maine Sunday Telegram,* 25 January, B1.

Portland Press Herald. 1998. 11 February, 6.

Quinn, Francis X. 1998. "Christian League Removes Leaders." *Bangor Daily News,* 1 October, 1.

Rawson, Davis. 1995. "Wyman Picks Religion Over Politics." *Waterville Morning Sentinel,* 3 September.

Rooks, Douglas. 1995. "No Room Left for Jasper Wyman in Maine." *Maine Times,* 7 September.

Rozell, Mark J., and Clyde Wilcox, eds. 1997. *God at the Grass Roots, 1996: The Christian Right in the American Elections.* Lanham, Md.: Rowman & Littlefield.

Saucier, Roxanne Moore. 1997. "Bangor Requests Picketing Hearing." *Bangor Daily News,* 3 January, B1.

Sorauf, Frank J. 1977. *The Wall of Separation: The Constitutional Politics of Church and State.* Princeton, N.J.: Princeton University Press.

"State Indicts Tax Activist on Charge of Petition Forgery." 1996. *Brunswick Times Record,* 21 October.

Vegh, Steven G. 1998a. "Diocese Clarifies Official Position on Gay-Rights Vote." *Portland Press Herald,* 30 January, 1.

————. 1998b. "Groups Organizing to Get Out the Vote." *Maine Sunday Telegram,* 1 January, 1.

Weinstein, Joshua L. 1994. "Wyman Bucks Stereotypes to Reshape Image." *Portland Press Herald,* 7 May, 1.

16

Conclusion: The Christian Right in Campaign '98

Clyde Wilcox and Mark J. Rozell

Although the movement won several individual victories, overall the 1998 elections constituted a defeat for the Christian Right. Movement leaders joined with others from the GOP's ideological wing to pressure Newt Gingrich to focus a national attack on President Clinton's character and to push for impeachment. Gingrich reluctantly agreed, and the party aired advertisements in many areas attacking Clinton. The result was a mobilization of the Democratic base in the final weeks of the campaign, and a loss of seats for House Republicans—only the second time the out-party has lost seats in an off-year election in the twentieth century. By 1999, Newt Gingrich was a private citizen, as was Bob Livingstone, who had won party election to be speaker, but Bill Clinton was still in office.

The Christian Right was preoccupied with Clinton's impeachment in 1998, featuring it in its mail, its magazines, and its Web pages. Impeachment was a natural issue for Christian conservatives, many of whom believe that God punishes nations for the sins of their leaders. Yet the general public did not share the Christian Right's zeal to remove Clinton from office—indeed, nearly two-thirds of the public consistently indicated that they did *not* want Clinton to be impeached. The Christian Right pushed the House Republicans hard on impeachment, but today many political strategists in both parties believe that the Democrats have a real chance to retake the House of Representatives in 2000 as a consequence.

In the end, Clinton remained president as moderate Republicans in the Senate joined a unanimous Democratic Party in voting not to remove the president from office. This visible defeat of the Christian Right seemed to demoralize the movement and caused considerable internal debate about the usefulness of political action. As the country turned toward a two-year campaign for the presidency, the Christian Right was in some disarray, and its future remained somewhat ambiguous. To understand possible futures for the movement, it is useful to first consider the movement's history.

The Christian Right in Twentieth-Century America: A Brief History

Conservative Protestants have long been ambivalent about political action. The fundamentalist and to a lesser extent pentecostal wings of evangelicalism have long held to a doctrine called "premillennial dispensationalism," a belief that worldwide conditions will inevitably worsen and that there will be "wars and rumors of wars" and other disasters before Christ comes again. Yet Christ can come any day, for "no man knows the hour" of the Second Coming. As a consequence, they have preached that political action is futile, that compromise over principles is sinful, and that it is better to remain apart from the world than to get involved in politics.

Despite these doctrinal views, fundamentalists have enlisted in three distinct Christian Right crusades in the twentieth century. In the 1920s they rallied to oppose the teaching of evolution in schools and managed to enact laws in several states to ban the practice. This movement, fueled by the religious enthusiasm generated by the birth of fundamentalism, used a relatively sophisticated mix of tactics but stayed out of electoral politics. Indeed, William Jennings Bryan, the perennial Democratic presidential candidate with populist economic views, became the most visible movement spokesperson, but his embarrassment in the Scopes trial stopped the movement's momentum cold. As the Great Depression descended, most fundamentalists withdrew into privatized religious activity.

In the 1950s, a second wave of fundamentalist activity focused on opposition to communism. The anticommunist crusades hitched their wagon to the star of Senator Joseph McCarthy, Republican from Wisconsin, but persisted after his demise to find a new hero in Republican Senator Barry Goldwater of Arizona. The 1964 Goldwater presidential campaign constituted the first real electoral activity by the Christian Right. Goldwater's landslide defeat marked the effective end to the Christian Right of that era.

In 1978, secular and social conservatives helped found a third wave of Christian Right organizations centered in fundamentalist Christianity.

The Moral Majority was the most famous of these groups, but the Christian Voice, Religious Roundtable, and others were visible for several years. The Moral Majority was active in elections from the start; indeed, it was formed precisely to rally fundamentalists into Republican political action. The organization and others like it held voter registration drives in white evangelical churches, it formed a PAC to give money to Republican candidates, and its leaders were visible at GOP national conventions.

Ultimately this wave of the fundamentalist Right failed for two important reasons. First, although the organizations paid lip service to building at the grass roots, they seldom had active organizations below the state level. Instead, most organizations were primarily national offices and large direct-mail lists. Without organizational strength in local communities, the Christian Right was ill equipped to survive the drop in direct-mail giving by conservatives in the mid 1980s. President Ronald Reagan proclaimed it was "morning in America" and many activists believed that they had won and that there was no longer any need to contribute to conservative organizations.

Second, the Christian Right of the 1970s built its organizations around fundamentalist preachers whose religious intolerance prevented the building of ecumenical coalitions. The Moral Majority leadership and membership were largely confined to Rev. Jerry Falwell's Baptist Bible Fellowship denomination, and its leaders were sharply critical of the religious beliefs of pentecostals, evangelicals, mainline Protestants, and especially Catholics.

In 1988, the Rev. Marion (Pat) Robertson sought the presidential nomination of the Republican Party. Robertson raised record amounts of money and did well in caucuses and conventions but lost badly in all primary elections. Nonetheless, his candidacy mobilized a wider coalition of conservative religious activists, especially pentecostals and charismatic Christians. The charismatic movement is truly ecumenical—there are charismatic caucuses in most Protestant denominations and in the Catholic Church, and most African American worship styles are charismatic. Robertson sought votes among such traditionally Democratic constituencies as Catholics and blacks, and although his campaign failed to convince these groups to register as Republicans and support his candidacy, it was a marked change from the religious particularism of the Moral Majority (Hertzke 1993).

Soon after Vice President George Bush clinched the 1988 presidential nomination, Robertson announced the formation of the Christian Coalition, and its pronouncements highlighted a major change from the fundamentalist crusades that had come before. Robertson invited Baptists and Catholics, white pentecostals and black charismatics, and mainline Protestants and fundamentalists all to unite behind political goals and candidates that they might all agree on. Early Coalition literature stressed that

God would decide who got to heaven, but that conservative Christians had a common interest in electing certain conservative (Republican) candidates (Wilcox 1992; Wilcox, Rozell, and Gunn 1996).

Together with other groups such as the Concerned Women for America and the Family Research Council, the Christian Coalition was unabashedly partisan, although it disguised its Republican affiliation to conform to tax law. The promise of this new, ecumenical wave of Christian Right activism was that if conservative Christians could deliver a Republican majority, then policies on abortion, homosexuality, schools, and traditional families would all change.

The history of the Christian Right in the twentieth century is one of mobilization and disintegration. Each wave of activity began with a large mobilization, formed social movement organizations, and used the technology of the time to communicate with potential members. In each case the principal movement organizations either disbanded or lived on as shadows of their former selves.

Why has the Christian Right ebbed and flowed throughout the twentieth century? It is likely that there is no single unifying explanation, but there are some common themes (for an interesting single explanation see Jelen 1991). First, new movements have arisen in times when social norms were becoming more pluralistic and behavior and groups previously sanctioned were increasingly accepted. In addition, these movements have formed when resources were available from some other source—national religious organizations in the case of the first two waves, sympathetic political organizations in the case of the second two.

The movements have ebbed away for different reasons. The first wave declined significantly after the humiliation of William Jennings Bryan at the hands of Clarence Darrow in the Scopes trial. The second wave began to lose steam with the demise of Senator Joseph McCarthy and almost disappeared after the defeat of Senator Barry Goldwater for president in 1964. The third wave ebbed away when the financial resources that supported the organizations eroded—primarily because it was difficult to convince people to continue to give money when President Reagan was reassuring them that all was now right with the world. The latest wave of the Christian Right, formed from the wreckage of the Robertson campaign, is still in existence and has done a far better job than earlier waves at building grassroots organizations and infrastructure.

In 1999, the contemporary Christian Right faced an internal crisis, as movement leaders and many activists began to question the utility of political action. Important figures in the Christian Right began to urge conservative Christians to focus their attention on religious rather than political issues. It appeared possible that significant portions of the movement might become disenfranchised with politics and return to their theological roots of separatism.

Kingdom of Heaven, Kingdom on Earth

Although the Christian Coalition was part of the mobilization that helped create the GOP majority in 1994 (Rozell and Wilcox 1995), many social conservatives grumbled that the party was quick to pay off economic conservatives but gave only limited rhetorical support to the Christian Right. Some bills, such as the Defense of Marriage Act, were primarily policies that legislated the status quo. Others were overturned: Clinton vetoed bans on partial-birth abortion, and the Supreme Court struck down legislation limiting Internet pornography.

Perhaps more important, it was soon evident that moderate Republicans were not happy with Christian conservative influence in their party. Moderates did not always endorse Christian Right candidates (Rozell and Wilcox 1996; Wilcox 2000), and appeared to want to keep social conservatives at arm's length. GOP presidential candidate Bob Dole didn't talk about abortion during the campaign, although he defended tobacco and attacked milk as being potentially unhealthy. He opposed "special rights" for gays and lesbians in a presidential debate but hastily added that his office had never discriminated on the basis of sexual preference and that his administration would follow the same policy. Dole lobbied hard to include in the GOP platform language proclaiming the party's "tolerance" of diverse views. This effort was clearly aimed at mollifying pro-choice activists in the GOP. When he lost that battle, Dole publicly proclaimed that he had not read the platform and did not expect to have the time to do so. By 1998 and 1999, Republican strategists were openly talking about the need to keep social conservatives happy without passing any policies that would alienate the median American.

In 1999, the Christian Right was a great paradox in the history of American social movements. It had achieved greater institutional influence within a political party than any other movement, with virtual control over the presidential party platform and veto power over vice presidential nominees. Yet on its policy agenda—limits on abortion and on civil rights for gays and lesbians, more religion in the classroom, more support for traditional families where women stay home to care for children—the movement had made little progress (Rozell 1997).

Social movements are most effective when they persuade the public of the validity of their claims. The labor movement, the civil rights movement, the feminist movement, and increasingly the gay and lesbian rights movements have altered public thinking and public discourse. Yet after a decade of activity by the ecumenical Christian Right, and after two decades of continual political involvement stretching back to the Moral Majority, public opinion is not more conservative on abortion and is actually substantially more liberal on gay rights and women's roles (Wilcox and Wolpert 2000).

All of this has led many of the original activists in the Christian Right to begin to question the utility of political involvement. During the 1996 campaign, Moral Majority activist Cal Thomas complained that despite all the movement had given the Republican party, Bob Dole spent far more time defending tobacco than he did talking about abortion. In early 1999, Paul Weyrich, instrumental in the founding of both the Moral Majority and the Christian Coalition, proclaimed that the culture wars were lost, and that conservative Christians should withdraw from political action and form self-contained communities within which they could maintain their moral values (Neibuhr and Berke 1999).

Soon after Weyrich's views were circulated, Cal Thomas joined with Ed Dobson (a preacher who wrote with Falwell) to write a book titled *Blinded by the Might* (1999). They argued that the Christian mission in politics has been lost amid the compromise. Thomas was long an insider critic of the movement, asking Falwell to produce more positive direct-mail letters. Dobson was a Moral Majority insider who decided that the Christian Right was intoxicated by the desire for fame and power, and resigned from the organization to accept the job of pastor of a Baptist church in Grand Rapids, Michigan.

The authors criticized the impact of partisan politics on what was originally a movement designed to inspire a return of Christian values to politics. They argued that partisan rhetoric soon created an atmosphere in which it was assumed that Democrats could not be Christians, and that Bill and Hillary Clinton were the Antichrist. Ultimately, they argued by embracing politics, Christian conservatives lost their ability to serve as prophetic witnesses. Dobson calls his version of this argument the "Mother Teresa test"—when Mother Teresa spoke, people listened because of her personal sacrifice and love and compassion and lack of a political agenda (Rosin 1999).

Thomas and Dobson have received harsh criticism from other movement activists, who have invited them to sever all contact. The authors' doubts resonate among many of the older movement activists, but younger movement leaders are quick to portray Thomas and Dobson as having the thoughts of old, tired men who have lost the heart for the competition. Whether this presages the end of the current wave of Christian Right activity is a question we will return to below.

Yet it is clear that the movement is in some turmoil as the next presidential election approaches. Its leaders are divided and its leading organization—the Christian Coalition—has experienced a significant exodus of personnel. With a multitude of candidates seeking the GOP presidential election, there is little chance that the Christian Right will speak with a single voice.

In 1998 it had appeared that the movement would unite behind a presidential campaign by Republican Senator John Ashcroft of Missouri.

Ashcroft actively solicited movement support and produced a biography to coincide with a launching of a national campaign, and it appeared that Christian Right leaders were ready to support him. Then Ashcroft suddenly dropped out of consideration and cited as a major reason a likely tough campaign to merely keep his Senate seat. Once Ashcroft declared he would not run, there was a mad scramble among several Republican presidential aspirants for the support of the Christian Right.

The Christian Right and the 2000 Elections

The open presidential election once again presents the Christian Right with an opportunity to influence the selection of the man or woman who will win the highest elected office in the land. In late 1999, several GOP candidates were running, many with explicit appeals to the Christian Right.

Ashcroft's decision not to run left the Christian Right with a plethora of candidate suitors. Movement activist Gary Bauer, longtime director of the Family Research Council and former domestic policy adviser to President Ronald Reagan, was the second movement activist to seek the presidency. Bauer's uncompromising rhetoric had led him to clash openly with Ralph Reed, then the pragmatic head of the Christian Coalition. As a consequence, Bauer's candidacy did not experience a wave of endorsements from movement leaders.

Perennial candidate Pat Buchanan announced he would try again for the presidency, but many of his staff had already defected to multimillionaire Steve Forbes, who had moved to the far right on social issues and attracted the backing of leading social conservatives. At first it appeared an unusual choice for many social conservative leaders to unite behind Forbes. He had run for the GOP presidential nomination in 1996 largely shunning the social conservative agenda. Yet by the time of the next presidential campaign, he had been converted on social issues, and his rhetoric on those issues was as angry and forceful as that of any new convert. Many social conservatives, however, complained that Forbes had converted merely as a strategy to win the presidency to enact his flat tax, and noted that conservative social views were a small investment in a policy that would personally benefit Forbes greatly. Indeed, many social conservatives are also highly suspicious of economic conservative candidates who suddenly "find religion" when it is politically beneficial to do so.

Alan Keyes, an African American social conservative and former ambassador in the Reagan administration, also announced his third bid for the White House. Keyes has impeccable conservative credentials and in the 1996 campaign during candidate appearances before various GOP groups, he frequently received the most enthusiastic crowd responses of all the nomination contenders. Despite enthusiastic receptions from party activists, few actually supported his bid for the presidency. He is a radio talk-show host and a twice defeated candidate for the Senate who has never held elective office. He stirs audiences with fiery rhetoric but few take him seriously as presidential timber.

International Red Cross Director and former cabinet official Elizabeth Dole, also the wife of 1996 candidate Bob Dole, campaigned briefly for the presidency and had hoped to attract the support of social conservatives. Although Elizabeth Dole's exact positioning on some social issues was unclear, her Southern Baptist roots and strong pro-life background allowed her to hope for support from some Christian Right activists. Dole nonetheless quit the campaign, citing a lack of fundraising success.

None of this set of candidates has ever held elected office. Nonetheless, they all trumpeted their appointed positions in presidential administrations as evidence of their political experience and qualifications to be president.

The diversity of candidates makes it very likely that the movement will remain divided in the 2000 presidential elections. Former GOP chairman Rich Bond has suggested that the movement will inevitably be fragmented in the presidential primaries, creating opportunities for moderate candidates to emerge.

The moderate candidate with the most support in late 1999 is George W. Bush, who is in his second term as governor of Texas. Bush is the son of a former president, and his "compassionate conservatism" has attracted support from women and racial minorities in his Texas campaigns. Bush has garnered a wave of early endorsements, and Christian Right leader Pat Robertson gave the seal of approval to his abortion views—banning all abortions except to save the life and health of the mother, and in cases of rape, incest, or fetal defect—calling them "profoundly pro-life."

The other leading centrist candidate is Arizona Senator John McCain. Although generally conservative on social issues, he couches his stands with soft rhetoric. He has never been nationally recognized as a leader on the social agenda, and most perceive McCain as strongest in foreign policy. McCain's efforts to enact campaign finance legislation and to regulate the tobacco industry have clearly angered many conservative activists.

The front-loaded nature of GOP primaries and caucuses makes raising substantial sums quickly an important factor in the 2000 race. Forbes's personal wealth assures him the ability to spend whatever he perceives can help his campaign. Bauer should be able to make substantial sums by renting the Family Research Council direct-mail lists, but he will be competing with Patrick Buchanan for Christian Right mail money. Texas Governor Bush in 1999 is the strong party front runner and that status—as well as the Bush family network—has assured him substantial funding. McCain chairs the prestigious commerce committee in the Senate, and he has not been reluctant to use that position to successfully tap into a network of PAC contributions for his presidential bid. So it is likely that several candidates will be able to raise enough money to compete in 2000. Pat Buchanan quit the GOP in late 1999 to run for the Reform Party nomination. If the GOP nominates a moderate, Buchanan may make a strong appeal to social conservatives from the Reform Party.

At the congressional level, the Christian Right can be expected to continue the recent practice of challenging in most open party primaries and of helping social conservative candidates in close races. A number of House GOP incumbents are likely to face close elections, partially as a result of the unpopular impeachment effort. Moreover, growing numbers of Senators have announced their retirement, creating a slew of open seats that should create highly competitive and expensive races. Clearly the Christian Right will have many elections in which they will play an active roll.

The Christian Right in the New Millennium

Yet the growing doubts among longtime movement leaders may well presage a weakening of the Christian Right in the new century. Pat Robertson has announced a shakeup of the Christian Coalition staff and has invited Dick Weinhold, campaign finance director of his presidential bid, to help launch an ambitious fundraising effort. Robertson announced a plan to raise and spend $21 million in the 2000 election cycle to dramatically increase the coalition's field staff across the country. He promised to distribute 75 million voter guides and to attract some 15 million new voters to the polls.

Robertson also promised that his organization "would continue to be a permanent fixture on the American political scene." Yet the resignation of Chuck Cunningham, director of national operations, and Donald Hodel, chief executive, made the future of the organization less clear. One GOP strategist compared Robertson's promises to a hypothetical promise by the Chicago Bulls' coach to repeat the championship without Michael Jordon, Scotty Pippen, or Dennis Rodman (Baltz 1999).

Although the media seem ready to write a new obituary to the Christian Right, many such notices have appeared in the past and yet the movement remains quite alive. Predicting the future of the Christian Right is risky business, as sociologists who predicted the election of Pat

Robertson in 1988 or the immediate death of the Christian Right in 1990 learned. We are not ready to announce the death of the movement, or even its serious illness.

Nonetheless we see evidence that the movement enthusiasm of the Christian Right may be fading, leaving behind weakened interest groups that will be active in politics for some time. This is often the fate of social movements, which generate fervor in their early stages but eventually either fade away or institutionalize into permanent organizations. The early passion of the labor movement left behind the AFL-CIO and other unions, the early enthusiasm of second-wave feminism left behind NOW and other groups, and the early massive marches of the civil rights movement have faded, with the NAACP and other civil rights organizations as institutional reminders. In each case, the remaining organizations are active in lobbying and in electoral politics, but the energy and passion surrounding the movements have ebbed away.

Although there remains considerable ideological fervor within the Christian Right, its transition from strictly a disorganized social movement into part social movement, part interest groups, and part GOP faction has had profound consequences. This transition does not mean that the Christian Right will lose its influence in Republican politics—witness the importance of labor, feminists, and African Americans in the Democratic Party. It may mean, however, that some activists might withdraw from Christian Right organizations because interest groups and party politics are less exciting than social movements. Furthermore, interest groups and parties negotiate with other interests instead of demonizing them, and the benefits of incremental change seem insignificant next to the grand vision of the early days of the movement.

The Christian Right has brought many conservative Christians to the polls, and for many adults voting is a habit that continues over their life spans. Regardless of whether movement leaders withdraw or whether the movement fragments, Christian conservatives will play an important role in politics for many years to come.

REFERENCES

Baltz, Dan. 1999. "Christian Coalition: A Staff to Match Its Goals?" *Washington Post,* 12 March, A15.

Hertzke, Allen D. 1993. *Echoes of Discontent.* Washington, D.C: Congressional Quarterly Press.

Jelen, Ted G. 1991. *The Political Mobilization of Religious Beliefs.* New York: Praeger.

Neibuhr, Gustav, and Richard Berke. 1999. "Unity Is Elusive as Religious Right Ponders 2000 Vote." *New York Times,* 7 March.

Rosin, Hanna. 1999. "The Moral Minority: Thomas Was Among the Right, Now They Find Him in the Wrong." *Washington Post,* 18 March, C1.

Rozell, Mark J., and Clyde Wilcox, eds. 1995. *God at the Grass Roots: The Christian Right in the 1994 Elections.* Lanham, Md.: Rowman & Littlefield.

Rozell, Mark J., and Clyde Wilcox. 1996. *Second Coming: The New Christian Right in Virginia Politics.* Baltimore: Johns Hopkins University Press.

Rozell, Mark J. 1997. "Growing Up Politically: The New Politics of the New Christian Right." In Corwin E. Smidt and James M. Penning, eds. *Sojourners in the Wilderness: The Christian Right in Comparative Perspective,* 235–48. Lanham, Md.: Rowman and Littlefield.

Wilcox, Clyde. 1992. *God's Warriors: The Christian Right in Twentieth-Century America.* Baltimore: Johns Hopkins University Press.

———. 2000. "They Did it Their Way." *Campaigns & Elections.*

Wilcox, Clyde, Mark J. Rozell, and Roland Gunn. 1996. "Religious Coalitions in the New Christian Right." *Social Science Quarterly* 77: 543–59.

Wilcox, Clyde, and Robin Wolpert. 2000. "Gay Rights in the Public Arena." In *The Politics of Gay Civil Rights,* edited by Craig Rimmerman, Kenneth Wald, and Clyde Wilcox. Chicago: University of Chicago Press.

INDEX